Microsoft® WSH and VBScript Programming for the Absolute Beginner Second Edition

JERRY LEE FORD, JR.

THOMSON
COURSE TECHNOLOGY™
Professional ■ Trade ■ Reference

ISBN: 1-59200-731-7

Library of Congress Catalog Card Number: 2004114912

Printed in the United States of America

05 06 07 08 09 BH 10 9 8 7 6 5 4 3 2 1

THOMSON

COURSE TECHNOLOGY

Professional ■ Trade ■ Reference

Thomson Course Technology PTR,
a division of Thomson Course Technology
25 Thomson Place
Boston, MA 02210
http://www.courseptr.com

Publisher and General Manager of PTR:
Stacy L. Hiquet

Associate Director of Marketing:
Sarah O'Donnell

Marketing Manager:
Heather Hurley

Manager of Editorial Services:
Heather Talbot

Acquisitions Editor:
Mitzi Koontz

Senior Editor:
Mark Garvey

Marketing Coordinator:
Jordan Casey

Project Editor:
Tarida Anantachai,
Argosy Publishing

Technical Reviewer:
Zac Hester

PTR Editorial Services Coordinator:
Elizabeth Furbish

Copy Editor:
Linda Seifert

Interior Layout Tech:
Shawn Morningstar

Cover Designer:
Mike Tanamachi

Indexer:
Linda Buskus

Proofreader:
Jan Cocker

To Alexander, William, Molly, and Mary.

ACKNOWLEDGMENTS

The second edition of *Microsoft WSH and VBScript Programming for the Absolute Beginner* represents the culmination of efforts provided by a number of individuals over the last two years. Todd Jensen served as the acquisitions editor for the first edition. Estelle Manticas and Zac Hester were also key contributors to the first edition. Estelle served as both the book's development and copy editor and Zac provided valuable guidance as technical editor.

I also want to acknowledge Mitzi Koontz for serving as the acquisitions editor for the second edition of the book. Special recognition also goes to Linda Seifert for her copyediting services. I'd be remiss if I did not thank Zac Hester one more time for returning as technical editor. Finally, I'd like to thank everyone else at Course PTR for all their hard work.

About the Author

Jerry Lee Ford, Jr. is an author, educator, and IT professional with over 16 years' experience in information technology, including roles as an automation analyst, technical manager, technical support analyst, automation engineer, and security analyst. Jerry has a master's degree in business administration from Virginia Commonwealth University in Richmond, Virginia. He also is the author of 13 other books, including *VBScript Professional Projects*, *Microsoft Windows Shell Scripting and WSH Administrator's Guide*, *Learn VBScript in a Weekend*, *Microsoft Windows Shell Scripting for the Absolute Beginner*, *Learn JavaScript in a Weekend*, and *Microsoft Windows XP Professional Administrator's Guide*. He has over five years' experience as an adjunct instructor teaching networking courses in Information Technology. Jerry lives in Richmond, Virginia, with his wife, Mary, and their children William, Alexander, and Molly.

Contents

INTRODUCTION

Welcome to the second edition of *Microsoft WSH and VBScript Programming for the Absolute Beginner*. VBScript (Visual Basic Scripting language) is a member of the Visual Basic family of programming languages. Other members of this family of programming languages include Visual Basic and VBA. Visual Basic is a very powerful and complex programming language used by programming professionals all over the world. VBA (Visual Basic for Applications) is a programming language based on Visual Basic that is designed to provide a programming environment for Microsoft Office applications such as Excel and Access.

Like VBA, VBScript represents a subset of the Visual Basic programming language. VBScripts can be run on any computer running Windows 95 or later as long as the Windows Script Host (WSH) is installed. The WSH represents one of several environments in which VBScripts can be run. Other environments where VBScripts can run include inside HTML pages processed by Internet Explorer-compatible Web browsers and within Microsoft Outlook or ASP (Active Server Pages). Of all the environments in which VBScript can run, the WSH is the most commonly used. However, by learning to write VBScripts using the WSH, you are also learning much of the prerequisite knowledge required to write VBScripts that will run in each of these other environments.

The WSH provides VBScripts with the capability to execute on Windows computers and to directly access and manipulate Windows resources such as the Windows desktop, file system, Registry, printers, network resources, and so on. You can think of the relationship between VBScript and the WSH as follows: VBScript provides the capability to create scripts and apply logic to perform specific tasks that manipulate Windows resources, which are made available to the script via the WSH.

WHY VBSCRIPT?

VBScript is an excellent first programming language to learn. Its simplicity makes learning basic programming concepts easy. Yet VBScript is a powerful scripting language from which you can learn even the most complex programming concepts such as how to perform object-based programming. Unlike Visual

Basic, VBA, and many other programming languages, there is no complex development environment to learn. In fact, you can create all your VBScripts using a simple text editor such as Windows Notepad.

VBScript provides a foundation that will later make learning Visual Basic and VBA a lot easier. VBScript is a great language for developing small but powerful scripts that perform all sorts of tasks. In fact, you'll find that many VBScripts are not very big at all when compared to programs written using more traditional programming languages. I think that as you read through this book you will be amazed at just what you can do with only a handful of lines of VBScript code. This makes VBScript the perfect language for rapid development, meaning that you can often write a VBScript to perform a task in a fraction of the time that it might take to write a program that performs the same task using a different programming language. Best of all, VBScript is free.

Who Should Read This Book?

This book is designed to teach you how to begin developing VBScripts using the WSH. It does not assume that you have a programming background. However, a basic understanding of computers and Microsoft Windows is assumed.

So, if you are a first timer looking for a friendly language with which to begin a programming career or a more experienced programmer who is looking for a book that provides you with a quick WSH and VBScript learning curve, then give this book a try. This book's games-based teaching approach makes it very different from other books. This approach is not only more fun, but is also an extremely helpful technique for learning a new programming language.

What You Need to Begin

To follow along and complete all the exercises that you'll find in this book, you'll need a number of things. First, you need a computer running Windows. You also need the current version of the WSH, which is version 5.6. If your computer is running Windows XP Home Edition or Windows XP Professional, then you already have the version of WSH that you need. Otherwise, you can download and install the latest version of the WSH from http://www.msdn.microsoft.com/scripting.

You also need an editor that supports the creation of plain text files in order to create and work with your VBScripts. For starters, you can use the Windows Notepad application. You'll also find a number of good VBScript editors on this book's companion Web site. These editors provide advanced features such as statement color-coding and line numbering.

How This Book Is Organized

The second edition of *Microsoft WSH and VBScript Programming for the Absolute Beginner* has been improved in a number of ways. For starters, it has two new chapters. One of these chapters provides expanded coverage of file processing and administration while the other provides an in-depth review of built-in VBScript objects. In addition, I've expanded coverage of many topics spread throughout the book to provide an even better learning experience.

This book is organized into four parts with the intention that you read it sequentially from beginning to end. If you are a new or inexperienced programmer, you will want to read this book in this manner. However, if you already know another programming language and feel that you have a strong enough background in basic programming concepts, you might want to skip around and tackle each chapter in the order that best suits your particular requirements.

Part I of this book consists of two chapters and provides an introduction to both VBScript and the WSH. Part II's five chapters cover the programming statements that make up the VBScript scripting language. In addition, you'll find coverage of the WSH woven throughout these chapters. Part III's five chapters, including the two new chapters, are dedicated to covering a collection of advanced topics that include file and folder administration, error handling, interaction with the Windows Registry, working with built-in VBScript objects, and using XML to create WSH files. Part IV is a collection of four appendixes that provide you with additional avenues of exploration, including examples of real-world scripts and recommended places to go to learn more.

The basic outline of the book is as follows:

- **Chapter 1, "Getting Started with the WSH and VBScript."** This first chapter provides you with a high-level introduction to both the WSH and VBScript. This includes how to install the WSH and how to create and execute your first VBScript. In addition, this chapter includes a range of information about both the WSH and VBScript.
- **Chapter 2, "Overview of the Windows Script Host."** This chapter provides you with an overview of the WSH architecture and introduces the concept of working with an object model. This includes a detailed explanation of WSH object methods and properties. You'll also learn how to configure the WSH and how to specify a default script execution host.
- **Chapter 3, "VBScript Basics."** This chapter begins your VBScript education. You'll learn about VBScript's core and run-time objects and their properties and methods. You'll learn about other VBScript elements including VBScript's built-in functions, syntax rules, and output methods. You'll also learn about various WSH output functions.

- **Chapter 4, "Constants, Variables, and Arrays."** This chapter shows you how to create and reference data stored in the computer's memory using constants, variables, and arrays. You'll learn about VBScript's built-in collection constants. This chapter also presents the rules for variable creation and the enforcement of variable use as well as the techniques required to store and retrieve collections of data in arrays.
- **Chapter 5, "Conditional Logic."** This chapter expands your scripting background to include an understanding of how to add conditional logic to your scripts to provide alternative execution paths for script execution. You'll examine both the VBScript `If` and `Select Case` statements. In addition, you'll learn about VBScript operators and operator precedence.
- **Chapter 6, "Processing Collections of Data."** This chapter teaches you how to process collections of data and resources using various VBScript looping statements (`For...Next`, `Do While`, `Do...Until`, `While...End`, and `For Each...Next`). You'll learn how to write small scripts that can add shortcuts to your scripts on the Windows desktop, Start menu, and Quick Launch Toolbar.
- **Chapter 7, "Using Procedures to Organize Scripts."** In this chapter, you learn how to improve the organization of your scripts using procedures. You'll also be introduced to the concept of creating reusable procedures. This will help you create scripts that are more complicated and easier to modify.
- **Chapter 8, "Storing and Retrieving Data."** This is an entirely new chapter that has been added to the second edition of this book. This chapter teaches you how to create VBScripts that can write to and read from text files. In addition to learning how to create reports and log files, this chapter shows you how to store and retrieve script configuration settings in `.ini` files, thus allowing you to externalize key script settings.
- **Chapter 9, "Handling Script Errors."** This chapter focuses on teaching you how to deal with the errors that occur during script development and execution. This chapter introduces errors during script development and shows you how to troubleshoot them. In addition, you'll learn how to bypass errors and to develop code that handles specific error conditions.
- **Chapter 10, "Using the Windows Registry to Configure Script Settings."** This chapter provides you with an overview of the Windows Registry and shows you how to develop scripts that store and retrieve data in Registry keys and values. Because most Windows functionality is controlled from the Registry, this knowledge will provide you with the basic building blocks required to manipulate any number of Windows settings.

- **Chapter 11, "Working with Built-In VBScript Objects."** This is an entirely new chapter that has been added to the second edition of this book. This chapter expands your understanding of object-based programming by reviewing VBScript's built-in collection of objects. Specifically, you'll learn new techniques for parsing and extracting data from strings.
- **Chapter 12, "Combining Different Scripting Languages."** In this chapter, you learn how to take advantage of the WSH's support for Windows Script Files. Windows Script Files allow you to combine two or more WSH-supported scripting languages (such as VBScript and JScript) into a single script using XML. You'll also learn a little about XML and the XML tags supported by the WSH.
- **Appendix A, "WSH Administrative Scripting."** In this appendix, I show you some practical examples that demonstrate the use of VBScript and the WSH in real-world situations. This appendix will assist you in making a transition form the book's game-based approach to real-world script development.
- **Appendix B, "Built-In VBScript Functions."** In this appendix, I list and define all the functions that are available as you develop your VBScripts.
- **Appendix C, "What's on the Companion Web Site?"** In this appendix, I provide you with more information about the sample scripts provided on the book's companion Web site. I also talk about the VBScript editors supplied on the book's companion Web site.
- **Appendix D, "What Next?"** In this appendix, I provide you with some final advice on how to continue your WSH and VBScript education.

Conventions Used in This Book

This book uses a number of conventions that are designed to make it easier for you to read and work with the information. These conventions are described here:

As you read along, I'll offer suggestions for different or better ways of doing things that will help make you a better and more efficient programmer.

I'll also point out places where it's easy to make mistakes and provide you with advice for avoiding them.

Whenever possible, I'll share shortcuts and techniques that will make things easier.

In the Real World

Throughout the book, I'll stop along the way to point out how the knowledge and techniques that you are learning can be applied to real-world scripting projects.

Challenges

At the end of every chapter, I'll provide you with a collection of small project suggestions that you can do to continue to build upon the skills you've learned.

Part I

Introducing the WSH and VBScript

GETTING STARTED WITH THE WSH AND VBSCRIPT

In this chapter, you'll be introduced to a number of topics. These topics include a high-level overview of the Windows Script Host (WSH) and VBScript. You will learn how the WSH and VBScript work together to provide a comprehensive scripting environment. In addition, you'll learn a little bit about VBScript's history and its relationship to other languages in the Visual Basic programming family of languages. As a wrap-up, you'll also learn how to create and execute your very first VBScript.

Specifically, you will learn

- The basic mechanics of the WSH
- How to write and execute VBScripts using the WSH
- Background information about VBScript and its capabilities
- How to create your first VBScript game

Project Preview: The Knock Knock Game

In this chapter, as in all the chapters to follow, you will learn how to create a computer game using VBScript. This chapter's game is called the Knock Knock game. Actually it's more of a riddle than a game, but it provides a great starting point for demonstrating how VBScript works and how it can be used to develop games and other useful scripts.

The Knock Knock game begins by displaying a pop-up dialog box that reads Knock Knock; it then waits for the user to respond with "Who's there?" The dialog between the game and the player continues until the computer finally displays the game's punch line. Figures 1.1 through 1.3 demonstrate the flow of the conversation between the game and the player. Figure 1.4 shows the message that appears if the player does not play the game correctly.

Figure 1.1

The game begins by knocking on the door and waiting for the player to respond.

Figure 1.2

The first clue is provided.

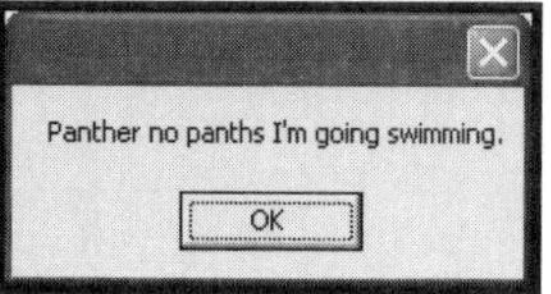

Figure 1.3

The joke's punch line is delivered.

Figure 1.4

If the user makes a mistake when playing the game, an error message providing another invitation to play the game appears.

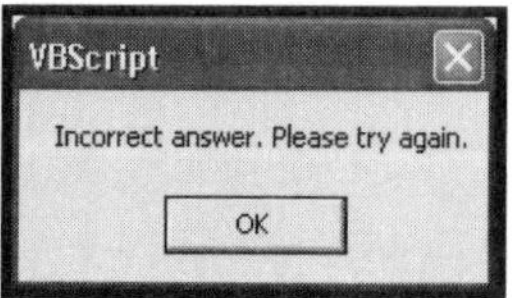

By the time you have created and run this game, you'll have learned the fundamental steps involved in writing and executing VBScripts. At the same time, you will have prepared yourself for the more advanced programming concepts developed in later chapters, including how to use the WSH and VBScript to develop some really cool games.

What Is the WSH?

The WSH (*Windows Script Host*) is a programming environment that allows you to write and execute scripts that run on Windows operating systems. You can use the WSH to create and execute *scripts*, which are small text-based files written in an English-like programming language, from the Windows command prompt or directly from the Windows desktop. Scripts provide quick and easy ways to automate lengthy or mundane tasks that would take too much time or effort using the Windows GUI (*graphical user interface*). Scripts are also better suited for automating tasks that are not complex enough to justify the development of an entire application using a language such as C++ or Visual Basic.

The WSH is a 32-bit application that is made up of a number of different components. These components include the following:

- Script engines
- Script execution hosts
- The WSH core object model

The relationship of each of the components to one another is shown in Figure 1.5.

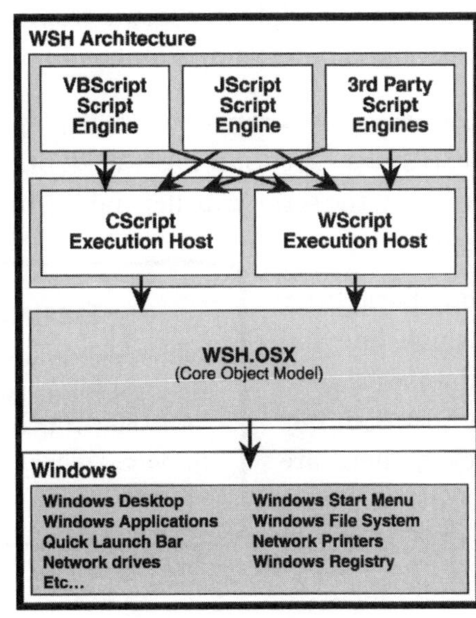

FIGURE 1.5

The components that comprise the WSH.

WSH Scripting Engines

A *script execution engine* is a program that processes (interprets) the statements that make up scripts and translates them into machine-readable code that the computer can understand and execute. By creating an environment in which scripts can execute, the WSH makes script development a straightforward task.

The WSH provides each script with a number of resources. First, the WSH provides script engines for processing scripts. By default, Microsoft provides two script engines for the WSH:

- **VBScript.** A scripting language based on Microsoft's Visual Basic programming language.
- **JScript.** A scripting language based on Netscape's JavaScript Web-scripting language.

Therefore, by default, the WSH can process scripts written in either VBScript or JScript. The WSH is designed in a modular fashion, allowing Microsoft and third-party software developers to add support for additional scripting engines. For example, script execution engines have already been developed for Perl, Python, and Rexx.

Selecting a WSH Script Execution Host

To actually run a script, the WSH uses a script execution host to process a script after a script engine has interpreted that script. The WSH supplies two different script execution hosts:

- **CScript.exe.** An execution host that enables scripts to execute from the Windows command prompt and display text-based messages.
- **WScript.exe.** An execution host that enables scripts to execute from the Windows desktop, display messages, and collect user input using graphical pop-up dialogs.

With the exception of the WScript.exe execution host's capability to display graphical pop-up dialogs, the functionality provided by WSH's two execution hosts is identical. In fact, if you run a script using the CScript.exe execution host, the script can, depending on how it is written, still display messages using pop-up dialogs.

> **DEFINITION**
>
> Within the context of this discussion, the term host describes an environment that provides all the resources required for VBScript to execute.

As both execution hosts provide the same basic functionality, you're probably wondering which one you should use. There's no right or wrong answer here, and often the selection of an execution host is simply a matter of personal preference. However, there are some circumstances in which you may want to choose one over the other. For example, if you plan to run your scripts in the background, or want to schedule the execution of your scripts using the Windows Task Scheduler service and have no requirement for interacting with the user, you might want to use CScript.exe. However, if your scripts need to interact with the user—which will be the case with the games you'll create with this book—you'll want to use the WScritp.exe execution host. Another factor that may affect your selection of a script execution host is your personal comfort level in working with the Windows command prompt.

Introducing the WSH Core Object Model

The WSH provides one final component, called the *core object model*, which is critically important to the development and execution of scripts. The WSH core object model provides VBScript with direct access to Windows resources.

Examples of the types of Windows resources to which the WSH core object model provides access include

- Windows desktop
- Windows Start menu
- Windows applications
- Windows file system
- Windows Quick Launch Toolbar
- Network printers
- Network drives
- Windows Registry

The Windows operating system can be viewed as a collection of objects. For example, a file is an object. So is a folder, disk drive, printer, or any other resource that is part of the computer. What the core object model does is expose these objects in a format that allows scripts to view, access, and manipulate them. Each exposed object has associated properties and methods that scripts can then use to interact with an object, as well as affect its behavior or status. For example, a file is an object, and a file has a number of associated properties, such as its name and file extension. By exposing the Windows file system, the WSH enables scripts to access files and their properties and to perform actions, such as renaming a particular file or its file extension. Files also have methods associated with them. Examples of these methods are those that perform the copy and move operations. Using these methods, you can write scripts that can move or copy files from one folder to another or, if you are working on a network, from one computer to another.

Don't worry if the WSH core object model seems a little confusing right now. I'll go over it in greater detail in Chapter 2, "Overview of the Windows Script Host," and will provide examples of how to use it within your scripts throughout this book. The important thing to understand for now is that the WSH enables scripts to access Windows resources (objects) and to change their attributes (properties) or perform actions that affect them (using object methods).

DEFINITION

In this book, the term *property* refers to an object-specific attribute, such as a file's name, that can be used to affect the status of the object.

How Does the WSH Compare to Windows Shell Scripting?

If you work on a computer running a Windows NT, 2000, XP, or .NET operating system, then Microsoft has supplied you with a second option for developing scripts, known as *Windows shell scripting*. Unfortunately, Windows 95, 98, and Me do not support this scripting option. This makes the WSH Microsoft's only universal scripting solution, and as you are about to find out, the WSH is the more powerful of the two scripting options.

DEFINITION

In this book, the term *method* is used to refer to a built-in function that your scripts can execute to perform an action on an object such as to copy or move a file to another location.

Windows shell scripts are plain text files that have a `.bat` or `.cmd` file extension. Unlike scripts written to work with the WSH, which are written using specific scripting languages like VBScript and JScript, Windows shell scripts are developed using regular Windows commands and a collection of shell-scripting statements. The WSH provides a more complete scripting environment due in large part to its core object model. However, Windows shell scripts still offer a powerful scripting solution. This is partly because you can execute any Windows command or command-line utility from within a shell script. Windows shell scripting also provides a complete collection of programming statements that include support for variables, looping, conditional logic, and procedures. For non-programmers, shell scripts may be easier to read, understand, and modify.

Another difference between script written using the WSH and Windows shell scripts is that Windows shell scripts only support text-based communications with the user. In other words, shell scripts cannot display messages or prompt the user for information using graphical pop-up dialogs. Windows shell scripting does not provide support for any type of object model, like the WSH does. Therefore Windows shell scripts are not capable of directly interacting with many Windows resources. For example, Windows shell scripts cannot directly edit the Windows Registry or create desktop shortcuts. However, Windows Resources kits provide Windows shell scripts with access to a number of command-line utilities that provide indirect access to many Windows resources.

To write shell scripts, you must have a good understanding of Windows commands and their syntax. You must also be comfortable working with the Windows command prompt. Conversely, to effectively use the WSH, you must be well versed in one of its supported scripting languages. There are many cases in which you can accomplish the same task using either Windows shell scripting or the WSH. As a general rule, however, the more complex the task, the more likely that you'll want to, or need to, use the WSH. This is true unless you need to develop scripts that will run on computers using Windows 95, 98, and Me; in which case, you'll have no choice but to use the WSH.

DEFINITION

Microsoft is notorious for finding ways to make money off its customers. One way it does so is by supplying command-line utilities as part of resource kits instead of as part of its operating systems. A *resource kit* is a combination of additional utilities and documentation designed for a particular Windows operating system and is sold as a separate package.

If you're really interested in learning more about Windows shell scripting, read the *Microsoft Windows Shell Scripting and the WSH Administrator's Guide* (ISBN 1-931841-26-8).

You also might want to check out *Microsoft Windows Shell Script Programming for the Absolute Beginner* (ISBN 1-592000-85-1).

Understanding How the Windows Shell Works

Even if you have used Windows operating systems for many years, chances are that you have only limited experience working with the Windows shell. To become a really efficient and proficient script programmer, you'll need a solid understanding of what the Windows shell is and how to work with it.

An understanding of how to work with the Windows shell is also important when learning how to work with the Cscript.exe execution hosts, because scripts run by this execution host are generally started from the Windows command prompt. It's also important to understand the Windows shell when working with the WScript.exe execution host because it provides support for command-line script execution.

You cannot touch the Windows operating system itself. This would be far too complex and difficult. Instead, you must go through an interface. Windows operating systems support two such interfaces, the Windows GUI and the Windows Shell. The Windows GUI is provided in the form of the Windows desktop, Start menu, and other graphical elements with which you normally interact when using your computer. The purpose of the GUI is to make the operating system easier to work with. Likewise, the Windows shell is a text-based interface between you or your scripts and the operating system (see Figure 1.6). You communicate with the Windows shell using the Windows command prompt by typing in Windows commands, which the Windows shell then translates into a format that the operating system can process. The operating system then returns any results to the Windows shell, which displays them in the Windows Console.

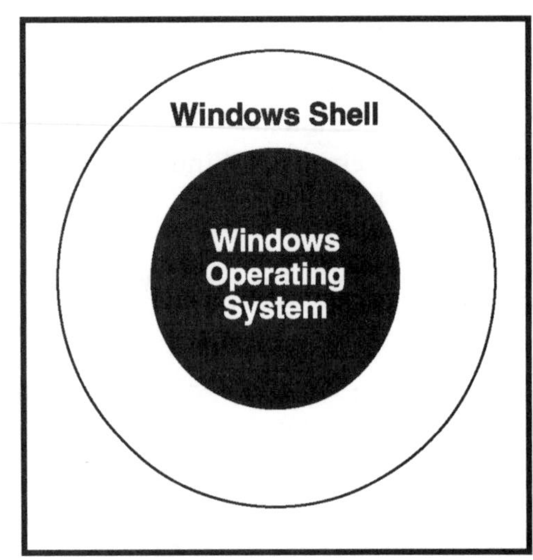

FIGURE 1.6

The Windows shell provides a text-based interface for working with the operating system.

To access the Windows shell and begin working with it using the command prompt, you must first open a Windows Command Console. For example, to open a Windows Command Console on a computer running Windows XP, you can click on Start, All Programs, Accessories, and then choose the command prompt, as shown in Figure 1.7.

DEFINITION

The Windows *command prompt* enables you to submit commands to the Windows shell for processing. By default, the command prompt appears in the form of a drive letter followed by a colon, the backslash character, and then the greater than character (for example, C:\>).

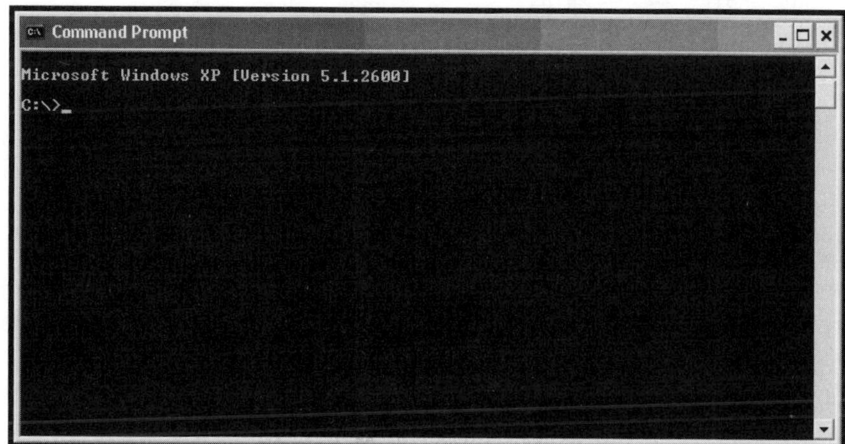

FIGURE 1.7

The Windows Command Console provides access to the Windows command prompt.

A program called CMD.exe provides the Windows Console. A quick way to open a Windows Console is to click on Start, Run, and then type `CMD` and press the Enter key.

As you can see, when the Windows Console first opens, it displays information about the version of Windows in use and Microsoft's copyright information; then the command prompt appears. Just to the right of the command prompt, you'll see a blinking cursor or underscore character. This character indicates that the command prompt is ready to accept input. For example, type the command `DIR` and then press the Enter key. The `DIR`, or `directory` command, instructs Windows to display a list of all the files and folders in the current working directory. The following output shows the results that were returned when I executed this command on my computer:

```
C:\>dir
 Volume in drive C has no label.
 Volume Serial Number is B497-7B65

 Directory of C:\

08/15/2002  10:01 AM    <DIR>          meteor
05/24/1999  01:31 PM    <DIR>          Documents and Settings
05/28/2002  10:04 AM    <DIR>          Program Files
05/24/1999  09:29 PM                 0 CONFIG.SYS
05/24/1999  09:29 PM                 0 AUTOEXEC.BAT
08/23/2002  11:11 PM                81 test.bat
```

```
11/11/2002  08:53 PM    <DIR>          Rexx
05/28/1999  09:34 AM    <DIR>          WINDOWS
06/04/2002  08:52 AM    <DIR>          Collage
               3 File(s)             81 bytes
               6 Dir(s)   2,388,291,584 bytes free

C:\>
```

As you can see, the last line in the output is the Windows command prompt. The Windows shell redisplayed the command prompt as soon as the `DIR` command completed, allowing for the entry of another command. For example, if I have a VBScript named `Hello.vbs` located in a folder named Scripts on the computer `C:` drive, I could now execute it by typing `CScript C:\Scripts\Hello.vbs` and pressing the Enter key. After the script finishes its execution, you can type additional commands, run more scripts, or end your Window shell session by closing the Windows Console. The Windows Console is closed just as any other Windows application—by either clicking on the Close button (X) in the upper-right corner of the Windows screen or by right-clicking on the icon in the upper-left corner of the screen and selecting Close.

You also can close the Windows Console by typing `Exit` and pressing the Enter key.

How Does It All Work?

To execute a script using the WSH, you must first create the script using one of the WSH's supported scripting languages. In this book, that language is VBScript. Windows operating systems recognize the type of data stored in files based on the file extension assigned to the file. For example, a file with a `.txt` file extension is a text file. Windows automatically associates files with this file extension with its Notepad application. Therefore, when you double-click on a `.txt` file to open it, Windows automatically loads the file into Notepad.

When you create your VBScripts, you need to save them as plain text files and assign them a `.vbs` file extension. That way, Windows will know that the file contains VBScripts. In a similar fashion, to write a script using JScript, you must save the file with a `.js` file extension, so that Windows can properly identify it as well.

As long as the WSH has been installed on your computer, all you have to do to execute a script that has been saved with the appropriate file extension is to run it. There are several ways to run a script. One way is to simply double-click on the file. Windows will recognize the file as a script and then automatically process it using the appropriate WSH script engine (based on the script's file extension). What happens next depends on how you have configured the WSH. By default, the WSH is configured to run all scripts using the `WScript.exe` execution host; you can modify this default behavior to make the `CScript.exe` execution host the default if you want. However, the `WScript.exe` execution host allows scripts to display messages and to collect text input using graphical pop-up dialogs, but the `CScript.exe` execution host does not. As the script runs in the execution host, it can access and manipulate Windows resources, thanks to the core object model.

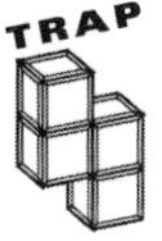

Windows runs a script based on the authority of the person who starts it. Therefore, your scripts have no more access to Windows and its resources than you do. If you try to create a script to perform a task that you cannot perform manually via the GUI, your script will not work. If this is the case, you might want to talk with your system administrator to see if you can be assigned additional access permissions and user rights.

Operating System Compatibility

The current version of the WSH is 5.6; this is the third version of the WSH released by Microsoft. The two previous versions were versions 2.0 and 1.0. Depending on which operating system your computer runs, you may already have access to one of these versions. For example, if you are using Windows XP Home Edition or Windows XP Professional, then you already have WSH 5.6. However, if you work with other Windows operations, you may or may not have an older version of the WSH installed. Table 1.1 provides a list of Windows operating systems and the version of the WSH that is supplied with them.

TABLE 1.1 VERSIONS OF THE WSH FOUND ON MICROSOFT OPERATING SYSTEMS

Operating System	WSH Version
Windows 95	None
Windows 98	1.0
Windows Me	2.0
Windows NT	1.0 Installed with SP4
Windows 2000	2.0
Windows XP	5.6
Windows .Net	5.6

As Table 1.1 shows, Microsoft did not equip Windows 95 with the WSH, whereas Windows 98 was shipped with WSH 1.0. Windows NT 4.0 did not ship with a copy of the WSH. However, Microsoft added its installation to Service Pack 4 (*SP4*) for that operating system. Other versions of Windows, including Windows Me and 2000, provide WSH 2.0.

How Do You Install It?

You can install or upgrade to WSH 5.6 on any of the operating systems listed in Table 1.1. You'll find a downloadable copy of the WSH 5.6 at http://msdn.microsoft.com/scripting. The steps involved in installing the WSH or upgrading to version 5.6 are as follows:

1. Start your Internet browser, type http://msdn.microsoft.com/scripting in the URL field, and then click on Go. The MSDN Scripting Web site appears.
2. Click on the `Microsoft Windows Script 5.6 Download` link. The Microsoft Windows Script 5.6 page appears.
3. Click on a version of the WSH to download. For example, to download the English version of the WSH for Windows 2000, click on the `English Download for Win 2000` link. Likewise, to download a version of the WSH compatible with Windows 98, Me, and NT 4.0, click on the `English Download for Win 98, Me, NT 4.0` link.
4. When the license agreement appears, click on Yes to accept the terms of the agreement.
5. Click on Save when prompted to download the documentation, select the location where you want to store the download, and then click on Save.
6. Double-click on the file that you just downloaded to begin the installation process.
7. When the Windows Script 5.6 dialog box appears, click on Yes to begin the installation process.
8. When another license agreement appears, click on Yes to accept the terms of this agreement, and then follow the instructions presented to complete the installation process.

How Does It Work with VBScript?

Microsoft originally designed VBScript to operate as a Web-scripting language. This means that it could only run when embedded within HTML pages that were executed by Internet Explorer. VBScript's success as a Web-scripting language has always been limited. One reason for this is that Netscape never provided support for it in its Internet browser. In addition, from the beginning, Netscape provided JavaScript free of charge, and there was a hesitation on the part of many programmers to abandon JavaScript in favor of VBScript, which Microsoft maintained as a proprietary technology, meaning that Microsoft and Microsoft alone owned and controlled VBScript.

Microsoft has since created a modified version of VBScript that is designed to work with the WSH. This version of VBScript lacks many of the features found in browser-based versions of VBScript. For example, it does not work with forms and frames. Then again, as a WSH scripting language, VBScript doesn't need this functionality because these types of resources are beyond the scope of its environment.

Hello World: Creating and Executing Your First VBScript

Instead of being embedded within HTML pages, VBScripts run by the WSH are saved as stand-alone files with a `.vbs` file extension. For example, take a look at the following VBScript:

```
MsgBox "Hello World!"
```

As you can see, the script consists of just one line of code. To create this script, open your editor and type the line of code exactly as I've shown it here and then save the script as `Hello.vbs`. That's it. Now run it: First locate the folder in which you saved the script, and then double-click on it. You should see a graphical pop-up dialog similar to the one shown in Figure 1.8.

Let's talk about the script that you just wrote and executed. First of all, because you executed it by double-clicking on it, you ran it using the default execution host. The default execution host is `WScritp.exe` unless you've changed it (I'll go over how to change the execution host in the next chapter). The script itself executes a VBScript function called `MsgBox()`.

FIGURE 1.8

Viewing the pop-up dialog box created by your first VBScript.

> **DEFINITION**
>
> A *function* is a collection of statements that is called and executed as a unit.

The `MsgBox()` function is a built-in VBScript function that you can call within your scripts to display messages in pop-up dialog boxes. As you can see, the text "Hello World" was displayed when you ran the script. This VBScript was run using a WSH execution engine (for example VBScript) and one of the WSH's two execution hosts (either `WScript.exe` or `CScript.exe`); however, the code itself was all VBScript.

Let's modify the script just a little bit to demonstrate how to incorporate the WScript object. The WScript object is one of a small number of objects that make up the WSH core object model (I'll go over this object and the rest of the WSH core object model in greater detail in Chapter 2). Using your editor, open the Hello.vbs script and modify it so that it looks exactly like the following example:

```
Set WshShl = WScript.CreateObject("WScript.Shell")
WshShl.Popup "Hello World!"
```

Now save the script and run it again. This time, unless you made a typo, you should see a pop-up dialog box similar to the one shown in Figure 1.9.

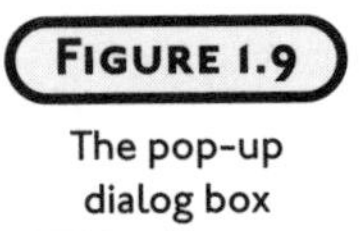

FIGURE 1.9 The pop-up dialog box created by your modified VBScript.

As you can see, things look pretty much the same. The same message is displayed, although the word "VBScript" in the pop-up dialog's title bar has now been replaced with the words "Windows Script Host." Let's break it down and examine exactly how the script is now written. Don't worry if you don't fully understand everything that is covered here—it's fairly complex and you'll be better prepared to understand it by the end of Chapter 2. For now, I'd like you to just read along with the steps I'll present, so that you'll understand the process involved in creating and executing scripts using VBScript and the WSH.

First, the script uses the Set command to define a variable named WshShl. This variable is then assigned a value using the following expression:

```
WScript.CreateObject("WScript.Shell")
```

This statement executes the WScript object's CreateObject() method. This method is used to instantiate (that is, create a new instance of) the WshShell object, which is another WSH core object. The second line of code in the example uses the WshShell object's Popup() method to display a pop-up dialog.

The WScript object is one of the WSH's core objects. Do not confuse it with the WSH WScript.exe execution host. It is unfortunate that they share the same name because they are very different.

As the two versions of the previous script show, many times you can perform the same task using either a VBScript function or a WSH method. This script also demonstrates how easy script creation and execution can be, and how even a one- or two-line script can perform some pretty neat tricks—such as displaying pop-up dialogs.

In the Real World

In the previous example, you created your first VBScript by following the steps that I set down. Often, depending on the size and complexity of the script that you're going to develop, you can get away with simply sitting down and writing the script as you go. More often than not, however, you'll want to take a more methodical approach to script development. First, make sure that you know exactly what you want to achieve. Then break the task down into specific steps that, when combined, complete the task. Spend a little time sketching out the design of your script and try to break the script into different sections. Then develop a section at a time, making sure that one section works before moving on to the next. I'll try to point out ways to do this throughout the book.

Executing Your Script from the Command Prompt

In the previous example, you executed your script by double-clicking on it, and everything worked fine because the scripts were written so that they could run from the Windows desktop. However, sometimes the execution host that you use to run your script has a big impact on how the script operates. Let's take a look at an example. First, open the `Hello.vbs` scripts again and replace the contents of the script with the following statement:

```
WScript.Echo "Hello World"
```

This statement uses the `WScript` object's `Echo()` method to display a text message. Save the script and execute it by double-clicking on it. Unless you have modified the default WSH configuration, the script will run using the `WScript.exe` execution host. The result is that the message is displayed in a pop-up dialog. Now copy the file to the `C:` drive on your computer and open a Windows Console. At the command prompt, type `CD \` and press the Enter key. This command changes the current working directory to the root of the `C:` drive where `Hello.vbs` script now resides. Now type the following command and press the Enter key:

```
CScript Hello.vbs
```

What you see this time is quite different. Instead of a pop-up dialog, the script's output is written to the Windows console, as shown in Figure 1.10.

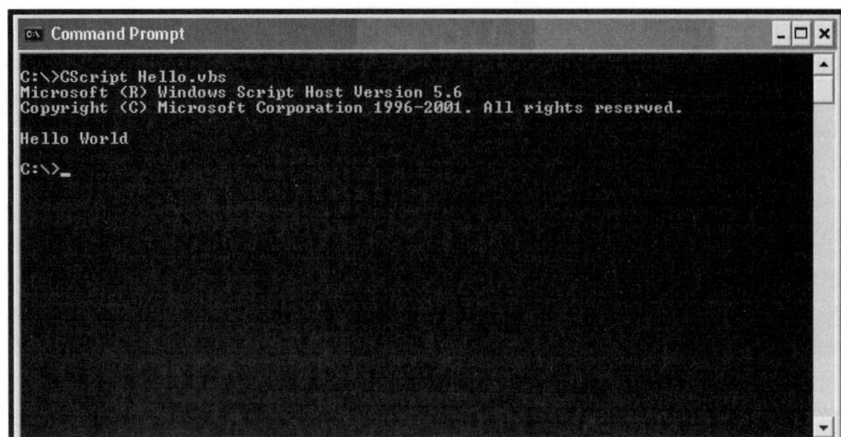

FIGURE 1.10

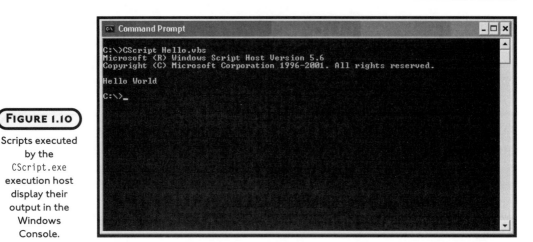

Scripts executed by the `CScript.exe` execution host display their output in the Windows Console.

As a final experiment, type the following command at the Windows command prompt:

```
WScript Hello.vbs
```

As you see, the message produced by the script is once again displayed in a pop-up dialog because even though the script was run from the Windows command prompt, the `WScript.exe` execution host displays its output graphically.

What Other Scripting Languages Does the WSH Support?

As I have already alluded to, the WSH supports other languages besides VBScript. Microsoft ships the WSH with both JScript and VBScript, and in addition to these scripting languages, a number of third-party scripting languages are also designed to work with the WSH. These languages include Perl, Python, and REXX.

JScript

JScript is Microsoft's implementation of Netscape's JavaScript language. Like VBScript, the version of JScript that is shipped with the WSH is a modified version of the browser-based scripting language. Also like VBScript, JScript is a complete programming language replete with support for variables, conditional logic, looping, arrays, and procedures.

JScript's overall syntax structure is a little more difficult to master than VBScript's, unless you are already familiar with JavaScript. VBScript provides better support for arrays whereas JScript provides a stronger collection of mathematical functions. JScripts are created as plain text files and saved with a `.js` file extension.

All in all, JScript and VBScript are very similar and provide the same level of functionality. Microsoft is equally committed to the continued development of both scripting languages and is working hard to make sure that both languages provide equivalent functionality. As a result, the differences between the two languages have become very small and are likely to continue to decrease.

To learn more about JScript, check out the JScript Documentation link on http://msdn.microsoft.com/scripting.

Perl

Perl (*Practical Extraction and Reporting Language*) is a scripting language that traces its roots to the Unix operating system. It has been ported over to every major computer operating system. A WSH-compatible version of Perl, called ActivePerl, is available at http://www.activestate.com. ActivePerl runs as a stand-alone language on Windows, Linux, and Unix operating systems. The Windows implementation of ActivePerl includes a Perl scripting engine, PerlScript, that works with the WSH.

Python

Python is a scripting language named after the Monty Python comedy troupe. Python was originally made popular with Linux users. It has also been ported over to Windows and Unix. A WSH-compatible version of Python is available at http://www.activestate.com. Like ActiveState's versions of ActivePerl, ActivePython is a free download.

REXX

REXX (*Restructured Extended Extractor language*) is a scripting language first made popular on IBM mainframe and OS2 desktop computers. IBM provides a version of REXX called Object REXX that works with the WSH. To learn more about Object REXX, check out http://www-4.ibm.com/software/ad/obj-rexx.

Introducing VBScript

As you now know, VBScript is a scripting language that allows you to develop scripts that automate tasks that would otherwise have to be manually performed in the environment in which they execute. VBScripts are stored as plain text files with a `.vbs` file extension and can be created using any text editor. This makes them easy and quick to develop.

Unlike the stand-alone implementations of many scripting languages, such as Perl or Python, VBScripts cannot execute without an execution host. VBScript was originally designed to execute as text embedded within HTML pages inside the Internet Explorer browser. However, over the years Microsoft has extended VBScript's capabilities to allow it to function in numerous different settings. VBScript is now supported in a number of different environments, including

- **Windows Script Host.** VBScript provides a host automation language for performing system and network tasks.
- **Internet Explorer.** VBScript supplies a client-side Web-scripting language.
- **Microsoft Windows Script Console.** Allows VBScript to be added to third-party applications to incorporate its scripting capabilities.
- **IIS (*Internet Information Server*) and ASP (*Active Server Pages*).** VBScript can be embedded into ASP to access local databases and help deliver dynamic Web content.
- **Outlook Express.** VBScript provides the ability to automate a number of Outlook's functions.

As you can see, after you master VBScript within the context of WSH script development, you'll have a number of other avenues in which you can begin using your new VBScript programming skills.

VBScript Capabilities

VBScripts cannot execute without an execution host. Therefore, the language's capabilities vary greatly based on where they are run. For example, when embedded within HTML pages, VBScript can access and manipulate forms, frames, links, images, and other objects that are based on Web pages. When placed inside ASP pages, VBScripts have access to server-based resources such as databases. However, because the purpose of this book is to teach you how to program using VBScript within the context of the WSH, I think it's best that we focus on the capabilities that VBScript has when executed in this environment.

As I'll show you throughout this book, you can create games using VBScript and the WSH. While game development is a great way to have fun while learning a new language, it's important to understand the reason Microsoft enabled VBScript to operate in the WSH, and to be familiar with the capabilities that Microsoft has given to VBScript within the context of WSH script development.

VBScript provides programmers with a quick development tool for creating small applications and utilities, and for prototyping new applications. System and network administrators use these tools to automate system administrative tasks, such as

- Creating user and group accounts
- Configuring the desktop

- Creating ad hoc reports
- Automating network file, folder, and drive administration
- Managing Windows services
- Administering local and network printers

Some tasks simply take a long time to perform manually or must be done so often that they become bothersome. By providing the ability to automate these tasks, VBScript provides a powerful yet easy way to use programming tools. Once developed, script execution can be automated using the Windows scheduling service. This allows you to run your scripts at the times that are most convenient for you. For example, suppose you wrote a script that reorganizes the locations of files on your computer by moving them from various folders into a centralized location. This way, at the end of each month, you can run the script and reorganize a month's worth of messy file placement. The number of files to be moved may be such that it takes the script a while to complete its work, during which time the computer runs slowly and is no fun to use. Fortunately for you, however, VBScripts can be scheduled—you can set up the execution of this script to run at night, over the weekend, or at any time that you don't plan on using your computer.

VBScript's Roots

Microsoft first released VBScript in 1996 as a Web-based, client-side scripting language for Internet Explorer 3.0. At the time, another Web-based client-side scripting language, called JavaScript was already making big waves in the Internet community. Despite the similarity in name, JavaScript had very little in common with Java, which was also fast becoming popular in the mid-to-late 1990s.

As I've already mentioned, JavaScript's popularity as a client-side Web-scripting language has continued over the years, while VBScript's stalled. Even today, the only way to perform client-side Web scripting and to be sure that everyone with an Internet browser has access is to use JavaScript.

Still, Microsoft has remained committed to the development of VBScript over the years. It released VBScript 2.0, along with IIS 3.0, turning VBScript into a server-side Web-development language. Now Web developers could embed VBScripts into their ASP pages, giving them the ability to access local databases and create dynamic HTML pages.

VBScript's big break came with VBScript 3.0. This version was packaged with multiple Microsoft products, including

- Internet Explorer 4.0
- IIS 4.0

- Outlook 98
- Windows Scripting Host

VBScript 3.0 now could be used as a scripting language for Microsoft's e-mail client. However, VBScript really took off when it was included as a scripting language for the WSH. Visual Basic programmers, computer administrators, and technology enthusiasts with a background in Visual Basic found VBScript easy to learn. It quickly proved to be a great language for developing small scripts to perform tasks that did not merit the development of a complete stand-alone application.

Microsoft later released VBScript 4.0 as part of its Microsoft Visual Studio application-development suite. Microsoft gave VBScript 4.0 the capability to access the Windows file system; otherwise, VBScript 4.0 remained pretty much unchanged from the previous version.

In 2000, Microsoft released VBScript 5.0 as a component of Windows 2000, which included Internet Explorer 5 and WSH 2.0. In 2001, Microsoft released Windows XP Professional, Windows XP Home Edition, and Internet Explorer 6.0. Along with these goodies came WSH 5.6 and VBScript 5.6. As you can see, Microsoft decided to sync up its version numbers with this release. Because WSH 5.6 and VBScript 5.6 are the most current releases, I will focus on their use throughout this book.

VBScript's Cousins: Visual Basic and VBA

VBScript is the third member in a family of three closely related programming languages:

- Visual Basic
- Visual Basic for Applications (VBA)
- VBScript

Visual Basic is the original member of this family; Microsoft first introduced it in 1991. In the past 12 years, Microsoft has steadily improved Visual Basic, releasing a number of versions along the way. The most current version of Visual Basic is Visual Basic .NET 2003. As a .NET-compliant language, Visual Basic supports Microsoft's .NET framework.

> **DEFINITION**
>
> .NET is a Microsoft framework that has been designed by Microsoft from the ground up to support integrated desktop, local area network, and Internet-based applications. Microsoft's .NET framework assists in developing applications by facilitating data exchange over a network—including the Internet.

If you want to learn more about .NET visit http://www.microsoft.com/net.

Visual Basic is generally used to create stand-alone programs. This means that once written and compiled into executable code, a Visual Basic application does not need anything other than a Windows operating system to execute. Visual Basic earned a reputation very early on for being easy to learn. As a result, it did not take Visual Basic long to become one of the most popular programming languages ever developed. Today Visual Basic is taught in colleges around the world and is used to build applications in companies of all sizes and types.

Visual Basic applications are created using Visual Basic's built-in IDE (*Integrated Development Environment*). Visual Basic's IDE includes a built-in compiler, debugger, help system, and tools for managing Visual Basic projects. Although Visual Basic's IDE provides a rich and powerful programming development environment, it takes a substantial amount of time and effort to learn. Because of the complexities of its IDE, Visual Basic is not well suited to the development of small scripts. Visual Basic's strength lies in aiding the development of larger and more complex programs that justify the time and effort required to develop them.

To learn more about Microsoft Visual Basic .NET, check out *Microsoft Visual Basic .Net Programming for the Absolute Beginner*, by Jonathan Harbour.

DEFINITION

An *IDE* is an application development program that gives programmers the tools required to create applications using a particular programming language. An IDE provides tools such as a compiler, which translates application code into a finished executable program; a debugger, which assists in tracking down and fixing programs; and tools for managing projects, which may consist of multiple applications.

The next language in the Visual Basic family is VBA (*Visual Basic for Applications*), which Microsoft first released in 1993. VBA represents a subset of Visual Basic, and is designed to provide applications with a Visual Basic–like programming language. For example, using VBA for Microsoft Excel, programmers can use VBA to develop entire applications using features provided by Excel. Similarly, VBA for Microsoft Access provides a powerful programming language for creating applications that require a Microsoft Access database.

Like Visual Basic applications, VBA applications are created using a sophisticated IDE program. Unlike Visual Basic applications, which can be compiled into fully executable programs, VBA can only be compiled into a format known as p-code, which you can think of as *partial compilation*. Using p-code, VBA code can load and run faster than VBScript, which is an interpreted language, but will still run slower than a Visual Basic application. VBA also requires a host application such as Microsoft Excel or Microsoft Access.

VBA 6.3 was released in 2001 and is still the current version. Using VBA, you can develop programs for any of the following Microsoft applications:

- Word
- PowerPoint
- Excel
- Outlook
- Access
- FrontPage

To learn more about VBA and Microsoft Excel, check out *Microsoft Excel VBA Programming for the Absolute Beginner*, by Duane Birnbaum. To learn more about VBA and Microsoft Access, check out *Microsoft Access VBA Programming for the Absolute Beginner*, by Michael Vine.

How Do Visual Basic and VBA Compare to VBScript?

Like VBA, VBScript represents a subset of Visual Basic. Unlike Visual Basic or VBA, VBScripts cannot be compiled prior to their execution. Thus, VBScript is the slowest of the three languages. However, because VBScripts don't have to be compiled prior to execution, you can save a lot of time during development because you don't have to stop and compile your scripts every time you make a change and want to see how it affects the application. Similar to VBA, VBScript, as you have learned, requires an execution host such as the WSH or Internet Explorer to run.

Microsoft maintains a strong commitment to VBScript. Over the years, Microsoft has ported it over to a number of different development environments. As a result, VBScripts can execute in any of the following execution environments:

- **WSH.** Provides an execution environment for running VBScripts directly on the Windows desktop that can interact directly with Windows resources.
- **Internet Explorer.** Provides the capability to embed VBScripts inside HTML pages to create dynamic Web content and facilitate direct interaction with visitors to your Web pages.

- **Outlook.** Provides the capability to automate a number of different e-mail operations.
- **Microsoft Windows Script Console.** Provides third-party application developers with the ability to integrate VBScript support into their applications.
- **IIS and ASP.** Provides the ability to embed VBScripts within ASP to facilitate the development of dynamic content and the accessing of data stored on Web server databases.

As you can see, by learning to develop VBScripts that work with the WSH, you are also laying a programming foundation that can lead you down a number of different paths. For example, widespread support for VBScript makes it an excellent scripting language for supporting Web page development. Although not supported by Netscape browsers, VBScript is supported by these Internet Explorer-compatible browsers:

- Internet Explorer
- AOL
- NeoPlanet
- Smart Explorer
- UltraBrowser
- EarthLink LiteAOL
- Oligo
- CrystalPort
- CompuServe
- MSN Explorer

You'll also find that learning to develop VBScripts will provide you with a head start should you decide to tackle VBA or Visual Basic programming. Table 1.2 provides a high-level comparison of the features of Visual Basic, VBA, and VBScript.

Table 1.2 Comparing VBScript to VBA and Visual Basic

Programming Language	Stand-alone	IDE	Compiled
Visual Basic	Yes	Yes	Yes
VBA	No	Yes	Yes
VBScript	No	No	No

In the Real World

Unlike Visual Basic and VBA, VBScript does not come with an IDE. However, you can find some perfectly good third-party script editors that will provide you with an advanced script development environment. For example, check out VBSedit at http://www.adersoft.com. It provides all the following features:

- **Line numbering**
- **Automatic color-coding of keywords**
- **Script execution from within the editor using `WScript.exe`**
- **Script execution from within the editor using `CScript.exe`**

Appendix C, "What's on the CD-ROM?" provides additional information about other script editors that you may find helpful.

Microsoft Scripting Technologies Web Page

I would be remiss if I did not point you to the Microsoft MSDN Scripting Web site, shown in Figure 1.11. This is Microsoft's official Web site for the WSH.

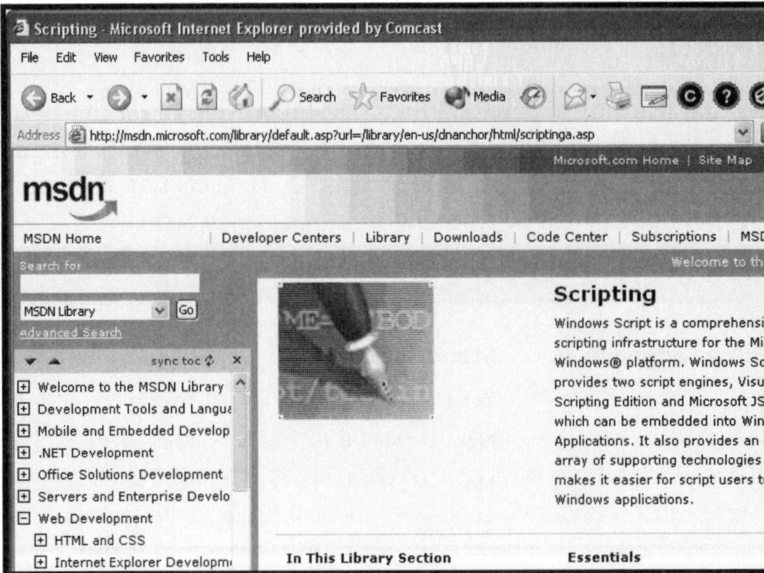

Figure 1.11

Visit `http://msdn.microsoft.com/scripting` to stay current on the latest information Microsoft publishes about its scripting technologies.

Microsoft publishes a great deal of information about both VBScript and the WSH at this site. Included among the information you'll find here is

- VBScript documentation
- JScript documentation
- WSH documentation
- The latest version of WSH ready for download
- Scripting newsgroups
- Information about third-partying scripting languages
- Sample scripts

You'll find both the VBScript and WSH documentation particularly helpful. The VBScript documentation is divided into two parts. The first part is a User's Guide that defines VBScript and explains how it can be used within a Web page. It also provides a basic overview of VBScript scripting. The second part of Microsoft's VBScript documentation is a VBScript language reference. Here you will find every VBScript statement fully documented, as well as an outline of its syntax and short coding examples.

In addition to the online version of these help files, Microsoft allows you to download and install a local copy for easy access. To do so, follow these steps:

1. Start your Internet browser, type **http://msdn.microsoft.com/scripting** in the URL field, and then click Go. The MSDN Scripting Web site appears.
2. Click on the Downloads link. The Microsoft Windows Script Downloads page appears.
3. Click on the Microsoft Windows Script 5.6 Documentation link.
4. The Windows Script 5.6 Documentation appears. Click on Download.
5. Click Save when prompted to download the documentation and select the location where you want to store the download; then click on Save.
6. Double-click the file that you just downloaded to begin the documentation installation process. The Windows Script 5.6 Documentation dialog box appears, as shown in Figure 1.12.
7. Click OK to perform the install.

After it's installed, you can view the documentation from the Windows Start menu. For example, on a computer running Windows XP, you would click on Start, All Programs, Windows Script Host, and then select Windows Script V5.6 Documentation. The Windows Script Technologies help dialog box then appears, as shown in Figure 1.13.

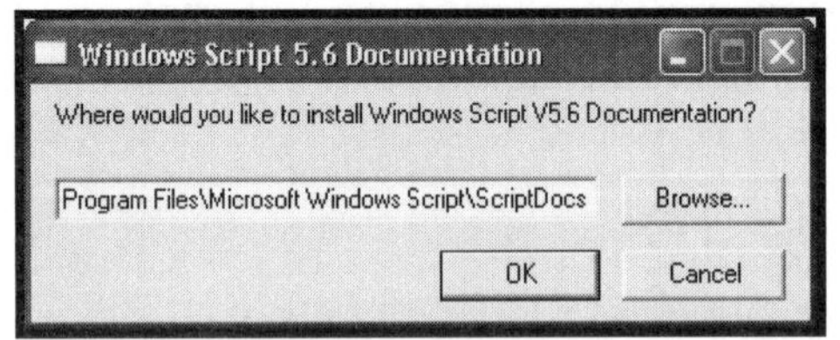

FIGURE 1.12

Specify the location where the WSH documentation should be installed.

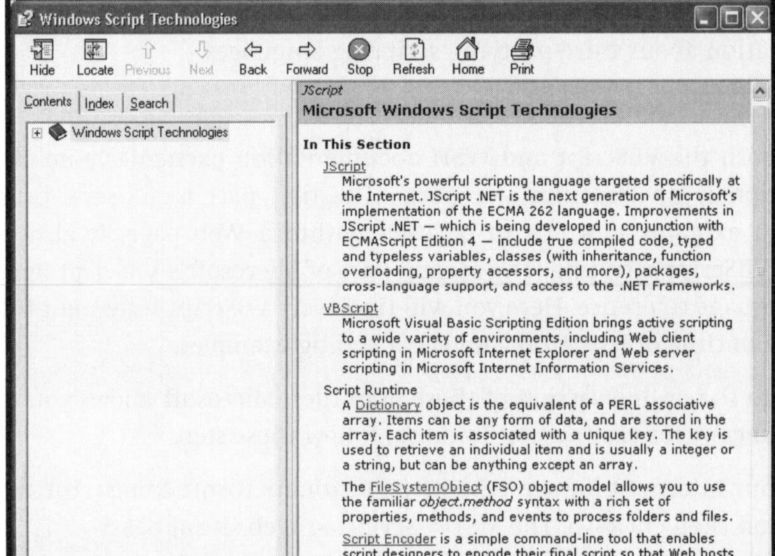

FIGURE 1.13

Viewing a local copy of Microsoft VBScript and WSH documentation is a lot faster and more convenient than using the online version.

BACK TO THE KNOCK KNOCK GAME

Let's turn the focus of this chapter back to the development of your first VBScript, the Knock Knock game. This project will demonstrate the steps involved in creating and running your first VBScript game. Along the way, you'll learn how to use VBScript to create a script that can communicate with the user via pop-up dialogs. You will also learn a little about conditional programming logic.

Designing the Game

The Knock Knock game's design is very straightforward, involving basic programming techniques. The game begins by displaying the message "Knock Knock" in a pop-up dialog box. It then waits for the player to reply by typing "Who's there?" The game then replies "Panther" and waits for the player to respond by typing "Panther who?" at which time the punch line,

"Panther no panths, I'm going swimming" is displayed. If the player fails to exactly type the proper responses at any point of the game, an error message will be displayed inviting the player to try again.

This project will be completed in five steps, as follows:

1. Present the player with the Knock Knock pop-up dialog box and collect the player's response.
2. Validate the player's reply and continue the game if appropriate. Otherwise, display an error message.
3. Present the player with the name of the person at the door and collect his or her reply.
4. Validate the player's reply and continue the game if appropriate. Otherwise display an error message.
5. Display the game's punch line.

Starting the Script Development Process

The first step in creating the Knock Knock game is to start your script editor and use it to create an empty VBScript file. For example, to create the script using the Notepad text editor on a computer running Windows XP, you would execute the following steps:

1. Click Start, All Programs, Accessories, Notepad. The Notepad application opens.
2. Click File, Save. The Save As dialog box appears. Specify the location where you want the script to be stored and then type `KnockKnock.vbs` in the File name field at the bottom of the dialog box. Click Save.

The Notepad editor should now display the name of the Knock Knock script in its title bar.

Starting the Game and Collecting Initial User Input

Now let's begin the script by writing its first VBScript statement. The first thing that the game is supposed to do is display a pop-up dialog box displaying the "Knock Knock" message and then wait for the user response. This task is performed surprisingly easily using VBScript, and can be done with a single line of code:

```
Reply1 = InputBox("Knock Knock!")
```

In plain English, this VBScript statement displays a pop-up dialog box with a "Knock Knock" message and then waits for the player to type something into the dialog box's text field and click the OK button.

> **DEFINITION**
>
> A *statement* is a line of code. Statements generally consist of a single line of code but can be spread over two or more lines depending on the size of the statement.

Let's break this statement down into pieces and see how it works. First of all, the statement executes a built-in VBScript function called `InputBox()`. This function displays a pop-up dialog box with a text entry field that allows the script to collect text input from the player.

The VBScript `InputBox()` function is just one of a number of options for collecting input. The `InputBox()` function facilitates direct interaction with users. When direct user interaction is not required, you can also develop VBScripts that can read input from text files or the Windows Registry. I'll show you how to read data from text files in Chapter 8 "Storing and Retrieving Data" and how to interact with the Windows Registry in Chapter 10 "Using the Windows Registry to Configure Script Settings." You can also create VBScripts that process data passed to them at run-time. I'll show you how this works in Chapter 4 "Constants, Variables, and Arrays."

To communicate with the player, the `InputBox()` function allows you to display a message. In the case of this example, the message is simply "Knock Knock," but could just as easily be "Hello, what is your name?" or any other question that helps the player understand the type of information the script is trying to collect.

Finally, the text typed by the player in the pop-up dialog box's text field is temporarily assigned to a variable called `Reply1`. Variables provide scripts with the capability to store and later reference data used by the script.

Functions and variables are fundamental components of VBScript. Unfortunately, it is difficult to write even the simplest scripts without using them. For now, don't worry too much about them and keep your focus on the overall steps used to create and run the Knock Knock game. I'll go over the use of variables in great detail in Chapter 4, "Constants, Variables, and Arrays," and the use of functions in Chapter 7, "Using Procedures to Organize Scripts."

Validating User Input

The player's role in this game is to first type in the phrase "Who's there?" Any variation in spelling or case will result in an error. After the player has typed in this message and clicked on the OK button, the script needs to perform a test that validates whether the player is playing the game properly. The following three lines of code accomplish this task:

```
If Reply1 = "Who's there?" Then
.
.
.
End If
If Reply1 <> "Who's there?" Then MsgBox "Incorrect answer. Try again."
```

The first two lines of code go together. The three dots that you see in between these lines of code are placeholders for more statements that will be inserted in the next section. The first of these two lines tests the value of `Reply1`. Remember that Reply1 is a variable that contains the response typed in by the player. This statement checks to see if the values stored in `Reply1` match the phrase "Who's there?" If there is an exact match, then the lines of code that you will soon place within the first two statements are executed. Otherwise, these statements are not processed. The third line of code inverts the test performed by the first two lines of code by checking to see if the player's reply is not equal to (that is, <>) the expected phrase. If this is the case, then the rest of the third statement executes displaying an error message. The text performed by the third statement may prove true for a number of reasons, including

- The player clicked the Cancel button.
- The player clicked the OK button without typing a response.
- The player typed an incorrect response.

Finishing Input Collection

If you are creating the script as you read along, then your script should now contain the following statements:

```
Reply1 = InputBox("Knock Knock!")
If Reply1 = "Who's there?" Then
.
.
.
End If
If Reply1 <> "Who's there?" Then MsgBox "Incorrect answer. Try again."
```

It's now time to add three lines of code that will reside within the second and third lines of code just shown. The first of these three lines of code is as follows:

```
Reply2 = InputBox("Panther!")
```

This statement is very similar to the first statement in the script, except that instead of displaying the message "Knock Knock," it displays the message "Panther" and then waits for the player to type in a response (that is, "Panther who?"). The text typed in by the player is then stored in a variable named `Reply2`.

Validating the User's Last Response

The following two lines of code need to be inserted just after the previous statement:

```
If Reply2 = "Panther who?" Then _
  MsgBox "Panther no panths I'm going swimming."
If Reply2 <> "Panther who?" Then MsgBox "Incorrect answer. Try again."
```

The first line checks to see if the value stored in `Reply2` is equal to the phrase "Who is it?" and if it is, then the rest of the statement displays the joke's punch line. If the player typed in something other than "Who is it?", then the second of these two statements executes displaying a message that informs the player that he or she did not provide the correct response.

The Final Result

Now let's take a look at the fully assembled script.

```
Reply1 = InputBox("Knock Knock!")

If Reply1 = "Who's there?" Then

  Reply2 = InputBox("Panther!")

  If Reply2 = "Panther who?" Then _
    MsgBox "Panther no panths I'm going swimming."

  If Reply2 <> "Panther who?" Then MsgBox "Incorrect answer. Try again."

End If

If Reply1 <> "Who's there?" Then MsgBox "Incorrect answer. Try again."
```

As you can see, the script only has seven lines of code, and yet it displays multiple graphical pop-up dialogs that collect player text input and display any of three additional messages in pop-up dialogs. In addition, this script demonstrates one way of testing player input and then altering the execution of the script based on that input.

Save and then run the script, and make sure everything works as expected. If not, open the script and double-check each statement to make sure that you typed it in correctly.

Summary

This chapter has covered a lot of ground for an introductory chapter. Not only did you create your first VBScript, but you also learned how to use the WSH to execute it and to incorporate WSH elements within your scripts. In addition, you learned a lot about VBScript and how it relates to other languages that make up the Visual Basic family of programming languages. Finally, you created your first computer game, learning how to collect and validate user input and to display output. All in all, I'd say that this has been a very good start.

Challenges

1. **The Knock Knock game is a very simple game. Its main purpose was to introduce you to the basics of script and game development. Try to improve the game by adding additional jokes so that the game does not end after the first joke.**
2. **Try running the Knock Knock game using both the CScript and WScript WSH execution hosts. How does the execution of the script change and why?**
3. **See if you can create a new script that prompts you for your name and then displays a personalized greeting message that includes your name. Hint: When displaying the customized greeting message, you will need to concatenate (glue together) the name of the user with a greeting message as follows:**

```
MsgBox "Greetings " & UserName
```

Overview of the Windows Script Host

Because VBScripts cannot execute without an execution host of some type, the WSH is at the heart of any VBScript that you run from the Windows desktop or command line. The WSH not only provides an environment in which VBScripts can execute, but it also provides scripts with direct access to Windows resources such as the Windows desktop, Start menu, Registry, event logs, and network resources. To effectively create and execute VBScripts in this environment, it's essential to have a good understanding of the WSH core object model. This includes knowing about the methods and properties associated with WSH objects, as well as how to configure the WSH to best suit your needs. In this chapter, you will learn

- About the objects that make up the WSH core object model
- How to use WSH object methods within your VBScripts
- How to use WSH object properties within your VBScripts
- How to configure the execution of the WScript and CScript execution hosts

Project Preview: The Rock, Paper, and Scissors Game

In this chapter, you will learn how to create a computer version of the Rock, Paper, and Scissors game that you played as a child. The game begins by displaying its rules and then it asks the player to choose between one of the three possible choices. After the player makes a selection, the game randomly makes its own selection and displays the results. Figure 2.1 through 2.3 demonstrate the flow of the game.

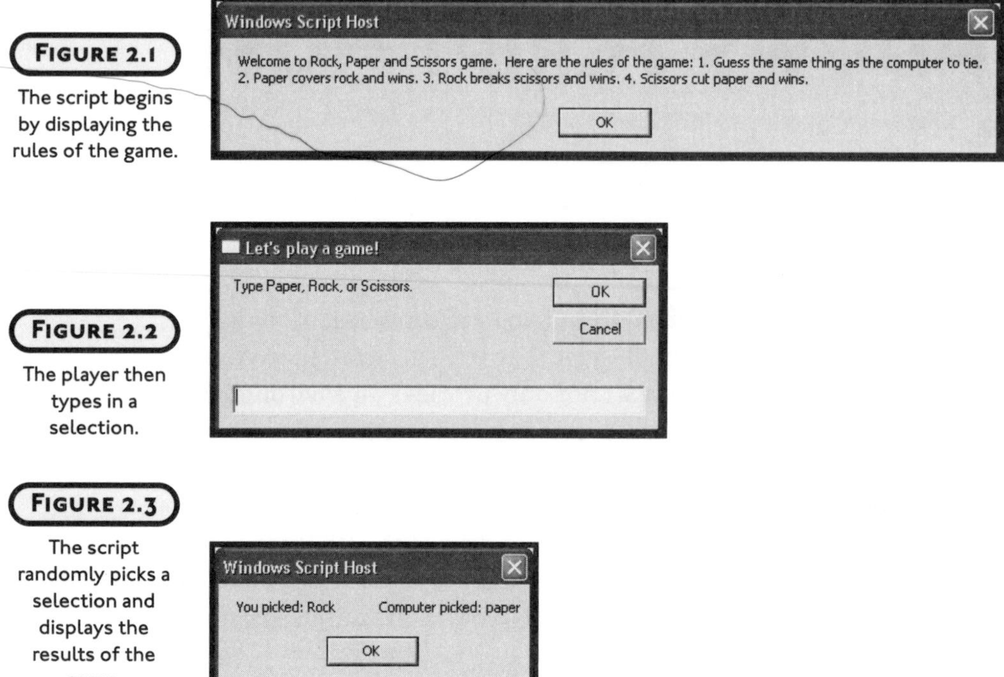

Figure 2.1 The script begins by displaying the rules of the game.

Figure 2.2 The player then types in a selection.

Figure 2.3 The script randomly picks a selection and displays the results of the game.

Through the development of this game, you'll get a chance to practice incorporating WSH objects and their methods into VBScripts. You'll also learn how to perform a little simple conditional logic, as well as take a peek at using a number of built-in VBScript functions.

A Detailed Examination of WSH Components

Think of a computer, its operating system, and its hardware and software as being a collection of objects such as files, disk drives, printers, and so on. To automate tasks on Windows operating systems, VBScript needs a way of interacting with these objects. This is provided by the WSH's core object model.

An understanding of the WSH core object model is essential to your success as a VBScript programmer. Not only will it provide you with the technical insights you'll need to develop scripts that will run on Windows operating systems, but by introducing you to working with objects, it will also prepare you to work with other object models. For example, many Windows applications, including Microsoft Office applications, expose their own object models, allowing VBScript to programmatically manipulate them. In addition, other VBScript execution hosts, such as Internet Explorer, provide VBScript with access to other object models. The WSH core object model is complex and may at first seem rather daunting. As a result, you may not leave this chapter feeling 100 percent confident that you fully understand it. But don't worry—you'll continue to develop your understanding of this complex topic as you go through the rest of this book.

DEFINITION

An *object model* is a representation of a number of related objects that provide a script or program with the capability to view and interact with each of the objects (files, disks, printers, and so on) represented in the object model.

The Core Object Model

The WSH core object model provides programmatic access to Windows resources. There are 14 objects in the WSH core object model, as depicted in Figure 2.4. Each of these objects provides access to a particular category of Windows resources.

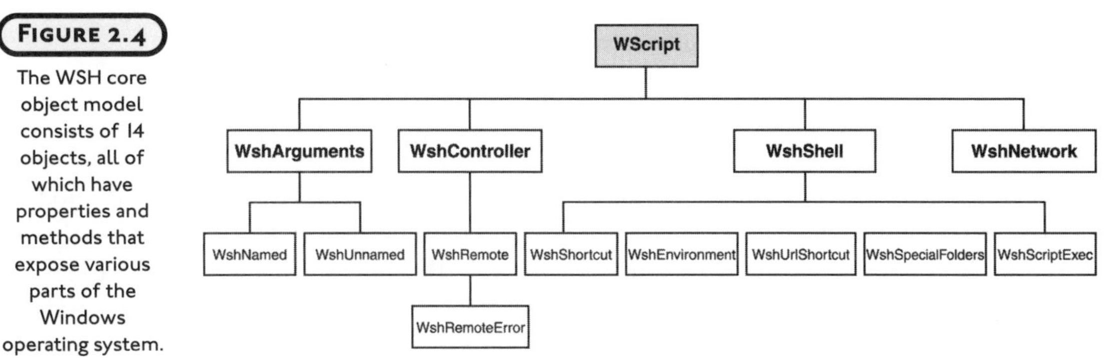

FIGURE 2.4

The WSH core object model consists of 14 objects, all of which have properties and methods that expose various parts of the Windows operating system.

At the top, or *root*, of the WSH core object model is the `WScript` object. All other objects are instantiated from this object. The `WScript` object is automatically established during the startup of the execution host and can therefore be referenced without first being instantiated within your scripts. For example, let's create a short one-line script called `Greeting.vbs`.

```
WScript.Echo "Example: Using the WScript object's Echo() method"
```

To test this script, open your script editor and type in this statement. Now save the script, and then run it by double-clicking on it. The pop-up dialog , shown in Figure 2.5, should appear. As this script demonstrates, you can automatically access any of the properties and methods belonging to the `WScript` object directly from within your scripts.

> **DEFINITION**
>
> *Instantiation* describes the process of creating a reference to an object. To work with an object, you must first create, or instantiate, a reference to it within your scripts.

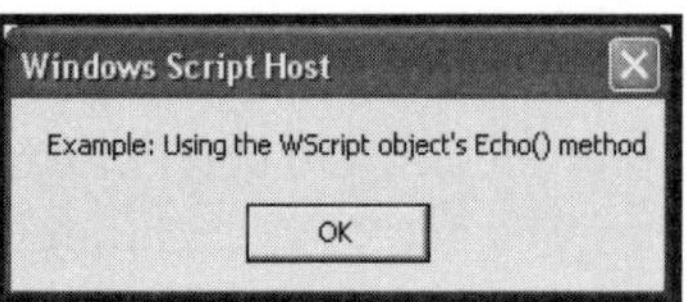

FIGURE 2.5

A pop-up dialog created using the `WScript` object's `Echo()` method.

The `WScript` object provides access to a number of very useful methods that you'll see used throughout this book. These methods include

- **`CreateObject()`** Establishes an instance of the specified object.
- **`DisconnectObject()`** Prevents a script from accessing a previously instantiated object.
- **`Echo()`** Displays a text message in the Windows Console or as a pop-up dialog depending on which execution host runs the script.
- **`Quit()`** Terminates a script's execution.
- **`Sleep()`** Pauses the execution of a script for a specified number of seconds.

The `WScript` object is referred to as a public or exposed object. The WSH core object model has three other public objects: `WshController`, `WshShell`, and `WshNetwork`. Each of these three objects must be instantiated within your scripts using the `WScript` object's `CreateObject()` method. All the other objects in the WSH core object model can only be instantiated by using properties or methods associated with the `WScript`, `WshController`, `WshShell`, and `WshNetwork` objects.

Table 2.1 lists the rest of the objects in the WSH core object model, as well as the object properties or methods required to instantiate them.

Table 2.1 Working with Lower-Level WSH Objects

Object	Method of Instantiation
WshArguments	WScript.Arguments
WshNamed	WScript.Arguments.Named
WshUnnamed	WScript.Arguments.Unnamed
WshRemote	WshController.CreateScript()
WshRemoteError	WshRemote.Error
WshShortcut	WshShell.CreateShortcut()
WshUrlShortcut	WshShell.CreateShortcut()
WshEnvironment	WshShell.Environment
WshSpecialFolders	WshShell.SpecialFolders
WshScriptExec	WshShell.Exec()

WSH Objects and Their Properties and Methods

Each object in the WSH core object model provides access to, or exposes, a particular subset of Windows functionality. Table 2.2 lists all 14 of the WSH core objects, provides a high-level description of these objects, and lists all the properties and methods associated with each object.

Table 2.2 WSH Core Objects

Object	Description
WScript	This is the WSH root object. It provides access to a number of useful properties and methods. It also provides access to the rest of the objects in the WSH core object model. **Properties:** Arguments, FullName, Interactive, Name, Path, ScriptFullName, ScriptName, StdErr, StdIn, StdOut, and Version. **Methods:** ConnectObject(), CreateObject(), DisconnectObject(), Echo(), GetObject(), Quit(), and Sleep().
WshArguments	This object enables you to access command-line arguments passed to the script at execution time. **Properties:** Count, Item, and Length, Named, and Unnamed. **Methods:** Count() and ShowUsage().

(continues)

Table 2.2 WSH Core Objects (continued)

Object	Description
WshNamed	This object provides access to a set of named command-line arguments. **Properties:** Item and Length. **Methods:** Count() and Exists().
WshUnnamed	This object provides access to a set of unnamed command-line arguments. **Properties:** Item and Length. **Methods:** Count().
WshController	This object provides the capability to create a remote script process. **Properties:** This object does not support any properties. **Methods:** CreateScript.
WshRemote	This object provides the capability to administer remote computer systems using scripts over a network. **Properties:** Status and Error. **Methods:** Execute() and Terminate().
WshRemoteError	This object provides access to information on errors produced by remote scripts. **Properties:** Description, Line, Character, SourceText, Source, and Number. **Methods:** This object does not support any methods.
WshNetwork	This object provides access to a number of different network resources such as network printers and drives. **Properties:** ComputerName, UserDomain, and UserName. **Methods:** AddWindowsPrinterConnection(), AddPrinterConnection(), EnumNetworkDrives(), EnumPrinterConnection(), MapNetworkDrive(), RemoveNetworkDrive(), RemovePrinterConnection(), and SetDefaultPrinter().
WshShell	This object provides access to the Windows Registry, event log, environmental variables, shortcuts, and applications. **Properties:** CurrentDirectory, Environment, and SpecialFolders. **Methods:** AppActivate(), CreateShortcut(), ExpandEnvironmentStrings(), LogEvent(), Popup(), RegDelete(), RegRead(), RegWrite(), Run(), SendKeys(), and Exec().
WshShortcut	This object provides scripts with methods and properties for creating and manipulating Windows shortcuts. **Properties:** Arguments, Description, FullName, Hotkey, IconLocation, TargetPath, WindowStyle, and WorkingDirectory. **Method:** Save().

Table 2.2 WSH Core Objects (continued)

Object	Description
WshUrlShortcut	This object provides scripts with methods and properties for creating and manipulating URL shortcuts. **Properties:** FullName and TargetPath. **Method:** Save().
WshEnvironment	This object provides access to Windows environmental variables. **Properties:** Item and Length. **Methods:** Remove() and Count().
WshSpecialFolders	This object provides access to special Windows folders that allow scripts to configure the Start menu, desktop, Quick Launch Toolbar, and other special Windows folders. **Properties:** Item. **Methods:** Count().
WshScriptExec	This object provides access to error information from scripts run using the Exec method. **Properties:** Status, StdOut, StdIn, and StdErr. **Methods:** Terminate().

There are too many properties and methods supported by objects in the WSH core object model to include them all in this table. I will cover them separately a little later in this chapter.

Examining Object Properties

By accessing object properties, your scripts can gather all kinds of information when they execute. For example, using the properties associated with the WshNetwork object, your scripts can collect information about the Windows domain that the person who ran the script has logged in to, as well as the computer's name and the user's name. This information could then be used, for example, to prevent the script from executing on certain domains or computers.

More than three dozen properties are associated with various WSH objects. In many cases, properties are associated with more than one object. Refer to Table 2.2 to see which properties are associated with which objects.

Table 2.3 provides a complete review of WSH object properties.

TABLE 2.3 WSH OBJECT PROPERTIES

Property	Description
Arguments	Sets a pointer reference to the WshArguments collection.
AtEndOfLine	Returns either true or false depending on whether the end-of-line maker has been reached in the stream.
AtEndOfStream	Returns either true or false depending on whether the end of the input stream has been reached.
Character	Identifies the specific character in a line of code where an error occurs.
Column	Returns the current column position in the input stream.
ComputerName	Retrieves a computer's name.
CurrentDirectory	Sets or retrieves a script current working directory.
Description	Retrieves the description for a specified shortcut.
Environment	Sets a pointer reference to the WshEnvironment.
Error	Provides the ability to expose a WshRemoteError object.
ExitCode	Returns the existing code from a script started using Exec().
FullName	Retrieves a shortcut or executable program's path.
HotKey	Retrieves the hotkey associated with the specified shortcut.
IconLocation	Retrieves an icon's location.
Interactive	Provides the ability to programmatically set script mode.
Item	Retrieves the specified item from a collection or provides access to items stored in the WshNamed object.
Length	Retrieves a count of enumerated items.
Line	Returns the line number for the current line in the input stream or identifies the line number within a script on which an error occurred.
Name	Returns a string representing the name of the WScript object.
Number	Provides access to an error number.
Path	Returns the location of the folder where the CScript or WScript execution hosts reside.
ProcessID	Retrieves the process ID (PID) for a process started using the WshScriptExec object.
ScriptFullName	Returns an executing script's path.
ScriptName	Returns the name of the executing script.
Source	Retrieves the identity of the object that caused a script error.

Table 2.3 WSH Object Properties (continued)

Property	Description
SourceText	Retrieves the source code that created the error.
SpecialFolders	Provides access to the Windows Start menu and desktop folders.
Status	Provides status information about a remotely executing script or a script starting with Exec().
StdErr	Enables a script to write to the error output stream or provides access to read-only error output from an Exec object.
StdIn	Enables read access to the input stream or provides access to the write-only input stream for the Exec object.
StdOut	Enables write access to the output stream or provides access to the write-only output stream of the Exec object.
TargetPath	Retrieves a shortcut's path to its associated object.
UserDomain	Retrieves the domain name.
UserName	Retrieves the currently logged-on user's name.
Version	Retrieves the WSH version number.
WindowStyle	Retrieves a shortcut's window style.
WorkingDirectory	Returns the working directory associated with the specified shortcut.

Working with Object Properties

Now let's take a look at an example of a VBScript that demonstrates how to instantiate an instance of the WshNetwork object and access its properties. The script is called NetInfo.vbs and is as follows:

```
Set WshNtwk = WScript.CreateObject("WScript.Network")

PropertyInfo = "User Domain" & vbTab & "= " & WshNtwk.UserDomain & _
  vbCrLf & "Computer Name" & vbTab & "= " & WshNtwk.ComputerName & _
  vbCrLf & _ "User Name" & vbTab & "= " & WshNtwk.UserName & vbCrLf

MsgBox PropertyInfo, vbOkOnly , "WshNtwk Properties Example"
```

As you can see, it isn't a very big script. It begins by using a Set statement to create an instance of the WshNetwork object, which is associated with a variable name of WshNtwk. After you have established an instance of the WshNetwork object in this manner, you can reference the object's properties and methods using its variable name assignment.

The next statement is so long, that to improve the script's readability, I decided to break it into three lines and end each of the first two lines with the & and _ characters. The `&` character is a concatenation character and is used to append two strings. The _ character is a continuation character and is used to indicate that a statement is continued on the next line. This statement displays the values of the following `WshShell` properties:

> **DEFINITION**
>
> The **`Set`** statement is used to create a reference to a specified object. Using this reference, you can refer to the object and its properties and methods over and over again throughout your script.

- **WshNetwork.UserDomain.** The name of the domain into which the person running the script is logged in.
- **WshNetwork.ComputerName.** The name of the computer on which the script is being executed.
- **WshNetwork.UserName.** The username of the person who ran the script.

To improve the presentation of the message, I formatted it using the VBScript `vbTab` and `vbCrLf` constants. The `vbTab` constant is used to line up the output at the point of the equals sign. The `vbCrLf` constant is used to execute a line feed and carriage return at the end of each line of output.

The last thing that the script does is display the message using the following statement:

```
MsgBox PropertyInfo, vbOkOnly , "WshNetwork Properties Example"
```

`MsgBox()` is a built-in VBScript function that displays a text message in a pop-up dialog. `PropertyInfo` is a variable that I used to store the output message. `VbOkOnly` is a VBScript constant that tells the `MsgBox()` function to only display the OK button in the pop-up dialog. The last part of the previous statement is a message that will be displayed in the pop-up dialog 's title bar. If you save and run this script yourself, you should see a pop-up dialog similar to the one shown in Figure 2.6.

> **DEFINITION**
>
> A *constant* is a VBScript construct that contains information that does not change during the execution of a script. VBScript provides a collection of built-in constants, such as the **`vbTab`** and **`vbCrLf`** constants, that you can incorporate into your scripts to control the formatting of your script output.

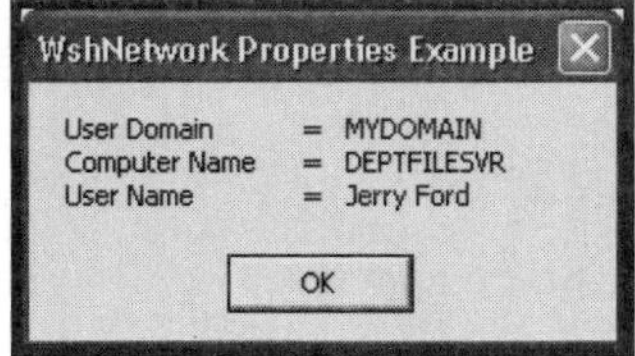

A pop-up dialog displaying properties associated with the `WshNetwork` object.

Examining Object Methods

The WSH also provides a large collection of object methods. By using these methods in your VBScripts, you'll be able to manipulate the Windows resources associated with objects.

You won't be able to do anything with your VBScripts that you don't have the appropriate set of security permissions and rights to do on a particular computer. For example, if you don't have the ability to manually create a new user account on your computer, then you won't be able to run a VBScript designed to perform this operation, either. However, if you have administrative privileges on the computer, your scripts should be able to run unhindered.

For example, using the `WshShell` object's `RegRead()`, `RegWrite()`, and `RegDelete()` methods, you can create scripts that can access and manipulate the contents of the Windows Registry. Using these methods, you can create scripts that can configure just about any Windows resource.

The Windows *Registry* is a repository used by the operating system to store information about every aspect of the computer's hardware and software. Making an incorrect configuration change to the Registry can have disastrous effects on the operation of the computer and may potentially prevent it from being able to start. I strongly recommend that, unless you're very sure of what you are doing, you never attempt to modify the Registry, either manually or by using a script.

Table 2.4 provides a complete review of WSH object methods.

Table 2.4 WSH Object Methods

Method	Description
AddPrinterConnection()	Creates printer mappings.
AddWindowsPrinterConnection()	Creates a new printer connection.
AppActivate()	Activates the targeted application window.
Close()	Terminates or ends an open data stream.
ConnectObject()	Establishes a connection to an object.
Count	Retrieves the number of switches found in the WshNamed and WshUnnamed objects.
CreateObject()	Creates a new instance of an object.
CreateScript()	Instantiates a WshRemote object representing a script that is running remotely.
CreateShortcut()	Creates a Windows shortcut.
DisconnectObject()	Terminates a connection with an object.
Echo()	Displays a text message.
EnumNetworkDrives()	Enables access to network drives.
EnumPrinterConnections()	Enables access to network printers.
Exec()	Executes an application in a child command shell and provides access to the environment variables.
Execute()	Initiates the execution of a remote script object.
Exists()	Determines a specified key exists within the WshNamed object.
ExpandEnvironmentStrings()	Retrieves a string representing the contents of the Process environmental variable.
GetObject()	Retrieves an Automation object.
GetResource()	Retrieves a resource's value as specified by the <resource> tag.
LogEvent()	Writes a message in the Windows event log.
MapNetworkDrive()	Creates a network drive mapping.
Popup()	Displays a text message in a pop-up dialog.
Quit()	Terminates, or ends, a script.
Read()	Retrieves a string of characters from the input stream
ReadAll()	Retrieves the s string that is made up of the characters in the input stream.

Table 2.4 WSH Object Methods (continued)

Method	Description
ReadLine()	Retrieves a string containing an entire line of data from the input stream.
RegDelete()	Deletes a Registry key or value.
RegRead()	Retrieves a Registry key or value.
RegWrite()	Creates a Registry key or value.
Remove()	Deletes the specified environmental variable.
RemoveNetworkDrive()	Deletes the connection to the specified network drive.
RemovePrinterConnection()	Deletes the connection to the specified network printer.
Run()	Starts a new process.
Save()	Saves a shortcut.
SendKeys()	Emulates keystrokes and sends typed data to a specified window.
SetDefaultPrinter()	Establishes a default Windows printer.
ShowUsage()	Retrieves information regarding the way that a script is supposed to be executed.
Skip()	Skips X number of characters when reading from the input stream.
SkipLine()	Skips an entire line when reading from the input stream.
Sleep()	Pauses script execution for X number of seconds.
Terminate()	Stops a process started by Exec().
Write()	Places a string in the output stream.
WriteBlankLines()	Places a blank in the output stream.
WriteLine()	Places a string in the output stream.

Working with Object Methods

To really understand how object methods work, you need to work with some examples. Let's take a look at two examples. In the first example, you'll see how to work with the WshShell object's Run() method to create a graphical front-end to the Windows NET SEND command. In the second example, you'll learn how to use the WshShell object's LogEvent() method to write messages directly to a Windows XP, .NET, 2000, or NT computer's application event log.

The `WshShell` object provides access to a number of Windows resources, including

- The Windows application log
- The Windows Registry
- Any Windows command-line command

Let's look at an example of how to use the `WshShell` object's `Run()` method. I've named this VBScript `NetMessenger.vbs`. `NetMessenger.vbs` provides a friendly graphical front end to the Windows `NET SEND` command-line command. The `NET SEND` command can be used to send text messages over a network to other currently logged-on users by specifying either the user's username or the computer name that the user is using. To use this command from the Windows command line, you might type something like

```
NET SEND jford Jerry, please stop by my office when you have a moment
```

`NET SEND` is the command being used. `Jford` is the username of the person to receive the message, and the rest of the statement is the message text that is to be sent.

Using the `NET SEND` command is not very complicated. Click on Start, Run, and then type `CMD` and click on OK. This opens the Windows Console. Now type the `NET SEND` command and press the Enter key. That's it. Within moments, your message should appear on the recipient's screen. Unfortunately, many people are intimidated by the very thought of using the Windows command prompt. So let's write a VBScript, shown here, that makes using this command easy:

```
Set WshShl = WScript.CreateObject("WScript.Shell")

Recipient = InputBox("Type the username or computer name " & _
  "that the message is to be sent: ")

MsgText = InputBox("Type your message: ")

WshShl.Run "Net Send " & Recipient & " " & MsgText
```

The first line of this script instantiates the `WshShell` object and associates with it a variable called `WshShl`. The next two lines display a pop-up dialog asking the user to type a username or computer name. The information typed in by the user is stored in a variable called `Recipient`. The next line allows the user to type in a text message and stores it in a variable called `MsgText`. The last line of this script executes the `WshShell` object's `Run()` method, passing it the `NET SEND` command, the name of the recipient, and the message to be sent.

Open your script editor and type in the script as just shown, and then save it as `Messenger.vbs`. Run the script and you'll see a pop-up dialog like the one in Figure 2.7, asking for the username or computer name of the recipient.

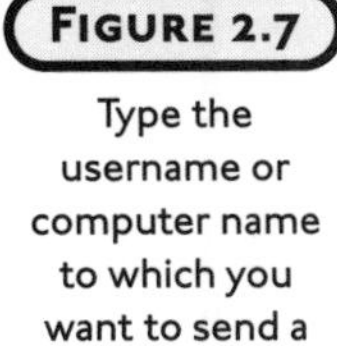

FIGURE 2.7

Type the username or computer name to which you want to send a message.

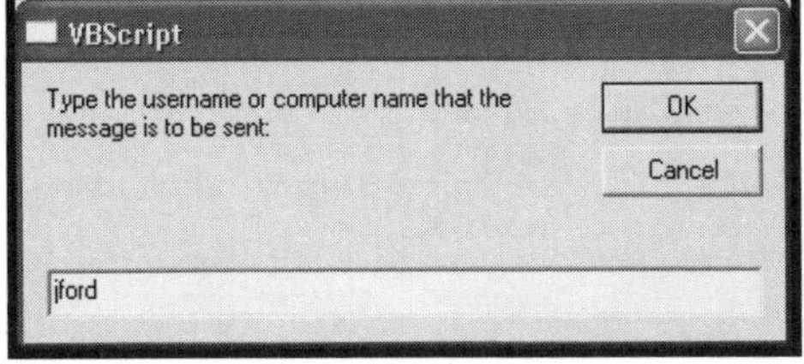

Type the required information and click on OK. The pop-up dialog shown in Figure 2.8 appears. Type the message you want to send and then click OK.

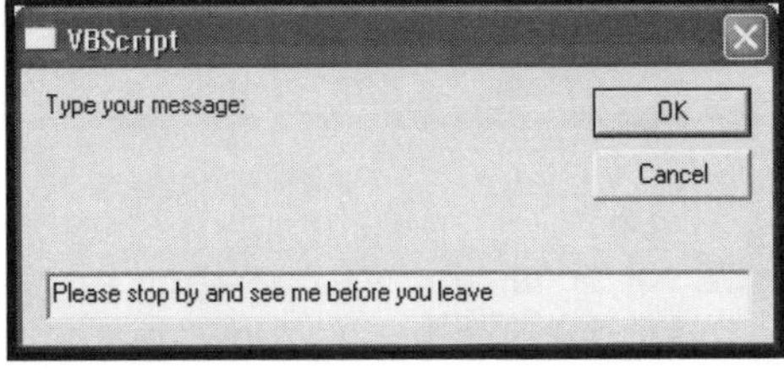

FIGURE 2.8

Type the message that you want to send.

Within a few moments, your message appears on the recipient's screen, as shown in Figure 2.9.

FIGURE 2.9

The recipient of the message sees your message, as well as your computer's name and the date and time of the message.

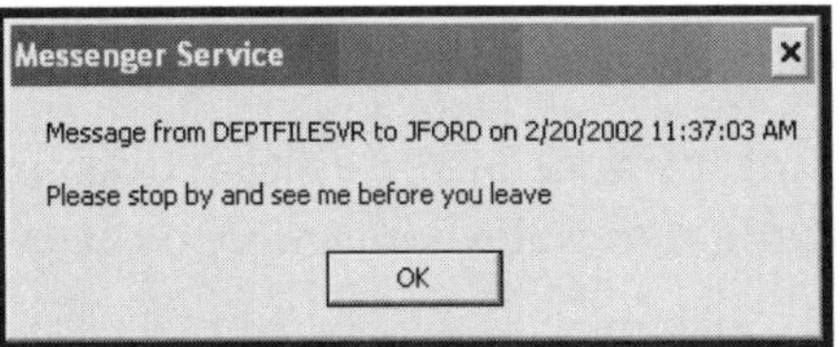

In the second example, you'll learn how to use the `WshShell` object's `LogEvent()` method to write a message to the Windows event log. The Windows event log is accessed differently, depending on which version of Windows you use. For example, on Windows 2000 and Windows XP, you can click Start and then right-click My Computer and select Manage to open the Computer Management console where the Event Viewer utility or snap-in resides. To view the application event log, expand the Event Viewer node and select Application, as shown in Figure 2.10. Double-click on an event entry in the event log to examine it.

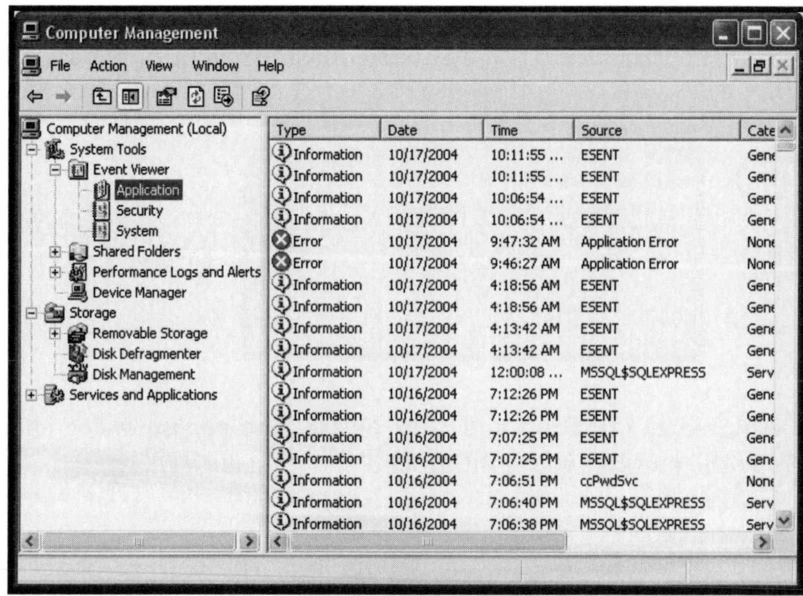

FIGURE 2.10

Examining the contents of the application event log.

Only the Windows .NET, XP, 2000, and NT operating systems support event logs. Don't try running this script on other Windows operating systems such as Windows 98 or Me.

The scripting logic to write a message to the Windows application event log is very simple:

```
Set WshShl = WScript.CreateObject("WScript.Shell")

WshShl.LogEvent 0, "EventLogger.vbs - Beginning script execution."
```

The first line of this script establishes an instance of the `WshShell` object. The second line uses the `WshShell` object's `LogEvent()` method to write a message to the event log.

One really good use of the `WshShell` object's `LogEvent()` method is to log the execution of scripts run using the Windows Event Scheduler service. This way, you can review the application event log each day and make sure that your scripts are executing when you expect them to.

Using your script editor, create a new script called `EventLogger.vbs` that contains the previous statements. Run the script and then check the application event log; you should find the message added by the script. Double-click it; you should see the Event Properties dialog for the event, as shown in Figure 2.11.

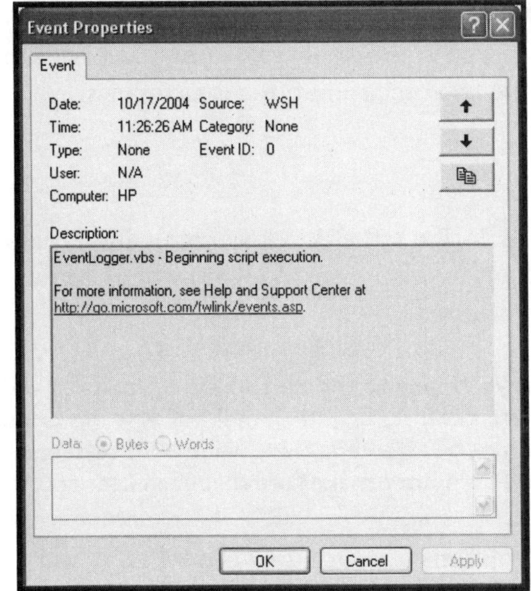

FIGURE 2.11

Viewing the event that the `EventLogger.vbs` script added to the Windows application event log.

CONFIGURING WSH EXECUTION HOSTS

So far you've used the CScript and WScript execution host default settings for each script that you've created and run. If you want to, you can modify these default settings to better suit your personal preferences. The WSH provides separate configuration settings for the WScript and CScript execution hosts. Because the WScript execution hosts can process scripts run from either the Windows GUI or the Windows command line, there are two different ways to configure them. The WSH also allows you to override execution host settings on-the-fly by passing configuration arguments to the execution host when starting a script's execution. Finally, the WScript execution host allows you to set execution host settings unique to a particular script using a `.wsh` file.

Each of these execution host configuration options is examined in detail in the sections that follow.

Configuring WScript and CScript Command-Line Execution

You can use either the WScript or CScript execution hosts to run any VBScript. Generally speaking, you'll use the WScript to run scripts that need to use pop-up dialogs, and the CScript execution host to run scripts silently in the background.

Even though they have their own separate configuration settings, both the WScript and CScript execution hosts are configured in the same way, using the exact same set of options. The syntax used to configure these two execution hosts is as follows:

```
wscript [//options]
cscript [//options]
```

Begin by opening a Windows Console. From the Windows command prompt, type the name of the execution host that you want to configure followed by one or more options, each of which is preceded by the // characters.

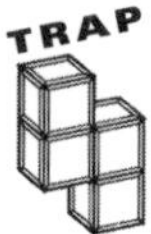

Any changes that you made to the default execution host will only affect your scripts—if you share a computer with somebody else, his or her WSH execution host settings will not be affected. If you want WSH settings to be standardized for all users of the computer, make sure that each user sets them accordingly.

Table 2.5 lists the configuration options supported by the WScript and CScript execution hosts.

Now let's look at some examples of how to modify the configuration of the execution hosts. By default, the WSH sets the WScript execution host up as the default execution host. However, you can change this by typing the following command and pressing the Enter key:

```
cscript //H:cscript //s
```

The `//H:cscript` option makes the CScript execution the default and the `//s` option makes the change permanent. If you left the `//s` option off the command, the change would have only been in effect for your current working session. Likewise, to change the default command-line execution host back to WScript, type the following command and press the Enter key:

```
wscript //H:wscript //s
```

Now let's try an example that sets more than one configuration option:

```
wscript //H:wscript //nologo //t:60 //s
```

In this example, the WScript execution host is set up as the default. In addition, the `//nologo` option prevents the display of the WScript logo during script execution. The `//t:60` option prevents any script from executing for more than 60 seconds. Finally, the `//s` option saves all specified settings.

Table 2.5 Command-Line Options for the WScript and CScript Execution Hosts

Configuration Option	Purpose
//?	Displays the command syntax for the CScript and WScript execution hosts.
//b	Runs a script in batch mode, where all errors and message output are suppressed.
//d	Turns on script debugging.
//e:jscript | e:vbscript	Sets the script engine that is to be used to run the script.
//h:wscript | h:script	Sets the execution host that is to be used to run the script.
//i	Runs the script interactively, displaying all errors and message output.
//job:*id*	Identifies a specific job within a Windows script file to be run.
//logo	Displays the CScript or WScript logo at the start of script execution.
//nologo	Suppresses the display of the CScript or WScript logo at the start of script execution.
//s	Saves the currently specified options and sets them as the default settings.
//t:*nn*	Establishes a timeout value that limits how long a script can execute. By default, these are not execution time limits imposed on script execution.
//x	Turns off script debugging.

Even the best programmers can make mistakes. Sometimes these mistakes cause scripts to behave in unexpected ways, such as getting stuck in a loop that executes forever. By setting the `//T:nn` option for both the WScript and CScript execution hosts, you can set up a sort of safety net that prevents any script that you run from executing for more than a minute.

Configuring WScript Desktop Execution

The WScript execution host's desktop configuration settings are different from its command-line configuring settings. First of all, there are only two configuration settings. The first specifies an optional time limit for script execution, and the second specifies whether or not the WScript logo is displayed when scripts are run from the Windows Console.

The steps involved in configuring the WScript execution host from the Windows desktop are as follows:

1. Click on Start, Run. The Run dialog appears.
2. Type `WScript` and then click on OK. The Windows Script Host Settings dialog appears, as shown in Figure 2.12.

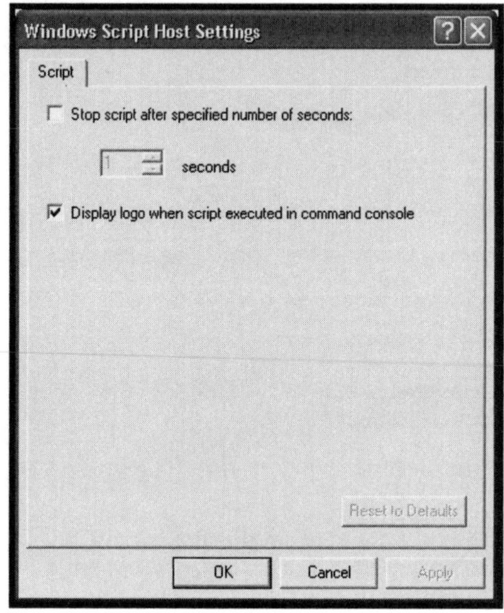

FIGURE 2.12

Modifying the WScript execution host's desktop configuration.

3. As you can see, by default, the WScript execution host does not have an execution time setting. To configure one, select the Stop script after specified number of seconds option and then specify a time limit (in seconds).
4. By default, the WScript execution host displays its logo when scripts are executed from the Windows Console. To prevent this behavior, clear the Display logo when script is executed in command console option.
5. Click on OK.

Overriding Command-Line Host Execution Settings

So far, you've learned how to configure the default execution of the WScript and CScript execution hosts from the Windows command-line and desktop. Now let's see how to override the default command-line settings without permanently changing them, in order to temporarily alter them for the execution of a specific script.

The syntax for temporarily overriding WScript and CScript execution is as follows:

```
wscript scriptname [//options] [arguments]
cscript scriptname [//options] [arguments]
```

First, open the Windows Console, and then type the name of the execution host you want to use to run the script. Next, type the name and path of the script to be executed; then type as many configuration settings as you want, preceding each with a pair of // characters. Finally, if the script that you're executing expects any input to be passed to it at execution time, specify the required arguments and then press the Enter key.

Now let's look at a few examples of how to override host script execution settings. First, let's assume that you're working with a script called `Test Script.vbs` and that you want to prevent it, using the WScript execution host, from executing for more than 30 seconds. Open the Windows Command Console and type the following command to run the script using the WScript execution hosts:

> **DEFINITION**
>
> In the context of this discussion, an *argument* is a piece of data passed to a script for processing. For example, if you wrote a VBScript to create new user accounts, your script might expect you to pass it one or more usernames to process.

```
wscript "Test Script.vbs" //T:30
```

Likewise, to execute the same script using the CScript execution host for a maximum of 30 seconds, type the following command, and then press the Enter key:

```
cscript "Test Script.vbs" //T:30
```

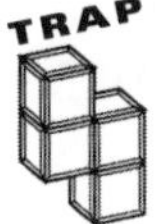

Windows operating systems support very large file names. They also allow you to include blank spaces as part of a file name to make those names more descriptive. If you choose to include blank spaces as part of your VBScript file names, then you'll need to enclose the file names inside a pair of quotation marks, as shown in the two previous examples, so that the script's file name will be correctly interpreted.

Now let's look at a slightly more complicated example, in which multiple configuration settings are overridden:

```
wscript "Test Script.vbs" //T:30 //nologo
```

In this example, the script is prevented from executing for more than 30 seconds using the WScript execution hosts. In addition, the WScript execution host's logo is suppressed to prevent it from being displayed at the beginning of the script's execution.

Customizing WScript Settings for Individual Desktop Scripts

The WSH also provides a way, using the WScript execution host, to permanently override configuration settings for specific scripts run from the Windows desktop. This is done by creating a text file with the same name as the script and giving the file a `.wsh` extension. Then, within the `.wsh` file, you can specify specific WSH configuration settings. For example, to set up a `.wsh` file for a script named `Test Script.vbs`, you would create a file called `Test Script.wsh` and save it in the same folder in which the `Test Script.vbs` script resides. You could then run the script by double-clicking on `the .wsh` file or by double-clicking on the script itself. If you double-click on the `.wsh` file, the WSH automatically finds the script that is associated with it, and, after processing the configuration settings stored in the `.wsh` file, runs the script. Conversely, whenever you double-click a script, the WSH first looks to see if it has an associated `.wsh` file before running it; if it does not, then the WSH processes it using the execution host's default configuration settings.

The following statements show the contents of a typical `.wsh` file:

```
[ScriptFile]
Path=C:\Test Script.vbs
[Options]
Timeout=30
DisplayLogo=0
```

The first line contains the section label called `[ScriptFile]`. The next statement provides the name and path of the script associated with this `.wsh` file. Next comes an `[Options]` section label. The last two lines contain configuration settings specific to the execution of this script. `Timeout=30` specifies that this script will not be allowed to process for more than 30 seconds, and `DisplayLogo=0` specifies that the WScript logo is to be suppressed. An alternative setting for this option would be `DisplayLogo=1`, which would enable the display of the WScript logo.

There are two ways to create a `.wsh` file. One way is to use a text editor, such as the Windows Notepad application, to manually create the file. The other option is to let Windows create the `.wsh` file for you using the following procedure:

1. Locate the folder in which the VBScript is stored.
2. Right-click on the script and select Properties from the menu that appears. The script's Properties dialog appears, as shown in Figure 2.13.

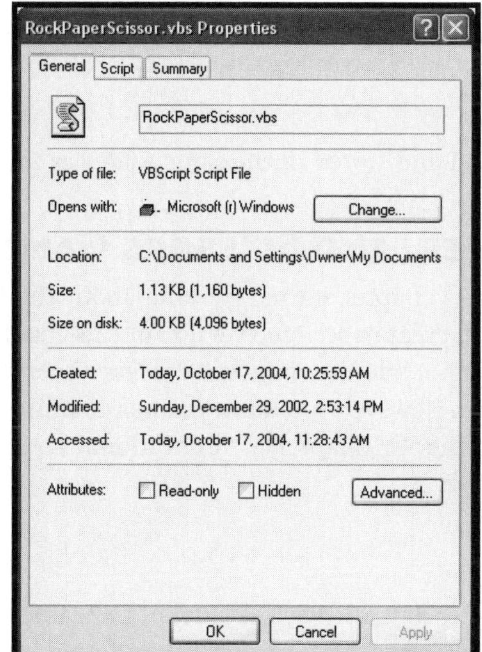

FIGURE 2.13

Examining the properties on the General property sheet of the scripts properties dialog.

3. Click on the Script property sheet, as shown in Figure 2.14.

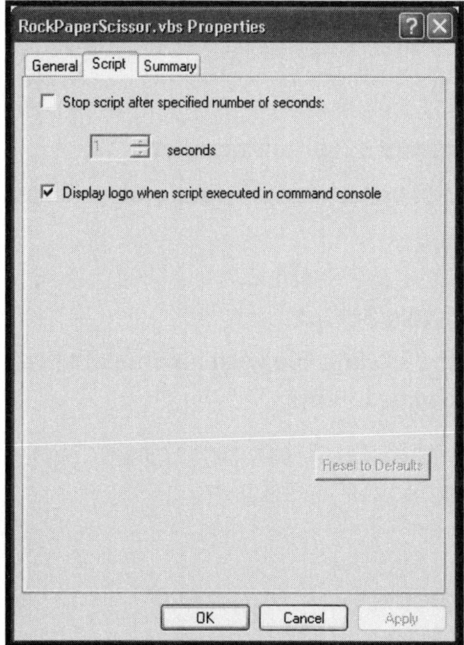

FIGURE 2.14

Creating a `.wsh` file via a script's Properties dialog.

4. Specify a script execution time limit, as required.
5. Enable or disable the display of the WScript logo as desired.
6. Click on OK.

A new `.wsh` file is then created for you and stored in the same folder as the script.

Back to the Rock, Paper, and Scissors Game

Now it's time to go back to where this chapter started—talking about the Rock, Paper, and Scissors game. In this project, you will create a scripted version of this classic game. This version is a bit limited, given that you've not had the chance yet to learn everything you'll need to create a more sophisticated version. However, you know enough to build the game's foundation and get a working model going. In Chapter 5, "Conditional Logic," you'll get the chance to return and spice things up a bit.

Designing the Game

The basic design of this game is simple. First, display the rules of the game, and then ask the player to type rock, `paper`, or `scissors`. Next, have the script randomly pick a choice of its own and display the results.

This project is completed in six steps:

1. Define the resources used by this script.
2. Display the game's instructions.
3. Provide a way for the user to select a choice.
4. Devise a way for the script to generate a random number.
5. Assign the computer's choice based on the script's randomly selected number.
6. Display the final results of the game.

Defining the Resources Used by the Script

Begin by opening your editor and saving a blank file with a name of `RockPaperScissors.vbs`. Next, add the first few lines of the script as follows:

```
'Formally declare variables used by the script before trying to use them

Dim WshShl, Answer, CardImage
```

```
'Create an instance of the WScript object in order to later use the
'Popup method
Set WshShl = WScript.CreateObject("WScript.Shell")
```

The first line begins with a ' character. This character identifies a VBScript comment. Comments can be used to document the contents of scripts. Comments have no affect on the execution of a script. The next line begins with the VBScript keyword `Dim`. This statement defines three variables that will be used by the script. A variable is simply a portion of the computer memory where your scripts can store and retrieve data. I'll provide more information about variables and how they work in Chapter 4, "Constants, Variables, and Arrays." The third statement is another comment, and the fourth statement uses the `WScript` object's `CreateObject()` method to set up an instance of the `WshShell` object. This statement allows the script to access `WshShell` properties and methods.

Displaying the Rules of the Game

Next, let's take advantage of the `WshShell` object that you just defined by using its `Popup()` method to display a message in a graphical pop-up dialog:

```
'Display the rules of the game
WshShl.Popup "Welcome to Rock, Paper and Scissors game. Here are the " & _
  "rules of the game: 1. Guess the same thing as the computer " & _
  "to tie. 2. Paper covers rock and wins. 3. Rock breaks " & _
  "scissors and wins. 4. Scissors cut paper and wins."
```

This is really just two lines of code, although it looks like five. The first line is a comment. However, the second line was so big that I chose to break it down into multiple pieces for easy display. To do so, I broke the message that I wanted to display into multiple segments of similar lengths, placing each segment within a pair of quotation marks. To tie the different segments into one logical statement, I added the VBScript `&` character to the end of each line, followed by the _ character.

Collecting the Player's Selection

When the player clicks on OK, the pop-up dialog displaying the game's rules disappears and is replaced with a new pop-up dialog that is generated by the following code:

```
'Prompt the user to select a choice
Answer = InputBox("Type Paper, Rock, or Scissors.", _
  "Let's play a game!")
```

The first statement is a comment and can be ignored. The second statement uses the VBScript `InputBox()` function to display a pop-up dialog into which the user can type either rock, paper, or scissors. The value typed by the user is then assigned to a variable called `Answer`.

Setting Up the Script's Random Selection

Now that the player has selected his or her choice, it's the script's turn to make a random selection on behalf of the computer. This can be done in two statements, as shown by the following statements:

```
'Time for the computer to randomly pick a choice
Randomize
GetRandomNumber = Int((3 * Rnd()) + 1)
```

The first line is a comment and can be ignored. The second line executes the `Randomize` statement, which ensures that the computer generates a random number. If you leave this line out and run the script several times, you'll notice that after making an initial random choice, the script always makes the exact same choice time and time again. The `Randomize` statement prevents this behavior by ensuring that a random number is generated each time the script executes.

The next statement generates a random number between 1 and 3. I'll break down the activity that occurs in this statement. First, the `Rnd()` function generates a random number between 0 and 1. Next, the `Int()` function, which returns the integer portion of a number, executes, multiplying 3 times the randomly generated number and then adding 1 to it. The final result is a randomly generated number with a value between 1 and 3.

Assigning a Choice to the Script's Selection

Next, you'll need to assign a choice to each of the three possible numeric values randomly generated by the script:

```
'Assign a value to the randomly selected number
If GetRandomNumber = 3 then CardImage = "rock"
If GetRandomNumber = 2 then CardImage = "scissors"
If GetRandomNumber = 1 then CardImage = "paper"
```

If the number 1 is generated, then a value of `rock` is assigned as the computer's selection. If the number 2 is generated, then a value of `scissors` is assigned as the computer's selection. Finally, if the number 3 is generated, then a value of `paper` is assigned as the computer's selection.

Displaying the Results of the Game

After the script comes up with the computer's selection, it's time to display the results of the game so that user can see who won:

```
'Display the game's results so that the user can see if he or she won
WshShl.Popup "You picked: " & Answer & Space(12) & "Computer picked: " & _
  CardImage
```

The `WshShell` object's `Popup()` method is used to display the results of the game. Using the `&` concatenation character, I pieced together the various parts of the message. These parts included text phrases enclosed within quotation marks; the `Answer` variable; the `CardImage` variable, which represents the user's and computer's choices; the `Space()` method, which added 12 blank spaces to the text messages; and the _ character, which allowed me to spread the message out over two separate lines.

The Final Result

Now let's put all the pieces of the script together and then save and run the scripts:

```
'Formally declare variables used by the script before trying to use them
Dim WshShl, Answer, CardImage

'Create an instance of the WScript object in order to later use the
'Popup method
Set WshShl = WScript.CreateObject("WScript.Shell")

'Display the rules of the game
WshShl.Popup "Welcome to Rock, Paper and Scissors game. Here are the " & _
  "rules of the game: 1. Guess the same thing as the computer " & _
  "to tie. 2. Paper covers rock and wins. 3. Rock breaks " & _
  "scissors and wins. 4. Scissors cut paper and wins."

'Prompt the user to select a choice
Answer = InputBox("Type Paper, Rock, or Scissors.", _
  "Let's play a game!")

'Time for the computer to randomly pick a choice
Randomize
GetRandomNumber = Round(FormatNumber(Int((3 * Rnd()) + 1)))
```

```
'Assign a value to the randomly selected number
If GetRandomNumber = 3 then CardImage = "rock"
If GetRandomNumber = 2 then CardImage = "scissor"
If GetRandomNumber = 1 then CardImage = "paper"

'Display the game's results so that the user can see if he or she won
WshShl.Popup "You picked: " & Answer & Space(12) & "Computer picked: " & _
  CardImage
```

SUMMARY

In this chapter, you learned a lot about the WSH core object model. This included a review of its 14 objects and their methods and properties. You also saw a number of example scripts that demonstrated the use of various objects and their methods and properties. This information and the examples that I covered here have given you the foundation required to complete the rest of this book, not to mention the games that you will learn. In addition, you learned how to configure both the WScript and CScript execution hosts to best suit your personal requirements and preferences.

CHALLENGES

1. **See whether you can expand `RockPaperScissors.vbs` by adding logic that compares the player's selection to the script's random selection to determine the winner.**
2. **Try adding logic to `RockPaperScissors.vbs` to see whether you can get the script to record its start time and completion time in the Windows event log. This way, you can monitor the event log and track the execution of the script.**
3. **See whether you can modify `NetMessenger.vbs` to execute different Windows commands. For example, try writing a script that uses the `NET START` and `NET STOP` commands to stop and start a Windows service.**

Part II

Learning VBScript & WSH Scripting

VBScript Basics

This chapter begins your VBScript education by teaching you a number of important concepts. You'll learn about the objects that make up the VBScript core and run-time object models. In addition, you'll learn about basic VBScript syntax, functions, reserved words, and special characters. You'll also learn about VBScript and WSH output functions and methods. Along the way, you'll create a Math Game while learning more about how VBScript works with the WSH. You also will learn

- The basic rules that you must follow when writing VBScripts
- The objects that make up the VBScript core and run-time object models
- How to enhance your scripts using built-in VBScript functions
- Different ways of displaying script output

PROJECT PREVIEW: THE MATH GAME

This chapter's game project shows you a programming technique that enables you to write VBScripts that can open and interact with other Windows applications. It's called `MathGame.vbs`, and it tests the player's understanding of the principle of *precedence* in solving a numeric expression. If the user gets the answer correct, he or she is congratulated for possessing superior math skills. If the player provides an incorrect answer, then the game offers to teach the player how to solve the expression.

To teach the player how to solve the equation, the program opens the Microsoft WordPad application and types out instructions that explain the steps required to solve the problem. To further demonstrate how the equation is solved, the program starts the Windows Calculator application and uses it to solve the equation. The WordPad and Calculator demonstrations play out almost like a movie or slide show, starting automatically, pausing as input and text are automatically keyed in, and finally automatically closing when the demonstrations end. Figures 3.1 through 3.6 demonstrate some of the screens that users will see when they play the Math Game.

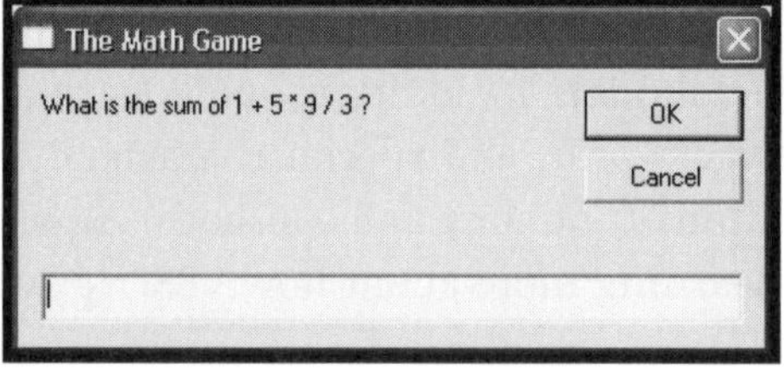

FIGURE 3.1

The game begins by asking the player to solve a mathematical equation.

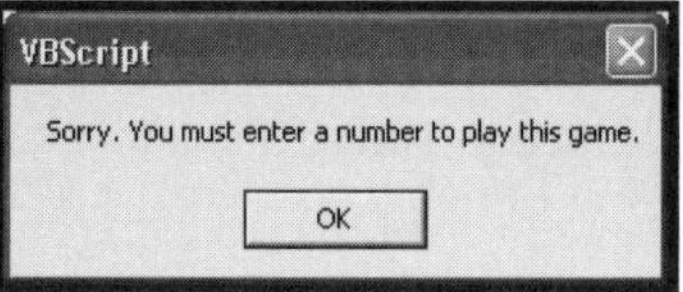

FIGURE 3.2

An error occurs if the player fails to enter a number.

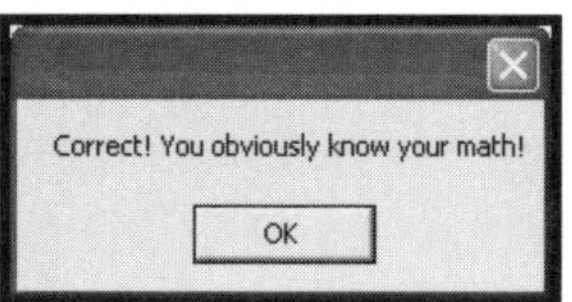

FIGURE 3.3

The player is praised if he or she correctly solves the equation.

FIGURE 3.4

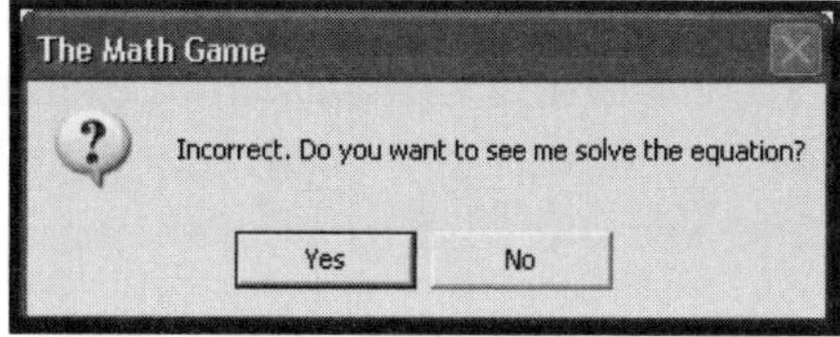

If the player provides an incorrect answer, the game offers to demonstrate how the equation is solved.

FIGURE 3.5

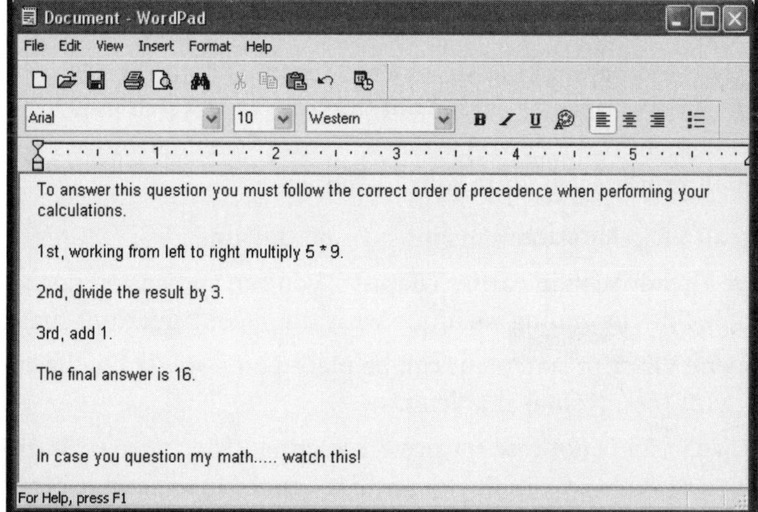

Using WordPad, the game types out detailed instructions for solving the problem.

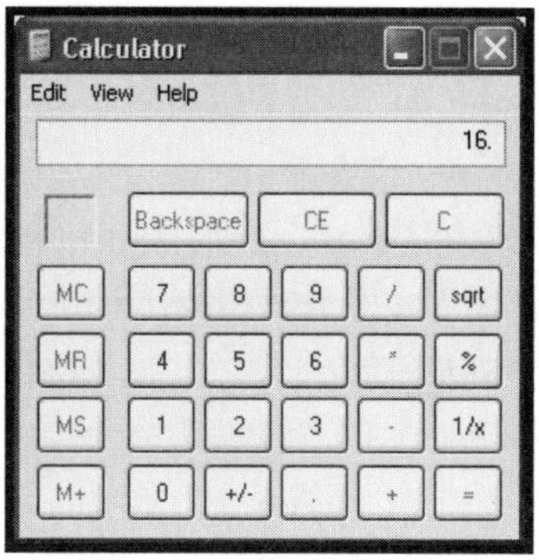

FIGURE 3.6

The game then starts the Calculator application and solves the equation again, just for fun.

As you go through the steps involved in creating this game, you'll learn how to use a number of `WScript` and `WshShell` object methods, and you'll get a brief introduction to VBScript's support for conditional programming logic.

VBScript Statements

Like any programming language, VBScript is comprised of programming statements. As you go through the chapters in this book, you'll be introduced to the statements that make up the VBScript's scripting language, learning a few different statements in every chapter, until, by the end of the book, you've seen and worked with most of them.

Table 3.1 lists the statements that make up the VBScript scripting language.

VBScript Syntax Rules

To properly apply the programming statements that make up the VBScript programming language, you must have an understanding of the syntax rules that govern these statements. Each VBScript statement has its own particular syntax. The following is a list of rules that you should keep in mind as you write your VBScripts:

- By default, all VBScript statements must fit on one line.
- As you have already seen in earlier chapters, you can spread a single statement out over multiple lines by ending each line with the _ (continuation) character.
- More than one VBScript statement can be placed on a single line by ending each statement with the : (colon) character.
- By default, VBScript is not case-sensitive, meaning VBScript regards different case spelling of words used by variables, constants, procedures, and subroutines as the same.
- You can enforce case-sensitivity by adding the `Option Explicit` statement to the beginning of your VBScripts. You'll learn more about this statement later in this chapter.
- By default, an error will halt the execution of any VBScript.
- You can prevent an error from terminating a VBScript's execution by adding the `On Error Resume Next` statement to your VBScripts. You'll learn more about working with this statement in Chapter 9, "Handling Script Errors."
- Extra blank spaces are ignored within scripts and can be used to improve scripts' format and presentation.

Every VBScript statement has its own specific syntax that must be exactly followed. Failure to properly follow a statement's syntax will result in an error. Let's look at an example. The following statement tries to use the VBScript's `MsgBox()` function to display a text message:

```
MsgBox "Thanks for playing!
```

TABLE 3.1 VBSCRIPT STATEMENTS

Statement	Description
Call	Executes a procedure
Class	Defines a class name
Const	Defines a constant
Dim	Defines a variable
Do...Loop	Repeatedly executes a collection of one or more statements as long as a condition remains True or until the condition becomes True
Erase	Reinitializes the elements stored in array
Execute	Executes a specified statement
ExecuteGlobal	Executes a specified statement in a script's global namespace
Exit	Ends a loop, subroutine, or function
For Each...Next	Processes all the elements stored in an array or collection
For...Next	Repeats a collection of one or more statements a specified number of times
Function	Defines a function and its associated arguments
If...Then...Else	Executes one or more statements depending on the value of a tested condition
On Error	Enables error handling
Option Explicit	Forces explicit variable declaration
Private	Defines a private variable
Property Get	Defines a property name and its arguments and then returns its value
Property Let	Defines a property procedure's name and its arguments
Property Set	Defines a property procedure's name and its arguments
Public	Defines a public variable
Randomize	Initializes VBScript's random-number generator
ReDim	Defines or redefines the dimension of an array
Rem	A comment statement
Select Case	Defines a group of tests, of which only one will execute if a matching condition is found
Set	Sets up a variable reference to an object
Sub	Defines a subroutine and its arguments
While...Wend	Executes one or more statements as long as the specified condition is True
With	Associates one or more statements that are to be executed for a specified object

Unfortunately, the statement's syntax requirements have not been followed. The `MsgBox()` function requires that all text messages be enclosed within a pair of quotation marks. If you look closely, you will see that the closing quotation mark is omitted. Figure 3.7 shows the error produced by this statement at run-time.

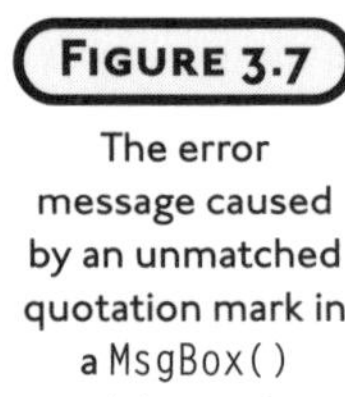

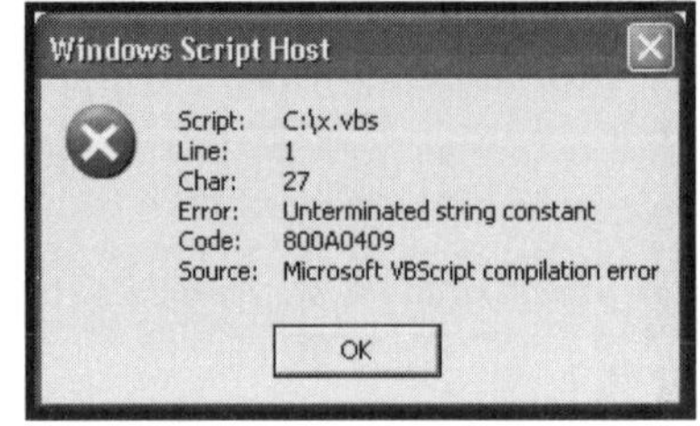

The error message caused by an unmatched quotation mark in a `MsgBox()` statement.

Reserved Characters

Like any programming language, VBScript has a collection of reserved words. *Reserved words* are words that you cannot use within your scripts because VBScript also assigns a special meaning to them. Some of these words are reserved because they are part of the language itself, and others are reserved for future use. Table 3.2 lists VBScript's reserved words. The important thing to remember when it comes to VBScript reserved words is that you can only use them as intended (that is, you cannot use them as variables, constants, and procedure names).

Adding Comments

One of the easiest VBScript statements to understand is the comment statement. The comment statement gives you the ability to add to your VBScripts descriptive text that documents why you wrote the script the way you did. Documenting your scripts with comments makes them easier to support and helps others who may come after you to pick up where you left off. Comments do not have any affect on the execution of your scripts and you should use them liberally.

Comments can be added to scripts using the VBScript `Rem` (short for remark) statement, as follows:

```
Rem Use the VBScript MsgBox() function to display a message
MsgBox "Thanks for playing!"
```

Comments also can be created using the `'` character:

```
' Use the VBScript MsgBox() function to display a message
MsgBox "Thanks for playing!"
```

Table 3.2 VBScript's Collection of Reserved Words

And	EndIf	LSet	RSet
As	Enum	Me	Select
Boolean	Eqv	Mod	Set
ByRef	Event	New	Shared
Byte	Exit	Next	Single
ByVal	False	Not	Static
Call	For	Nothing	Stop
Case	Function	Null	Sub
Class	Get	On	Then
Const	GoTo	Option	To
Currency	If	Optional	True
Debug	Imp	Or	Type
Dim	Implements	ParamArray	TypeOf
Do	In	Preserve	Until
Double	Integer	Private	Variant
Each	Is	Public	Wend
Else	Let	RaiseEvent	While
ElseIf	Like	ReDim	With
Empty	Long	Rem	Xor
End	Loop	Resume	

The ' character is my preferred style. I find it less visually intrusive and just as effective.

Also, you can add a comment to the end of any statement:

```
MsgBox "Thank you for playing"  'Display a thank you message
```

One sign of an experienced programmer is the amount of and usefulness of comments added to his or her scripts. Consider adding comments that describe the function of variables, constants, and arrays; also use them to explain complicated pieces of coding.

Comments also can be used to create a script template, which will provide additional structure to your VBScripts. For example, consider the following template:

```
'*************************************************************************
'Script Name: ScriptName.vbs
'Author: Author Name
'Created: MM/DD/YY
'Description: Xxxxxxxxxxxxxxxxxxxxxxxxx.
'*************************************************************************

'Initialization Section
Option Explicit
On Error Resume Next
Dim…
Const…
Set…

'Main Processing Section



'Procedure Section

'This function .....
Function Xxxxx(Zzzz)
  Xxxxxxxxxx
End Function
```

This template begins with a documentation section that provides a place to record the script's name, its author, its creation date, and a brief description. Other information that you might want to add here includes

- Instructions for running the script
- Documentation for any arguments the script expects to receive at execution time
- Documentation of the recent updates to the script, including when, by whom, and why
- Copyright information
- Contact or support information

The rest of the template is divided into three sections.

- **Initialization Section.** Contains statements that globally affect the scripts, including `Option Explicit` and `On Error` as well as the declaration of any variables, constants, script.
- ection contains the statements that control the main he statements in this section access the resources ction as necessary, and call on the procedures and lure Section.
- contains all the script's procedures. *Procedures* are be called and executed as a unit. You'll learn how to er 7, "Using Procedures to Organize Scripts."

IPT OBJECT MODEL

ows Script Host," you learned about the WSH core object ds. You also learned how to instantiate WSH objects to ies and methods. VBScript also provides two collections ipts. Table 3.3 provides an overview of VBScript's built-in

Built-in VBScript Objects" to learn more about VBScript's

SCRIPT BUILT-IN OBJECTS

	on
	ripts with access to class events
	ripts with access to information about run-time errors
	ripts with access to the read-only properties of a regular match
`Matches Collection`	A collection of regular expression `Match` objects
`RegExp`	Supports regular expressions
`SubMatches Collection`	Provides scripts with access to read-only values of regular expression submatch strings

WORKING WITH VBSCRIPT RUN-TIME OBJECTS

In addition to its core object model, VBScript's `FileSystemObject` object also provides a number of run-time objects. As Table 3.4 shows, your scripts can use these objects and their properties and methods to interface with the Windows file system.

The WSH core object model provides access to a number of Windows resources. Absent from this model is a file system object. Therefore, to access system files from your VBScripts, you'll need to learn how to work with VBScript's `FileSystemObject` object. With this object, your scripts will be able to

- Check for the existence of files and folders before attempting to work with them
- Create and delete files and folders
- Open and read files
- Write or append to files
- Close files
- Copy and move files and folders

TABLE 3.4 VBSCRIPT RUN-TIME OBJECTS

Object Name	Description
`Dictionary`	Stores data key, item pairs. Properties: `Count`, `Item`, Key. Methods: `Add`, `Exists`, `Items`, `Keys`, `Remove`, `RemoveAll`.
`Drive`	Provides script with access to disk properties. Properties: `AvailableSpace`, `DriveLetter`, `DriveType`, `FileSystem`, `FreeSpace`, `IsReady`, `Path`, `RootFolder`, `SerialNumber`, `ShareName`, `TotalSize`, `VolumeName`. Methods: This object does not support any methods.
`Drives Collection`	Provides script with access to information regarding a drive's location. Properties: `Count`, `Item`. Methods: This object does not support any methods.
`File`	Provides script with access to file properties. Properties: `Attributes`, `DateCreated`, `DateLastAccessed`, `DateLastModified`, `Drive`, `Name`, `ParentFolder`, `Path`, `ShortName`, `ShortPath`, `Size`, `Type`. Methods: `Copy`, `Delete`, `Move`, `OpenAsTextStream`.

Table 3.4 VBScript Run-Time Objects (continued)

Object Name	Description
Files Collection	Provides scripts with access to files stored in a specified folder. Properties: Count, Item. Methods: This object does not support any methods.
FileSystemObject	Provides scripts with access to the file system. Properties: Drives. Methods: BuildPath, CopyFile, CopyFolder, CreateFolder, CreateTextFile, DeleteFile, DeleteFolder, DriveExists, FileExists, FolderExists, GetAbsolutePathName, GetBaseName, GetDrive, GetDriveName, GetExtensionName, GetFile, GetFileName, GetFolder, GetParentFolderName, GetSpecialFolder, GetTempName, MoveFile, MoveFolder, OpenTextFile.
Folder	Provides scripts with access to folder properties. Properties: Attributes, DateCreated, DateLastAccessed, DateLastModified, Drive, Files, IsRootFolder, Name, ParentFolder, Path, ShortName, ShortPath, Size, SubFolders, Type. Methods: Copy, Delete, Move, OpenAsTextStream.
Folders Collection	Provides scripts with access to folders located within another folder. Properties: Count, Item. Methods: Add.

Properties

Like WSH objects, the VBScript run-time objects support a large number of properties. Table 3.5 provides a complete list of VBScript run-time properties.

Table 3.5 VBScript Run-Time Properties

Property Name	Description
AtEndOfLine	Returns a value of either true or false based on whether the file pointer has reached the TextStream file's end-of-line marker
AtEndOfStream	Returns a value of either true or false based on whether the end of a TextStream file has been reached
Attributes	Modifies or retrieves file and folder attributes
AvailableSpace	Retrieves the amount of free space available on the specified drive

(continues)

Table 3.5 VBScript Run-Time Properties (continued)

Property Name	Description
`Column`	Retrieves the current column position in a `TextStream` file
`CompareMode`	Sets or returns the comparison mode used to compare a `Dictionary` object's string keys
`Count`	Returns a value representing the number of the items in a collection or `Dictionary` object
`DateCreated`	Retrieves a file or folder's creation date and time
`DateLastAccessed`	Retrieves the date and time that a file or folder was last accessed
`DateLastModified`	Retrieves the date and time that a file or folder was last modified
`Drive`	Retrieves the drive letter where a file or folder is stored
`DriveLetter`	Retrieves the specified drive's drive letter
`Drives`	Establishes a `Drives` collection representing all the drives found on the computer
`DriveType`	Returns a value identifying a drive's type
`Files`	Establishes a `Files` collection to represent all the `File` objects located within a specified folder
`FileSystem`	Retrieves the name of the file system used on the specified drive
`FreeSpace`	Retrieves the amount of free space available on the specified drive
`IsReady`	Returns a value of either `true` or `false` based on the availability of the specified drive
`IsRootFolder`	Returns a value of either `true` or `false` based on whether the specified folder is the root folder
`Item`	Retrieves or sets an item based on the specified `Dictionary` object key
`Key`	Sets a `Dictionary` object key
`Line`	Retrieves the current line number in the `TextStream` file
`Name`	Gets or modifies a file or folder's name
`ParentFolder`	Returns a reference to the specified file or folder's parent folder object
`Path`	Retrieves the path associated with the specified file, folder, or drive
`RootFolder`	Retrieves the `Folder` object associated with the root folder on the specified drive
`SerialNumber`	Retrieves the specified disk volume's serial number
`ShareName`	Retrieves the specified network drive's share name
`ShortName`	Retrieves the specified file or folder's 8.3-character short name

Table 3.5 VBScript Run-Time Properties (continued)

Property Name	Description
ShortPath	Retrieves a file or folder's short pathname associated with a file or folder's 8.3-character name
Size	Returns the number of bytes that make up a file or folder
SubFolders	Establishes a Folders collection made up of the folders located within a specified folder
TotalSize	Retrieves a value representing the total number of bytes available on a drive
Type	Retrieves information about the specified file or folder's type
VolumeName	Gets or modifies a drive's volume name

Methods

VBScript run-time objects also support a larger number of methods, which you will find essential when working with the Windows file system. These methods are outlined in Table 3.6.

Table 3.6 VBScript Run-Time Methods

Method Name	Description
Add (Dictionary)	Adds a key and item pair to a Dictionary object
Add (Folders)	Adds a Folder to a collection
BuildPath	Appends a name to the path
Close	Closes an open TextStream file
Copy	Copies a file or folder
CopyFile	Copies one or more files
CopyFolder	Recursively copies a folder
CreateFolder	Creates a new folder
CreateTextFile	Creates a file and a TextStream object so that it can be read from and written to
Delete	Deletes a file or folder
DeleteFile	Deletes a file

(continues)

Table 3.6 VBScript Run-Time Methods (continued)

Method Name	Description
`DeleteFolder`	Deletes a folder's contents
`DriveExists`	Returns a value of `true` or `false` based on whether a drive exists
`Exists`	Returns a value of `true` or `false` based on whether a key exists in a `Dictionary` object
`FileExists`	Returns a value of `true` or `false` based on whether the specified file can be found
`FolderExists`	Returns a value of `true` or `false` based on whether the specified folder can be found
`GetAbsolutePathName`	Retrieves a complete pathname
`GetBaseName`	Retrieves a file name without its file extension
`GetDrive`	Returns the `Drive` object associated with the drive in the specified path
`GetDriveName`	Returns the name of a drive
`GetExtensionName`	Returns a file's extension
`GetFile`	Returns a `File` object
`GetFileName`	Returns the last file name or folder of the specified path
`GetFileVersion`	Returns a file's version number
`GetFolder`	Returns the `Folder` object associated with the folder in the specified path
`GetParentFolderName`	Returns the name of the parent folder
`GetSpecialFolder`	Returns a special folder's name
`GetTempName`	Returns the name of a temporary file or folder
`Items`	Returns an array where items in a `Dictionary` object are stored
`Keys`	Returns an array containing the keys in a `Dictionary` object
`Move`	Moves a file or folder
`MoveFile`	Moves one or more files
`MoveFolder`	Moves one or more folders
`OpenAsTextStream`	Opens a file and retrieves a `TextStream` object to provide a reference to the file
`OpenTextFile`	Opens a file and retrieves a `TextStream` object to provide a reference to the file
`Read`	Returns a string containing a specified number of characters from a `TextStream` file

Table 3.6 VBScript Run-Time Methods (continued)

Method Name	Description
ReadAll	Reads the entire TextStream file and its contents
ReadLine	Reads an entire line from the TextStream file
Remove	Deletes a Dictionary object's key, item pair
RemoveAll	Deletes all Dictionary object's key, item pairs
Skip	Skips a specified number of character positions when processing a TextStream file
SkipLine	Skips an entire line when processing a TextStream file
Write	Places a specified string in the TextStream file
WriteBlankLines	Writes a specified number of newline characters to the TextStream file
WriteLine	Writes the specified string to the TextStream file

Using VBScript Run-Time Objects in Your Scripts

Now seems like a good time to look at an example of how to incorporate the VBScript `FileSystemObject` into your scripts and use its properties and methods to work with the Windows file system. Take a look at the following script:

```
'*************************************************************************
'Script Name: FreeSpace.vbs
'Author: Jerry Ford
'Created: 11/22/02
'Description: This script demonstrates how to use VBScript run-time
'objects and their properties and methods.
'*************************************************************************

'Initialization Section

Option Explicit

Dim FsoObject, DiskDrive, AvailSpace
```

```
'Instantiate the VBScript FileSystemObject
Set FsoObject = WScript.CreateObject("Scripting.FileSystemObject")

'Use the FileSystem Object object's GetDrive method to set up a reference
'to the computer's C: drive
Set DiskDrive = FsoObject.GetDrive(FsoObject.GetDriveName("c:"))


'Main Processing Section

'Use the FileSystemObject FreeSpace property to determine the amount of
'free space (in MB) on the C: drive
AvailSpace = (DiskDrive.FreeSpace / 1024) / 1024

'Use the VBScript FormatNumber Function to format the results as a
'whole number
AvailSpace = FormatNumber(AvailSpace, 0)

'Display the amount of free space on the C: drive
WScript.Echo "You need 100 MB of free space to play this game. " & _
  vbCrLf & "Total amount of free space is currently: " & AvailSpace & " MB"
```

The script begins by instantiating the `FileSystemObject` as shown here:

```
Set FsoObject = WScript.CreateObject("Scripting.FileSystemObject")
```

The script then uses this instance of the `FileSystemObject` to execute its `GetDrive()` method and set up a reference to the computer's C: drive:

```
Set DiskDrive = FsoObject.GetDrive(FsoObject.GetDriveName("c:"))
```

The next statement uses the `FileSystemObject` object's `FreeSpace` property to retrieve the amount of free space on the C: drive:

```
AvailSpace = (DiskDrive.FreeSpace / 1024) / 1024
```

This statement divides this value by 1,024, and then again by 1,024, to present the amount of free space in megabytes.

The next statement formats this value further by eliminating any numbers to the left of the decimal point. Finally, the last statement displays the final result, as shown in Figure 3.8.

FIGURE 3.8

Using the `FileSystem Object` to access information about disk drives.

For more information on how to use the VBScript `FileSystemObject`, see Chapter 5, "Conditional Logic," in which I'll show you how to create and write to Windows files to produce reports and log files. In Chapter 8, "Storing and Retrieving Data," I'll cover how to open and read from Windows files.

Examining Built-in VBScript Functions

One of the real advantages of working with VBScript is having access to its large number of built-in functions. In the previous example, you saw how to use the `FormatNumber()` function. There are too many built-in VBScript functions to try and list them all here. For a complete list, refer to Appendix B "Built-in VBScript Functions."

Demo: The Square Root Calculator

By using functions, you can really streamline your scripts. VBScript's built-in functions provide built-in code that you don't have to write. The best way to illustrate this is by two examples. In the first example, I've written a small VBScript that prompts the user to type in a number so that the script can calculate its square root. The second script is a rewrite of the first script, using the VBScript `Sqr()` function in place of the original programming logic.

Here's the first example.

```
'*************************************************************************
'Script Name: SquareRoot-1.vbs
'Author: Jerry Ford
'Created: 11/22/02
'Description: This script demonstrates how to solve square root
'calculations using a mathematic solution devised by Sir Isaac Newton
'*************************************************************************

'Initialization Section

Option Explicit
```

```
Dim UserInput, Counter, X

UserInput = InputBox ("Type a number", "Square Root Calculator")

X = 1
For Counter = 1 To 15
  X = X - ((X^2 - UserInput) / (2 * X))
Next

MsgBox "The square root of " & UserInput & " is " & X
```

As you can see, the first part of the script displays a pop-up dialog to collect the number, and the last part displays the script's final results. The middle is where the real work results.

```
X = 1
For Counter = 1 To 15
  X = X - ((X^2 - UserInput) / (2 * X))
Next
```

I won't go into the mathematical logic behind these statements. Unless you're a math major, it's a bit of a challenge to understand. This solution is based on Sir Isaac Newton's solution for solving square root equations. Granted, it only took four lines of code to reproduce the formula, but would you like to have tried to write these four statements from scratch? I don't think so.

Demo: A New and Improved Square Root Calculator

Now let's look at a rewrite of the square root calculator script in which I use VBScript's built-in `Str()` function to perform square root calculations.

```
'*************************************************************************
'Script Name: SquareRoot-2.vbs
'Author: Jerry Ford
'Created: 11/22/02
'Description: This script demonstrates how to solve square root
'calculations using VBScript's Built-in Sqr() function
'*************************************************************************

'Initialization Section

Option Explicit
```

```
Dim UserInput

UserInput = InputBox ("Type a number", "Square Root Calculator")

MsgBox "The square root of " & UserInput & " is " & Sqr(UserInput)
```

As you can see, this time you don't have to be a mathematician to write the script. All you have to know is the correct way to use the `Sqr()` function, which is simply to pass it a number—in the case of this script, that number is represented by a variable named `UserInput`. These two examples show clearly the advantage of using VBScript's built-in functions. These functions can save you a lot of time and effort and perhaps a few headaches.

Figures 3.9 and 3.10 demonstrate the operation of either version of these two scripts.

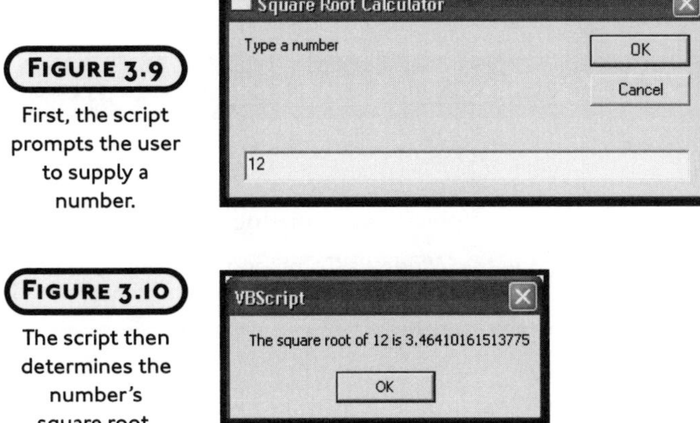

FIGURE 3.9

First, the script prompts the user to supply a number.

FIGURE 3.10

The script then determines the number's square root.

DISPLAYING SCRIPT OUTPUT

You've seen many examples already of how to display output messages in VBScripts. Output display is a critical tool in any programmer's toolbox. As a VBScript programmer working with the WSH, you have four different options for displaying script output. Two of these options are provided by the WSH in the form of object methods:

- **`Echo()`**. Displays text messages in the Windows Console when processed by the CScript execution hosts, and in pop-up dialog boxes when processed by the WScript execution hosts.
- **`Popup()`**. Displays text messages in the pop-up dialog boxes, giving you control over the icons and buttons that are displayed, and, optionally, returning a value representing the button that is pressed.

In addition to these two WSH options, VBScript gives you two functions of its own:

- **InputBox()**. Displays a text entry field in a pop-up dialog to collect user input.
- **MsgBox()**. Displays text messages in the pop-up dialog boxes, giving you control over the icons and buttons that are displayed, and, optionally, returning a value representing the button that is pressed.

The WScript's Echo() Method

The WScript object's Echo() method can display text output in the Windows Command Console or in a pop-up dialog, depending on the execution hosts that processes it. Table 3.7 outlines the Echo() method's behavior based on the execution host that processes it. Unlike other WSH output methods or VBScript functions, the Echo() method cannot collect user input.

TABLE 3.7 WSCRIPT ECHO() METHOD EXECUTION OPTIONS

WSH Execution Hosts	Output
WScript.exe	Displays text messages in graphical pop-up dialog boxes
CScript.exe	Displays text messages in the Windows Command Console

The syntax for the WScript Echo() method is as follows:

```
WScript.Echo [Arg1] [,Arg2] ...
```

The Echo() method can display any number of arguments:

```
WScript.Echo "This message appears differently depending on the " & _
  "execution host that runs it."
```

The WshShell Object's Popup() Method

The WshShell object's Popup() method displays messages in pop-up dialog boxes. You can customize its appearance by selecting the buttons and the icon to be displayed. You can also determine which button the user clicked on.

The WshShell object's Popup() method can be used in either of two ways. The syntax of the first option is as follows:

```
Response = WScript.Popup(StrText,[Time],[TitleBarMsg],[DialogSettings])
```

The syntax of the second option is as follows:

```
WScript.Popup StrText,[Time],[TitleBarMsg],[DialogSettings]
```

`Response` is a variable that stores a number representing the button that was clicked by the user. `StrText` represents the message text to be displayed. `Time` is a value that determines how long, in seconds, the pop-up dialog will be displayed; if omitted, the default is forever. `TitleBarMsg` is an optional message that is displayed in the pop-up dialog's title bar. Finally, `DialogSettings` is an option numeric value that specifies the buttons and the icon that are to appear on the pop-up dialog. If omitted, the pop-up dialog box displays the OK button without an icon.

To determine what numeric value to specify as the `DialogSettings` value, you'll need to reference Tables 3.8 and 3.9. Table 3.8 lists the different collections of buttons that can be displayed on pop-up dialogs created by the `Popup()` method, and Table 3.9 displays the different icons that you can display using the `Popup()` method.

Table 3.8 Popup() Method Button Types

Value	Button(s)
0	Displays the OK button
1	Displays the OK and Cancel buttons
2	Displays the Abort, Retry, and Ignore buttons
3	Displays the Yes, No, and Cancel buttons
4	Displays the Yes and No buttons
5	Displays the Retry and Cancel buttons

Table 3.9 Popup() Method Icon Types

Value	Icon
16	Displays the stop icon
32	Displays the question icon
48	Displays the exclamation mark icon
64	Displays the information icon

For example, to display a pop-up dialog that displays the OK button without any icon, you would specify a value of `0`. As this is the default option for the `Popup()` method, you do not have to specify this value at all. To display a pop-up dialog with the `Yes`, `No`, and `Cancel` button and no icon, you specify a value of `3` for `DialogSettings`. To display a pop-up dialog with OK and Cancel buttons and the information icon, you specify a value of `65` (that is, the collective sum of 1 and 64).

If you use the first form of the `Popup()` method (to be able to determine which button the user clicked), you'll need to examine the value of `Response` as demonstrated here:

```
Response = WshShl.Popup("This is a text message", ,"Test Script", 5)
If Response = 4 Then
  WshShl.Popup "You clicked on Retry"
End If
```

Table 3.10 lists the possible range of values that can be returned by the `Popup()` method.

TABLE 3.10 POPUP() METHOD RETURN VALUES

Value	Results
1	OK button
2	Cancel button
3	Abort button
4	Retry button
5	Ignore button
6	Yes button
7	No button

The VBScript InputBox() Function

VBScript provides two built-in functions that you can use to display text messages and interact with users. The `InputBox()` function displays your text message in a pop-up dialog that also includes an entry field. You have already seen the `InputBox()` function in action in both the Knock Knock game and the Rock, Paper, and Scissors game.

The syntax for this function is as follows:

```
Response = InputBox(StrText[, TitleBarMsg][, default][, xpos][, ypos]
[, helpfile, context])
```

`Response` is a variable that stores a number representing the input typed by the user. `StrText` is the message that you want to display. `TitlebarMsg` is an optional message that will be displayed in the pop-up dialog's title bar. `Default` is an optional default answer that you can display in the pop-up dialog. `Xpos` and `ypos` are optional arguments that specify, in twips, the horizontal and vertical location of the pop-up dialog on the screen. `Helpfile` and `context` are also optional. They specify the location of an optional context-sensitive help file.

The following statement provides another example of how to use the VBScript `InputBox()` function:

```
PlayerName = InputBox("Please type your name")
MsgBox "You typed: " & PlayerName
```

DEFINITION

Twip stands for Twentieth of a Point and represents a value of 1/1440 inch.

The VBScript MsgBox() Function

The VBScript `MsgBox()` function displays a pop-up dialog that is very similar to the pop-up dialog produced by the WSH `Popup()` method. It gives you the ability to customize the appearance of the dialog by selecting the buttons and the icon to be displayed. You also can use it to determine which button the user clicked on.

The syntax for the `MsgBox()` function is as follows:

```
MsgBox(TextMsg[, buttons][, TitleBarMsg][, helpfile, context])
```

`TextMsg` is the message to be displayed in the dialog . `Buttons` is a representation of the buttons and icon to appear in the pop-up dialog . `TitleBarMsg` is an optional message that will be displayed in the pop-up dialog's title bar, and `helpfile` and `context` are optional; when used, they specify the location of an optional context-sensitive help file.

Table 3.11 defines the different collections of buttons that can be displayed on pop-up dialogs displayed using the `MsgBox()` function.

TABLE 3.11 VBSCRIPT MSGBOX() FUNCTION BUTTONS

Constant	Value	Description
vbOKOnly	0	Displays the OK button
vbOKCancel	1	Displays the OK and Cancel buttons
vbAbortRetryIgnore	2	Displays the Abort, Retry, and Ignore buttons
vbYesNoCancel	3	Displays the Yes, No, and Cancel buttons
vbYesNo	4	Displays the Yes and No buttons
vbRetryCancel	5	Displays the Retry and Cancel buttons

Table 3.12 defines the list of icons that you can add to the `MsgBox()` pop-up dialog.

TABLE 3.12 VBSCRIPT MSGBOX() FUNCTION ICONS

Constant	Value	Description
vbCritical	16	Displays the critical icon
vbQuestion	32	Displays the question icon
vbExclamation	48	Displays the exclamation mark icon
vbInformation	64	Displays the information icon

You can use the `MsgBox()` function in your scripts like this:

```
MsgBox "Thanks for playing!"
```

You also can use the `MsgBox()` like this:

```
UserSelected = MsgBox(Would you like to play a game?)
```

The advantage to this last option is that you can interrogate the button that the user clicks on and use it to drive the execution flow of your script like this:

```
UserSelected = MsgBox("Would you like to play a game?", 4, "Text Script")
If UserSelected = 6 Then
  MsgBox "OK, The rules of this game are as follows:!"
End If
```

Alternatively, you could rewrite the previous statements as follows:

```
UserSelected = MsgBox("Would you like to play a game?", 4, "Text Script")
If UserSelected = vbYes Then
  MsgBox "OK, let's play!"
End If
```

Table 3.13 defines the list of return values associated with the various `MsgBox()` buttons.

TABLE 3.13 VBSCRIPT MSGBOX() FUNCTION RETURN VALUES

Constant	Value	Description
vbOK	1	User clicked on OK
vbCancel	2	User clicked on Cancel
vbAbort	3	User clicked on Abort
vbRetry	4	User clicked on Retry
vbIgnore	5	User clicked on Ignore
vbYes	6	User clicked on Yes
vbNo	7	User clicked on No

BACK TO THE MATH GAME

The Math Game is played by displaying a math equation and asking the player to provide the solution. If the player provides the correct answer, the game ends; however, if the player gets the answer wrong, then the script offers to show the player how to arrive at the correct answer. This is achieved in a slide slow or movie-like fashion, in which the script first starts WordPad, then starts the Calculator application, and finally uses the applications to solve the equation while the player sits back and watches. When the script is done with its presentation, it ends by closing both the WordPad and the Calculator applications.

A Quick Overview of the WshShell SendKeys() Method

Before I jump completely into the design of the Math Game, I need to give you one more piece of information. The Math Game's capability to interact with the WordPad and Calculator application depends on the use of the `WshShell` object's `SendKeys()` method. This method is used to send keystrokes to the currently active Windows application.

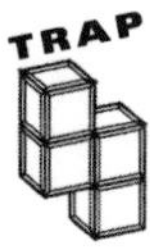

Because it sends keystrokes to the currently active Windows application, it is very important that, when the script is running, the player does not open any new windows (applications). If he or she does, the script will begin sending keystrokes to whatever applications the player opened, causing any of a number of unpredictable problems.

In the Real World

Because opening another window while the `SendKeys()` method is executing will divert the keystrokes to the new window, you will want to find another way of integrating your scripts with other applications whenever possible. Many applications, such as Excel and Word, provide their own built-in core object model. WSH scripts can interact directly with these applications by first instantiating references to the application's objects and then accessing their methods and properties. The only trick here is that you need to know the objects that make up the application's object model, as well as their associated methods and properties. You can often get this information from the application vendor's Web site or from searching the Internet. Of course, if the application that you want to work with does not expose an object model for your scripts to work with, you can always try using the `SendKeys()` method.

The syntax of the `SendKeys()` method is as follows:

```
SendKeys(string)
```

`String` is a value representing the keystrokes that are to be sent to the target application. You can send more keystrokes by simply typing them out, like this:

```
SendKeys "I am "
SendKeys 38
SendKeys " years old."
```

However, in many cases, you'll want to send other types of keystrokes. For example, to send an Enter key keystroke, you'll need to send the following:

```
SendKeys "~"
```

Table 3.14 provides a list of `SendKeys()` keystrokes that you're likely to want to use.

Table 3.14 SendKeys() Keystrokes

Key	Corresponding SendKeys() Codes
BACKSPACE	{BACKSPACE}, {BS}, or {BKSP}
BREAK	{BREAK}
CAPS LOCK	{CAPSLOCK}
DEL or DELETE	{DELETE} or {DEL}
DOWN ARROW	{DOWN}

Table 3.14 SendKeys() Keystrokes (continued)

Key	Corresponding SendKeys() Codes
END	{END}
ENTER	{ENTER} or ~
ESC	{ESC}
HELP	{HELP}
HOME	{HOME}
INS or INSERT	{INSERT} or {INS}
LEFT ARROW	{LEFT}
NUM LOCK	{NUMLOCK}
PAGE DOWN	{PGDN}
PAGE UP	{PGUP}
PRINT SCREEN	{PRTSC}
RIGHT ARROW	{RIGHT}
SCROLL LOCK	{SCROLLLOCK}
TAB	{TAB}
UP ARROW	{UP}
F1	{F1}
F2	{F2}
F3	{F3}
F4	{F4}
F5	{F5}
F6	{F6}
F7	{F7}
F8	{F8}
F9	{F9}
F10	{F10}
F11	{F11}
F12	{F12}
F13	{F13}
F14	{F14}
F15	{F15}
F16	{F16}

Besides the keystrokes outlined in Table 3.14, Table 3.15 lists three additional keystroke combinations that can be used to send keystrokes that require a special key to be pressed in conjunction with another key. For example, if you were working with an application that could be closed by holding down the Alt key and pressing the F4 key, you could perform this operation as follows:

```
SendKeys "%{F4}"
```

Table 3.15 Special SendKeys() Keystrokes

Key	Corresponding SendKeys() Codes
Shift	+
Alt	^
Ctrl	%

Designing the Game

Okay, let's start building the Math Game. This game will be assembled in five steps. The first three steps create the logic that interacts with the user and plays the game. The last two steps perform the game's application demonstrations. These steps are as follows:

1. Add the standard documentation template and define any variables, constants, or objects used by the script.
2. Present the player with the equation and then test the player's response to determine whether he or she provided an answer and whether that answer was numeric.
3. Test to see whether the player provided the correct answer. If not, then offer to show the user how to arrive at the correct answer.
4. Add the statements required to start and control the WordPad application.
5. Add the statements required to start and control the Calculator application.

Beginning the Math Game

Let's begin by adding the script template that I introduced earlier in this chapter. This includes initializing variables and constants, and setting up object declaration statements.

```
'*************************************************************************
'Script Name: Mathgame.vbs
'Author: Jerry Ford
'Created: 02/28/02
'Description: This script prompts the user to solve a mathematical
'expression and demonstrates how to solve it in the event that the user
'cannot
'*************************************************************************


'Initialization Section

Option Explicit

Dim WshShl, QuestionOne, ProveIt

'Define the title bar message to be displayed in the script's
'pop-up dialog
Const cTitlebarMsg = "The Math Game"

'Instantiate an instance of the WshShell object
Set WshShl = WScript.CreateObject("WScript.Shell")
```

Collect the Player's Answer and Test for Errors

Next, display the equation and store the player's answer in a variable called `QuestionOne`, like this:

```
'Present the player with the equation
QuestionOne = InputBox("What is the sum of 1 + 5 * 9 / 3 ?", cTitlebarMsg)
```

Now verify that the player actually typed in an answer instead of just clicking on OK or Cancel; if the player has not typed in an answer, display an error message and end the game.

```
'See if the player provided an answer
If Len(QuestionOne) = 0 Then
  MsgBox "Sorry. You must enter a number to play this game."
  WScript.Quit
End If
```

Another good test to perform is to make sure that the player is, in fact, typing in a number as opposed to a letter or other special character:

```
'Make sure that the player typed a number
If IsNumeric(QuestionOne) <> True Then
  MsgBox "Sorry. You must enter a number to play this game."
  WScript.Quit
End If
```

Check for the Correct Answer

Okay, now add a test to see if the player provided the correct answer. If the answer provided is correct, then compliment the player's math skills. Otherwise, offer to teach the player how to solve the equation.

```
'Check to see if the player provided the correct answer
If QuestionOne = 16 Then
  MsgBox "Correct! You obviously know your math!"
Else
  ProveIt = MsgBox("Incorrect. Do you want to see me solve the " & _
  "equation?", 36, cTitlebarMsg)

  If ProveIt = 6 Then 'Player wants to see the solution

    .
    .
    .
  End If

End If
```

As you can see, I left space in the previous statements. This space marks the spot where the rest of the script's statements will be written as you continue to develop the script.

Interacting with WordPad

For the script to work with the WordPad application, WordPad must first be started. This can be done using the `WshShell` object's `Run()` method.

```
WshShl.Run "WordPad"
```

It may take a moment or two for the application to finish starting, so pause the script's execution for two seconds and wait using the WScript object's Sleep() method, like this:

```
WScript.Sleep 2000
```

Next add a series of statements that use the SendKeys() method to write text to WordPad. To slow things down a bit and make the process run more like a slide show, add the Sleep() method after each write operation. Finally, pause for a couple seconds and then close WordPad.

```
WshShl.SendKeys "To answer this question you must follow the " & _
  "correct order of precedence when performing your calculations."
WScript.Sleep 2000
 WshShl.SendKeys "~~"
 WshShl.SendKeys "1st, working from left to right multiply 5 * 9."
 WScript.Sleep 2000
 WshShl.SendKeys "~~"
 WshShl.SendKeys "2nd, divide the result by 3."
 WScript.Sleep 2000
 WshShl.SendKeys "~~"
 WshShl.SendKeys "3rd, add 1."
 WScript.Sleep 2000
 WshShl.SendKeys "~~"
 WshShl.SendKeys "The final answer is 16."
 WScript.Sleep 2000
 WshShl.SendKeys "~~"
 WshShl.SendKeys "~~"
 WshShl.SendKeys "In case you question my math..... watch this!"
 WScript.Sleep 2000
 WshShl.SendKeys "%{F4}"
 WshShl.SendKeys "%{N}"
```

Take notice of the last two statements. The first statement closed WordPad by sending the F4 keystroke. As a new document was just opened, WordPad displays a dialog asking if you want to save it. The last statement responds by sending the CTRL+N keystrokes indicating a "no" response.

Interacting with the Calculator

The final piece of the game opens the Windows Calculator application and resolves the equation, just in case the player has any doubts as to the answer you presented using WordPad. The statements required to write this portion of the script are as follows:

```
'Start the Calculator application
WshShl.Run "Calc"

'Use the Calculator application to solve the equation
WScript.Sleep 2000
WshShl.SendKeys 5 & "{*}"
WScript.Sleep 2000
WshShl.SendKeys 9
WScript.Sleep 2000
WshShl.SendKeys "~"
WScript.Sleep 2000
WshShl.SendKeys "{/}" & 3
WScript.Sleep 2000
WshShl.SendKeys "~"
WScript.Sleep 2000
WshShl.SendKeys "{+}" & 1
WScript.Sleep 2000
WshShl.SendKeys "~"
WScript.Sleep 2000
WshShl.SendKeys "%{F4}"
```

As you can see, the same techniques have been used here to work with the Windows Calculator as were used to control WordPad.

The Final Result

Well, that's it. Let's assemble all the pieces of the script and see what it looks like:

```
'*************************************************************************
'Script Name: Mathgame.vbs
'Author: Jerry Ford
'Created: 02/28/02
'Description: This script prompts the user to solve a mathematical
'expression and demonstrates how to solve it in the event that the user
'cannot
'*************************************************************************
```

```
'Initialization Section

Option Explicit

Dim WshShl, QuestionOne, Proveit

'Define the title bar message to be displayed in the script's
'pop-up dialog
Const cTitlebarMsg = "The Math Game"

'Instantiate an instance of the WshShell object
Set WshShl = WScript.CreateObject("WScript.Shell")

'Present the player with the equation
QuestionOne = InputBox("What is the sum of 1 + 5 * 9 / 3 ?", cTitlebarMsg)

'See if the player provided an answer
If Len(QuestionOne) = 0 Then
  MsgBox "Sorry. You must enter a number to play this game."
  WScript.Quit
End If

'Make sure that the player typed a number
If IsNumeric(QuestionOne) <> True Then
  MsgBox "Sorry. You must enter a number to play this game."
  WScript.Quit
End If

'Check to see if the player provided the correct answer
If QuestionOne = 16 Then
  MsgBox "Correct! You obviously know your math!"
Else
  ProveIt = MsgBox("Incorrect. Do you want to see me solve the " & _
  "equation?", 36, cTitlebarMsg)

  If ProveIt = 6 Then 'Player wants to see the solution
```

```
'Start the WordPad application
WshShl.Run "WordPad"

'Pause script execution to give Windows enough time to load WordPad
WScript.Sleep 2000

'Use WordPad to show the player how to solve the equation
WshShl.SendKeys "To answer this question you must follow the " & _
  "correct order of precedence when performing your calculations."
WScript.Sleep 2000
WshShl.SendKeys "~~"
WshShl.SendKeys "1st, working from left to right multiply 5 * 9."
WScript.Sleep 2000
WshShl.SendKeys "~~"
WshShl.SendKeys "2nd, divide the result by 3."
WScript.Sleep 2000
WshShl.SendKeys "~~"
WshShl.SendKeys "3rd, add 1."
WScript.Sleep 2000
WshShl.SendKeys "~~"
WshShl.SendKeys "The final answer is 16."
WScript.Sleep 2000
WshShl.SendKeys "~~"
WshShl.SendKeys "~~"
WshShl.SendKeys "In case you question my math..... watch this!"
WScript.Sleep 2000
WshShl.SendKeys "%{F4}"
WshShl.SendKeys "%{N}"

'Start the Calculator application
WshShl.Run "Calc"

'Use the Calculator application to solve the equation
WScript.Sleep 2000
WshShl.SendKeys 5 & "{*}"
WScript.Sleep 2000
WshShl.SendKeys 9
```

```
    WScript.Sleep 2000
    WshShl.SendKeys "~"
    WScript.Sleep 2000
    WshShl.SendKeys "{/}" & 3
    WScript.Sleep 2000
    WshShl.SendKeys "~"
    WScript.Sleep 2000
    WshShl.SendKeys "{+}" & 1
    WScript.Sleep 2000
    WshShl.SendKeys "~"
    WScript.Sleep 2000
    WshShl.SendKeys "%{F4}"
  End If
End If
```

I suggest that you run and test this script to make sure that it works as expected. For example, try typing in a letter instead of a number for the answer. Then try typing nothing at all and just click on OK or Cancel. Finally, try both a correct and then an incorrect answer and see what happens. This is a fairly lengthy script, so the odds of typing it in correctly the first time are slim. If you get errors when you run the script, read them carefully and see if the error message tells you what's wrong and then go fix it. Otherwise, you may need to double-check your typing again.

As your scripts grow more complex, you're going to run into more and more errors while developing them. I recommend that you learn to develop your scripts in a modular fashion, writing one section at a time and then testing it before moving on to the next section. In Chapter 9, "Handling Script Errors," I'll demonstrate how to do this.

Summary

In this chapter, you learned about the core and run-time VBScript objects and their associated properties and methods, and were shown how to use them within your VBScripts. You also learned about VBScript syntax, reserved words, and special characters. In addition, you learned about and saw the power and convenience of VBScript functions. Finally, you learned four different ways to display script output.

CHALLENGES

1. Change the Math Game to use a different equation and modify the logic required to adapt the statements that work with the WordPad and Calculator applications.
2. Try using the `SendKeys()` method to work with other Windows applications, such as Notepad.
3. Spend some time reviewing VBScript built-in math functions and see if you can create a new calculator similar to the Square Root calculator.
4. Modify the VBScript template presented earlier in this chapter and adapt it to suit your personal preferences, and then use it as you begin developing new VBScripts.

Constants, Variables, and Arrays

This is the second of five chapters in this book that teaches the fundamentals of VBScript. One of the key concepts that you need to understand when working with VBScript, or any programming language, is how to store, retrieve, and modify data. This chapter will teach you a number of different ways to perform these tasks. By the time you have completed this chapter, you will know how to write scripts that can collect and manipulate data. Specifically, you will learn how to

- Process data passed to the script at execution time
- Store data that does not change
- Work with data that can change during script execution
- Process collections of related data as a unit

Project Preview: The Story of Captain Adventure

In this chapter, you will learn how to create a game that builds a comical adventure story based on user input. The game begins by collecting answers to a series of questions without telling the user how the answers will be used. After all the information that the script needs is collected, the story is displayed, as shown in Figures 4.1 through 4.7.

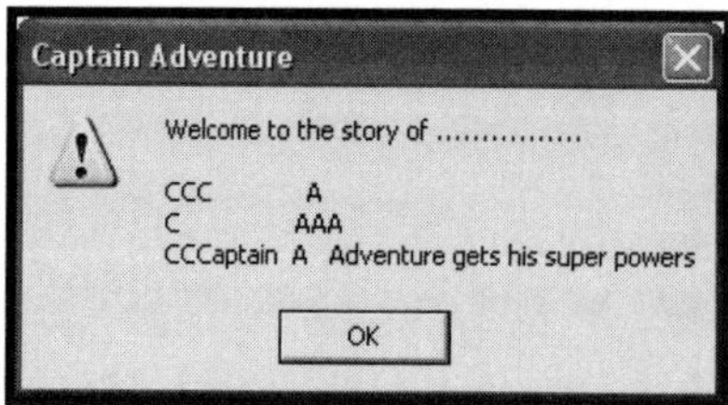

FIGURE 4.1

The story's initial splash screen.

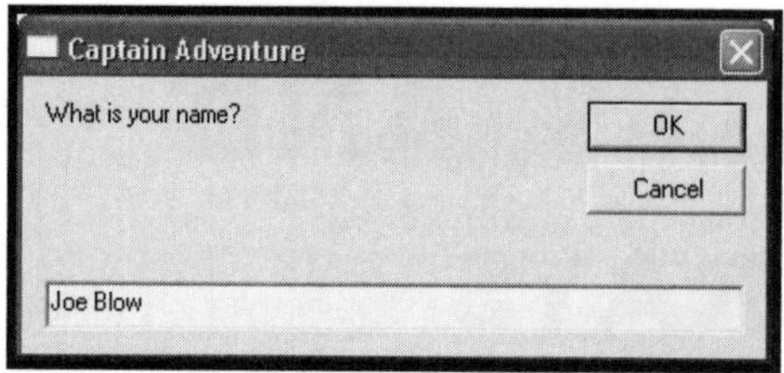

FIGURE 4.2

The user is the star of the story.

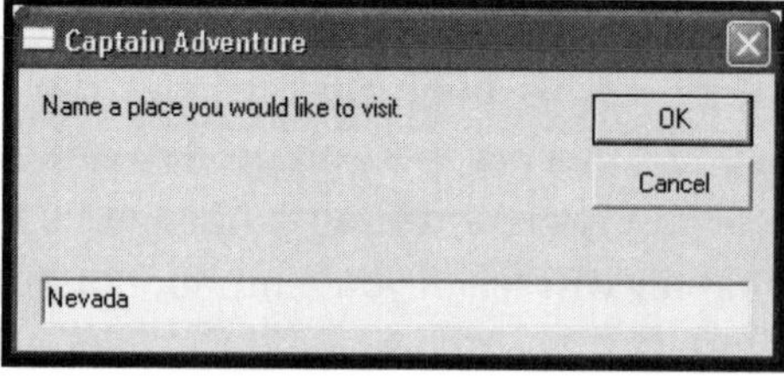

FIGURE 4.3

The story begins anywhere the user specifies.

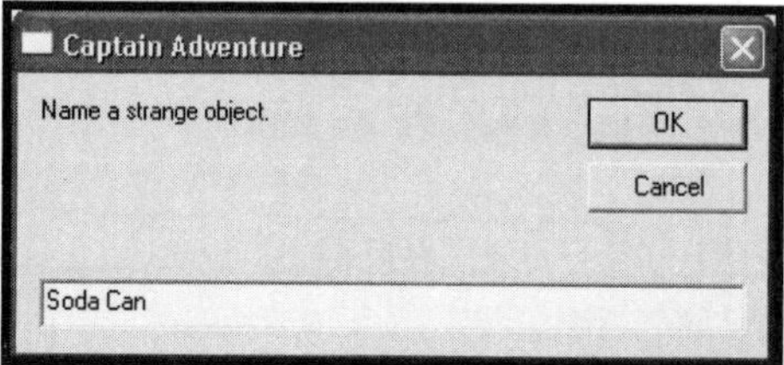

FIGURE 4.4

The user must specify the object that provides our hero with his superpowers.

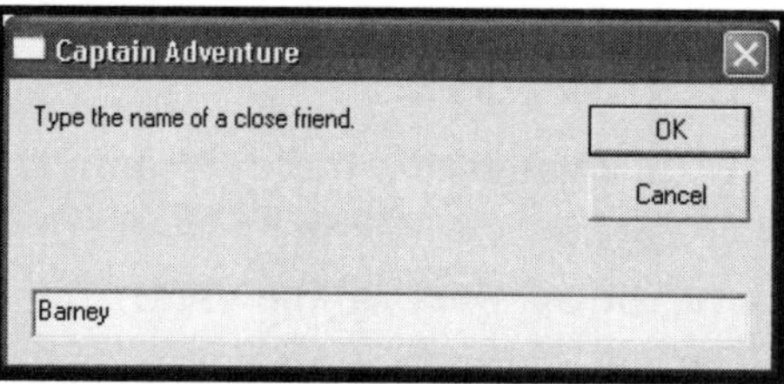

FIGURE 4.5

The user specifies the story's co-star.

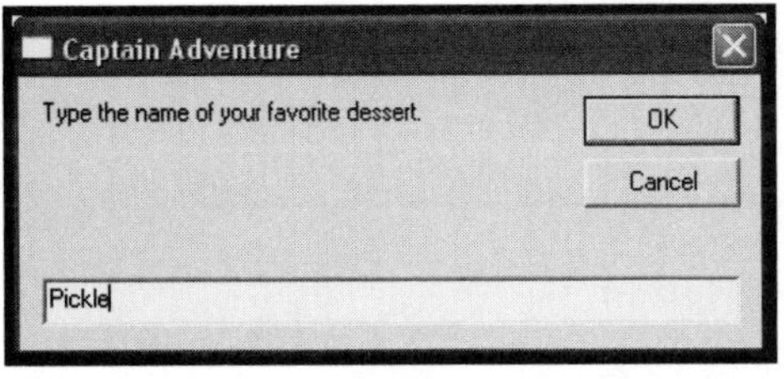

Finally, the user specifies a magic word.

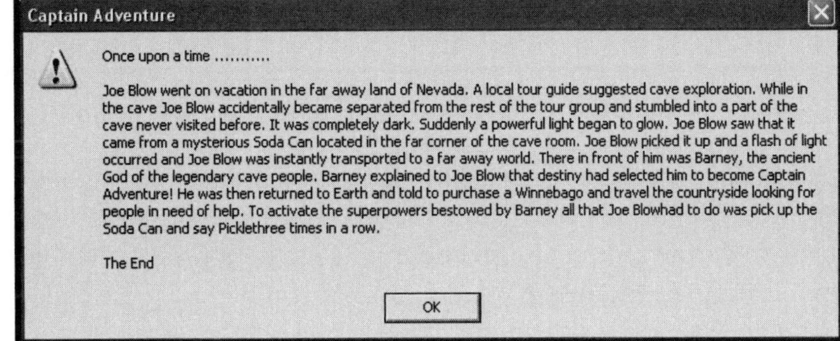

FIGURE 4.7

After the script has all the information it needs, the story is told.

Through the development of this story-building game, you will learn a number of important programming techniques, including how to collect, store, and reference data. In addition, you will learn how to control the presentation of script output.

Understanding How Scripts View Data

VBScript, like other programming languages, needs a way of storing data so that it can be accessed throughout the execution of a script. Up to this point in the book, you have seen a number of examples of how VBScript temporarily stores and references data. Now I'll explain how this works.

VBScript supplies a number of different statements that allow you to define several different types of data. These VBScript statements are outlined in Table 4.1.

> **DEFINITION**
>
> *Data* is information that a computer program collects, modifies, stores, and retrieves during execution.

TABLE 4.1 VBSCRIPT STATEMENTS THAT DETERMINE HOW DATA IS DEFINED

Statement	Description
`Const`	Defines a VBScript constant
`Dim`	Defines a VBScript variable or array
`ReDim`	Defines a dynamic VBScript array

The `Const` statement is used to define data that never changes throughout the execution of a script. For example, in this book you will sometimes see constants used to define strings that are used to define a standard greeting message in pop-up dialog boxes. The `Dim` statement is used to define a variable. A *variable* stores an individual piece of data such as a name, number, or date. The `ReDim` statement is used to create an array. *Arrays* are used to store groups of related information. For example, instead of defining 20 different variables to store information about 20 different people, a single array could be defined and then information about each person can be stored in it. Each of these statements will be examined in greater detail throughout the rest of this chapter.

WORKING WITH DATA THAT NEVER CHANGES

Data should be defined within a script according to the manner in which it will be used. If the script only needs to reference a piece of data that has a value that is known during script development, then the data can be defined as a constant. An example of a constant is the mathematical value of pi. Other examples of constants include specific dates of history, the name of places, and so on.

There are two sources of constants within scripts. First, you can define your own constants within your scripts. Another option is to reference a built-in collection of readily available constants provided by VBScript.

Assigning Data to Constants

If you're going to write a script and know for a fact that you need to reference one or more values that will not change during the execution of the script, then you can define each piece of data as a constant. One of the nice features of constants is that, once defined, their value cannot be changed. This prevents their values from being accidentally modified during the execution of the script.

If your script attempts to modify the value assigned to a constant after it has been initially assigned, you will see an "Illegal assignment: 'XXXXXXXX'" error message when the script executes. XXXXXXXX will reference the name of the constant. Open your script and do a search on this word and look for the statements that have attempted to modify its value to find the source of the error.

To define a constant within a VBScript, you must use the `Const` statement. This statement has the following syntax:

```
[Public | Private] Const ConstName = expression
```

`Public` and `Private` are optional keywords and are used to determine the availability of constants throughout a script. Defining a constant as `Public` makes it available to all procedures within the scripts. Defining a constant as `Private` makes it available only within the procedure that defines them. `ConstName` is the name of the constant being defined, and `expression` is the value that identifies the data being defined. To make sense of all this, let's look at an example.

DEFINITION

A *procedure* is a collection of script statements that are processed as a unit. In Chapter 7, "Using Procedures to Organize Scripts," you will learn how to use procedures to improve the overall organization of your scripts and to create reusable units of code.

```
'*************************************************************************
'Script Name: LittlePigs.vbs
'Author: Jerry Ford
'Created: 02/28/02
'Description: This script demonstrates how to use a constant to create a
'standardized title bar message for pop-up dialogs displayed by the script
'*************************************************************************

'Specify the message to appear in each pop-up dialog title bar

Const cTitleBarMsg = "The Three Little Pigs"

'Display the story

MsgBox "Once upon a time........", vbOkOnly, cTitleBarMsg
MsgBox "There were 3 little pigs", vbOkOnly, cTitleBarMsg
MsgBox "Who liked to build things.", vbOkOnly, cTitleBarMsg
```

In this example, I wrote a small VBScript that tells a very brief story about three little pigs. The script begins by defining a constant named `cTitleBar`. I then used three `MsgBox()` statements to display the text that makes up the story. The first argument in each `MsgBox()` statement is a text message, which is then followed by a VBScript `MsgBox()` constant `vbOkOnly`. This constant tells VBScript to only display the OK button on the pop-up dialog (a complete listing of `MsgBox()` constants is available in Chapter 3, "VBScript Basics." The last part of each `MsgBox()` statement is the `cTitleBarMsg` constant. VBScript automatically substitutes the value assigned to the `cTitleBarMsg` constant whenever the script executes. Figure 4.8 shows how the first pop-up dialog appears when the script is executed.

FIGURE 4.8

By referencing the value assigned to a constant, you can create a standard title bar message for every pop-up dialog displayed by your script.

I strongly recommend that you apply a naming convention for your constants that will uniquely identify them within your scripts. A good naming convention will make your constants easy to locate and identify and will improve the overall readability of your scripts. For example, in this book I will use the following constant naming convention:

- Constant names begin with the lowercase letter c.
- Constant names describe their contents using English words or easily identifiable parts of words.

Other examples of tasks related to working with constants include assigning values such as numbers, strings, and dates. For example, the following statement assigns a value of `1000` to a constant called `cUpperLimit`:

```
Const cUpperLimit = 1000
```

To define a text string, you must place the value being assigned within a pair of quotes, like this:

```
Const cMyName = "Jerry Lee Ford, Jr."
```

In a similar fashion, you must use a pair of pound signs to store a date value within a constant, like this:

```
Const cMyBirthday = #11-20-64#
```

VBScript Run-Time Constants

VBScript supplies you with an abundance of built-in constants. In Chapter 3 you learned about the constants associated with the `MsgBox()` function. For example, the following VBScript statement executes the `MsgBox()` function using the `vbOkOnly` constant:

```
MsgBox "Welcome to my VBScript game!", vbOkOnly
```

This statement displays a pop-up dialog that contains a single OK button. In addition to these constants, VBScript supplies constants that help when you're working with dates and times. VBScript also supplies a number of constants that can help you manipulate the display of text output and test the type of data stored within a variable.

Using Date and Time Constants

Table 4.2 lists VBScript Date and Time constants.

TABLE 4.2 VBSCRIPT DATE AND TIME CONSTANTS

Constant	Value	Description
`vbSunday`	1	Sunday
`vbMonday`	2	Monday
`vbTuesday`	3	Tuesday
`vbWednesday`	4	Wednesday
`vbThursday`	5	Thursday
`vbFriday`	6	Friday
`vbSaturday`	7	Saturday
`vbFirstFourDays`	2	First full week with a minimum of 4 days in the new year
`vbFirstFullWeek`	3	First full week of the year
`vbFirstJan1`	1	Week that includes January 1
`vbUseSystemDayOfWeek`	0	Day of week as specified by the operating system

The following script demonstrates how the vbFriday constant, listed in Table 4.2, can be used to determine whether the end of the workweek is here:

```
'*************************************************************************
'Script Name: HappyHour.vbs
'Author: Jerry Ford
'Created: 10/26/02
'Description: This script tells the user if it's Friday
'*************************************************************************

'Perform script initialization activities

Dim TodaysDate

' Weekday is a VBScript function that gets the day of the week
TodaysDate = Weekday(Date)

If TodaysDate = vbFriday then MsgBox "Hurray, it is Friday. Time " & _
  "to get ready for happy hour!"
```

You may have noticed the use of the & character in the previous example. The & character is a VBScript string concatenation operator. It allows you to combine two pieces of text into a single piece of text.

The first two lines of the script define a variable (we'll discuss variables in detail in the next section). The third line assigns a numeric value to the variable. In this case, the script used the VBScript `Weekday()` function to execute the VBScript `Date()` function. The `Date()` function retrieves the current date from the computer. The `Weekday()` function then provides a numeric value to represent the weekday for the date. Table 4.2 provides a list of the possible range of values in its Value column. If the current day of the week is Friday, then the value returned by the `Weekday()` function will be `6`. Because the `vbFriday` constant has a value of `6`, all that has to be done to determine if it is Friday is to compare the value returned by the `Weekday()` function to the `vbFriday`. If the two values are equal, a pop-up dialog displays the message `"Hurray, it is Friday. Time to get ready for happy hour!"`.

Using String Constants

Another group of constants that you may find useful are the VBScript string constants listed in Table 4.3.

TABLE 4.3 VBSCRIPT STRING CONSTANTS

Constant	Value	Description
vbCr	Chr(13)	Executes a carriage return
vbCrLf	Chr(13) and Chr(10)	Executes a carriage return and a line feed
vbFormFeed	Chr(12)	Executes a form feed
vbLf	Chr(10)	Executes a line feed
vbNewLine	Chr(13) and Chr(10)	Adds a newline character
vbNullChar	Chr(0)	Creates a 0 or null character
vbNullString	String with no value	Creates an empty string
vbTab	Chr(9)	Executes a horizontal tab
vbVerticalTab	Chr(11)	Executes a vertical tab

Using the constants shown in Table 4.3, you can control the manner in which output text is displayed. For example, take a look at the following script:

```
'*************************************************************************
'Script Name: MsgFormatter.vbs
'Author: Jerry Ford
'Created: 02/28/02
'Description: This script demonstrates how to use VBScript string constants
'to control how text messages are displayed.
'*************************************************************************

'Specify the message to appear in each pop-up dialog title bar

Const cTitleBarMsg = "The three little pigs"

'Specify variables used by the script

Dim StoryMsg

'Specify the text of the message to be displayed
```

```
StoryMsg = "Once upon a time there were 3 little pigs" & vbCrLf & _
           "who liked to build things." & vbCrLf & vbCrLf & _
           vbTab & "The End"

'Display the story to the user

MsgBox StoryMsg, vbOkOnly + vbExclamation, cTitleBarMsg
```

The text message that is displayed by the script is

```
Once upon a time there were 3 little pigs who liked to build things.
The End
```

Notice how the `vbCrLf` and `vbTab` constants have been placed throughout the text to specify how VBScript should display message text. Figure 4.9 shows the output that is displayed when this script is executed.

FIGURE 4.9 Using VBScript string constants to manipulate the display of text in pop-up dialogs.

If the `vbCrLf` and `vbTab` constants were removed from the formatted message, the text displayed in the pop-up dialog would look completely different, as shown in Figure 4.10.

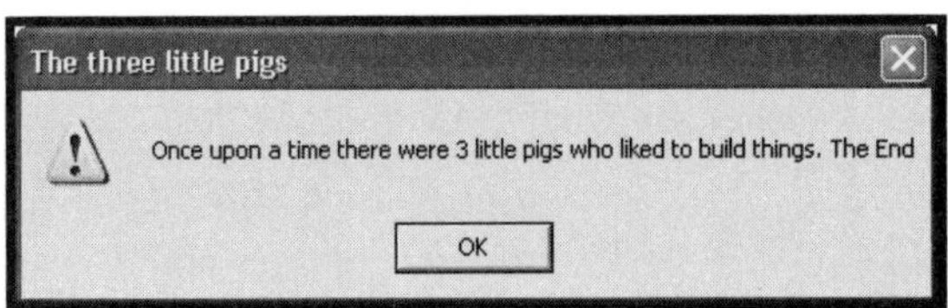

FIGURE 4.10 Displaying the same output as the previous example without the use of the `vbCrLf` and `vbTab` constants.

For more information about VBScript constants, go to http://www.msdn.microsoft.com and click on the VBScript Documentation link.

Storing Data That Changes During Script Execution

Chances are most programs that you write will have data in them that will need to be modified. For example, you may write a script that asks the user for input and then modifies the data while processing it. In this situation, you can define variables.

Two categories of variables are available to your scripts: variables that you define within your scripts and environment variables that are maintained by Windows that your scripts can reference. I'll demonstrate how to work with both categories of variables in the sections that follow.

VBScript Data Types

Unlike many other programming languages, VBScript only supports one type of variable, called a *variant*. However, a variant is very flexible and can be used to store a number of different types of data. Table 4.4 lists variant data types supported by VBScript.

Definition

A *variant* is a type of variable that can contain any number of different types of data.

Table 4.4 VBScript Supported Variant Subtypes

Subtype	Description
Boolean	A variant with a value of `True` or `False`
Byte	An integer whose value is between 0 and 255
Currency	A currency value between −922,337,203,685,477.5808 and 922,337,203,685,477.5807
Date	A number representing a date between January 1, 100 and December 31, 9999
Double	A floating-point number with a range of – 1.79769313486232E308 and −4.94065645841247E-324 or 4.94065645841247E-324 and 1.79769313486232E308
Empty	A variant that has not been initialized
Error	A VBScript error number
Integer	An integer with a value that is between −32,768 and 32,767
Long	An integer whose value is between −2,147,483,648 and 2,147,483,647
Null	A variant set equal to a null value
Object	An object
Single	A floating-point number whose value is between −3.402823E38 and – 1.401298E-45 or 1.401298E-45 and 3.402823E38
String	A string up to two billion characters long

Variants automatically recognize the types of data that are assigned to them and act accordingly. In other words, if a date value is assigned to a variant, then your script can use any of VBScript's built-in date functions to work with it. Likewise, if a text string is assigned to a variant, then your script can use any of VBScript's built-in string functions to work with it.

Like constants, VBScript provides you with some control over the way in which it identifies the types of values stored in a variant. For example, if you assign 100 as the variable value, then VBScript automatically interprets this value as a number. But if you enclose the value in quotation marks, VBScript treats it like a string.

VBScript also provides the capability to convert data from one type to another using built-in VBScript functions. You can use these functions within your scripts to change the way VBScript views and works with data. For example, the following VBScript statement defines a variable named `MyBirthday` and assigns it a text string of `"November 20, 1964"`:

> **DEFINITION**
>
> The term *string* and *text string* are used synonymously throughout this book to refer to text-based data or other types of data that have been enclosed within a pair of quotations.

```
MyBirthday = "November 20, 1964"
```

VBScript views this variable's value as a text string. However, using the `Cdate()` function, you can covert the string value to date format:

```
MyBirthday = CDate(MyBirthday)
```

Now, instead of seeing the variable's value as `"November 20, 1964"`, VBScript sees it as `11/20/1964`.

VBScript provides a large number of conversion functions that you can use to convert from one data type to another. These functions include `Asc()`, `Cbool()`, `Cbyte()`, `Cbur()`, `Cdate()`, `CDbl()`, `Chr()`, `Cint()`, `CLng()`, `CSng()`, and `CStr()`. For more information about how to use these functions, see Chapter 7.

Defining Variables

VBScript provides two ways of defining variables: dynamically, and formally, using the `Dim` statement. To dynamically create a variable within a script, you simply need to reference it like this:

```
MyBirthday = #November 20, 1964#
```

Using this method of programming, you can define variables anywhere within your script. However, I strongly recommend against creating variables in this manner. It is much better to formally define any variables used in a script all at once at the beginning of the script. This helps keep things organized and easier to read. In addition, I also strongly suggest that you use the Dim statement. The syntax of the Dim statement is as follows:

```
Dim VariableName
```

VariableName is the name of the variable being defined. For example, the following statement defines a variable named MyBirthday:

```
Dim MyBirthday
```

After a variable has been defined, you can assign a value to it, like this:

```
MyBirthday = #November 20, 1964#
```

Always use the Dim statement to make your code more readable and to explicitly show your intentions. You can define multiple variables within your scripts using multiple Dim statements:

```
Dim MyBirthday
Dim MyName
Dim MyAge
```

However, to reduce the number of lines of code in your scripts, you have the option of defining more than one variable at a time using a single Dim statement, by separating each variable with a comma and a space:

```
Dim MyBirthday, MyName, MyAge
```

As I already stated, it's better to formally define a variable before using it. One way to make sure that you follow this simple rule is to place the Option Explicit statement at the beginning of your scripts. The Option Explicit statement generates an error during script execution if you attempt to reference a variable without first defining it. Therefore, Option Explicit helps remind you to follow good programming practices when working with variables.

To test the use of the Option Explicit statement, let's take a look at another example:

```
'*************************************************************************
'Script Name: BigBadWolf.vbs
'Author: Jerry Ford
'Created: 02/29/02
'Description: This script demonstrates how to use the Option Explicit
'statement
'*************************************************************************
```

```
'For the explicit declaration of all variables used in this script

Option Explicit

'Create a variable to store the name of the wolf

Dim WolfName

'Assign the wolf's name to the variable

WolfName = "Mr. Wiggles"

'Display the story

MsgBox "Once upon a time there was a big bad wolf named " & WolfName & _
       " who liked to eat little pigs", vbOkOnly
```

In this example, the `Option Explicit` statement is the first statement in the script. By making it the first statement in the script, `Option Explicit` will affect all variables that follow. The next statement defines a variable representing the name of the wolf. The statement after that assigns a name to the variable, which is then used by the script's final statement to tell the story. Run the script and you'll see that everything works fine. Then modify the script by placing a comment in front of the `Dim` statement and run the script again. This time, instead of executing properly, the error shown in Figure 4.11 will appear, indicating that the script attempted to reference an undefined variable.

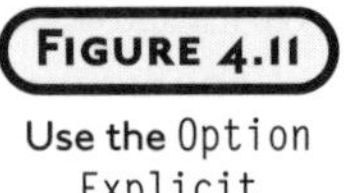

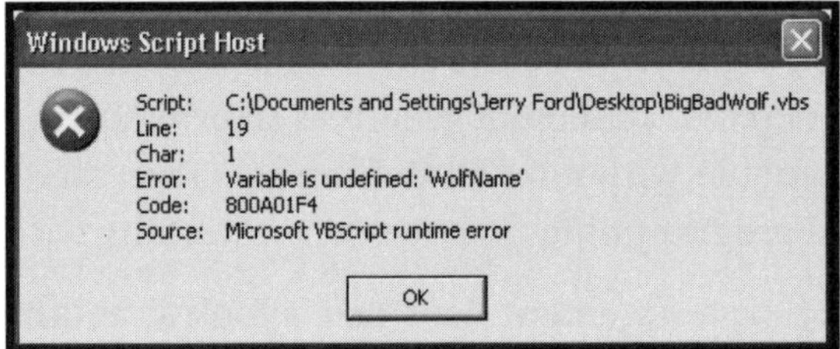

FIGURE 4.11 Use the `Option Explicit` statement in all your scripts to prevent the use of undefined variables.

To summarize, the following list provides the guidelines that you should follow when working with variables:

- Define your variables at the beginning of your scripts in one location.
- Use the `Option Explicit` statement to enforce formal variable declaration.
- Use the `Dim` statement to define each variable.

Up to this point in the chapter, I have not been following these rules because I had not gotten to them yet. However, from this point on, you'll find them applied consistently in every script that uses variables.

There is one exception to the set of rules that I want to point out. In certain cases, you can limit the availability of a variable and its value to a specific portion of your scripts. This is called *creating a local variable* and can be useful when manipulating a sensitive variable to make sure that its value is not accidentally modified by other parts of the script. I'll provide more information about local variables a little later in this chapter.

Variable Naming Rules

Another important issue that merits attention is the proper naming of variables. VBScript has a number of rules that you must follow to avoid errors from inappropriately named variables. These rules include

- Variable names must be less than 256 characters long.
- Variable names must begin with an alphabetic character.
- Only letters, numbers, and the _ character can be used when creating variable names.
- Reserved words cannot be used as variable names.
- Variable names cannot contain spaces.
- Variable names must be unique.

One more important thing to know about VBScript variables is that they are case-insensitive. This means that capitalization does not affect VBScript's capability to recognize a variable. Therefore, if a script defines a variable as `Dim MyBirthday` and then later references it as `MYBIRTHDAY`, VBScript recognizes both spellings of the variable name as the same. However, mixing cases in this manner can be confusing and you should do your best to use a consistent case throughout your scripts.

In the Real World

You should assign descriptive variable names in your scripts to make them easier to identify and understand. Select a standard approach in the way that you use case in the spelling of your variables. Up to this point in the book, I have defined variables using complete words or parts of words, and I began each word or part of a word with a capital letter, as in `Dim MyBirthday`.

Another approach that many programmers take when naming variables is to add a three-character prefix, sometimes referred to as Hungarian Notation, to the beginning of each variable name to identify the type of data stored in the variable. For example, instead of naming a variable `Mybirthday`, you would name it `dtmMyBirthday`. This way by examining the first three characters of the variable name, you'll be able to tell that it contains a date. The following list identifies typical prefixes associated with each of the variable subtypes supported by VBScript.

- Boolean – bln
- Byte – byt
- Currency – cur
- Date – dtm
- Double – dbl
- Error – err
- Integer – int
- Long – lng
- Object – obj
- Single – sng
- String – str
- Variant – var

Now that I have formally introduced you to Hungarian Notation, I'll begin using it when naming variables in all the script examples you'll see throughout the rest of this book.

Variable Scope

Another key concept that you need to understand when working with variables is *variable scope*. In this context, *scope* refers to the ability to reference a variable and its assigned value from various locations within a script.

VBScript supports two different variable scopes, global and local. A variable with a global scope can be accessed from any location within the script. However, a variable with a local scope can only be referenced from within the procedure that defines it. VBScript supports two types of procedures, subroutines and functions, both of which are discussed in detail in Chapter 7.

As you know, a procedure is a collection or group of statements that is executed as a unit. Without getting too far ahead of myself, for now just note that a variable defined outside a procedure is global in scope, meaning that it can be accessed from any location within the script, including from within the script's procedures. A variable that is local in scope is defined within a procedure.

Modifying Variable Values with Expressions

Throughout this chapter, you have seen the equals sign (=) used to assign value to variables, like this:

```
strMyName = "Jerry Lee Ford, Jr."
```

To change the value assigned to a variable, all you have to do is use the equals sign again, along with a new value, like this:

```
strMyName = "Jerry L. Ford, Jr."
```

The two previous examples set and then modified the value assigned to a text variable. However, this same approach works just as well for other types of variables, such as those that contain numeric values:

```
Option Explicit
Dim intMyAge
intMyAge = 37
intMyAge = 38
```

In this example, the variable is defined and then assigned a numeric value. The value assigned to that variable is then modified to a different number. VBScript provides additional ways of modifying the value of numeric variables using the equals sign and VBScript arithmetic operators. Table 4.5 lists the VBScript arithmetic operators.

Table 4.5 VBScript Arithmetic Operators

Operator	Description
+	Addition
-	Subtraction
*	Multiplication
/	Division
-	Negation
^	Exponentiation
\	Integer division
Mod	Modulus

The best way to explain how these arithmetic operators are used is to show you an example. Take a look at the following script:

```
'*************************************************************************
'Script Name: MathDemo.vbs
'Author: Jerry Ford
'Created: 02/29/02
'Description: This script demonstrates how to use various VBScript
'arithmetic operators
'*************************************************************************


'Force the explicit declaration of all variables used in this script

Option Explicit

'Create a variable to store the name of the wolf

Dim intMyAge

'Assign my initial starting age
```

```
intMyAge = 37
WScript.Echo "I am " & intMyAge

'Next year I will be

intMyAge = intMyAge + 1
WScript.Echo "Next year I will be " & intMyAge

'But I am not that old yet

intMyAge = intMyAge - 1
WScript.Echo "But I still am " & intMyAge

'This is how old I'd be if I were twice as old as I am today

intMyAge = intMyAge * 2
WScript.Echo "This is twice my age " & intMyAge

'And if I took that value, divided it by 5, added 3, and multiplied it
'by 10

intMyAge = intMyAge / 5 + 3 * 10
WScript.Echo "This says that I will be " & intMyAge
```

If you run this script, you'll see the results shown in Figure 4.12.

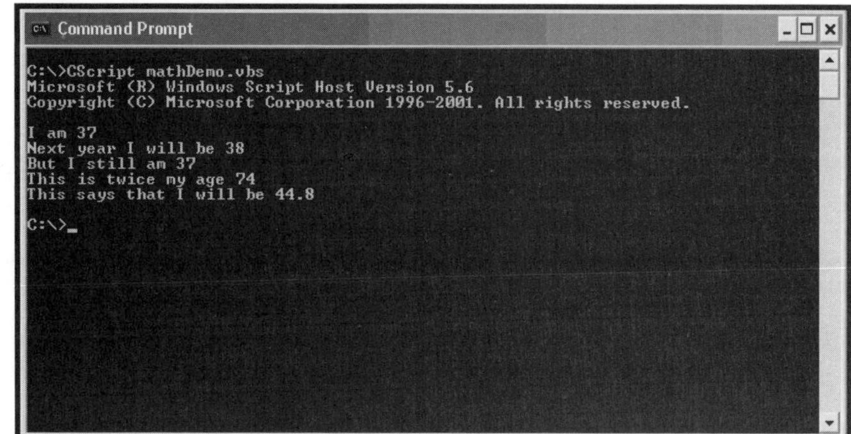

FIGURE 4.12

Using VBScript arithmetic operators to modify numeric variables.

The first four calculations should be fairly easy to understand. In the first calculation, I took the value of intMyAge and added 1 to it. Similarly I subtracted 1 in the next calculation and then multiplied intMyAge times 2 in the third statement. The final calculation requires a little more explanation. You may have been surprised by this calculation's result. At first glance, it appears that VBScript will try to solve the equation as follows:

```
Step 1: Divide intMyAge, which is currently 74 by 5 yielding 14.8
Step 2: Add 14.8 to 3 getting 17.8.
Step 3: Multiple 17.8 and 10 getting as the final result 178
```

However, VBScript says that the answer is actually 44.8. How could this be? The answer lies in something called the order of precedence, which tells VBScript the order in which to perform individual calculations within an equation or expression. Table 4.6 outlines the order in which VBScript order of precedence occurs.

TABLE 4.6 ORDER OF PRECEDENCE FOR VBSCRIPT ARITHMETIC OPERATORS

Operator	Description
^	Exponentiation
-	Negation
*	Multiplication
/	Division
\	Integer division
Mod	Modulus
+	Addition
-	Subtraction

Note: Operators appearing at the beginning of the table have precedence over operators appearing later in the table.

Exponentiation occurs before negation. Negation occurs before multiplication, and so on. So when applied to the last calculation in the previous example, VBScript solves the equation as follows:

```
Step 1: Multiple 3 * 10 to get 30
Step 2: Divide intMyAge by 5 to get 14.8
Step 3: Add 14.8 to 30 getting the final result of 44.8
```

You can add parentheses to your VBScript expressions to exercise control over the order in which individual calculations are performed. For example, you could rewrite the last expression in the previous example as follows:

```
inMyAge = ((intMyAge / 5) + 3) * 10
```

VBScript now performs individual calculation located within parentheses first, like this:

```
Step 1: Divide intMyAge by 5 to get 14.8
Step 2: Add 14.8 and 3 to get 17.8
Step 3: Multiple 17.8 times 10 to get a final result of 178
```

Using the WSH to Work with Environment Variables

Thus far, the scripts that you have worked with in this chapter have used variables that are defined by the scripts themselves. A second type of variable, known as an *environment variable*, is also available to your VBScripts. Windows operating systems automatically create and maintain environment variables. The two types of environment variables are user and computer. User environment variables are created during user login and provide information specific to the currently logged on user. Computer environment variables, on the other hand, are created based on what Windows learns about the computer; they are available at all times, as opposed to user variables, which are only available when you're logged in to the computer.

You may end up writing scripts that are designed to run when no one is logged on to the computer. This can be done using the Windows Scheduler Service to automate the execution scripts. In this case, user environment variables will not be available to your scripts and it will be up to you to make sure that your scripts do not depend on them.

User and computer environment variables can be viewed from the Windows Environment Variables dialog. For example, on Windows XP you can access this dialog using the following procedure:

1. Click on Start.
2. Right-click on My Computer and select Properties. The System Properties dialog appears.
3. Select the Advanced property sheet.
4. Click on Environment Variables. The Environment Variables dialog appears, as shown in Figure 4.13.

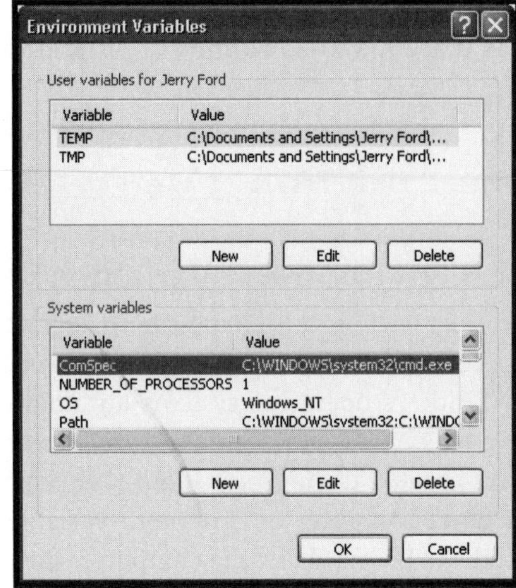

FIGURE 4.13

Examining Windows environment variables

Examples of user environment variables include

- **TEMP**. A folder where temporary files can be stored.
- **TMP**. Another folder where temporary files can be stored.

Examples of computer environment variables include

- **ComSpec**. Specifies the location of the Windows shell.
- **NUMBER_OF_PROCESSORS**. Displays a value of 1 for single processor computers.
- **OS**. Displays the operating system's name.
- **Path**. Specifies the current search path.

- **PATHEXT**. Specifies a list of extensions that identify executable files.
- **PROCESSOR_ARCHITECTURE**. Identifies the computer's processor type.
- **PROCESSOR_IDENTIFIER**. Displays a detailed description of the computer's processor.
- **PROCESSOR_LEVEL**. Displays the processor's stepping level.
- **PROCESSOR_REVISION**. Displays the processor's revision number.
- **TEMP**. A folder in which temporary files can be stored.
- **TMP**. Another folder in which temporary files can be stored.
- **Windir**. Identifies the location of the Windows folder.

To access environment variables, you need to use the WSH. For example, take a look at the following script:

```
'*************************************************************************
'Script Name: ComputerAnalyzer.vbs
'Author: Jerry Ford
'Created: 02/29/02
'Description: This script demonstrates how to access environment
'variables using the WSH
'*************************************************************************

'Force the explicit declaration of all variables used in this script

Option Explicit

'Create a variable to store the name of the wolf

Dim objWshObject

'Set up an instance of the WScript.WshShell object
Set objWshObject = WScript.CreateObject("WScript.Shell")

'Use the WScript.Shell object's ExpandEnvironmentScrings() method to view
'environment variables
MsgBox "This computer is running a version of " & _
       objWshObject.ExpandEnvironmentStrings("%OS%") & vbCrLf & _
       "and has " & _
       objWshObject.ExpandEnvironmentStrings("%NUMBER_OF_PROCESSORS%") & _
       " processor(s)."
```

The first statement in this example creates an instance of the WSH `WScript.Shell` object using the WScript's `CreateObject()` method. The next part of the script uses the `WScript.Shell` object's `ExpandEnvironmentStrings()` method to display the value of specific environment variables.

In the Real World

Although the script demonstrates how to access environment variables, it really isn't very useful. Another use for environment variables might be to validate the operating system on which the script has been started and to terminate script execution if it has been started on the wrong operating system like this:

```
If objWshObject.ExpandEnvironmentStrings("%OS%") <> "Windows_NT" Then
  MsgBox "This script is designed to only run on " & _
    "Windows NT, 2000, XP or .NET"
  WScript.Quit
End If
```

In this example, the first line of code checks to see if the script is being run on an NT, 2000, XP, or .NET system. If it isn't, then the second and third lines of code execute, informing the user of the situation and terminating the script's execution.

Working with Collections of Related Data

When using variables, you can store an incredible amount of information during the execution of your scripts; you're limited only by the amount of memory available on your computer. However, keeping up with large numbers of variables can be difficult and may make your scripts difficult to maintain.

Often, data items processed by a script have a relationship to one another. For example, if you write a script that collects a list of names from the user in order to generate a list of personal contacts, it would be more convenient to store and manage the list of names as a unit instead of as a collection of individual names. VBScript provides support for arrays so that such a task can be performed.

Definition

An *array* is an indexed list of related data. The first element, or piece of data, stored in the array is assigned an index position of 0. The second element is assigned an index position of 1 and so on. Thus, by referring to an element's index position, you can access its value.

For example, you can think of an array as being like a collection of numbered index cards, where each card contains the name of a person who has been sent an invitation to a party. If you assigned a name of `ItsMyParty` to the collection of cards, you could then programmatically refer to any card in the collection as `ItsMyParty(`*`index#`*`)`, where index# is the number written on the card.

The `ItsMyParty` collection is an example of a single-dimension array. VBScript is capable of supporting array with as many as 60 dimensions. In most cases, all you'll need to work with are single dimension arrays, so that's where I'll focus most of my attention.

Single-Dimension Arrays

To create a single-dimension array, you use the `Dim` statement. When used in the creation of arrays, the `Dim` statement has to have the following syntax:

```
Dim ArrayName(dimensions)
```

`Dimensions` is a comma-separated list of numbers that specifies the number of dimensions that make up the array. For example, the following VBScript statement can be used to create a single dimension array named `ItsMyParty` that can hold up to 10 names:

```
Dim ItsMyParty(9)
```

Notice that I used the number `9` to define an array that can hold up to 10 elements. This is because the first index number in the array is automatically set to 0, thus allowing the array to store 10 elements (that is, 0–9).

After an array is defined, it can be populated with data.

Because the first element stored in an array has an index of 0, its actual length is equal to the number supplied when the array is first defined, plus one.

The following VBScript statements demonstrate how you can assign data to each element in the array:

```
ItsMyParty (0) = "Jerry"
ItsMyParty (1) = "Molly"
ItsMyParty (2) = "William"
ItsMyParty (3) = "Alexander"
.
.
.
ItsMyParty(9) = "Mary"
```

As you can see, to assign a name to an element in the array, I had to specify the element's index number. After you populate the array, you can access any array element by specifying its index number, like this:

```
MsgBox ItsMyParty(1)
```

In this example, `ItsMyParty(1)` equates to `Molly`.

If you like the suggestions I made earlier in this chapter about naming constants and about using Hungarian Notation when creating names for your variables, then you might want to combine these two approaches when naming your arrays. For example, instead of naming an array `ItsMyParty()`, you might want to name it `astrItsMyParty()`. The first character of the name identifies that it's an array and the next three characters identify the type of data that stored in the array. This is the naming standard that I'll use when naming arrays throughout the rest of this book.

Multiple-Dimension Arrays

As I previously stated, VBScript can support arrays with as many as 60 dimensions, although one or two dimensions are usually sufficient. Let's take a look at how to define a two-dimensional array, which you can think of as being like a two-column table. The first column contains the name of the guests invited to the party and the second column stores the guest's phone numbers.

```
Dim astrItsMyParty(3,1)

astrItsMyParty(0,0) = "Jerry"
astrItsMyParty(0,1) = "550-9933"
astrItsMyParty(1,0) = "Molly"
astrItsMyParty(1,1) = "550-8876"
astrItsMyParty(2,0) = "William"
astrItsMyParty(2,1) = "697-4443"
astrItsMyParty(3,0) = "Alexander"
astrItsMyParty(3,1) = "696-4344"
```

In this example, a two-dimensional array is created that is four rows deep and two columns wide, allowing it to store up to eight pieces of data. To refer to any particular element in this two-dimensional array, you must supply both its row and column coordinates, like this:

```
WScript.Echo astrItsMyParty(1,0)
WScript.Echo astrItsMyParty(1,1)
```

The first of the two previous statements refer to the `Molly` element. The second statement refers to the phone number associated with `Molly`.

Another way of thinking about a two-dimensional array is to consider it a one-dimensional array made up of a collection of one-dimensional arrays.

Processing Array Contents

So far, in all the examples, I have accessed each array element by specifically referencing its index position. This works fine as long as the array is small, but it's not a practical approach for processing the contents of large arrays, which may contain hundreds or thousands of entries. To handle arrays of this size, a different approach is needed. VBScript's solution to this issue is the `For Each...Next` loop. The syntax of the `For Each...Next` loop is as follows:

```
For Each element In group
  Statements . . .
Next [element]
```

Element is a variable that the loop uses to iterate through each array element. *Group* identifies the name of the array. *Statements* are the VBScripts statements that you add to process the contents of each array element. The `For Each...Next` loop continues processing until every element in the array has been examined.

The `For Each...Next` loop lets your scripts process the entire contents of an array using just a few statements. The number of statements required does not increase based on array size. Therefore, you can use a `For Each...Next` loop to process extremely large arrays with very little programming effort. For example, the next script defines an array named `GameArray()` and populates it with five elements. It then processes the entire array using just one line of code located within a `For Each...Next` loop.

```
'*************************************************************************
'Script Name: ArrayDemo.vbs
'Author: Jerry Ford
'Created: 02/28/02
'Description: This script demonstrates how to store and retrieve data
'using a single-dimension VBScript array.
'*************************************************************************


'Perform script initialization activities
```

```
Option Explicit

'Define variables used in the script

Dim intCounter          'Variable used to control a For...Each loop
Dim strMessage   'Message to be displayed in a pop-up dialog

strMessage = "The array contains the following default game " & _
    "information: " & vbCrLf & vbCrLf

Dim astrGameArray(4)  'Define an array that can hold 5 index elements
astrGameArray(0) = "Joe Blow"  'The default username
astrGameArray(1) = "Nevada"    'A place worth visiting
astrGameArray(2) = "Soda Can"  'An interesting object
astrGameArray(3) = "Barney"    'A close friend
astrGameArray(4) = "Pickle"    'A favorite dessert

For Each intCounter In astrGameArray
  strMessage = strMessage & intCounter & vbCrLf
Next
WScript.Echo strMessage
```

If you run this script using the `CScript.exe` execution host, you receive the output shown in Figure 4.14.

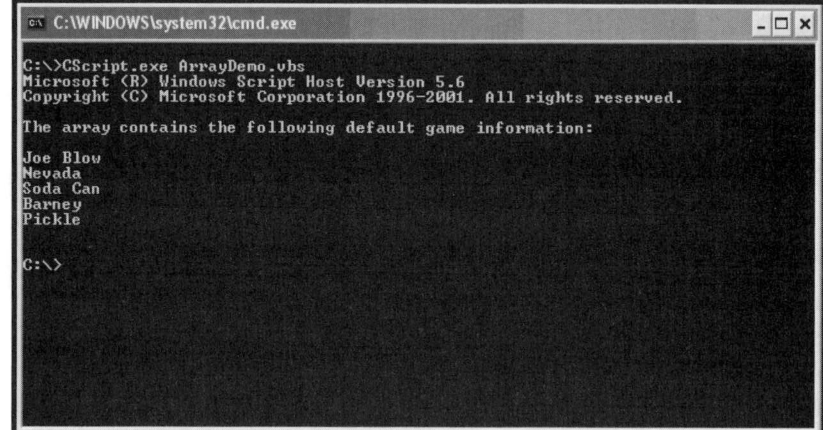

FIGURE 4.14

Iteratively processing all the contents of an array.

These same few lines of code can just as easily process the array, even if it has a hundred or a thousand elements. The alternative to the `For...Each...Next` loop is to write an individual statement to access each element stored within the array, like this:

```
'Display the contents of the array
WScript.Echo strMessage
WScript.Echo astrGameArray(0)
WScript.Echo astrGameArray(1)
WScript.Echo astrGameArray(2)
WScript.Echo astrGameArray(3)
WScript.Echo astrGameArray(4)
```

Writing statements for individual access array contents may not seem like a lot of work in a small program, but imagine trying to process an array with 1,000 elements!

For more information on how to work with the `For...Each...Next` loop, see Chapter 6, "Processing Collections of Data."

Getting a Handle on the Size of Your Arrays

VBScript provides you with two built-in functions that make it easier to work with arrays:

- **Ubound().** Returns a numeric value indicating the array's upper bound or its highest element.
- **Lbound().** Returns a numeric value indicating the array's lower bound or its lowest element.

The `Lbound()` function isn't really that useful because the lower bound of all VBScript arrays is always set equal to 0. On the other hand, the `Ubound()` function can be quite handy, especially when working with dynamic arrays. I'll cover dynamic arrays a little later in this chapter.

`Lbound()` is a function common to VBScript, VBA, and Visual Basic. It's a lot more useful in VBA and Visual Basic because these programming languages allow you to specify the lower bounds of arrays.

The syntax of the `Ubound()` function is

```
Ubound(ArrayName, Dimension)
```

`ArrayName` is the name of the array whose upper bound is to be returned. `Dimension` is used to specify the array dimension whose upper bound is to be returned. For example, you could retrieve the upper bound of a single dimension array called `astrItsMyparty` as shown here:

```
intSize = Ubound(astrItsMyParty)
```

In this case, the upper bound of the array is assigned to a variable named `intSize`. Let's look at a quick example of the `Ubound()` function in action:

```
Dim intCounter   'Define a variable to be used when processing array
                  'contents
Dim strMessage   'Define a variable to be used to store display output

Dim astrGameArray(2)  'Define an array that can hold 3 index elements
astrGameArray(0) = "Joe Blow"   'The default username
astrGameArray(1) = "Nevada"     'A place worth visiting
astrGameArray(2) = "Soda Can"   'An interesting object

intSize = UBound(astrgameArray)

For intCounter = 0 to intSize
  strMessage = strMessage & astrGameArray(intCounter) & vbCrLf
Next

MsgBox strMessage
```

Run this example and you'll see that the script displays all three elements in the array in a pop-up dialog.

Resizing Arrays

Sometimes it's impossible to know how many elements an array will need to store when developing your scripts. For example, you might develop a script that uses the `InputBox()` function to prompt the user to specify the data to be stored in the array. You might expect the user to specify only a few pieces of data, but the user may have an entirely different idea. To handle this type of situation, you need a way of resizing the array to allow it to store the additional data.

One way of dealing with this situation is to define the array without specifying its size, like this:

```
Dim astrGameArray()
```

This lets you define the array's size later in the script. For example, you might want to define the array and later ask the user how many pieces of data he or she intends to provide. This is accomplished by using the `ReDim` statement:

```
ReDim astrGameArray(9)
```

This `ReDim` statement has set up the array to store up to 10 elements. After its size has finally been defined, you can begin populating the array with data.

If you use the `ReDim` statement to set up a new array by accidentally specifying the name of an existing array, the data stored in the existing array will be lost.

Another, more flexible way of setting up an array so that it can be later resized is to replace the array's original `Dim` definition statement with the `ReDim` statement. For example, the following statement sets up a new array capable of holding up to 10 elements:

```
ReDim astrTestArray(9)
```

However, if you populate this array with data and then later attempt to resize it, as shown next, you'll lose all the data originally stored in the array.

```
ReDim astrTestArray(19)
```

To prevent this from happening, you can add the `Preserve` keyword to the `ReDim` statement, like this:

```
ReDim Preserve astrTestArray(19)
```

This statement instructs VBScript to expand the size of the array while preserving its current contents. After the array is expanded, you can then add additional elements to it. For example, take a look at the next script. It defines an array with the capability to store five elements and then resizes the array to increase its storage capacity to eight elements. The script then uses a `For...Each...Next` loop to display the contents of the expanded array.

```
'*************************************************************************
'Script Name: ResizeArray.vbs
'Author: Jerry Ford
'Created: 02/28/02
```

```
'Description: This script demonstrates how to resize an array during
'execution
'*************************************************************************

'Perform script initialization activities

Option Explicit

'Define variables used in the script

Dim intCounter          'Variable used to control a For...Each loop
Dim strMessage   'Message to be displayed in a pop-up dialog

strMessage = "The array contains the following default game " & _
    "information: " & vbCrLf & vbCrLf

ReDim astrGameArray(4)  'Define an array that can hold 5 index elements
astrGameArray(0) = "Joe Blow"  'The default username
astrGameArray(1) = "Nevada"    'A place worth visiting
astrGameArray(2) = "Soda Can"  'An interesting object
astrGameArray(3) = "Barney"    'A close friend
astrGameArray(4) = "Pickle"    'A favorite dessert

'Insert additional script code here........

ReDim Preserve astrGameArray(7) 'Change the array to hold 8 entries
astrGameArray(5) = "Lard Tart"  'Default villain name
astrGameArray(6) = "Water Gun"  'Default villain weapon
astrGameArray(7) = "Earth"      'Planet the villain wants to conquer

'Display the contents of the array

For Each intCounter In astrGameArray
  strMessage = strMessage & intCounter & vbCrLf
Next
WScript.Echo strMessage
```

Be careful not to accidentally lose any data if you decide to resize an array to a smaller size. For example, if you defined an array that can hold 100 elements and then later resize it to hold 50 elements using the `Preserve` keyword, only the first 50 elements in the array will actually be preserved.

Building Dynamic Arrays

Up to this point, all the arrays demonstrated in this book have been static, meaning that their size was predetermined at execution time. But in the real world, you won't always know how many elements your arrays will need to store. For example, you might write a script that enables the user to supply a list of names of people to be invited to a party. Depending on the number of friends the user has, the amount of data to be stored in the array can vary significantly. VBScript's solution to this type of situation is dynamic arrays. A *dynamic array* is an array that can be resized during execution as many times as necessary.

You can use the `Dim` statement to define a dynamic array as shown here:

```
Dim astrItsMyParty()
```

Note that an index number for the array was not supplied inside the parentheses. This allows you to come back later on in the script and resize the array using the `ReDim` statement as demonstrated here:

```
ReDim astrItsMyParty(2)
```

Once resized, you can add new entries:

```
astrItsMyParty(0) = "Molly"
astrItsMyParty(1) = "William"
astrItsMyParty(2) = "Alexander"
```

If the script later needs to add additional elements to the array, you can resize it again:

```
ReDim Preserve astrItsMyParty(4)
```

This statement has increased the size of the array so that it can now hold an additional two elements. Note the use of the `Preserve` keyword on the `ReDim` statement. This parameter was required to prevent the array from losing any data stored in it before increasing the array's size.

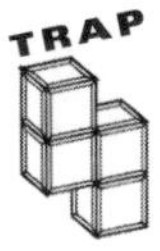

Dynamic arrays can be increased or decreased in size. If you decrease the size of a dynamic array, all elements stored in the array are lost even if the `Preserve` keyword is added to the `ReDim` statement.

Now, let's look at one more example of how to work with dynamic arrays. In this example, an array named `astrItsMyParty` is initially set up with the capability to store one element. The user is then prompted to provide a list of names to be added to the array. Each time a new name is supplied, the script dynamically increases the size of the array by 1, allowing it to hold additional information.

```
Dim astrItsMyParty()

ReDim astrItsMyParty(0)

Dim intCounter, strListOfNames

intCounter = 0

Do While UCase(strListOfNames) <> "QUIT"
  strListOfNames = InputBox("Enter the name of someone to be invited: ")

  If UCase(strListOfNames) <> "QUIT" Then
    astrItsMyParty(intCounter) = strListOfNames
  Else
    Exit Do
  End If

  intCounter = intCounter + 1
  ReDim Preserve astrItsMyParty(intCounter)

Loop
```

In this example, the array is named `astrItsMyParty`. A `Dim` statement is used to define it and then a `ReDim` statement is used to set its initial size, thus allowing it to store a single element. After setting up a couple of variables used by the script, I added a `Do...While` loop to collect user input. The loop runs until the user types `Quit`.

`UCase()` is a VBScript function that converts string characters to uppercase. Using `UCase()`, you can develop scripts that process user input regardless of how the user employs capitalization when entering data.

Assuming that the user does not type `Quit`, the script adds the names entered by the user to a string, which is stored in a variable named `strListOfNames`. Otherwise, the `Do...While` loop terminates. Each time a new name is entered, the `ReDim` statement is executed to redimension the array by increasing its size by one.

Erasing Arrays

When your script is done working with the data stored in an array, you can erase or delete it, thus freeing up a small portion of the computer's memory for other work. This is accomplished using the `Erase` statement, which has the following syntax:

```
Erase ArrayName
```

For example, the following statement could be used to erase an array named `astrGameArray`:

```
Erase astrGameArray
```

PROCESSING DATA PASSED TO A SCRIPT AT RUN-TIME

Up to this point, every script you have seen in this chapter expects to have its data hard-coded as constants, variables, and arrays. Another way for a script to access data for processing is to set up the script so that the user can pass it arguments for processing at execution time.

> **DEFINITION**
>
> An *argument* is a piece of data passed to the script at the beginning of its execution. For example, a script that is designed to copy a file from one location to another might accept the name of the file to be copied as an argument.

Passing Arguments to Scripts

To pass arguments to a script, you must start the script from the command line, as follows:

```
CScript DisplayArgs.vbs tic tac toe
```

In the previous statement, the `CScript.exe` execution host is used to start a VBScript named `DisplayArgs.vbs`. Three arguments have been passed to the script for processing. Each argument is separated by a blank space.

The next example shows a slight variation of the statement. In this case, the script still passes three arguments, but because the second argument contains a blank space, it must be enclosed in quotation marks:

```
CScript DisplayArgs.vbs tic "super tac" toe
```

Of course, for a script to accept and process arguments at execution time, it must be set up to do so, as demonstrated in the next section.

Designing Scripts That Accept Argument Input

To set a script up to accept arguments, as demonstrated in the previous section, you can use the WSH's `WshArguments` object as shown in the following script:

```
'*************************************************************************
'Script Name: ArgumentProcessor.vbs
'Author: Jerry Ford
'Created: 02/29/02
'Description: This script demonstrates how to work with arguments passed
'to the script by the user at execution time
'*************************************************************************

'For the explicit declaration of all variables used in this script

Option Explicit

'Define variables used during script execution

Dim objWshArgs, strFirstArg, strSecondArg, strThirdArg

'Set up an instance of the WshArguments object
Set objWshArgs = WScript.Arguments

'Use the WshArguments object's Count property to verify that 3 arguments
'were received. If 3 arguments are not received then display an error
'message and terminate script execution.
If objWshArgs.Count <> 3 then
  WScript.Echo "Error: Invalid number of arguments."
  WScript.Quit
End IF

'Assign each argument to a variable for processing
strFirstArg = objWshArgs.Item(0)
strSecondArg = objWshArgs.Item(1)
strThirdArg = objWshArgs.Item(2)

'Display the value assigned to each variable
WScript.Echo   "The first argument is " & strFirstArg & vbCrLf &_
               "The second argument is " & strSecondArg & vbCrLf & _
               "The third argument is " & strThirdArg & vbCrLf
```

To use the `WshArguments` object, the script must first create an instance of it, like this:

```
Set objWshArgs = WScript.Arguments
```

Next, the script uses the `WshArguments` object's `Count` property to make sure that three arguments have been passed to the script. If more than or fewer than three arguments have been received, an error message is displayed and the script terminates its execution. Otherwise, the script continues and assigns each of the arguments to a variable. Each argument is stored in an indexed list by the `WshArguments` object and is referenced using the object's `Item()` method. `Item(0)` refers to the first arguments passed to the script. `Item(1)` refers the second argument, and `Item(2)` refers to the third argument.

Finally, the `WScript.Echo` method is used to display each of the arguments passed to the script. The following shows how the script's output appears when executed using the `CScript.exe` execution host and three arguments (`tic`, `tac`, and `toe`):

```
C:\>CScript.exe ArgumentProcessor.vbs tic tac toe
Microsoft (R) Windows Script Host Version 5.6
Copyright (C) Microsoft Corporation 1996-2001. All rights reserved.

The first argument is tic
The second argument is tac
The third argument is toe

C:\>
```

Similarly, the following output shows what happens when only two arguments are passed to the script:

```
C:\>CScript.exe ArgumentProcessor.vbs tic tac
Microsoft (R) Windows Script Host Version 5.6
Copyright (C) Microsoft Corporation 1996-2001. All rights reserved.

Error: Invalid number of arguments.

C:\>
```

Back to the Story of Captain Adventure

Now let's return to the chapter's programming project, the Story of Captain Adventure. In this programming project, you'll develop a script that displays a story describing how the story's hero, Captain Adventure, first gets his superpowers. Through the development of this script, you'll have the opportunity to put your knowledge of how to work with VBScript constants, variables, and string formatting constants to the test.

Designing the Game

The basic design of this project is to ask the user a bunch of questions (without telling the player what the answers will be used for) and then to use the information provided by the player to build a comical action story about a fictional hero named Captain Adventure.

This project will be completed in five steps.

1. Add the standard documentation template and fill in its information.
2. Define the constants and variables that will be used by the script.
3. Create the splash screen that welcomes the user to the story.
4. Use the `InputBox()` function to create variables that store user-supplied data.
5. Write the story, adding the data stored in the script's variables and constants. In addition, use VBScript string constants to control the manner in which the story text is formatted before finally displaying the story using the `MsgBox()` function.

Beginning the Captain Adventure Script

The first step in putting this project together, now that an outline of the steps involved has been defined, is to open your editor and set up your script template as follows:

```
'*************************************************************************
'Script Name: Captain Adventure.vbs
'Author: Jerry Ford
'Created: 02/28/02
'Description: This script prompts the user to answer a number of questions
'and then uses the answers to create a comical action adventure story.
'*************************************************************************


'Perform script initialization activities

Option Explicit
```

This template, introduced in the last chapter, gives you a place to provide some basic documentation about the script that you're developing. In addition, the template also includes the `Option Explicit` statement, based on the assumption that just about any script that you'll develop will use at least one variable.

Setting Up Constants and Variables

The next step in creating the Captain Adventure script is to specify the constants and variables that will be used by the script:

```
'Specify the message to appear in each pop-up dialog title bar

Const cGameTitle = "Captain Adventure"

'Specify variables used by the script

Dim strWelcomeMsg, strName, strVacation, strObject, strFriend
Dim strFood, strStory
```

The first line of code defines a constant name `cGameTitle`. This constant will be used to define a message that will be displayed in the title bar area of any dialog boxes displayed by the script. This allows you to define the title bar message just once, and to apply it as needed throughout the script without having to retype it each time.

The last line of code defines seven variables that the script will use. The first variable, `strWelcomeMsg`, will store the message text that will be displayed in a splash screen displayed when the script first executes.

In the Real World

Sometimes splash screens are used to remind the user to register the application. In other instances, splash screens are meant to distract the user when applications take a long time to load or may be used to advertise the Web site of the application or script developer. Adding a splash screen to your script gives you the chance to communicate with the user before the script begins its execution, and they can be used to display instructions or other useful information.

The next five variables (`strName`, `strVacation`, `strObject`, `strFriend`, and `strFood`) are used to store data collected from the user; they will be used later in the script in assembling the Captain Adventure story. The last variable, `strStory`, is used to store the fully assembled Captain Adventure story.

Creating a Splash Screen

As I said, adding a splash screen to your script gives you an opportunity to display your Web site, game instructions, or other information you think will be useful to the user.

The following statements show one way of building a splash screen. The `StrWelcomeMsg` variable is used to define the text that will be displayed in the splash screen. The message text to be displayed is formatted using VBScript string constants to make it more attractive.

```
'Specify the message to be displayed in the initial splash screen

strWelcomeMsg = "Welcome to the story of ..............." & vbCrLf & _
            vbCrLf & "CCC" & space(14) & "A" & vbCrLf & _
             "C" & space(17) & "AAA" & vbCrLf & _
             "CCCaptain  A   Adventure gets his super powers" & _
             vbCrLf

' Welcome the user to the story

MsgBox strWelcomeMsg, vbOkOnly + vbExclamation, cGameTitle
```

Finally, the VBScript `MsgBox()` function is used to display the splash screen. In this case, the `vbOkOnly + vbExclamation` `MsgBox()` constants instruct VBScript to display only the OK button and the exclamation mark graphic on the pop-up dialog. In addition, the `cGameTitle` constant has been added to display the script's custom title bar message.

Collecting User Input

The next five lines of code, shown next, use the VBScript `InputBox()` function to collect data provided by the user. This code contains the following five questions/instructions:

- What is your name?
- Name a place you would like to visit.
- Name a strange object.
- Type the name of a close friend.
- Type the name of your favorite dessert.

```
'Collect story information from the user

strName = InputBox("What is your name?", cGameTitle,"Joe Blow")
strVacation = InputBox("Name a place you would like to visit.", _
  cGameTitle,"Nevada")
```

```
strObject = InputBox("Name a strange object.", cGameTitle,"Soda Can")
strFriend = InputBox("Type the name of a close friend.", _
  cGameTitle,"Barney")
strFood = InputBox("Type the name of your favorite dessert.", _
  cGameTitle,"Pickle")
```

Notice that the user is only given a little bit of information about the type of information the script is looking for. This is intentional, and is meant to provide a certain amount of unpredictability to the story line.

You may have also noticed the final argument on each of the `InputBox()` statements. I have added the argument so that each dialog that is displayed by the script will automatically display a default answer. Providing a default answer in this way helps the user, by giving an idea of the kind of information you're trying to collect.

Assembling and Displaying the Story

The last step in putting together the Captain Adventure script is to assemble the story. This is done by typing out the story's text while inserting references to the script's variables at the appropriate locations in the story. In addition, the `vbCrLf` string constant is used to improve the display of the story.

The entire story is assembled as a single string, which is stored in a variable called `Story`. Finally, the completed story is displayed using the VBScript `MsgBox()` function.

```
' Assemble the Captain Adventure story

strStory = "Once upon a time .........." & vbCrLf & vbCrLf & _
  strName & " went on vacation in the far away land of " & strVacation & _
  ". A local tour guide suggested cave exploration. While in the cave " & _
  strName & " accidentally became separated from the rest of the tour " & _
  "group and stumbled into a part of the cave never visited before. " & _
  "It was completely dark. Suddenly a powerful light began to glow. " & _
  strName & " saw that it came from a mysterious " & strObject & " " & _
  "located in the far corner of the cave room. " & strName & " picked " & _
  "it up and a flash of light occurred and " &strName & " was " & _
  "instantly transported to a far away world. There in front of him " & _
  "was " & strFriend & ", the ancient God of the legendary cave " & _
  "people. " & strFriend & " explained to " & strName & " that " & _
  "destiny had selected him to become Captain Adventure! He was " & _
  "then returned to Earth and told to purchase a Winnebago and travel " & _
```

```
  "the countryside looking for people in need of help. To activate " & _
  "the superpowers bestowed by " & strFriend & " all that " & strName & _
  "had to do was pick up the " & strObject & " and say " & strFood & _
  "three times in a row." & vbCrLf & vbCrLf & _
  "The End"
'Display the story

MsgBox strStory, vbOkOnly + vbExclamation, cGameTitle
```

The Final Result

Okay, now that you've written all the various parts of the programs, put them all together into a single script, as follows:

```
'*************************************************************************
'Script Name: Captain Adventure.vbs
'Author: Jerry Ford
'Created: 02/28/02
'Description: This script prompts the user to answer a number of questions
'and then uses the answers to create a comical action adventure story.
'*************************************************************************

'Perform script initialization activities

Option Explicit

'Specify the message to appear in each pop-up dialog title bar

Const cGameTitle = "Captain Adventure"

'Specify variables used by the script

Dim strWelcomeMsg, strName, strVacation, strObject, strFriend
Dim strFood, strStory
'Specify the message to be displayed in the initial splash screen

strWelcomeMsg = "Welcome to the story of ..............." & vbCrLf & _
              vbCrLf & "CCC" & space(14) & "A" & vbCrLf & _
              "C" & space(17) & "AAA" & vbCrLf & _
              "CCCaptain  A   Adventure gets his super powers" & _
              vbCrLf
```

```
' Welcome the user to the story

MsgBox strWelcomeMsg, vbOkOnly + vbExclamation, cGameTitle

'Collect story information from the user

strName = InputBox("What is your name?", cGameTitle,"Joe Blow")
strVacation = InputBox("Name a place you would like to visit.", _
  cGameTitle,"Nevada")
strObject = InputBox("Name a strange object.", cGameTitle,"Soda Can")
strFriend = InputBox("Type the name of a close friend.", _
  cGameTitle,"Barney")
strFood = InputBox("Type the name of your favorite dessert.", _
  cGameTitle,"Pickle")

' Assemble the Captain Adventure story

strStory = "Once upon a time .........." & vbCrLf & vbCrLf & _
  strName & " went on vacation in the far away land of " & strVacation & _
  ". A local tour guide suggested cave exploration. While in the cave " & _
  strName & " accidentally became separated from the rest of the tour " & _
  "group and stumbled into a part of the cave never visited before. " & _
  "It was completely dark. Suddenly a powerful light began to glow. " & _
  strName & " saw that it came from a mysterious " & strObject & " " & _
  "located in the far corner of the cave room. " & strName & " picked " & _
  "it up and a flash of light occurred and " &strName & " was " & _
  "instantly transported to a far away world. There in front of him " & _
  "was " & strFriend & ", the ancient God of the legendary cave " & _
  "people. " & strFriend & " explained to " & strName & " that " & _
  "destiny had selected him to become Captain Adventure!. He was " & _
  "then returned to Earth and told to purchase a Winnebago and travel " & _
  "the countryside looking for people in need of help. To activate " & _
  "the superpowers bestowed by " & strFriend & " all that " & strName & _
  "had to do was pick up the " & strObject & " and say " & strFood & _
  "three times in a row." & vbCrLf & vbCrLf & _
  "The End"

'Display the story

MsgBox strStory, vbOkOnly + vbExclamation, cGameTitle
```

Now, run the script and test it to make sure that everything works as expected. Be aware that this script pushes the string length allowed by VBScript to the limit. If the information that you supply to the script is too long, some of the story may end up truncated.

Summary

You covered a lot of ground in this chapter. You now know how to define and work with constants and variables, including VBScript's built-in constants and Windows environment variables. In addition, you learned how to apply VBScript string constants to script output to control the manner in which output is displayed. You also learned about the VBScript variant and how to use built-in VBScript functions to convert data from one variant subtype to another. Finally, you learned how to store related collections of data in arrays for more efficient storage and processing, and to develop scripts that can process input passed to them at execution time.

Challenges

1. **Modify the Captain Adventure story by collecting additional user input and adding more text to the story line.**
2. **Try using an array to store the user input collected in the Captain Adventure story instead of storing data in individual variables.**
3. **Develop your own story for someone you know, and e-mail it to your friend as a sort of living greeting card.**
4. **Experiment with the VBScript string constants when developing your own story to improve the format and presentation of your story's output.**

Conditional Logic

Every programming language allows you to perform tests between two or more conditions. This capability is one of the cornerstones of programming logic. It lets you develop scripts that collect input from the user or the user's computer and compare it to one or more conditions. Using the results of the tests, you can alter the execution of your scripts and create dynamic scripts that can adjust their execution according to the data with which they're presented.

By the time you have completed this chapter, you'll know how to:

- Write scripts that test two conditions
- Write scripts that can test two or more conditions against a single value
- Write scripts that can test for a variety of different types of conditions
- Write scripts that work with a variety of built-in VBScript functions

Project Preview: The *Star Trek* Quiz Game

In this chapter, you'll create a game that administers and scores a quiz based on various *Star Trek* TV shows and movies. The game asks the player a series of questions and then assigns a rank of Ensign, Lieutenant, Lieutenant Commander, Commander, Captain, or Admiral, based on the player's final score. Besides displaying the final results, the game also creates a report that shows every question that was asked, the player's answer, the correct answer for any incorrectly answered question, the total number of questions answered correctly, and the player's assigned rank.

Figures 5.1 through 5.4 show some of the interaction between the player and the game.

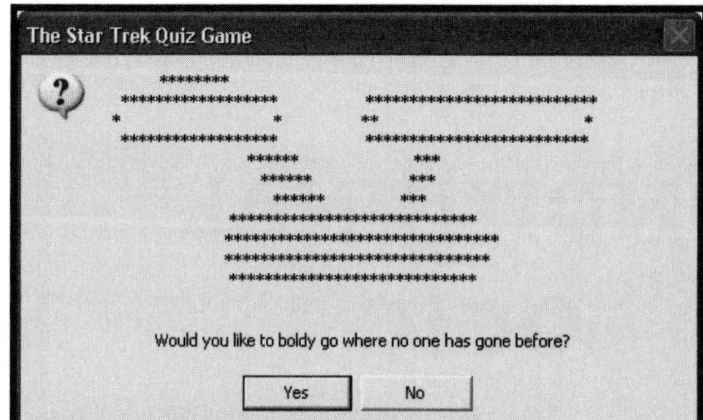

FIGURE 5.1

The game's splash screen invites the user to take the quiz.

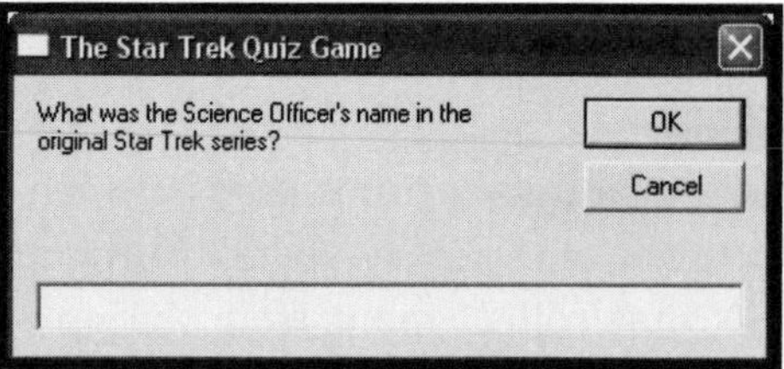

FIGURE 5.2

This dialog appears if the user decides not to play.

FIGURE 5.3

This figure shows an example of the types of questions asked by the game.

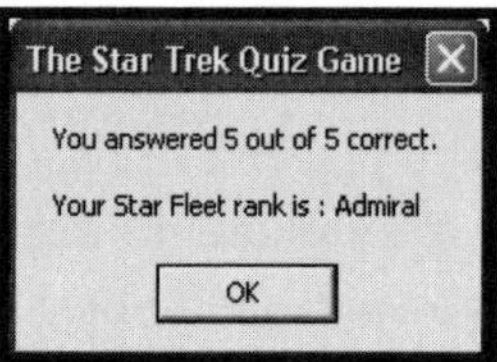

FIGURE 5.4

When the player finishes the questions, his or her score is tallied, and a rank is assigned based on the number of questions correctly answered.

During the development of this game, you will learn how to apply sophisticated conditional logic. In addition, you'll also learn how to work with a number of built-in VBScript functions.

Examining Program Data

In any programming language, you need to be able to test whether a condition is true or false to develop complex logical processes. VBScript provides two different statements that perform this function. These statements are

- `If`. A statement that allows or skips the execution of a portion of a program based on the results of a logical expression or condition.
- `Select Case`. A formal programming construct that allows a programmer to visually organize program flow when dealing with the results of a single expression.

You've already seen short demonstrations of the `If` statement in earlier chapters of this book. This is because even the simplest scripts require some form of conditional logic.

The power and importance of these two statements cannot be overstated. For example, let's say you took a job from someone without knowing exactly what you'd be paid, and now you're finished with the job and are waiting to be paid. As you're waiting, you think about what you want to do with your newfound fortune. After a few moments, you decide that if you're paid $250, then you'll by a TV. If you're paid less, you think, you'll buy a radio instead. This kind of test lends itself well to an `If` statement. Let's rewrite this scenario into a more program-like format.

```
If your pay is equal to $250
  Then Buy a TV
Else
  Buy a Radio
EndIf
```

As you can see, the logic is very straightforward and translates well from English into pseudo code. I used bold text to identify portions of the example to point out the key VBScript language programming components that are involved. I'll go into greater detail about what each of these keywords means a little later in the chapter.

Definition

Pseudo code is a rough, English-like outline or sketch of a script. By writing out the steps you think will be required to write a script in pseudo code, you provide yourself with an initial first-level script design that will serve as a basis for building the final product.

Back to our scenario: Perhaps after thinking about it a few more minutes, you decide that there are a number of things that you might do with your pay, depending on how much money you receive. In this case, you can use the VBScript `Select Case` statement to outline the logic of your decisions in pseudo code format.

```
Select Case Your Pay
  Case If you get $250 you'll buy a TV
  Case If you get $200 you'll buy a VCR
  Case If you get $100 you'll buy a radio
  Case Else You'll just buy lunch
End Select
```

Again, I have used bold text to identify portions of the example to point out key VBScript language programming components involved. In the next two sections of this chapter, I'll break down the components of the `If` and `Select Case` statements into greater detail and show you exactly how they work.

The If Statement

The VBScript `If` statement lets you test two values or conditions and alter the execution of the script based on the results of the test. The syntax of this statement is as follows:

```
If condition Then
   statements
ElseIf condition-n Then
   statements
.
.
.
Else
   statements
End If
```

Working with the If Statement

The `If` statement begins with the `If` keyword and ends with `End If`. *condition* represents the comparison being performed. For example, you might want to see whether the value of `X` is equal to `250`, like this:

```
If X = 250 Then
```

The keyword `Then` identifies the beginning of a list of one or more *`statements`*. *`statements`* is a placeholder representing the location where you would supply whatever script statements you want executed. For example, the following example displays a complete `If` statement that tests to see whether a variable has a value of 250, and if it does (that is, the test provides equal to true), a message is displayed:

```
If X = 250 Then
  WScript.Echo "Go and by that TV!"
End If
```

You may add as many statements as you want between the `Then` and `End If` keywords.

```
If X = 250 Then
  WScript.Echo "Go and buy that TV!"
  WScript.Echo "Buy a TV Guide while you are at it."
  WScript.Echo "And do not forget to say thank you."
End If
```

But what happens if the tested condition proves false? Well, in the previous test, nothing. However, by adding the `Else` keyword and one or more additional *`statements`*, the script is provided with an additional execution path.

```
If X = 250 Then
  WScript.Echo "Go and buy that TV!"
  WScript.Echo "Buy a TV Guide while you are at it."
  WScript.Echo "And do not forget to say thank you."
Else
  WScript.Echo "OK. Just purchase the radio for today."
End If
```

Figure 5.5 provides a flowchart view of the logic used in this example.

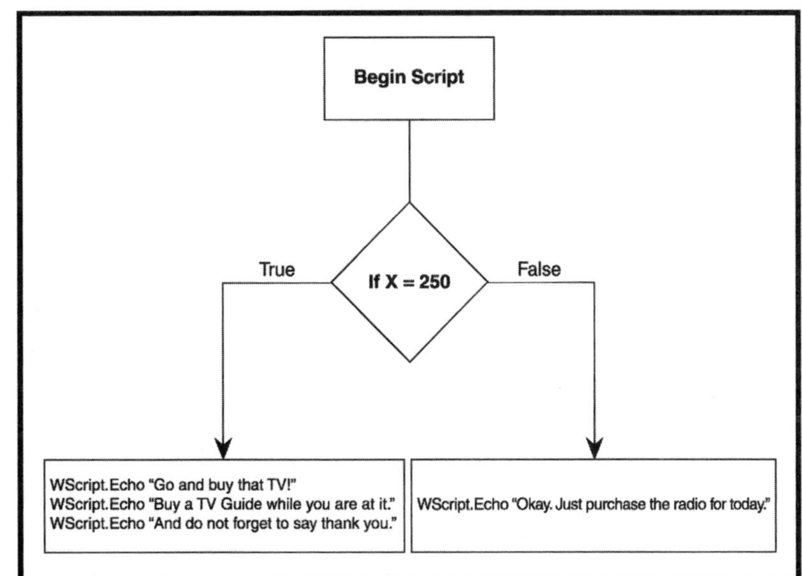

FIGURE 5.5

A flowchart outlining the logic behind a typical `If` statement.

In the Real World

A *flowchart* is a graphical depiction of the possible logical flow of a script or program. Programmers sometimes begin script development by first creating a flowchart. The flowchart serves as a visual tool for script development and provides a valuable documentation tool. Flowchart development can be a big help in the creation of complex scripts. Flowcharts help programmers formalize their thoughts before script development begins. Sometimes an automation task requires the development of several scripts, all of which must work together. Flowcharts provide a way of designing and documenting the logical flow between each script. Flowcharts can also facilitate script development when multiple programmers are involved, as they can be used to break down a task into discrete parts, each of which can then be assigned to a different person to work on.

You can expand the `If` statement by adding one or more `ElseIf` keywords, each of which can test another alternative condition. For example, look at the following VBScript statements:

```
If X = 250 Then
  WScript.Echo "Go and buy that TV!"
  WScript.Echo "Buy a TV Guide while you are at it."
  WScript.Echo "And do not forget to say thank you."
ElseIf X = 200 Then
  WScript.Echo "Buy the VCR"
ElseIf X = 100 Then
  WScript.Echo "Buy the Radio."
Else
  WScript.Echo "OK. Maybe you had best just eat lunch."
End If
```

Nesting If Statements

Another way to use `If` statements is to embed them within one another. This enables you to develop scripts that test for a condition and then further test other conditions based on the result of the previous test. To see what I mean, look at the following example (I have bolded the embedded `If` statement to make it easier to see):

```
X = 250
If X = 250 Then
```

```
  If Weekday(date()) = 1 Then
    WScript.Echo "It's Sunday. The TV store is closed on Sundays."
  Else
  WScript.Echo "Go and buy that TV!" & vbCrLf & _
     "Buy a TV Guide while you are at it." & vbCrLf & _
     "And do not forget to say thank you."
  End If
Else
  WScript.Echo "OK. Just purchase the radio for today."
End If
```

In this example, the first statement performs a test to see whether the value assigned to a variable named `X` is equal to `250`. If it's not equal to `250`, the script skips all the statements located between the `If X = 250 Then` line and the `Else` line and displays the message `"OK. Just purchase the radio for today."` However, if the value of `X` is equal to `250`, then the embedded `If` statement executes. This `If` statement begins by determining whether the current day of the week is Sunday, and if it is, the script informs the user that the TV store is closed. Otherwise, it tells the user to go and make the purchase.

The test performed by the `If` statement in the previous example deserves a little extra explanation. As you saw, it retrieved a numeric value representing the current day of the week. Here's how to break down the logic used by this statement: First, it executed the built-in VBScript `Date()` function. The value retrieved by this function was then used by the built-in VBScript `Weekday()` function to determinate the numeric value that represents the current day of the week. These values are 1 = Sunday, 2 = Monday, 3 = Tuesday, 4 = Wednesday, 5 = Thursday, 6 = Friday, 7 = Saturday. Once this value was established, the `If` statement simply checked to see if it was equal to 7 (Sunday).

As you can see, by taking advantage of built-in VBScripts functions you can perform some fairly complex tasks with minimal coding. It's a good idea to always check to see whether VBScript has a built-in function before attempting to write a piece of code to perform a generic task, such as date manipulation or checking.

By *embedding*, or nesting one `If` statement within another `If` statement, you can develop complex programming logic. There's no limit on the number of `If` statements you can embed within one another, although going more than a few layers deep can become confusing and difficult to follow.

RockPaperScissors.vbs Revisited

Okay. You've now learned a lot about the If statement, including its syntax and various ways in which it can be used. One of the biggest challenges that I faced in coming up with the VBScript examples for the first four chapters of this book was how to create VBScript-based games without using VBScript programming statements that I had not yet covered. For the most part I was successful, but there was one exception: I just could not avoid using the If statement—although I tried to use it as little as possible. In most cases, this meant limiting the completeness of the games presented.

One such game was the RockPaperScissors.vbs game. Now that I've finally provided a complete review of the If statement, let's revisit the game and see how we can make it better.

```
'Formally declare each variable used by the script before trying to
'use them
Dim objWshShell, strAnswer, strCardImage, intGetRandomNumber

'Create an instance of the WScript object in order to later use
'the Popup method
Set objWshShell = WScript.CreateObject("WScript.Shell")

'Display the rules of the game
objWshShell.Popup "Welcome to Rock, Paper, and Scissors game. " & _
  "Here are the " & _
  "rules of the game: 1. Guess the same thing as the computer " & _
  "to tie. 2. Paper covers rock and wins. 3. Rock breaks " & _
  "scissors and wins. 4. Scissors cut paper and win."

'Prompt the user to select a choice
strAnswer = InputBox("Type Paper, Rock, or Scissors.", _
  "Let's play a game!")
'Time for the computer to randomly pick a choice
Randomize
intGetRandomNumber = Round(FormatNumber(Int((3 * Rnd) + 1)))

'Assign a value to the randomly selected number
If intGetRandomNumber = 3 then strCardImage = "rock"
If intGetRandomNumber = 2 then strCardImage = "scissors"
If intGetRandomNumber = 1 then strCardImage = "paper"

'Display the game's results so that the user can see if he won
```

```
objWshShell.Popup "You picked: " & strAnswer & Space(12) & _
"Computer picked: " & strCardImage
```

Figure 5.6 shows the output of a complete game as the script currently is written.

FIGURE 5.6

Playing Rock, Paper, and Scissors.

First off, let's update the script by adding the script template that was introduced back in Chapter 3, "VBScript Basics."

```
'*************************************************************************
'Script Name: RockPaperScissors-2.vbs
'Author: Jerry Ford
'Created: 11/16/02
'Description: This script revisits the RockPaperScissors.vbs script, first
'introduced in Chapter 2, and updates it using advanced conditional logic.
'*************************************************************************
```

Next, let's rewrite the `Dim` statement by adding another variable called `Results`.

```
Dim objWshShell, strAnswer, strCardImage, strResults
```

`Results` is used later in the scripts to store the results of the game (that is, who wins and who loses). Next let's add the following statement to the script:

```
Set objWshShell = WScript.CreateObject("WScript.Shell")
```

This statement creates an instance of the `objWshShell` object. This object's `Quit()` method is used later in the script to terminate its execution in the event that the user fails to provide a valid selection (that is, the player does not pick rock, paper, or scissors).

Now that the variables and objects to be used by the script have been defined, let's assign a default value of `None` to the `strResults` variable, like this:

```
strResults = "None"
```

Unless the player provides a correction selection, this value will remain equal to `None` throughout the script's execution, and will eventually cause the script to terminate and display an error message. However, if the player supplies a correct response, the response will be assigned to the `strResults` variable and then will be analyzed by the script.

The original RockPaperScissors.vbs script displayed the game's instructions in one popup dialog, and then prompted the player to specify a selection of rock, paper, or scissors in a second pop-up dialog. This works, but using two pop-up dialogs is a bit clunky. Let's modify the scripts to display the game's directions and collect the player's input at the same time, like this:

```
strAnswer = InputBox("Please type paper, rock, or scissors." & _
          vbCrLf & vbCrLf & "Rules:" & vbCrLf & vbCrLf & _
          "1. Guess the same thing as the computer to tie." & vbCrLf & _
          "2. Paper covers rock and wins." & vbCrLf & _
          "3. Rock breaks scissors and wins." & vbCrLf & _
          "4. Scissors cut paper and win." & vbCrLf, "Let's play a game!")
```

As you can see, I used the VBScript InputBox() function to display the pop-up dialog, and I formatted the instructions for better presentation using the vbCrLf constant.

The next two sections of the script remain the same as in the original script.

```
Randomize
intGetRandomNumber = Round(FormatNumber(Int((3 * Rnd) + 1)))

If intGetRandomNumber = 3 then strCardImage = "rock"
If intGetRandomNumber = 2 then strCardImage = "scissors"
If intGetRandomNumber = 1 then strCardImage = "paper"
```

As explained in Chapter 2, "Overview of the Windows Script Host," the first pair of statements results in the selection of a random number with a value between 1 and 3. The next three lines assign a value of rock, paper, or scissors to each of these values. The rest of the script will be comprised of all new code. Instead of simply displaying the player's and the script's selection of rock, paper, or scissors and then leaving it up to the player to figure out who won, the script now performs the analysis. To begin, add the following lines to the bottom of the script:

```
If strAnswer = "rock" Then

   If intGetRandomNumber = 3 Then strResults = "Tie"
   If intGetRandomNumber = 2 Then strResults = "You Win"
   If intGetRandomNumber = 1 Then strResults = "You Lose"

End If
```

This set of statements executes only if the player typed **rock**. Three `If` statements then compare the user's selection to the script's randomly selected decisions and determine the results of the game. Now replicate this collection of statements two times, and then modify each set as follows to add tests for the selection of both scissors and paper:

```
If strAnswer = "scissors" Then

  If intGetRandomNumber = 3 Then strResults = "You Lose"
  If intGetRandomNumber = 2 Then strResults = "Tie"
  If intGetRandomNumber = 1 Then strResults = "You Win"

End If

If strAnswer = "paper" Then

  If intGetRandomNumber = 3 Then strResults = "You Win"
  If intGetRandomNumber = 2 Then strResults = "You Lose"
  If intGetRandomNumber = 1 Then strResults = "Tie"

End If
```

Now add the following statements to the script:

```
If strResults = "None" Then
  objWshShell.Popup "Sorry. Your answer was not recognized. " & _
      "Please type rock, paper, or scissors in all lowercase letters."
  WScript.Quit
End If
```

These statements only execute if the player fails to provide a correct response when playing the game. If this happens, the value of `strResults` is never changed and will still be set equal to `None` as assigned at the beginning of the script. In this case, the `objWshShell` object's `Popup()` and `Quit()` methods are used to display an error message and then end the game.

Now let's wrap up this script by adding these last few lines of code.

```
objWshShell.Popup "You picked: " & space(12) & strAnswer & vbCrLf & _
    vbCrLf & "Computer picked: " & space(2) & strCardImage & vbCrLf & _
    vbCrLf & "================" & vbCrLf & vbCrLf & "Results: " & _
    strResults
```

These statements are only executed if the player provided a valid response. They used the `objWshShell` object's `Popup()` method to display the results of the game, including both the player's and the script's selections.

The fully assembled script should now look like the following:

```
'*************************************************************************
'Script Name: RockPaperScissor-2.vbs
'Author: Jerry Ford
'Created: 11/16/02
'Description: This script revisits the RockPaperScissors.vbs script first
'introduced in Chapter 2 and updates it using advanced conditional logic.
'*************************************************************************


'Perform script initialization activities


Dim objWshShell, strAnswer, strCardImage, strResults

Set objWshShell = WScript.CreateObject("WScript.Shell")


strResults = "None"


'Prompt the user to select a choice


strAnswer = InputBox("Please type paper, rock, or scissors." & _
          vbCrLf & vbCrLf & "Rules:" & vbCrLf & vbCrLf & _
          "1. Guess the same thing as the computer to tie." & vbCrLf & _
          "2. Paper covers rock and wins." & vbCrLf & _
          "3. Rock breaks scissors and wins." & vbCrLf & _
          "4. Scissors cut paper and win." & vbCrLf, "Let's play a game!")


'Time for the computer to randomly pick a choice
Randomize
intGetRandomNumber = Round(FormatNumber(Int((3 * Rnd) + 1)))


If intGetRandomNumber = 3 then strCardImage = "rock"
If intGetRandomNumber = 2 then strCardImage = "scissors"
If intGetRandomNumber = 1 then strCardImage = "paper"
```

```
'When you select rock
If strAnswer = "rock" Then

  If intGetRandomNumber = 3 Then strResults = "Tie"
  If intGetRandomNumber = 2 Then strResults = "You Win"
  If intGetRandomNumber = 1 Then strResults = "You Lose"

End If

'When you select scissors
If strAnswer = "scissors" Then

  If intGetRandomNumber = 3 Then strResults = "You Lose"
  If intGetRandomNumber = 2 Then strResults = "Tie"
  If intGetRandomNumber = 1 Then strResults = "You Win"

End If

'When you select paper
If strAnswer = "paper" Then

  If intGetRandomNumber = 3 Then strResults = "You Win"
  If intGetRandomNumber = 2 Then strResults = "You Lose"
  If intGetRandomNumber = 1 Then strResults = "Tie"

End If

If strResults = "None" Then
  objWshShell.Popup "Sorry. Your answer was not recognized. " & _
      "Please type rock, paper, or scissors in all lowercase letters."
  WScript.Quit
End If

objWshShell.Popup "You picked: " & space(12) & strAnswer & vbCrLf & _
    vbCrLf & "Computer picked: " & space(2) & strCardImage & vbCrLf & _
    vbCrLf & "================" & vbCrLf & vbCrLf & "Results: " & _
    strResults
```

Save and execute the script. Figure 5.7 shows the initial pop-up dialog displayed by the script.

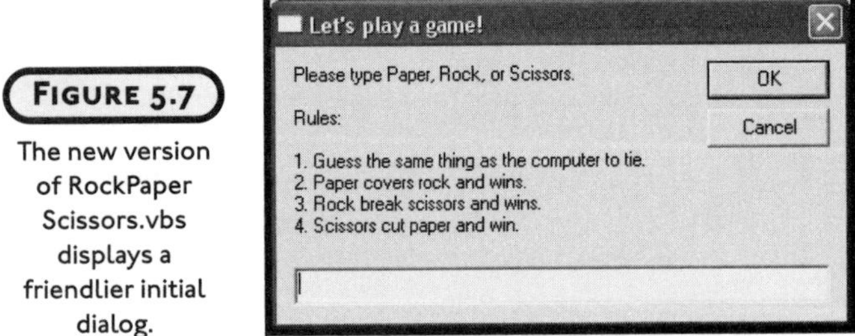

FIGURE 5.7

The new version of RockPaper Scissors.vbs displays a friendlier initial dialog.

Figure 5.8 shows the results of a typical game.

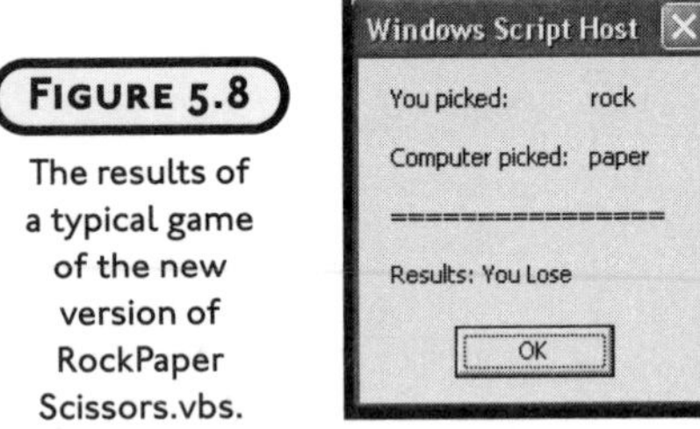

FIGURE 5.8

The results of a typical game of the new version of RockPaper Scissors.vbs.

The Select Case Statement

The `If` statement provides a great tool for testing two expressions. Using `ElseIf` you can modify the `If` statement to perform additional tests. VBScripts supplies another statement, called `Select Case`, which also lets you perform comparative operations. Functionally, it's not really very different from the `If` statement. However, the `Select Case` statement is better equipped to perform large numbers of tests against a single expression.

Here is the syntax of the `Select Case` statement:

```
Select Case expression
  Case value
    statements
      .
      .
      .
  Case value
    statements
  Case Else
    statements
End Select
```

The `Select Case` statement begins with `Select Case`, and then specifies the expression to be compared against one or more values specified in `Case` statements that follow the `Select Case` statement and precede the End Select statement. Optionally, a `Case Else` statement can also be added to provide an alternative course of action should none of the `Case` statement's values match up against the expression specified by the `Select Case` statement.

Look at the following example:

```
Select Case strAnswer
  Case "rock"
    If intGetRandomNumber = 3 Then strResults = "Tie"
    If intGetRandomNumber = 2 Then strResults = "You Win"
    If intGetRandomNumber = 1 Then strResults = "You Lose"
  Case "scissors"
    If intGetRandomNumber = 3 Then strResults = "You Lose"
    If intGetRandomNumber = 2 Then strResults = "Tie"
    If intGetRandomNumber = 1 Then strResults = "You Win"
  Case "paper"
    If intGetRandomNumber = 3 Then strResults = "You Win"
    If intGetRandomNumber = 2 Then strResults = "You Lose"
    If intGetRandomNumber = 1 Then strResults = "Tie"
  Case Else
    objWshShell.Popup "Sorry. Your answer was not recognized. " & _
      "Please type rock, paper, or scissors in all lowercase letters."
    WScript.Quit
End Select
```

Here I have rewritten most of the logic implemented in the `RockPaperScissors.vbs` script. As the following complete script shows, not only did I reduce the number of lines of code required by the script to work, but I also improved the script's readability:

```
'*************************************************************************
'Script Name: RockPaperScissors-3.vbs
'Author: Jerry Ford
'Created: 11/16/02
'Description: This script revisits the RockPaperScissors-2.vbs script,
'replacing some of the If statement's logic with a Case Select statement.
'*************************************************************************


'Perform script initialization activities
```

```
Dim objWshShell, strAnswer, strCardImage, strResults, intGetRandomNumber

Set objWshShell = WScript.CreateObject("WScript.Shell")

strResults = "None"

'Prompt the user to select a choice

strAnswer = InputBox("Please type Paper, Rock, or Scissors." & _
          vbCrLf & vbCrLf & "Rules:" & vbCrLf & vbCrLf & _
          "1. Guess the same thing as the computer to tie." & vbCrLf & _
          "2. Paper covers rock and wins." & vbCrLf & _
          "3. Rock break scissors and wins." & vbCrLf & _
          "4. Scissors cut paper and win." & vbCrLf, "Let's play a game!")

'Time for the computer to randomly pick a choice
Randomize
intGetRandomNumber = Round(FormatNumber(Int((3 * Rnd) + 1)))

If intGetRandomNumber = 3 then strCardImage = "rock"
If intGetRandomNumber = 2 then strCardImage = "scissors"
If intGetRandomNumber = 1 then strCardImage = "paper"

Select Case strAnswer
  Case "rock"
    If intGetRandomNumber = 3 Then strResults = "Tie"
    If intGetRandomNumber = 2 Then strResults = "You Win"
    If intGetRandomNumber = 1 Then strResults = "You Lose"
  Case "scissors"
    If intGetRandomNumber = 3 Then strResults = "You Lose"
    If intGetRandomNumber = 2 Then strResults = "Tie"
    If intGetRandomNumber = 1 Then strResults = "You Win"
  Case "paper"
    If intGetRandomNumber = 3 Then strResults = "You Win"
    If intGetRandomNumber = 2 Then strResults = "You Lose"
    If intGetRandomNumber = 1 Then strResults = "Tie"
  Case Else
    objWshShell.Popup "Sorry. Your answer was not recognized. " & _
```

```
      "Please type rock, paper, or scissors in all lowercase letters."
    WScript.Quit
End Select

objWshShell.Popup "You picked: " & space(12) & strAnswer & vbCrLf & _
    vbCrLf & "Computer picked: " & space(2) & strCardImage & vbCrLf & _
    vbCrLf & "===============" & vbCrLf & vbCrLf & "Results: " & _
    strResults
```

Performing More Complex Tests with VBScript Operators

Up to this point in the book every example of the `If` or a `Select Case` statement that you have seen has involved a single type of comparison, equality. This is a powerful form of comparison, but there will be times when your scripts will need to test for a wider range of values. For example, suppose you wanted to write a script that asked the user to type in their age so that you could determine whether the user was old enough to play your game (say you didn't want a user to play the game if he or she was younger than 19). It would be time-consuming to write a script that used a 100 `If` statements, or 1 `Select Case` statement with 100 corresponding `Case` statements, just to test a person's age. Instead, you could save a lot of time by comparing the user's age against a range of values. To accomplish this task, you could use the VBScript `Less Than` operator as follows:

```
intUserAge = InputBox("How old are you?")

If intUserAge < 19 Then
  MsgBox "Sorry but you are too young to play this game."
  WScript.Quit()
Else
  MsgBox "OK. Let's play!"
End If
```

In this example, the VBScript `InputBox()` function was used to collect the user's age and assign it to a variable called `intUserAge`. An `If` statement then checks to see whether `intUserAge` is less than `19`, and if it is, the game is stopped. Another way you could write the previous example is using the VBScript `Less Than or Equal To` operator, like this:

```
If intUserAge <= 18 Then
```

If you use the `Less Than or Equal To` operator, this statement will not execute if the user is 18 or fewer years old. VBScript also supplies `Greater Than` and `Greater Than or Equal To` operators, allowing you to invert the logic used in the preceding example.

```
intUserAge = InputBox("How old are you?")

If intUserAge > 18 Then
  MsgBox "OK. Let's play!"
Else
  MsgBox "Sorry but you are too young to play this game."
  WScript.Quit()
End If
```

Table 5.1 lists VBScript comparison operators.

TABLE 5.1 VBSCRIPT COMPARISON OPERATORS

Operator	Description
=	Equal
<>	Not equal
<	Less than
>	Greater than
<=	Less than or equal to
>=	Greater than or equal to

VBScript does not impose an order or precedence on comparison operators like it does with arithmetic operators. Instead, each comparison operation is performed in the order in which it appears, going from left to right.

BACK TO THE *Star Trek* QUIZ GAME

Now let's return to where we began this chapter, by developing the *Star Trek* Quiz game. In this program, you will create a VBScript that presents the player with a quiz about *Star Trek*. The game presents questions, collects the player's answers, scores the final results, assigns a rank to the player based on his or her score, and finally creates a summary text report. By working your way through this project, you will work more with both the `If` and `Select Case` statements. You'll also learn how to work with a number of built-in VBScript functions.

Game Development

The following steps outline the process you'll need to go through to complete the development of the game:

1. Add the standard documentation template and fill in its information.
2. Define the constants and variables that will be used by the script.
3. Create the splash screen that welcomes the user to the story and determines whether the user wants to play the game.
4. Use the `InputBox()` function to display questions and collect the player's answers and to add logic to determine whether the player's answers are right or wrong.
5. Use the `Select Case` statement to determine the rank to be assigned to the player, based on the number of correctly answered questions.
6. Display the player's score and rank.

Beginning the *Star Trek* Quiz Game

Begin this script by opening your script editor and cutting and pasting your script template from another script; then go back and modify the template with information relevant to the *Star Trek* Quiz game.

```
'*************************************************************************
'Script Name: StarTrekQuiz.vbs
'Author: Jerry Ford
'Created: 11/17/02
'Description: This script creates a Star Trek Quiz game.
'*************************************************************************


'Perform script initialization activities

Option Explicit
```

Setting Up Constants and Variables

The next step is to define the variables and constants used by the script.

```
Dim intPlayGame, strSplashImage, strAnswerOne, strAnswerTwo, strAnswerThree
Dim strAnswerFour, strAnswerFive, intNumberCorrect, strFederationRank
Dim objFsoObject
```

```
Const cTitlebarMsg = "The Star Trek Quiz Game"

'Start the user's score at zero
intNumberCorrect = 0
```

The `intNumberCorrect` variable is used to count the number of quiz answers the player gets right. I set `intNumberCorrect` equal to zero here to ensure that it has a value because it is always possible that the player will miss every answer and this variable might not otherwise get set. I'll explain what each of these variables is used for as we go through the rest of the script development process.

Creating a Splash Screen

Let's create a spiffy splash screen that asks the user whether he or she wants to play the game. As you can see, I added a graphic to spice up things a bit. Graphic development of this type takes a little time, as well as some trial and error.

```
'Display the splash screen and ask the user if he or she wants to play
strSplashImage = space(11) & "********" & vbCrLf & _
  "  ******************" & space(20) & "*************************" & _
  space(20) & vbCrLf & "*" & space(35) & "*" & space(18) & _
  "**" & space(46) & "*" & vbCrLf & "  ******************" & _
  space(20) & "************************" & vbCrLf & space(31) & _
  "******" & space(26) & "***" & vbCrLf & _
  space(34) & "******" & space(22) & "***" & vbCrLf & _
  space(37) & "******" & space(17) & "***" & vbCrLf & _
  space(26) & " ***************************" & vbCrLf & _
  space(26) & "******************************" & vbCrLf & _
  space(26) & "*****************************" & vbCrLf & _
  space(26) & " ***************************" & vbCrLf & vbCrLf & vbCrLf &_
  space(10) & "Would you like to boldly go where no one has gone before?"

intPlayGame = MsgBox(strSplashImage, 36, cTitlebarMsg)
```

The splash screen is created using the VBScript `InputBox()` function. It displays the invitation to play the game as well as Yes and No buttons. The value of the button the user clicks is assigned to the `PlayGame` variable (that is, `PlayGame` will be set equal to 6 if the player clicks on the `Yes` button).

Now let's check to see whether the user wants to play the game.

```
If intPlayGame = 6 Then 'User elected to play the game
'Insert statements that make up the game here
.
.
.
Else 'User doesn't want to play
  MsgBox "Thank you for taking the Star Trek Quiz © Jerry Ford 2002." & _
    vbCrLf & vbCrLf & "Live long and prosper!", , cTitlebarMsg
  WScript.Quit()
End If
```

As you can see, the first statement checks to see whether the user clicked on the `Yes` button. I left some room to mark the area where you will need to add the statements that actually make up the game, in case the user does want to play. If the user clicked No, then the VBScript displays a "thank you" message and terminates its execution using the `WScript` object's `Quit()` method.

Display Quiz Questions and Collect the Player's Answers

The next step is to add the questions that make up the game. The following questions make up the quiz:

- What was the Science Officer's name in the original *Star Trek* series?
- What *Star Trek* villain appeared in both the original series and a *Star Trek* movie?
- What was the numeric designation of Voyager's on-board Borg?
- Name the only *Star Trek* character to regularly appear on two series and at least two *Star Trek* movies.
- What is the last name of your favorite Captain?

The statements that display and grade the first quiz questions are as follows:

```
strAnswerOne = InputBox("What was the Science Officer's name in the " & _
  "original Star Trek series?", cTitlebarMsg)

If LCase(strAnswerOne) = "spock" Then
  intNumberCorrect = intNumberCorrect + 1
End If
```

First the VBScript `InputBox()` function displays the question. The answer typed by the user is then assigned to a variable named `strAnswerOne`. Next, an `If` statement is used to interrogate the player's answer and determine whether it's correct. The VBScript `LCase()` function is used to convert the answer the player types to all lowercase . This way, it doesn't matter how the player types in the answer. For example, **SPOCK**, **spock**, **SpOcK**, and **Spock** would all end up as `spock`. Finally, if the player provides the correct answer, then the value of `intNumberCorrect` is increased by 1.

As you can see, the second quiz question, shown next, is processed exactly like the first question. The only difference is the content of the question itself and the name of the variable used to store the player's answer to the question.

```
strAnswerTwo = InputBox("What Star Trek villain appeared in both the " & _
  "original series and a Star Trek movie?", cTitlebarMsg)

If LCase(strAnswerTwo) = "khan" Then
  intNumberCorrect = intNumberCorrect + 1
End If
```

The statements that make up and process the quiz's third question are shown next. As you can see, I have altered the logic a bit by adding an `ElseIf` statement to accommodate either of two possible answers to this question.

```
strAnswerThree = InputBox("What was the numeric designation of " & _
  "Voyager's on-board Borg?", cTitlebarMsg)

If CStr(strAnswerThree) = "7" Then
  intNumberCorrect = intNumberCorrect + 1
ElseIf CStr(strAnswerThree) = "7 of 9" Then
  intNumberCorrect = intNumberCorrect + 1
End If
```

The statements that make up the fourth question follow the same pattern as the first two questions.

```
strAnswerFour = InputBox("Name the only Star Trek character to " & _
  "regularly appear on two series and at least two Star Trek " & _
  "movies?", cTitlebarMsg)
If LCase(strAnswerFour) = "worf" Then
  intNumberCorrect = intNumberCorrect + 1
End If
```

The construction of the fifth question, shown next, merits some additional examination. First of all, the fourth statement uses the VBScript `LCase()` function to convert the player's answer to all lowercase. The VBScript `Instr()` function then takes the answer and searches the string `"kirkpicardsiscojanewayarcher"` to see whether it can find a match. This string contains a list of last names belonging to various Star Fleet captains.

```
strAnswerFive = InputBox("What is the last name of your favorite " & _
  "Captain?", cTitlebarMsg)


If Len(strAnswerFive) > 3 Then
  If Instr(1, "kirkpicardsiscojanewayarcher", LCase(strAnswerFive), 1) _
  <> 0 Then
    intNumberCorrect = intNumberCorrect + 1
  End If
End If
```

So the `InStr()` function begins its search starting with the first character of the string to see whether it can find the text string that it's looking for (that is, `kirk`, `picard`, `janeway`, `sisco`, or `archer`). The syntax of the `Instr()` function is as follows:

```
InStr([start, ]string1, string2[, compare])
```

`Start` specifies the character position in the script, from left to right, where the search should begin. `String1` identifies the string to search. `String2` identifies the text to search for, and `compare` specifies the type of search to perform. A value of `0` specifies a binary comparison, and a value of `1` specifies a textual comparison.

The `InStr()` function returns the location of the beginning location of a matching text string. If it does not find a matching text string in the list, then it will return to zero, in which case the user provided the wrong answer. Otherwise, it will return the starting character position where the search string was found. If the search string is found in the list, then the value returned by the `InStr()` function will be greater than 1, in which case the value of `intNumberCorrect` will be incremented by 1.

However, it is always possible that the player doesn't know the name of one Star Ship captain, and that he or she will just type a character or two, such as the letter "A." Because the letter "A" is used in at least one of the captain's last names, the player would end up getting credit for a correct answer to the question. Clearly, this is not good. To try to keep the game honest, I used the VBScript `Len()` function to be sure that the user provided at least a four-character name (that is, the length of the shortest last name belonging to any captain). This way, the player must know at least the first four characters of a captain's last name to get credit for a correct answer.

Scoring the Player's Rank

At this point, the script has enough logic to display all five questions and determine which ones the player got correct. In addition, it has been keeping track of the total number of correct answers. What you need to do next is add logic to assign the player a rank based on the number of correctly answered questions. This can be done using a `Select Case` statement, like this:

```
Select Case intNumberCorrect
  Case 5 'User got all five answers right
    strFederationRank = "Admiral"
  Case 4 'User got 4 of 5 answers right
    strFederationRank = "Captain"
  Case 3 'User got 3 of 5 answers right
    strFederationRank = "Commander"
  Case 2 'User got 2 of 5 answers right
    strFederationRank = "Lieutenant-Commander"
  Case 1 'User got 1 of 5 answers right
    strFederationRank = "Lieutenant"
  Case 0 'User did not get any answers right
    strFederationRank = "Ensign"
End Select
```

The variable `intumberCorrect` contains the number of answers that the player has correctly answered. The value of this variable is then compared against six possible cases, each of which represents a different score the player could have gotten from the game. When a match is found, the player's rank is assigned based on the values listed in Table 5.2.

TABLE 5.2 DETERMINING THE PLAYER'S FEDERATION RANK

Number of Correctly Answered Questions	Federation Rank
5	Admiral
4	Captain
3	Commander
2	Lieutenant-Commander
1	Lieutenant
0	Ensign

Displaying the Player's Score and Rank

The last thing the game does is display the player's score and rank in a pop-up dialog.

```
MsgBox "You answered " & intNumberCorrect & " out of 5 correct." & _
  vbCrLf & vbCrLf & "Your Star Fleet rank is : " & _
  strFederationRank, , cTitlebarMsg
```

As you can see, there is not much to this last statement. All you need to do is to use the VBScript `MsgBox()` function, the `strNumberCorrect`, and `strFederationRank` variables, as well as the `vbCrLf` constant, to display the message for the player to see.

The Fully Assembled Script

Okay, let's take a look at how the script looks now. Run it and be sure that everything is working as advertised.

```
'*************************************************************************
'Script Name: StarTrekQuiz.vbs
'Author: Jerry Ford
'Created: 11/17/02
'Description: This script creates a Star Trek Quiz game.
'*************************************************************************


'Perform script initialization activities

Option Explicit

Dim intPlayGame, strSplashImage, strAnswerOne, strAnswerTwo, strAnswerThree
Dim strAnswerFour, strAnswerFive, intNumberCorrect, strFederationRank
Dim objFsoObject

Const cTitlebarMsg = "The Star Trek Quiz Game"

'Start the user's score at zero
intNumberCorrect = 0

'Display the splash screen and ask the user if he or she wants to play
strSplashImage = space(11) & "********" & vbCrLf & _
  "  ******************" & space(20) & "***************************" & _
  space(20) & vbCrLf & "*" & space(35) & "*" & space(18) & _
```

```
  "**" & space(46) & "*" & vbCrLf & "  ******************" & _
  space(20) & "************************" & vbCrLf & space(31) & _
  "******" & space(26) & "***" & vbCrLf & _
  space(34) & "******" & space(22) & "***" & vbCrLf & _
  space(37) & "******" & space(17) & "***" & vbCrLf & _
  space(26) & " ***************************" & vbCrLf & _
  space(26) & "******************************" & vbCrLf & _
  space(26) & "*****************************" & vbCrLf & _
  space(26) & " ***************************" & vbCrLf & vbCrLf & vbCrLf &_
  space(10) & "Would you like to boldly go where no one has gone before?"

intPlayGame = MsgBox(strSplashImage, 36, cTitlebarMsg)

If intPlayGame = 6 Then 'User elected to play the game

strAnswerOne = InputBox("What was the Science Officer's name in the " & _
  "original Star Trek series?", cTitlebarMsg)

If LCase(strAnswerOne) = "spock" Then
  intNumberCorrect = intNumberCorrect + 1
End If

Else 'User doesn't want to play

  MsgBox "Thank you for taking the Star Trek Quiz © Jerry Ford 2002." & _
    vbCrLf & vbCrLf & "Live long and prosper!", , cTitlebarMsg
  WScript.Quit()

End If

strAnswerTwo = InputBox("What Star Trek villain appeared in both the " & _
  "original series and a Star Trek movie?", cTitlebarMsg)

If LCase(strAnswerTwo) = "khan" Then
  intNumberCorrect = intNumberCorrect + 1
End If
```

```
strAnswerThree = InputBox("What was the numeric designation of " & _
  "Voyager's on-board Borg?", cTitlebarMsg)

If CStr(strAnswerThree) = "7" Then
  intNumberCorrect = intNumberCorrect + 1
ElseIf CStr(strAnswerThree) = "7 of 9" Then
  intNumberCorrect = intNumberCorrect + 1
End If

strAnswerFour = InputBox("Name the only Star Trek character to " & _
  "regularly appear on two series and at least two Star Trek " & _
  "movies?", cTitlebarMsg)

If LCase(strAnswerFour) = "worf" Then
  intNumberCorrect = intNumberCorrect + 1
End If

strAnswerFive = InputBox("What is the last name of your favorite " & _
  "Captain?", cTitlebarMsg)

If Len(strAnswerFive) > 3 Then
  If Instr(1, "kirkpicardsiscojanewayarcher", LCase(strAnswerFive), 1) _
  <> 0 Then
    intNumberCorrect = intNumberCorrect + 1
  End If
End If

Select Case intNumberCorrect
  Case 5 'User got all five answers right
    strFederationRank = "Admiral"
  Case 4 'User got 4 of 5 answers right
    strFederationRank = "Captain"
  Case 3 'User got 3 of 5 answers right
    strFederationRank = "Commander"
  Case 2 'User got 2 of 5 answers right
    strFederationRank = "Lieutenant-Commander"
  Case 1 'User got 1 of 5 answers right
    strFederationRank = "Lieutenant"
```

```
  Case 0 'User did not get any answers right
    strFederationRank = "Ensign"
End Select

MsgBox "You answered " & intNumberCorrect & " out of 5 correct." & _
  vbCrLf & vbCrLf & "Your Star Fleet rank is : " & _
  strFederationRank, , cTitlebarMsg
```

Summary

This chapter covered a lot of ground. You learned how to use the `If` and `Case Select` statements in a number of different ways. Using this new information, you updated the Rock, Paper, and Scissors game and created the *Star Trek* Quiz game. In addition, you learned how to create VBScripts that could generate reports and log files.

Challenges

1. **Modify the *Star Trek* Quiz game so that it asks players for their names and then use the players' names at the end of the game to address them according to their ranks.**
2. **Modify the *Star Trek* Quiz so that it displays the correct answer for any question that the player misses.**
3. **Expand the *Star Trek* Quiz game by adding more questions. Store a list of questions in an array and then use a `For...Each...Next` loop to display and process both the questions and the player's answers.**

PROCESSING COLLECTIONS OF DATA

In this chapter, you'll learn how to use a number of VBScript statements that can help you develop scripts capable of processing extremely large amounts of information–in most cases with only a handful of script statements. Using these statements, you can establish loops within your scripts to let the user iteratively enter as much data as needed, to process the contents of array, to read the content's files, and to control the execution of VBScript games. I'll also show you how to create shortcuts for your scripts, as well as how to place them on the Windows desktop, Start Menu, and Quick Launch toolbar. Specifically, you will learn how to

- Work with five different types of VBScript loops
- Use loops to control the execution of your scripts (and games)
- Programmatically create Windows shortcuts and use them to configure Windows resources such as the desktop and Start Menu

PROJECT PREVIEW: THE GUESS A NUMBER GAME

In this chapter's project, you'll create a script that plays a number guessing game. The game generates a random number between 1 and 100, then instructs the player to try to guess it. As the player enters guesses, the game provides the player with hints to help him figure out the number. If the player types an invalid guess, the game will let him know that only numeric input is accepted.

The player may quit at any time by simply clicking on the Cancel button, or by failing to type a guess before clicking on OK. Once the player guesses the correct answer, the game displays the number of guesses it took him to find the correct answer. Figures 6.1 through 6.6 provide a sneak peek of the game's interaction.

FIGURE 6.1

The Guess a Number game begins by prompting the player to type a number between 1 and 100.

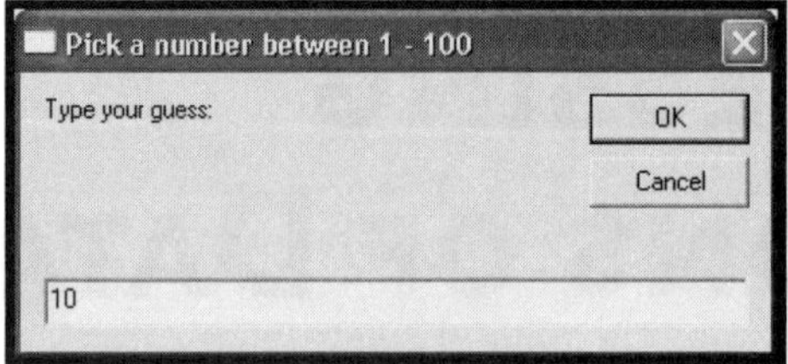

FIGURE 6.2

The game tells the player to try again if his or her guess is too low.

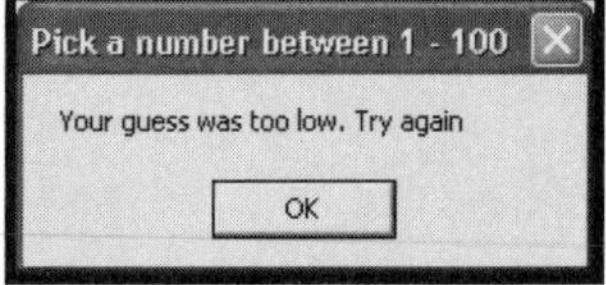

FIGURE 6.3

The game tells the player to try again if his or her guess is too high.

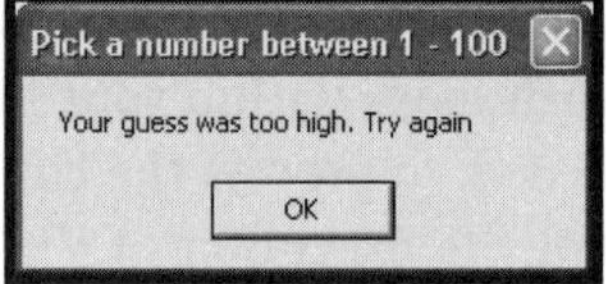

FIGURE 6.4

The game instructs the player to provide only numeric input.

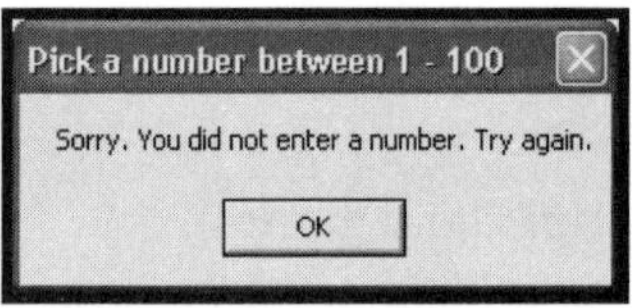

FIGURE 6.5

The game ends if the player clicks on Cancel or fails to provide a guess.

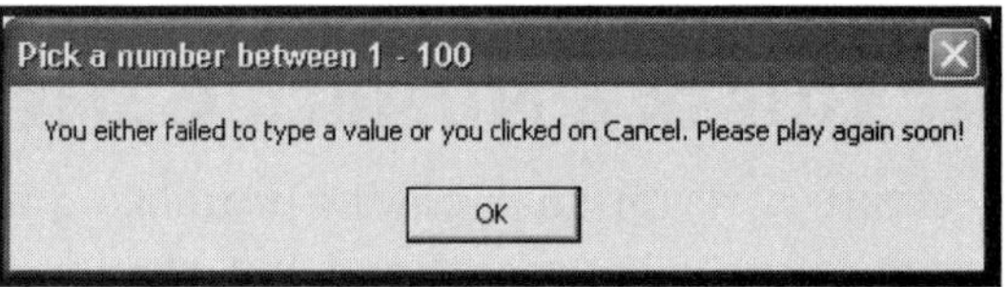

The game uses a VBScript loop to continue executing until either the player guesses the correct answer or quits. By developing and working with this game, you will solidify your understanding of iterative programming while also learning specifically how to apply a loop using VBScript.

FIGURE 6.6

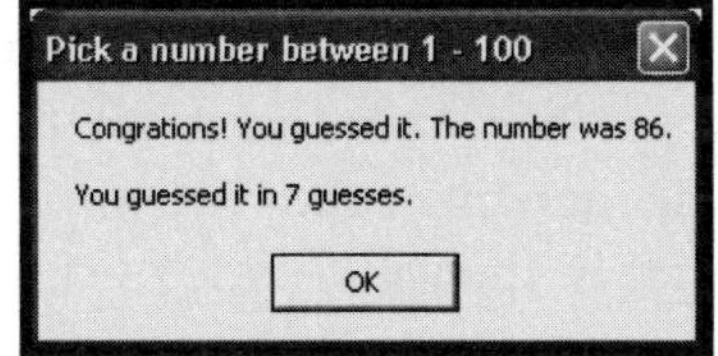
Pick a number between 1 - 100
Congrations! You guessed it. The number was 86.
You guessed it in 7 guesses.
OK

Once the player has correctly guessed the game's number, the player is congratulated.

ADDING LOOPING LOGIC TO SCRIPTS

One of VBScript's best programming features is its strong support for *looping* or *iterative statements*. VBScript provides five different statements that can create loops. Loops provide your scripts with the capability to process large collections of data using a minimal number of programming statements that are repeatedly executed, either for each member of the collection or for a specified number of times.

> **DEFINITION**
>
> A *loop* is a collection of statements repeatedly executed to facilitate the processing of large amounts of data.

The following list provides a high-level description of each of VBScript's looping statements:

- `For...Next`. Establishes a loop that iterates for a specified number of times.
- `For...Each...Next`. Establishes a loop that iterates through all the properties associated with an object.
- `Do...While`. Establishes a loop that iterates for as long as a stated condition continues to be true.
- `Do...Until`. Establishes a loop that iterates until a stated condition finally becomes true.
- `While...Wend`. Establishes a loop that iterates for as long as a condition continues to be true.

The For...Next Statement

The `For...Next` statement is used to create loops that execute a specific number of times. For example, if you're creating a game requiring the player to enter five guesses, you could use a `For...Next` loop to control the logic that supports the data collection portion of the script.

The syntax for the `For...Next` statement is as follows:

```
For counter = begin To end [Step StepValue]
   statements
Next
```

`counter` is a variable used to control the execution of the loop. *`begin`* is a numeric value that specifies the starting value of the *`counter`* variable. *end* specifies the ending value for the counter variable (that is, the value that, when reached, terminates the loop's execution). *`StepValue`* is an optional setting that specifies the increment that the `For...Next` statement uses when incrementing the value of *`counter`* (that is, the value added to `counter` at the end of each iteration). If omitted, the value assigned to *`StepValue`* is always 1.

To better understand the operation of a `For...Next` loop, look at one example that collects data without using a loop and one that collects the same data using a `For...Next` loop. In the following example, let's assume that you're creating a game in which the player is expected to enter the name of his or her five favorite foods. You could always handle this type of situation as follows:

```
Dim strFoodList
strFoodList = " "
strFoodList = strFoodList & " " & InputBox("Type the name of a food " & _
  "that you really like.")
strFoodList = strFoodList & " " & InputBox("Type the name of a food " & _
  "that you really like.")
strFoodList = strFoodList & " " & InputBox("Type the name of a food " & _
  "that you really like.")
strFoodList = strFoodList & " " & InputBox("Type the name of a food " & _
  "that you really like.")
strFoodList = strFoodList & " " & InputBox("Type the name of a food " & _
  "that you really like.")
MsgBox "You like : " & strFoodList
```

As you can see, this example repeats the same statement over and over again to collect user input. Then, as proof that it did its job, it displays the data it collected using the `MsgBox()` function.

Collecting five pieces of data like this is a bit of a chore. Now imagine a situation in which you want to collect a lot more data. Instead of typing the same statement over and over again, as done in the previous example, you can use the `For...Next` loop.

```
Dim intCounter, strFoodList
strFoodList = " "

For intCounter = 1 To 5
  strFoodList = strFoodList & " " & InputBox("Type the name of a " & _
    "food that you really like.")
```

```
Next

MsgBox "You like : " & strFoodList
```

Figure 6.7 demonstrates the output produced by this example.

FIGURE 6.7 Using a `For...Next` loop to collect and process user input.

Notice this new script is two lines shorter than the previous example. Unlike the previous example, other than the value of the loop's ending value, this script does not have to be modified to accommodate the collection of additional data. For example, to change the `For...Next` loop so that it can accommodate the collection of ten pieces of data, all you'd have to do is modify it like this:

```
For intCounter = 1 To 10
  strFoodList = strFoodList & " " & InputBox("Type the name of a " & _
    "food that you really like.")
Next
```

Optionally, you can use the `Exit For` statement to break out of a `For...Next` loop at any time, like this:

```
Dim intCounter, strFoodList, strNewFood
strFoodList = " "

For intCounter = 1 To 5
  strNewFood = InputBox("Type the name of a food that you really like.")
  If strNewFood = "beans" Then
    MsgBox "Sorry, but I don't want to talk to anyone who likes beans!"
    Exit For
  End If
  strFoodList = strFoodList & " " & strNewFood
Next

MsgBox "You like : " & strFoodList
```

In this example, the assignment of data has been split into two different statements. The first of these statements assigns the name of the food entered by the user to a variable called `strNewFood`. The value of `strNewFood` is then added to the list of foods liked by the user only if it is not "beans," in which case the script displays a message and then terminates the execution of the `For...Next` loop. As a result, only the foods entered by the user up to the point where beans was typed are displayed.

Let's look at one last example before we examine the other loop statements supported by VBScript. In this example, the `For...Next` statement's optional keyword `Step` has been added to change the behavior of the loop.

```
Dim intCounter
For intCounter = 1 To 9 Step 3
  WScript.Echo intcounter
Next
```

In this example, the script will display the value of the *`counter`* variable, which is used to control the loop's execution. Instead of counting to 9 by 1s, the script will count by 3s as demonstrated here.

```
C:\>CScript TextScript.vbs
Microsoft (R) Windows Script Host Version 5.1 for Windows
Copyright (C) Microsoft Corporation 1996-1999. All rights reserved.

1
4
7

C:\>
```

The For Each...Next Statement

VBScript's `For Each...Next` statement is a programming tool for working with all the properties associated with objects. Every object has a number of properties associated with it. Using the `For Each...Next` loop, you could write a script to loop through all an object's properties.

The syntax of the `For...Each...Next` statement is as follows:

```
For Each element In collection
  statements
Next [element]
```

element is a variable representing a property associated with the *collection* (or object). Look at the following example:

```
Dim objFsoObject, objFolderName, strMember, strFileList, strTargetFolder

Set objFsoObject = CreateObject("Scripting.FileSystemObject")
Set objFolderName = objFsoObject.GetFolder("C:\Temp")

For Each strMember in objFolderName.Files
  strFileList = strFileList & strMember.name & vbCrLf
Next

MsgBox strFileList, ,"List of files in " & objFolderName
```

This example begins by defining its variables and then establishing an instance of the `FileSystemObject`. It then uses the `FileSystemObject` object's `GetFolder()` method to set a reference to a folder. Next, using the folder reference, a `For Each...Next` loop processes all the files (which, in this case, are considered to be properties of the folder) stored within the folder. As the `For Each...Next` loop executes, it builds a list of files stored within the folder and uses the `vbCrLf` constant to format the list in an attractive manner. The final statement displays the results, as shown in Figure 6.8.

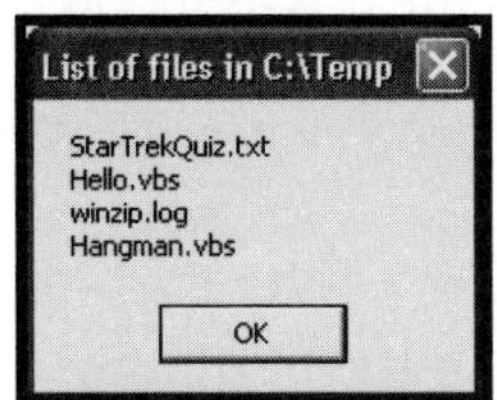

FIGURE 6.8 Using a `For Each...Next` loop to process the contents of a folder.

`For Each...Next` loops also are an excellent programming tool for processing the contents of arrays. For example, the following statements are all that are needed to process and display an array called `astrGameArray`, and to display each of its elements:

```
For Each intCount In astrGameArray
  strMessage = strMessage & intCounter & vbCrLf
Next
WScript.Echo strMessage
```

To learn more about arrays and see a more complete example of a script that uses the `For Each...Next` statement, refer to the Processing Array Contents section in Chapter 4, "Constants, Variables, and Arrays."

Do...While

The `Do...While` statement creates a loop that runs as long as a specified condition is true. VBScript supports two different versions of the `Do...While` loop. The syntax for the first version of the `Do...While` loop is as follows:

```
Do While condition
  statements
Loop
```

`Condition` is expressed in the form of an expression, like this:

```
intCounter = 0
Do While intCounter < 10
  intCounter = intCounter + 2
Loop
```

In this example, the expression (`intCounter < 10`) allows the loop to continue as long as the value of `intCounter` is less than `10`. The value of `intCounter` is initially set to `0`, but is increased by `2` every time the loop executes. As a result, the loop iterates five times.

As the `While` keyword has been placed at the beginning of the loop, the loop will not execute if the value of counter is already 10 or greater.

The syntax for the second format of the `Do...While` statement is as follows:

```
Do
  statements
Loop While condition
```

As you can see, the `While` keyword had been moved from the beginning to the end of the loop. Therefore, the loop will always execute at least once, even if the condition is initially false.

Let's look at another example of the `Do...While` loop in action. In this example, the `Do...While` loop is set up to collect names and phone numbers for an address book. The loop uses the VBScript `InputBox()` function to collect the names and phone numbers. The names and addresses are added to a variable string and formatted such that, when displayed, each entry is listed on a separate line. The user may enter as many names and numbers as he or she wishes. When done adding new address book entries, all he or she must do is type "Quit" as the final entry.

```
Dim intCounter, strAddressBook, strAddressEntry

intCounter = 0
```

```
Do While strAddressEntry <> "Quit"
  intCounter = intCounter + 1
strAddressEntry = InputBox("Please type a name, a space, and then " & _
  "the person's phone number", "Personal Address Book")
  If strAddressEntry <> "Quit" Then
    strAddressBook = strAddressBook & strAddressEntry & vbCrLf
  End If
Loop

MsgBox strAddressBook, ,"New Address Book Entries = " & intCounter - 1
```

Figure 6.9 displays a list of four names entered as this script executed.

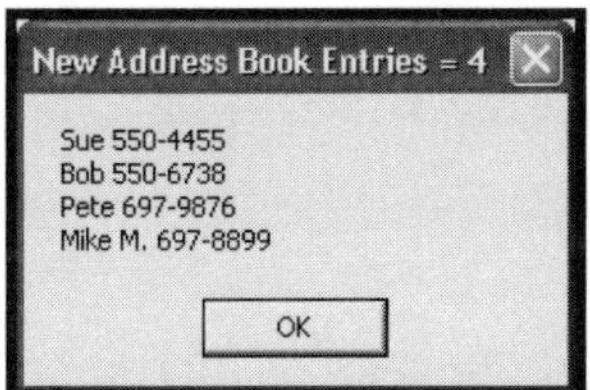

Using a `Do...While` loop to collect new address book entries.

Alternatively, you could have written this example as shown next. In this example the `While` keyword and its associated condition have been moved to the end of the loop. However, the script still operates exactly as in the previous example.

```
Dim intCounter, strAddressBook, strAddressEntry

intCounter = 0

Do
  intCounter = intCounter + 1
  strAddressEntry = InputBox("Please type a name, a space, and then " & _
    "the person's phone number", "Personal Address Book")  If strAddressEntry <>
"Quit" Then
    strAddressBook = strAddressBook & strAddressEntry & vbCrLf
  End If
Loop While strAddressEntry <> "Quit"

MsgBox strAddressBook, ,"New Address Book Entries = " & intCounter -1
```

One of the dangers of working with loops is that you may accidentally create a loop that has no way of terminating its own execution. This is an *endless loop*. Endless loops run forever, needlessly consuming computer resources and degrading a computer's performance. For example, look at the following:

```
intCounter = 0
Do While intCounter < 10
  intCounter = intCounter + 1
WScript.Echo intCounter
Loop
```

When executed this script counts from 1 to 10. Now look at the next script.

```
intCounter = 0
Do While intCounter < 10
  intCounter = intCounter - 1
  WScript.Echo intCounter
Loop
```

It looks almost exactly like the previous example, only instead of incrementing the value of `intCounter` by 1, it increments the value of `intCounter` by –1, creating an endless loop. One way to protect against the creation of an endless loop is to put in a safety net, like this:

```
intCounter = 0
Do While intCounter < 10
  intCounter = intCounter - 1
  intNoExecutions = intNoExecutions + 1
  WScript.Echo intCounter
  If intNoExecutions  > 99 Then
    Exit Do
  End If
Loop
```

As you can see, I added to the script a variable called `intNoExecutions` that I then used to keep track of the number of times that loop iterated. If the loop iterates 100 times, then something is wrong. So I added an `If` statement to test the value of `intNoExecutions` each time the loop is processed and to execute the `Exit Do` statement in the event that something goes wrong. Of course, there is no substitute for good program design and careful testing.

Do...Until

The VBScript `Do...Until` statement creates a loop that executes as long as a condition is false (that is, until it becomes true). VBScript supports two versions of the `Do...Until` statement. The syntax for the first version is as follows:

```
Do Until condition
  statements
Loop
```

Let's look at an example that demonstrates how this loop works. In this example, shown next, the script prompts the player to answer a question and uses a `Do...Until` loop to allow the user up to three chances to correctly answer the question.

```
Dim intMissedGuesses, strPlayerAnswer

intMissedGuesses = 1

Do Until intMissedGuesses > 3

  strPlayerAnswer = InputBox("Where does Peter Pan live?")

  If strPlayerAnswer <> "Neverland" Then

    intMissedGuesses = intMissedGuesses + 1

    If intMissedGuesses < 4 Then
      MsgBox "Incorrect: You have " & 4 - intMissedGuesses & _
      " guesses left. Please try again."
    Else
      MsgBox "Sorry. You have used up all your chances."
    End If

  Else

    intMissedGuesses = 4

    MsgBox "Correct! I guess that you must believe in Faith, Trust " & _
      "and Pixy Dust!"

  End If

Loop
```

In this example, the loop has been set up to execute until the value of a variable named `intMissedGuesses` becomes greater than 3. The variable is initially set equal to 1 and is incremented by 1 each time the loop executes, unless the player provides a correct answer, in which case the script sets the value of `intMissedGuesses` to 4 in order to arbitrarily terminate the loop's execution.

Figure 6.10 demonstrates the execution of this script by showing the pop-up dialog that appears if the player guesses incorrectly on his or her first attempt to answer the question.

FIGURE 6.10

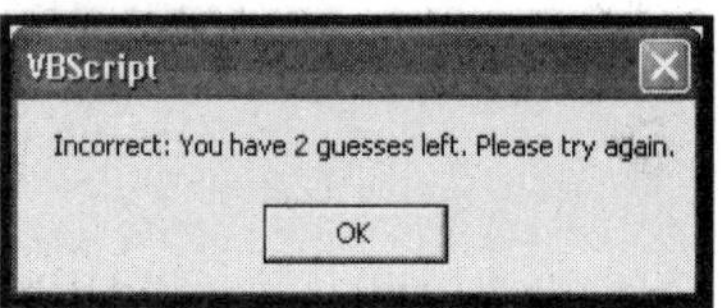

Using a `Do...Until` loop to provide the player with three chances to correctly answer a question.

The syntax of the second form of the `Do...Until` statement is as follows:

```
Do
  statements
Loop Until condition
```

As you can see, the `Until` keyword and its associated *`condition`* have been moved from the beginning to the end of the loop, thus ensuring the loop executes at least once.

While...Wend

The `While...Wend` statement creates a loop that executes as long as a tested condition is true.

The syntax for this loop is as follows:

```
While condition
  statements
Wend
```

The `Do...While` and `Do...Until` loops provide the same functionality as the `While...Wend` loop. The general rule of thumb, therefore, is that you should use one of the `Do` loops in place of this statement. However, I'd be remiss if I failed to show you how this statement works, so take a look at the following example:

```
Dim intCounter, strCountList
```

```
intCounter = 0

While intCounter < 10
  intCounter = intCounter + 1
  strCountList = strCountList & intCounter & vbCrLf
Wend

MsgBox "This is how to count to 10:" & vbCrLf & vbCrLf & _
  strCountList, , "Counting Example"
```

This example begins by initializing two variables. `intCount` is used to control the loop's execution. `strCountList` is used to build a formatted script containing the numbers counted by the script. The loop itself iterates 10 times. Figure 6.11 shows the output created by this example when run using the WScript execution host.

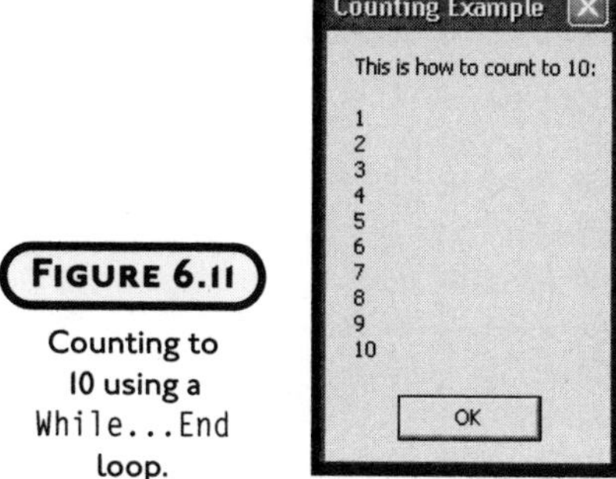

FIGURE 6.11

Counting to 10 using a `While...End` loop.

BACK TO THE GUESS A NUMBER GAME

Let's turn our attention back to the Guess a Number game. In this game, the player is prompted to guess a randomly generated number between 1 and 100. Each time the player takes a guess, the script will check to see if the correct number was guessed. If not, the script will provide a hint to help the player on his or her next guess.

Developing this script will enhance your knowledge and understanding of working with the `Do...Until` loop. You will also work with the `If` statement, and learn how to work with a number of new built-in VBScript functions.

Designing the Game

The Guess a Number game begins by asking the player to guess a number between 1 and 100, and then helps the user guess the number by providing hints. This project has five steps.

These steps are

1. Add the standard documentation template and define any variables, constants, or objects used by the script.
2. Generate a random number between 1 and 100.
3. Create a loop that runs until the player either guesses the correct answer or gives up.
4. Test the player's answer to see whether it's valid.
5. Test the player's answer to see whether it is too low, too high, or correct.

As a kind of project bonus, once you have completed the Guess a Number game, I'll show you how to create a VBScript desktop shortcut for it. I'll also show you how to use shortcuts to configure the Windows Start Menu and Quick Launch toolbar.

Beginning the Guess a Number Game

Begin by creating a new script and adding your script template.

```
'*************************************************************************
'Script Name: GuessANumber.vbs
'Author: Jerry Ford
'Created: 10/19/02
'Description: This script plays a number-guessing game with the user
'*************************************************************************

'Initialization Section

Option Explicit
```

Next, create a constant and assign it the text message to be used in the title bar of the script's pop-up dialogs.

```
Const cGreetingMsg = "Pick a number between 1 - 100"
```

Define four variables as shown. Use `intUserNumber` to store the player's numeric guess. `intRandomNo` stores the script's randomly generated number. `strOkToEnd` is a variable the script uses to determine whether the game should be stopped, and `intNoGuesses` keeps track of the number of guesses the player makes.

```
Dim intUserNumber, intRandomNo, strOkToEnd, intNoGuesses
```

Finally, set the initial value of `intNoGuesses` to 0, like this:

```
intNoGuesses = 0
```

Generating the Game's Random Number

The following statements are next and are responsible for generating the game's random number:

```
'Generate a random number
Randomize
intRandomNo = FormatNumber(Int((100 * Rnd) + 1))
```

The `Randomize` statement ensures that a random number is generated each time the game is played. The last statement uses the following built-in VBScript functions to generate a number between 1 and 100.

- **`Rnd()`**. Returns a randomly generated number.
- **`Int()`**. Returns the integer portion of a number.
- **`FormatNumber()`**. Returns an expression that has been formatted as a number.

Creating a Loop to Control the Game

Now you'll need to set up the `Do...Until` loop that controls the game's execution. In this example, the loop executes until the value assigned to the `strOkToEnd` variable is set to `yes`.

```
Do Until strOkToEnd = "yes"

  'Prompt users to pick a number
  intUserNumber = InputBox("Type your guess:",cGreetingMsg)
  intNoGuesses = intNoGuesses + 1
  .
  .
  .
Loop
```

As you can see, the only statement inside the loop, for now, prompts the player to guess a number and keeps track of the number of guesses made by the player.

Testing Player Input

Now let's put together the code that performs validation of the data supplied by the player.

```
'See if the user provided an answer
If Len(intUserNumber) <> 0 Then

  'Make sure that the player typed a number
  If IsNumeric(intUserNumber) = True Then
```

```
    .
    .
    .
  Else
    MsgBox "Sorry. You did not enter a number. Try again.", , cGreetingMsg
  End If
 Else
  MsgBox "You either failed to type a value or you clicked on Cancel. " & _
    "Please play again soon!", , cGreetingMsg
    strOkToEnd = "yes"
End If
```

The first validation test is performed using the built-in VBScript `Len()` function. It is used to ensure that the player actually typed in a number before clicking on the `OK` button. If the player's input is not `0` characters long, the game continues to the next test. Otherwise, an error message is displayed, and the value of `strOkToEnd` is set to `yes`, terminating the loop and ending the game. If the length test is passed, then the script performs a second validation test on the player's input. This time, the built-in VBScript `IsNumeric()` function is used to make sure that the player typed a number instead of a letter or other special character. If a number was typed, then the game continues. If a number was not typed, then an error message is displayed, but the game continues with the next iteration of the loop.

Determine Whether the Player's Guess Is High, Low, or Correct

There are three more sets of statements that need to be added to the script. They will be inserted one after another, just after the `If` statement that performs the game's second validation test.

The first of these three sets of statements is shown here. It begins by verifying that the user's guess matches the game's randomly selected number. Then it displays a message congratulating the player, showing the random number, and showing the number of guesses that it took for the player to guess it. Finally, the value of `strOkToEnd` is set equal to `yes`. This terminates the loop and allows the game to end.

```
'Test to see if the user's guess was correct
If FormatNumber(intUserNumber) = intRandomNo Then
MsgBox "Congratulations! You guessed it. The number was " & _
    intUserNumber & "." & vbCrLf & vbCrLf & "You guessed it " & _
    "in " & intNoGuesses & " guesses.", ,cGreetingMsg
  strOkToEnd = "yes"
End If
```

The second of the three sets of statements provides the player with help if his or her guess is too low. The value of `strOkToEnd` is set equal to `no`. This ensures that the loop that controls the game will continue.

```
'Test to see if the user's guess was too low
If FormatNumber(intUserNumber) < intRandomNo Then
  MsgBox "Your guess was too low. Try again", ,cGreetingMsg
  strOkToEnd = "no"
End If
```

Finally, the last collection of statements provides the player with help if his or her guess is too high. The value of `strOkToEnd` is set equal to `no`. This ensures that the loop that controls the game will continue.

```
'Test to see if the user's guess was too high
If FormatNumber(intUserNumber) > intRandomNo Then
  MsgBox "Your guess was too high. Try again", ,cGreetingMsg
  strOkToEnd = "no"
End If
```

The Final Result

Let's put all the pieces of the Guess a Number script together and see how it looks fully laid out.

```
'*************************************************************************
'Script Name: GuessANumber.vbs
'Author: Jerry Ford
'Created: 10/19/02
'Description: This script plays a number-guessing game with the user
'*************************************************************************

'Initialization Section

Option Explicit

Const cGreetingMsg = "Pick a number between 1 - 100"

Dim intUserNumber, intRandomNo, strOkToEnd, intNoGuesses

intNoGuesses = 0
```

```
'Main Processing Section

'Generate a random number
Randomize
intRandomNo = FormatNumber(Int((100 * Rnd) + 1))

'Loop until either the user guesses correctly or the user clicks on Cancel
Do Until strOkToEnd = "yes"

  'Prompt user to pick a number
  intUserNumber = InputBox("Type your guess:",cGreetingMsg)
  intNoGuesses = intNoGuesses + 1

  'See if the user provided an answer
  If Len(intUserNumber) <> 0 Then

    'Make sure that the player typed a number
    If IsNumeric(intUserNumber) = True Then

      'Test to see if the user's guess was correct
      If FormatNumber(intUserNumber) = intRandomNo Then
        MsgBox "Congratulations! You guessed it. The number was " & _
          intUserNumber & "." & vbCrLf & vbCrLf & "You guessed it " & _
          "in " & intNoGuesses & " guesses.", ,cGreetingMsg
        strOkToEnd = "yes"
      End If

      'Test to see if the user's guess was too low
      If FormatNumber(intUserNumber) < intRandomNo Then
        MsgBox "Your guess was too low. Try again", ,cGreetingMsg
        strOkToEnd = "no"
      End If

      'Test to see if the user's guess was too high
      If FormatNumber(intUserNumber) > intRandomNo Then
        MsgBox "Your guess was too high. Try again", ,cGreetingMsg
        strOkToEnd = "no"
      End If
```

```
      Else
        MsgBox "Sorry. You did not enter a number. Try again.", , _
          cGreetingMsg
      End If

    Else
      MsgBox "You either failed to type a value or you clicked on " & _
        "Cancel. Please play again soon!", , cGreetingMsg
      strOkToEnd = "yes"
    End If

  Loop
```

Okay, it's time to run the script and see whether it works as promised (don't worry, it will). After testing to see whether the script works as expected, retest it to see whether you can break it. For example, try feeding it special characters or letters instead of numbers. Once you're satisfied with the operation of the script, keep reading. I have one more little goodie for you in this chapter.

Creating Shortcuts for Your Game

Up until now you have been running your scripts in one of two ways. One is by opening the Windows Command Console and typing in the name of an execution host, followed by the path and filename of your scripts at the Windows Command Prompt. The other is by locating the folder in which the script resides and opening it (that is, double-clicking on it).

Windows provides shortcuts as a convenient alternative for executing Windows applications and scripts from the Windows desktop. A shortcut provides access to a Windows resource without requiring the user to find or even know the actual location of the resource that it represents. For example, just about any new application that you install on your computer automatically adds an application shortcut to the Programs menu located on the Windows Start Menu. In addition, most application installation procedures offer to add a shortcut for the application on the Windows desktop. Some application install processes go a step further and add a shortcut for the application on the Windows Quick Launch toolbar.

DEFINITION

Shortcuts are links or pointers to Windows objects. These objects can be just about anything, including Windows applications, folders, files, printers, disk drives, and scripts.

Using VBScript and the WSH, you can create a setup script that configures shortcuts for your VBScript games in any of these locations. Of course, you can always manually create shortcuts for your scripts, but the advantage of scripting their setup is that, once written, you can re-create these shortcuts on any computer. For example, if you purchase a new computer, all you'd have to do is copy your VBScripts from your older computer and then run your VBScript setup script, and all your shortcuts would be re-created. Likewise, if you give copies of your VBScript games to all your friends, all they'd have to do to set up shortcuts for the scripts is to run the setup script.

> **DEFINITION**
>
> The Windows Quick Launch toolbar is an optional toolbar located on top of the Windows taskbar. It provides single-click access to Windows applications. Applications typically found on this toolbar include Internet Explorer, Outlook Express, and Windows Media Player.

Examining Shortcut Properties

Windows shortcuts are identified by a small black arrow in the lower-left side of the icon that represents them. Shortcuts contain information, in the form of properties, about the Windows resources that they are associated with. The most important of these properties is the path and name of the Windows resources that the shortcut represents.

You can view the properties associated with any shortcut by right-clicking on the shortcut and selecting Properties. The shortcut's Properties dialog appears. Click the Shortcut property sheet to view these properties, as shown in Figure 6.12.

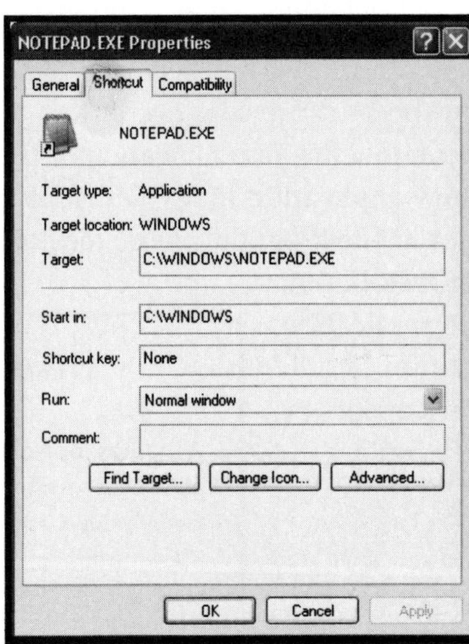

FIGURE 6.12

Examining the properties associated with a shortcut to the Windows Notepad application.

Creating Desktop Shortcuts

As you will see, you can create a desktop shortcut in just five simple steps. To demonstrate, let's create a shortcut for the `GuessANumber.vbs` game on the Windows desktop.

The first step in creating the game's shortcut is to establish an instance of the `WshShell` object. The script will need to use this object's SpecialFolders property to access the folder that represents the Windows desktop. In addition, you'll need to use the `WshShell` object to instantiate the `WshShortcut` object in order to set shortcut properties.

The following statement establishes an instance of the `WshShell` object:

```
Set objWshShl = WScript.CreateObject("WScript.Shell")
```

The second step in creating the shortcut is to set up a reference to the folder where the shortcut is to reside. In Windows, everything, including the Windows desktop and Start Menu, is represented as a folder. Therefore, to add a shortcut to the Windows desktop, all you have to do is save the shortcut in a special folder called `Desktop` by specifying a value for the `WshShell` object's `SpecialFolder` property.

```
strDesktopFolder = objWshShl.SpecialFolders("Desktop")
```

The third step required to set up the desktop shortcut is to use the `WshShell` object's `CreateShortcut()` method to define the shortcut and instantiate the `WshShortcut` object.

```
Set objNewShortcut = objWshShl.CreateShortcut(strDesktopFolder & _
  "\\GuessANumber.lnk")
```

`strDesktopFolder` provides a reference to the location of the Windows desktop and \\GuessANumber.lnk is the name to be assigned to the shortcut.

The fourth step in creating the new shortcut is to configure properties associated with the shortcut. The `WshShortcut` object provides access to these properties, which are listed in Table 6.1.

> **DEFINITION**
>
> *Special Folders* are a Windows management tool that is used to organize and manage the contents of a number of Windows features, including the Start Menu, the Quick Launch toolbar, and desktop.

Only the `TargetPath` property must be set to create a shortcut. Configuration of the remaining shortcut properties is optional. The following statement configures the `TargetPath` property by setting it to `C:\GuessANumber.vbs`:

```
objNewShortcut.TargetPath = "C:\ GuessANumber.vbs"
```

TABLE 6.1 PROPERTIES OF THE WSHSHORTCUT OBJECT

Property	Description
`Arguments`	Sets arguments to be passed to the application or script associated with the shortcut
`Description`	Adds a comment to the shortcut
`Hotkey`	Sets a keyboard keystroke sequence that can be used to activate the application associated with the shortcut
`IconLocation`	Sets the shortcut's icon
`TargetPath`	Sets the path and file name of the object associated with the shortcut
`WindowStyle`	Sets the window style used when the application associated with the shortcut is opened (e.g., normal, minimized, or maximized)
`WorkingDirectory`	Sets the default working directory or folder for the application associated with the shortcut

Examples of how to set other properties are

```
objNewShortcut.Description = "Guess a Number Game"
objNewShortcut.Hotkey = "CTRL+Alt+G"
```

The first of these two statements adds a description to the shortcut. Once created, this description can be viewed by moving the pointer over the shortcut's icon for a few moments. The second statement defines a keyboard keystroke sequence that, when executed, will activate the shortcut and thus open its associated Windows resources (that is, run your script). In this case, pressing the CTRL, ALT, and J keys at the same time will run the VBScript.

The fifth and final step in creating the shortcut is to save it using the `WshShortcut` object's `Save()` method, like this:

```
objNewShortcut.Save()
```

Let's put all five of these statements together to complete the script.

```
Set objWshShl = WScript.CreateObject("WScript.Shell")
strDesktopFolder = objWshShl.SpecialFolders("Desktop")
Set objNewShortcut = objWshShl.CreateShortcut(strDesktopFolder & _
  "\\GuessANumber.lnk")
objNewShortcut.TargetPath = "c:\GuessANumber.vbs"
objNewShortcut.Save()
```

It's just as easy to delete a shortcut using VBScript and the WSH, as it is to create one. For example, create and run the following script to delete the shortcut the previous script created:

```
Set objWshShl = WScript.CreateObject("WScript.Shell")
strTargetFolder = objWshShl.SpecialFolders("Desktop")
Set objFsoObject = CreateObject("Scripting.FileSystemObject")
Set objNewShortcut = objFsoObject.GetFile(strTargetFolder & "\\GuessANumber.lnk")
objNewShortcut.Delete
```

The first statement establishes an instance of the `WshShell` object. The second statement uses the `WshShell` object's `SpecialFolders` property to identify the location of the shortcut. The third statement creates an instance of the VBScript `FileSystemObject`. The fourth statement uses the `FileSystemObject` object's `GetFile()` method to instantiate the `File` object and create a reference to the shortcut, and the final statement deletes the shortcut using the `File` object's `Delete()` method.

Understanding How to Work with Special Folders

Windows operating systems use folders for a number of purposes. For example, folders are used to store system files. You also use folders to store your own personal files. As you just learned, the Windows desktop is a special folder. Windows XP is loaded with special folders as shown in the following list:

- Desktop
- Start Menu
- Programs
- Favorites
- Fonts
- NetHood
- PrintHood
- SendTo
- Recent
- Startup
- Templates
- My Documents

By adding and removing shortcuts to and from Windows special folders you can change their contents. Finding special folders is easy, just right-click on the Windows XP Start button and click on Explore. Windows displays the Explorer folder as demonstrated in Figure 6.13. The Document and Settings folder is automatically expanded. A folder containing your personal user profile settings is also expanded. From here you can view numerous special folders, including the Desktop and Start Menu special folders.

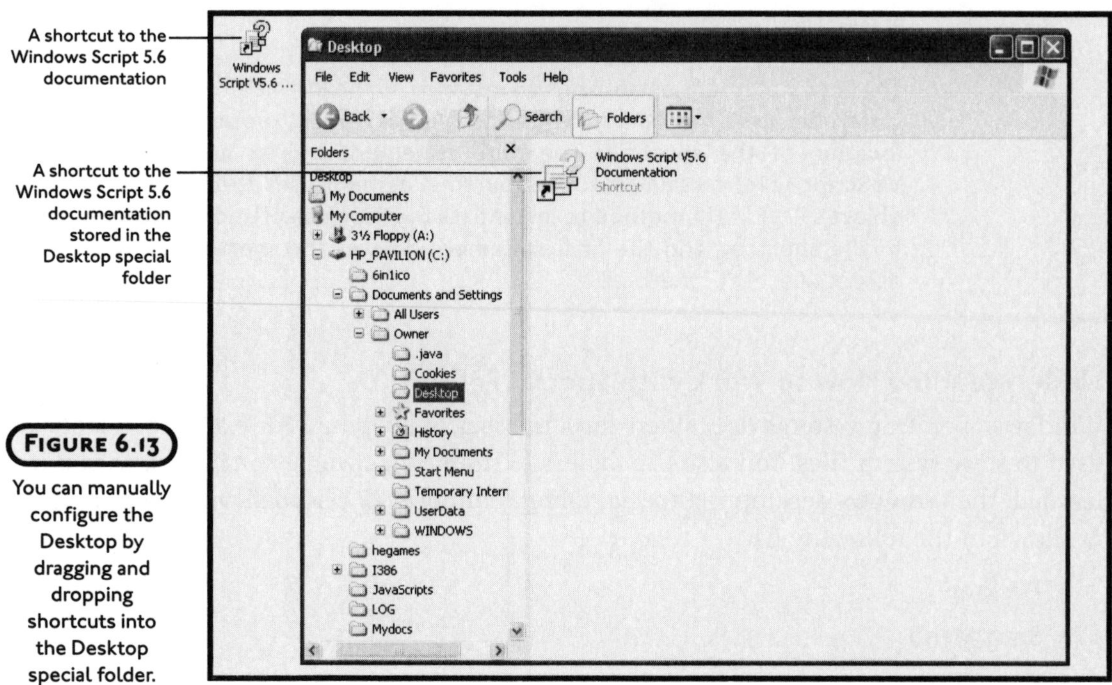

FIGURE 6.13

You can manually configure the Desktop by dragging and dropping shortcuts into the Desktop special folder.

So far, all the special folders that you've seen are associated with just one person—you. That's why they were stored in your personal profile. What's nice about this is that someone else who shares your computer can have his or her own custom profile settings without affecting you or any other user of your computer. Windows also lets you make configuration changes that can be applied to all users of your computer. To do this you must make the configuration changes to one of a collection of special folders that are shared by all users. You can find these shared special folders by expanding the All Users folder as demonstrated in Figure 6.14.

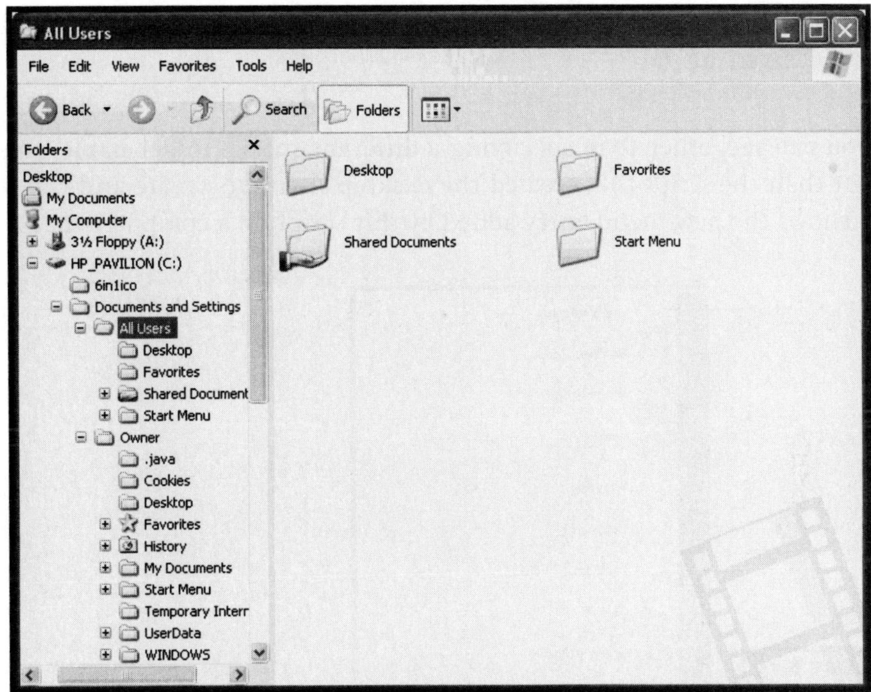

FIGURE 6.14

Any changes to one of the shared special folders affect every user of the computer.

Shared special folders are not as easy to identify as other special folders. To locate them you must first know their names, as shown in the following list.

- **AllUsersDesktop.** Stores items visible on every user's desktop.
- **AllUsersStartMenu.** Stores items visible on every user's Start Menu.
- **AllUsersPrograms.** Stores items visible on every user's All Programs menu.
- **AllUsersStartup.** Stores items that are automatically started any time a user logs on to the computer.

If you look closely at each of these folder's names, you will see that they can be derived by appending `AllUsers` to the beginning of the folder names shown in Figure 6.14.

Using Shortcuts to Add Your Script to the Windows Start Menu

To work with the folders that make up the Windows Start Menu, you need to create a reference to the `StartMenu` special folder. Using the following script, you can programmatically configure this menu:

```
Set objWshShl = WScript.CreateObject("WScript.Shell")
strTargetFolder = objWshShl.SpecialFolders("StartMenu")
```

```
Set objNewShortcut = objWshShl.CreateShortcut(strTargetFolder & "\\GuessANumber.lnk")
objNewShortcut.TargetPath = "c:\ GuessANumber.vbs"
objNewShortcut.Save
```

As you can see, other than specifying a different special folder name, this script is no different than the script that created the desktop shortcut. Create and run this script. Figure 6.15 shows the new menu entry added by this script on a computer that runs Windows XP.

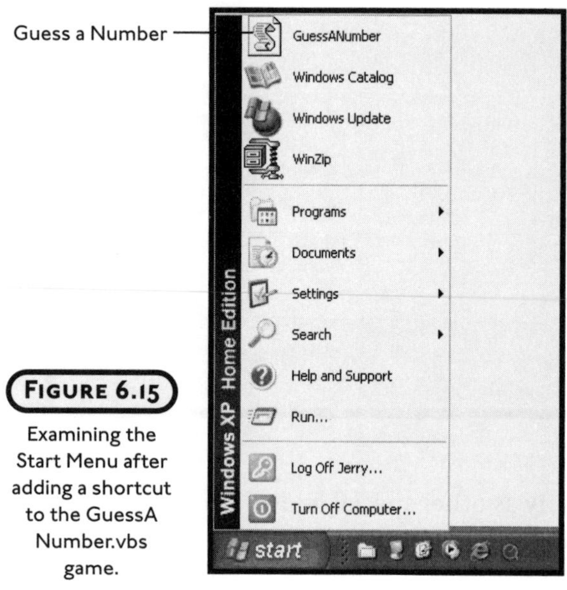

FIGURE 6.15

Examining the Start Menu after adding a shortcut to the GuessA Number.vbs game.

Using Shortcuts to Add Your Script to the Programs Menu

You can just as easily add shortcuts for your VBScripts to other menus located off the Windows Start Menu. For example, the following script adds a menu entry for the `GuessANumber.vbs` script on the Programs menu.

```
Set objWshShl = WScript.CreateObject("WScript.Shell")
strTargetFolder = objWshShl.SpecialFolders("Programs")
Set objNewShortcut = objWshShl.CreateShortcut(strTargetFolder & "\\GuessANumber.lnk")
objNewShortcut.TargetPath = "c:\ GuessANumber.vbs"
objNewShortcut.Save
```

Again, the only thing that changed in this script is the name of the special folder that represents the Programs menu. Figure 6.16 demonstrates how the Programs menu now looks with its new shortcut.

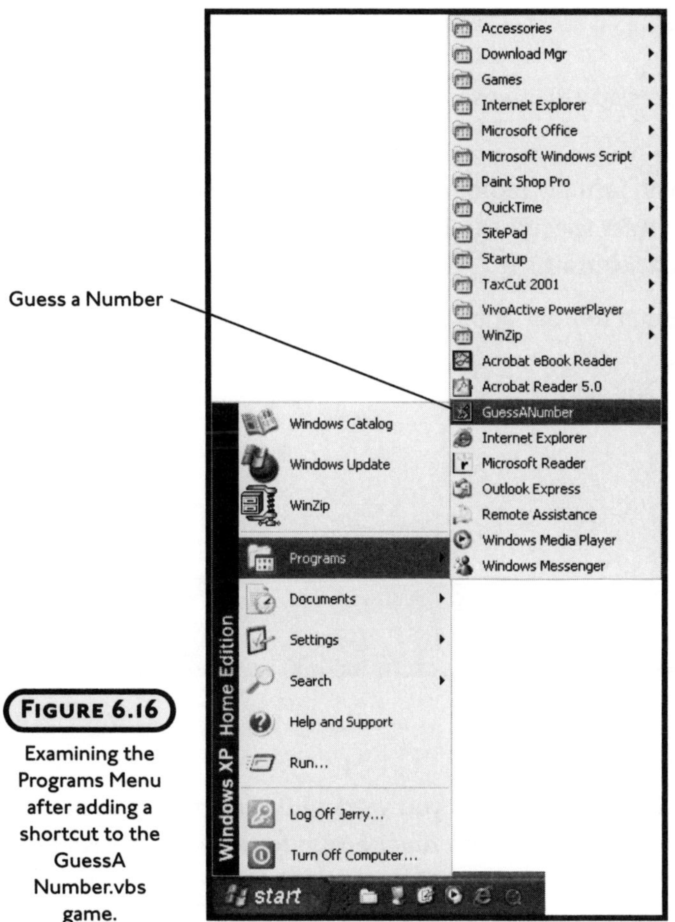

FIGURE 6.16

Examining the Programs Menu after adding a shortcut to the GuessA Number.vbs game.

Using Shortcuts to Add Your Script to the Quick Launch Toolbar

The Windows Quick Launch toolbar is an optional toolbar located on the Windows taskbar of computers running Windows 98, Me, 2000, and XP. It provides single-click access to Windows resources. The next script demonstrates how to add a shortcut for the `GuessANumber.vbs` script to the Quick Launch toolbar. For the most part, this script is no different than any of the previous examples. There is one key difference, however, which I have highlighted in bold.

```
Set objWshShl = WScript.CreateObject("WScript.Shell")
strQuickLaunchToolbar = objWshShl.SpecialFolders("AppData")
strAppDataPath = strQuickLaunchToolbar + _
  "\Microsoft\Internet Explorer\Quick Launch"
```

```
Set objNewShortcut = objWshShl.CreateShortcut(strAppDataPath + _
  "\\GuessANumber.lnk")
objNewShortcut.TargetPath = "C:\ GuessANumber.vbs"
objNewShortcut.Save
```

What makes working with the Quick Launch toolbar different than working with other Windows special folders is that you must specify the location of the Quick Launch toolbar within the special folder (`AppData`) that contains it.

Figure 6.17 shows how the Quick Launch toolbar appears once the shortcut of your VBScript game has been added to it.

FIGURE 6.17 Examining the Windows Quick Launch toolbar after adding a shortcut to the GuessANumber.vbs game.

A Complete Shortcut Script

Now let's put together some of the shortcut examples you worked on previously to make a new script that creates shortcuts for `GuessANumber.vbs` on the Windows desktop, Programs menu, and Quick Launch toolbar.

```
'*************************************************************************
'Script Name: ShortcutMaker.vbs
'Author: Jerry Ford
'Created: 11/28/02
'Description: This script creates shortcuts for the GuessANumber.vbs
'VBScript 'on the Windows desktop, Programs menu, & Quick Launch Toolbar.
'*************************************************************************

'Initialization Section

Option Explicit

Dim objWshShl, strTargetFolder, objDesktopShortcut, objProgramsShortcut
Dim strAppDataPath, objQuickLaunchShortcut
```

```
'Establish an instance of the WshShell object
Set objWshShl = WScript.CreateObject("WScript.Shell")

'Create the Desktop shortcut
strTargetFolder = objWshShl.SpecialFolders("Desktop")
Set objDesktopShortcut = objWshShl.CreateShortcut(strTargetFolder +
"\\GuessANumber.lnk")
objDesktopShortcut.TargetPath = "C:\ GuessANumber.vbs"
objDesktopShortcut.Description = "Guess a Number Game"
objDesktopShortcut.Hotkey = "CTRL+Alt+G"
objDesktopShortcut.Save

'Create the Programs menu shortcut
strTargetFolder = objWshShl.SpecialFolders("Programs")
Set objProgramsShortcut = objWshShl.CreateShortcut(strTargetFolder &
"\\GuessANumber.lnk")
objProgramsShortcut.TargetPath = "c:\ GuessANumber.vbs"
objProgramsShortcut.Save

'Create the Quick Launch Toolbar shortcut
strTargetFolder = objWshShl.SpecialFolders("AppData")
strAppDataPath = strTargetFolder + "\Microsoft\Internet Explorer\Quick Launch"
Set objQuickLaunchShortcut = objWshShl.CreateShortcut(strAppDataPath +
"\\GuessANumber.lnk")
objQuickLaunchShortcut.TargetPath = "C:\ GuessANumber.vbs"
objQuickLaunchShortcut.Save
```

I achieved a few economies of scale here. First of all, I only had to instantiate the `WshShell` object once. I also reused the `strTargetFolder` variable over and over again. However, I thought that it made the script more readable to assign a different variable to each special folder reference. Run this script and you should see shortcuts for `GuessANumber.vbs` added to the Windows desktop, Programs Menu, and Quick Launch toolbar.

SUMMARY

In this chapter you learned about loops and how to apply them to your VBScripts. You demonstrated your understanding of this fundamental programming concept through the development of the Guess a Number game. You also leaned how to programmatically work with Windows shortcuts, and how to use them to create shortcuts for your scripts, as well as how to configure a number of Windows features, including the Windows desktop, Start Menu, and Quick Launch toolbar.

Challenges

1. Modify the Guess a Number Game by providing the players with better hints. For example, if a user's guess is within 20 numbers of the answer, tell the player that he is getting warm. As the player gets even closer to the correct guess, tell him that he is getting very hot.
2. Change the Guess a Number game to increase the range of numbers from 1 to 100 to 1 to 1000.
3. Rewrite the Pick a Number Game so it uses a `Do...While` statement in place of a `Do...Until` statement.
4. Use `ShortcutMaker.vbs` as a starting point, and write a new script that creates one or more shortcuts for your favorite VBScript game. Alternatively, if you keep all your VBScripts in one location, create a shortcut to that folder.

Using Procedures to Organize Scripts

By now you've seen and worked on a number of VBScript projects in this book, and all of these scripts have been organized the same way. First, you've set up script initialization processes (defining variables, constants, objects, and so on), and then you sequentially wrote the rest of the script as one big collection of statements. You've then used the `If` and `Select Case` statements to organize your scripts. Finally, by embedding statements within one another you have further refined your scripts' organization. In this chapter, you will learn how to further improve the organization of your VBScripts, using procedures. Specifically, you will learn how to

- Create your own customized functions
- Create reusable collections of statements using subroutines
- Break down scripts into modules of code to make them easier to manage
- Control variable scope within your scripts using procedures

Project Preview: The BlackJack Lite Game

In this chapter, you create a game called BlackJack Lite. This game is based on the classic blackjack game played in casinos around the world. In this game, both the player and the computer are dealt a single card, face up. The object of the game is to try to get as close as possible to a value of 21 without going over. The player can ask for as many extra cards (hits) as desired and can stop (stick) at any time.

If the player goes over 21, he or she busts. Otherwise the computer plays its hand, stopping only after either reaching a total of 17 or more or busting. Figures 7.1 through 7.5 demonstrate the game in action.

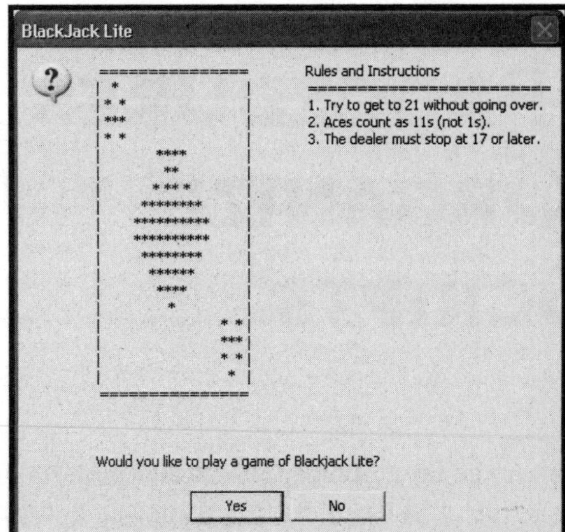

FIGURE 7.1

The game's splash screen invites the user to play a game of BlackJack Lite.

FIGURE 7.2

If the user declines, the game displays information about itself and its author and invites the user to play later.

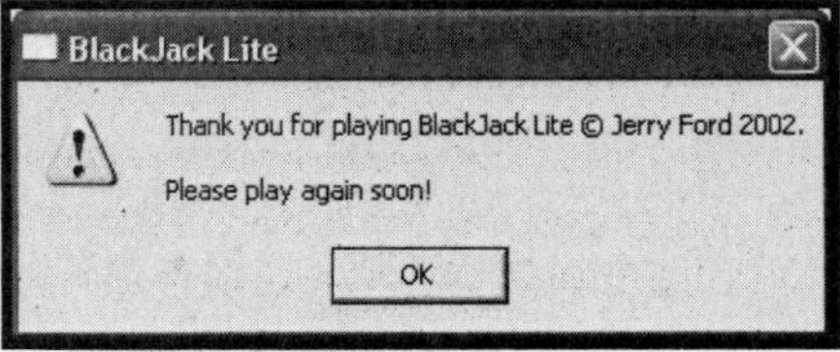

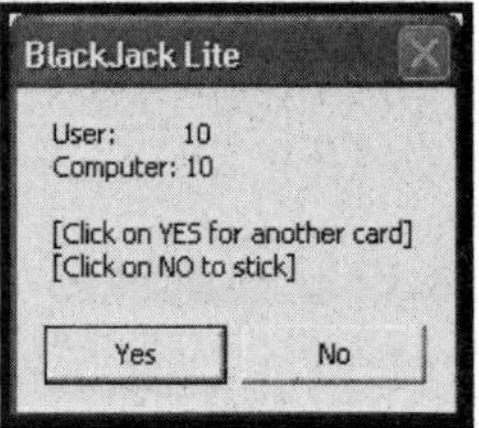

FIGURE 7.3

If the user accepts the offer to play, the initial hands are dealt.

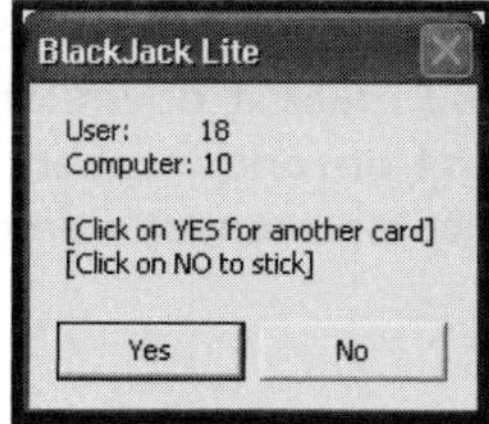

FIGURE 7.4

The user plays until either busting or holding.

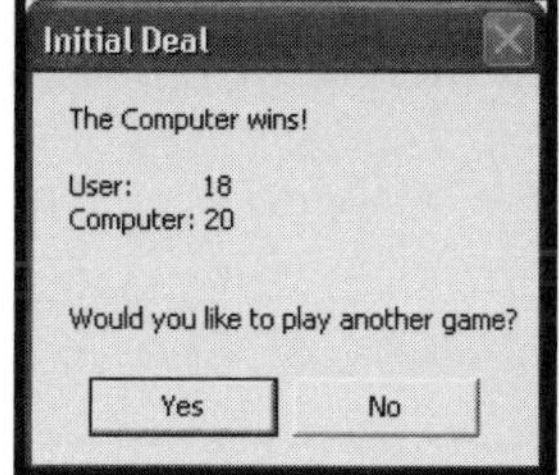

FIGURE 7.5

The computer then plays and the results of the game are shown.

By the time you've worked your way through this chapter and completed the BlackJack Lite game, you will have gained a solid understanding of how to use procedures. You will be able to improve the overall organization and functionality of your VBScripts and tackle even more challenging projects.

Improving Script Design with Procedures

VBScript procedures improve the overall organization and readability of scripts giving you a way to group related statements and execute them as a unit. Once written, a VBScript procedure can be called on from any location in your script and can be executed over and over again as needed. This enables you to create scripts that are smaller and easier to maintain.

> **DEFINITION**
>
> A *procedure* is simply a collection of VBScript statements that, when called, are executed as a unit.

VBScript provides support for two different types of procedures.

- **Sub.** A VBScript procedure that executes a set of statements without returning a result.
- **Function.** A VBScript procedure that executes a set of statements and, optionally, returns a result to the statement that called it.

I recommend using procedures as the primary organization tool for all VBScripts. By organizing a script into procedures, you break it down into a collection of units. This allows you to separate processes from one another, making it easier to develop scripts in a modular fashion, one component at a time.

Introducing Subroutines

The VBScript `Sub` procedure is used to create subroutines. Subroutines are great for grouping together statements that perform a common task from which a result is not required. When called, subroutines execute their statements and then return processing control back to the calling statement.

The syntax for this type of procedure is as follows:

```
[Public | Private] Sub name [(arglist)]
  statements
End Sub
```

`Private` is an optional keyword that specifies the subroutine cannot be called by other procedures within the script, thus limiting the ability to reference it. `Public` is an optional keyword that specifies the subroutine can be called by other procedures within the script. *`name`* is the name assigned to the subroutine. Like variables, a subroutine's name must be unique within the script that defines it. *`arglist`* represents a list of one or more comma-separated arguments that can be passed to the subroutine for processing, and *`statements`* represents the statements that make up the subroutine.

For example, the next subroutine is called `DisplaySplashScreen()`. It does not accept any arguments and it does not return anything back to the VBScript statement that calls it. What it does is display a script's splash screen any time it is called.

```
Sub DisplaySplashScreen()
  MsgBox "Thank you for playing the game. © Jerry Ford 2002." & _
  vbCrLf & vbCrLf & "Please play again soon!", 4144, "Test Game"
End Sub
```

You can execute this subroutine by calling it from anywhere within your script using the following statement:

```
DisplaySplashScreen()
```

The following example is a rewrite of the previous subroutine; only this time the subroutine has been rewritten to accept an argument. The argument passed to the subroutine will be a message. Using a subroutine in this manner, you can develop scripts that display all their pop-up dialogs using one subroutine.

```
Sub DisplaySplashScreen(strMessage)
  MsgBox strMessage, 4144, "Test Game"
End Sub
```

You can call this subroutine from anywhere within your script like this:

```
DisplaySplashScreen("Thank you for playing the game. © Jerry Ford " &_
  "2002." & vbCrLf & vbCrLf & "Please play again soon!")
```

Creating Custom Functions

Functions are almost exactly like subroutines. Functions can do anything that a subroutine can do. In addition, a function can return a result back to the statement that called it. As a result (to keep things simple), I usually use functions only within my VBScripts.

The syntax for a function is as follows:

```
[Public | Private] Function name [(arglist)]
  statements
End Function
```

`Private` is an optional keyword that specifies that the function cannot be called by other procedures within the script, thus limiting the ability to reference it. `Public` is an optional keyword that specifies that the function can be called by other procedures within the script. *`name`* is the name assigned to the function. Like variables, a function's name must be unique within the script that defines it. *`arglist`* represents a list of one or more comma-separated arguments that can be passed to the function for processing, and *`statements`* represents the statements that make up the function.

Let's look at an example of a function that does not return a result to its calling statement.

```
Function DisplaySplashScreen()
  MsgBox "Thank you for playing the game. © Jerry Ford 2002." & _
  vbCrLf & vbCrLf & "Please play again soon!", 4144, "Test Game"
End Function
```

As written, this function performs the exact same operation as the subroutine you saw previously. This function can be called from anywhere in your script using the following statement:

```
DisplaySplashScreen()
```

As with subroutines, you may pass any number of arguments to your functions, as long as commas separate the arguments, like this:

```
Function DisplaySplashScreen(strMessage)
  MsgBox strMessage, 4144, "Test Game"
End Function
```

Once again, this function is no different from the corresponding subroutine example you just saw, and can be called as follows:

```
DisplaySplashScreen("Thank you for playing the game. © Jerry Ford " &_
  "2002." & vbCrLf & vbCrLf & "Please play again soon
```

Functions also can be set up to return a result to their calling statement. This is achieved by creating a variable within the function that has the same name as the function, and by setting the variable equal to the result that you want the function to return.

Again, this technique can best be demonstrated with an example.

```
strPlayersName = GetPlayersName()
MsgBox "Greetings " & strPlayersName

Function GetPlayersName()
  GetPlayersName = InputBox("What is your first name?")
End Function
```

The first statement calls a function name `GetPlayersName()`. The second statement displays the results returned by the function and stored in the variable called `PlayersName`. The next three lines are the actual function, which consists of a single statement that collects the player's name and assigns it to a variable named `GetPlayersName` so that it can be passed back to the calling statement.

Another way to call a function is to reference it as part of another VBScript statement, like this:

```
MsgBox "Greeting " & GetPlayersName()
```

Improving Script Manageability

As I said before, by organizing your VBScripts into procedures, you make them more manageable, allowing you to create larger and more complex scripts without adding mounds of complexity. As an example, let's say that you're developing a game that performs the five major activities that follow:

- Initializes variables, constants, and objects used by the script
- Asks the player whether he or she wants to play the game
- Collects the player's name
- Displays a story, substituting the player's name at predetermined locations within the story
- Displays a closing dialog inviting the player to play again on another day

One way to design your script would be to first define the variables, constants, and object references, and then create a series of functions and subroutine calls from the script's main processing section. The rest of the script would then consist of individual functions and subroutines, each of which would be designed to perform one of the activities outlined in the previous list.

In the Real World

One sign of a world-class programmer is the path that he or she leaves behind—in other words, the professional way in which the programmer organizes and documents his or her scripts. One organizational technique used by experienced programmers is to group all functions and subroutines together in one place, apart from the initialization and main processing sections of the script. This makes them easy to locate and maintain. Usually, you'll find a script's functions and subroutines located at the bottom of the script. I suggest that you modify your script template to include a Procedure section for this purpose.

Writing Reusable Code

One of the biggest advantages provided by functions and subroutines is the capability to create reusable code within your VBScripts. Any time you find yourself needing to perform the same task over and over in a script—such as displaying messages in popup dialogs or retrieving random numbers—consider creating a function or subroutine. Then, by using a single statement to call the appropriate procedure, you can reuse the statements located within the procedure over and over again.

Functions and subroutines help make for smaller scripts. They also make script maintenance and enhancement much easier and quicker. For example, it's a lot easier to change one line of code located in a procedure than it is to make that same change in numerous places throughout a script.

The Guess a Number Game Revisited

So far, you have seen examples of small pieces of code that work with functions and subroutines. Now let's take a look at how to apply procedures to a larger script. To begin, take a moment to go back and review the Guess a Number game at the end of Chapter 6. This script, like all other scripts earlier in this book, was written without the use of procedures.

As I deliberately avoided using procedures in the script from Chapter 6, I had to use other techniques for organizing the script's programming logic. What I chose to do was put everything in the script's main processing section as follows:

- Added statements that generate a random number
- Added a `Do...Until` loop that controls the game's execution
- Embedded an `If` statement within the `Do...Until` loop that ensures that the player typed a number
- Embedded a second `If` statement within the previous `If` statement that makes sure that the data the player typed was numeric
- Embedded three more `If` statements within the previous `If` statement to determine whether the player's guess was low, high, or correct

As you can see, I had to embed a lot of statements within one another to organize the script into a workable game. As the script itself was not exceptionally large, this was a manageable task. However, had the script been much larger or more complex, it would have been difficult to keep track of all the embedded logic.

Now that you understand what procedures are and what they're used for, let's take a moment and go back and redesign the Guess a Number game using them. One way of doing this is as follows:

```
'*************************************************************************
'Script Name: GuessANumber-2.vbs
'Author: Jerry Ford
'Created: 11/29/02
'Description: This script plays a number-guessing game with the user
'*************************************************************************

'Initialization Section

Option Explicit
```

```
Const cGreetingMsg = "Pick a number between 1 - 100"

Dim intUserNumber, intRandomNo, strOkToEnd, intNoGuesses, strBadData

strOkToEnd = "no"
intNoGuesses = 0


'Main Processing Section

RandomNumber()     'Get the game's random number

PlayTheGame()       'Start the game

WScript.Quit()      'End the game


'Procedure Section

'Generate the game's random number
Function RandomNumber()

  'Generate a random number
  Randomize
  intRandomNo = FormatNumber(Int((100 * Rnd) + 1))

End Function

'Set up a Do...Until loop to control the execution of the game
Function PlayTheGame()

  'Loop until either the user guesses correctly or the user clicks on
  'Cancel
  Do Until strOkToEnd = "yes"

    'Prompt user to pick a number
    intUserNumber = InputBox("Type your guess:", cGreetingMsg)
    intNoGuesses = intNoGuesses + 1
    strBadData = "no"
```

```
    'Go see if there is anything wrong with the player's input
    ValidateInput()


    If strOkToEnd <> "yes" Then     'The player typed in something
      If strBadData <> "yes" Then   'The player typed in a number
        TestAnswer()            'Let's see how good the player's guess was
      End If
    End If

  Loop

End Function



'Determine if there are any problems with the data entered by the player
Function ValidateInput()

  'See if the player provided an answer
  If Len(intUserNumber) = 0 Then
    MsgBox "You either failed to type a value or you clicked on " & _
      "Cancel."
    "Please play again soon!", , cGreetingMsg
    strOkToEnd = "yes"
  Else
    'Make sure that the player typed a number
    If IsNumeric(intUserNumber) = False Then
      MsgBox "Sorry. You did not enter a number. Try again.", , _
        cGreetingMsg
      strBadData = "yes"
    End If
  End If

End Function
```

```
'Determine if the player's guess is too low, too high or just right
Function TestAnswer()

  'Test to see if the user's guess was correct
  If FormatNumber(intUserNumber) = intRandomNo Then
MsgBox "Congratulations! You guessed it. The number was " & _
      intUserNumber & "." & vbCrLf & vbCrLf & "You guessed it " & _
      "in " & intNoGuesses & " guesses.", ,cGreetingMsg
    strOkToEnd = "yes"
  End If

  'Test to see if the user's guess was too low
  If FormatNumber(intUserNumber) < intRandomNo Then
    MsgBox "Your guess was too low. Try again", ,cGreetingMsg
    strOkToEnd = "no"
  End If

  'Test to see if the user's guess was too high
  If FormatNumber(intUserNumber) > intRandomNo Then
    MsgBox "Your guess was too high. Try again", ,cGreetingMsg
    strOkToEnd = "no"
  End If

End Function
```

As you can see, the script's initialization section remained unchanged, except for the addition of one more variable, which will be used to indicate that the player has typed an invalid character. However, the main processing section is now quite different. Instead of having all the script's statements embedded within it, this section now drives the script by maintaining high-level control over a collection of functions, each of which performs a specific process for the script.

The main processing section now does three things: It calls a function that gets the game's random number (`RandomNumber()`), it calls a function that controls the play of the game (`PlayTheGame()`), and then it ends the game by executing the `WScript` object's `Quit()` method.

The `RandomNumber()` function generates the random number used by the game. The `PlayTheGame()` function controls play of the game itself. Instead of making this a really large function, I simplified it a bit by removing and modifying the two `If` statements that perform input validation and placing them within their own function called `ValidInput()`. Likewise, I moved and modified the three `If` statements that determine whether the player's guess was low, high, or correct to their own function called `TestAnswer()`. The only other modification made to the script was the addition of the following statements in the `PlayTheGame()`. These statements were needed to test the values of variables manipulated in the `ValidateInput()` and `TestAnswer()` functions.

```
If strOkToEnd <> "yes" Then     'The player typed in something
  If strBadData <> "yes" Then   'The player typed in a number
    TestAnswer()              'Let's see how good the player's guess was
  End If
End If
```

Working with Built-In VBScript Functions

VBScript provides a large collection of built-in functions that you can add to your scripts to save yourself time and effort. Obviously, leveraging the convenience and power of these built-in VBScript functions is a smart thing to do.

In fact, VBScript's built-in functions are so essential to VBScript development that it's difficult to write a script of any complexity without using them. I have already demonstrated this fact many times throughout the book. A complete list of all VBScript built-in functions appears in Appendix B, "Built-In VBScript Functions."

Limiting Variables Scope with Procedures

You have seen and worked with variables throughout this book. Thus far, all the variables that you have worked with have had a *global* or *script-level* scope, meaning they could be accessed from any point within the script. Any variable that is defined outside of a VBScript procedure (that is, function or subroutine) is global in scope.

In contrast, any variable defined within a procedure is *local in scope*, meaning it exists and can only be referenced within the procedure that defines it. The best way to demonstrate the concept of global and local variable scope is in an example. The following script creates two variables, one at the beginning of the script and the other within a function:

```
Option Explicit

Dim intFirstRandomNumber
```

```
intFirstRandomNumber = GetRandomNumber()
MsgBox "The first random number is " & intFirstRandomNumber

GenerateLocalizedVariable()
MsgBox "The second random number is " & intSecondRandomNumber

WScript.Quit()


Function GenerateLocalizedVariable()

  Dim intSecondRandomNumber
  intSecondRandomNumber = GetRandomNumber()

  MsgBox "The second random number is " & intSecondRandomNumber

End Function

Function GetRandomNumber()

  'Generate a random number between 1 and 10
  Randomize
  GetRandomNumber = FormatNumber(Int((10 * Rnd) + 1))

End Function
```

When you run this script, the first variable is defined at the beginning of the script, making it a global variable. The value of the variable is then immediately displayed. The second variable is defined within a function named `GenerateLocalizedVariable()`. As a result, the variable can be referenced only within this function, as proven when the function's `MsgBox()` statement displays its value. When the `GenerateLocalizedVariable()` function completes its execution, processing control returns to the statement that called the function. This statement is immediately followed by another `MsgBox()` statement, which attempts to display the value of the variable defined in the `GenerateLocalizedVariable()` function. However, this variable was destroyed as soon as that function ended, so instead of seeing the variable's value, an error message is displayed, as shown in Figure 7.6.

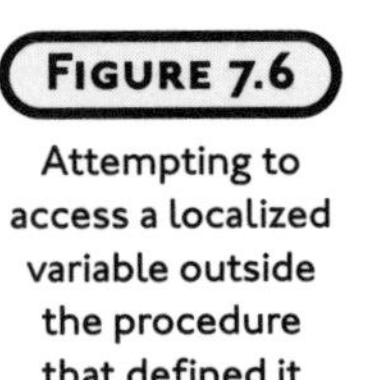
FIGURE 7.6

Attempting to access a localized variable outside the procedure that defined it results in an error.

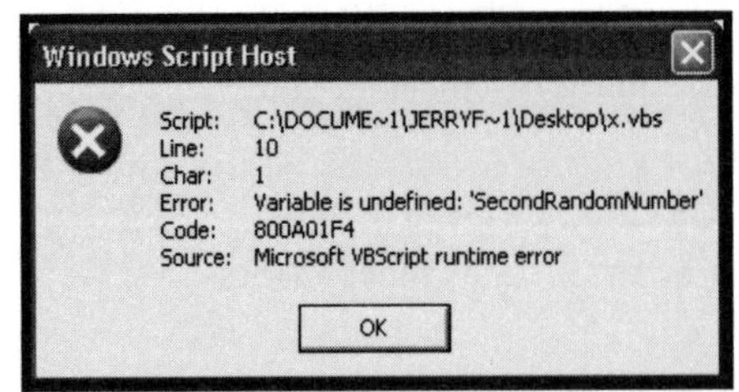

BACK TO THE BLACKJACK LITE GAME

Now let's return to the development of the BlackJack Lite game. In this game, you'll develop your own version of the casino game blackjack. BlackJack Lite is a card game that pits the player against the computer. The object of the game is to come as close to 21 as possible without going over, to beat the computer's hand. The computer, like a real casino blackjack dealer, waits for the player to finish before playing. The computer must then take hits until its hand busts (goes over 21) or reaches at least 17, at which time it must stop.

Designing the Game

The BlackJack Lite game is more complex than the other VBScripts that you've seen in this book. The game itself has a large number of different functions to perform. For example, the initial hand must be dealt for both the player and the computer. Then the game has to facilitate the dealing of cards to the player and later to the computer. In addition, numerous smaller processes must occur along the way.

Because this script is rather complex, I've decided to organize it into procedures. Each procedure will be assigned a specific activity to perform. As part of my preparation for the design of the game, I have drawn a high-level flowchart of the game's overall structure and processing logic; the flowchart is shown in Figure 7.7.

The script consists of nine functions. These functions and their purposes are as follows:

1. `DoYouWantToPlay()`. Displays the game's splash screen and invites the user to play the game.
2. `NowGoPlay()`. Controls the overall execution of the game, calling upon other procedures as required.
3. `DealFirstHand()`. Presents the initial cards for both the player and the computer.
4. `PlayTheGame()`. Asks the player whether he or she would like another card and determines when the player has either busted or decided to hold.

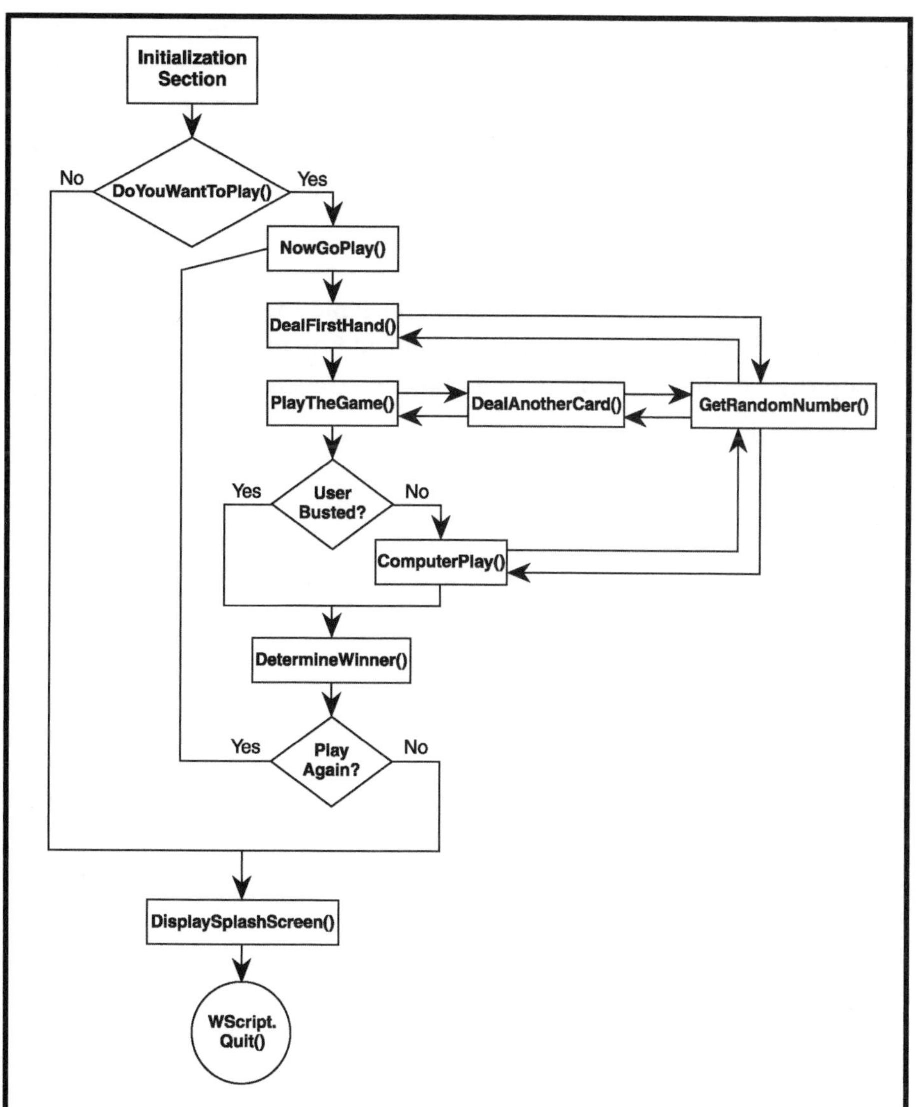

FIGURE 7.7

A flowchart outlining the overall design and execution flow of the BlackJack Lite game.

5. `DealAnotherCard()`. Retrieves another card for the player's hand.
6. `GetRandomNumber()`. This function is called by several other functions in the script. It returns a random number between 1 and 13 representing the value of a playing card.
7. `ComputerPlay()`. Plays the computer hand, taking hits until either the computer's hand is busted or is greater than 17.

8. **DetermineWinner().** Compares the player's hand against the computer's hand to determine who has won. It then offers to let the player play another hand. If the player accepts, the `NowGoPlay()` function is called, starting a new hand.
9. **DisplaySplashScreen().** Displays information about the game and its author, and invites the player to return and play again before finally ending the game.

Setting Up the Initialization Section

Begin the development of the BlackJack Lite game the same way that you've begun all your other games, by first creating a new file and adding in your VBScript template, and then setting up the variables, constants, and object references in the script's Initialization Section.

```
'*************************************************************************
'Script Name: BlackJack.vbs
'Author: Jerry Ford
'Created: 11/28/02
'Description: This script creates a scaled down version of the casino
'version of the BlackJack card game
'*************************************************************************


'Initialization Section

Option Explicit

Dim intPlayGame, strCardImage, intUserCard, intComputerCard, intAnotherCard
Dim intUserNextCard, strUserDone, intNewComputerCard, intPlayAgain
Dim strUserBusted, strTextMsg

strUserDone = "False"
strUserBusted = "False"
```

This game is fairly lengthy and requires a number of variables.

- **intPlayGame.** Stores the player's reply when asked if he or she wants to play a game.
- **strCardImage.** Stores the message displayed in the game's initial pop-up dialog.
- **intUserCard.** Stores the total value of the cards dealt to the user.
- **intComputerCard.** Stores the total value of the cards dealt to the computer.
- **intAnotherCard.** Stores the player's reply to the question of whether he or she wants another card.

- **intUserNextCard.** Stores the value returned by the function that retrieves a random number and is later added to the value of the intUserCard variable.
- **strUserDone.** Stores a value indicating whether the player is ready to hold.
- **intNewComputerCard.** Stores the value returned by the function that retrieves a random number and is later added to the value of the intComputerCard variable.
- **intPlayAgain.** Stores the player's reply when asked whether he or she wants to play another game.
- **strUserBusted.** Stores a value indicating whether the player has busted.
- **strTextMsg.** Stores text to be displayed in pop-up dialogs displayed by the game.

Developing the Logic for the Main Processing Section

The script's Main Processing section is very small and consists only of a call to the DoYouWantToPlay() function to determine whether the player wants to play the game, followed by the Select Case statement, which determines the player's reply.

```
'Main Processing Section

  'Ask the user if he or she wants to play
  intPlayGame = DoYouWantToPlay()

  Select Case intPlayGame
    Case 6 'User clicked on Yes
      NowGoPlay()
    Case 7 'User clicked on No
      DisplaySplashScreen()
  End Select
```

If the player clicks on the Yes button, then the NowGoPlay() function is called. Otherwise, the DisplaySplashScreen() function is called. This function displays a pop-up dialog providing information about the game and then terminates the game's execution.

Creating the DoYouWantToPlay() Function

This function displays the game's initial pop-up dialog and invites the player to play a game of BlackJack Lite. Much of the text displayed in this pop-up dialog is dedicated to creating an image depicting the ace of spades. Also included in this pop-up dialog is a brief set of instructions.

```
function DoYouWantToPlay()

  strCardImage = " ===============" & Space(15) & "Rules and " & _
        "Instructions" & vbCrLf & _
        "|    *   " & Space(32) & "|" & Space(15) & "================" & _
        "========" & vbCrLf & _
        "| *   * " & Space(31) & "|" & Space(15) & "1. Try to get to " & _
        "21 without going over." & vbCrLf & _
        "| *** " & Space(31) & "|" & Space(15) & "2. Aces count as " & _
        "11s (not 1s)." & vbCrLf & _
        "| *   * " & Space(31) & "|" & Space(15) & "3. The dealer " & _
        "must stop at 17 or later." & vbCrLf & _
        "|" & Space(15) & "****" & Space(16) & "|" & vbCrLf & _
        "|" & Space(17) & "**" & Space(18) & "|" & vbCrLf & _
        "|" & Space(14) & "* ** *" & Space(15) &"|" & vbCrLf & _
        "|" & Space(11) & "********" & Space(12) &"|" & vbCrLf & _
        "|" & Space(9) & "**********" & Space(10) & "|" & vbCrLf & _
        "|" & Space(9) & "**********" & Space(10) & "|" & vbCrLf & _
        "|" & Space(11) & "********" & Space(12) & "|" & vbCrLf & _
        "|" & Space(13) & "******" & Space(14) & "|" & vbCrLf & _
        "|" & Space(15) & "****" & Space(16) & "|" & vbCrLf & _
        "|" & Space(17) & " *" & Space(19) & "|" & vbCrLf & _
        "|" & Space(32) & "*   * |" & vbCrLf & _
        "|" & Space(32) & "*** |" & vbCrLf & _
        "|" & Space(32) & "*   * |" & vbCrLf & _
        "|" & Space(33) & " *    |" & vbCrLf & _
        " ===============" & vbCrLf & vbCrLf & vbCrLf & vbCrLf & _
        "Would you like to play a game of Blackjack Lite?            "
  DoYouWantToPlay = MsgBox(strCardImage, 36, "BlackJack Lite")

End Function
```

If the player clicks on the `Yes` button, the value of `DoYouWantToPlay` is set to 6. This value will later be tested in the script's main processing section to determine whether the game should continue.

Creating the NowGoPlay() Function

The `NowGoPlay()` function is called when the player clicks on the `Yes` button on the script's initial pop-up dialog, indicating that he or she wants to play the game.

```
function NowGoPlay()

  DealFirstHand()
  PlayTheGame()
  If strUserBusted = "False" Then
    ComputerPlay()
  End If
  DetermineWinner()

End Function
```

This function controls the actual play of the game. It is made up of calls to several other functions. First it calls the `DealFirstHand()` function, which deals both the user and the computer their initial cards. Next it calls the `PlayTheGame()` function, which allows the user to continue to take hits or hold, and determines whether the player busted. The `NowGoPlay()` function then checks the value of the `strUserBusted` variable to see whether the game should continue. If the user decides to hold, then the `ComputerPlay()` function is called so the computer's (or dealer's) hand can finish being dealt. Regardless of whether the user busts or the `ComputerPlay()` function is called, eventually control returns to the `NowGoPlay()` function and the `DetermineWinner()` function is called. This function determines the winner of the hand and gives the player an opportunity to play another hand.

Creating the DealFirstHand() Function

The `DealFirstHand()` function makes two calls to the `GetRandomNumber()` function to deal both the player's and the computer's initial cards.

```
function DealFirstHand()

  intUserCard = GetRandomNumber()
  intComputerCard = GetRandomNumber()

End Function
```

Creating the PlayTheGame() Function

The `PlayTheGame()` function, shown next, sets up a `Do...Until` loop that executes until either the player busts or decides to hold. The first statement in the loop prompts the player to decide whether he or she wants another card. If the player clicks `Yes`, the `DealAnotherCard()` function is called. The `PlayTheGame()` function then checks to see whether the player has busted, setting the value of the `strUserBusted` and `strUserDone` variables if appropriate (`True`). If the player decides to hold and clicks the `No` button, the value of `strUserDone` is also set to `True`.

```
function PlayTheGame()

  Do Until strUserDone = "True"

  intAnotherCard = MsgBox("User: " & Space(8) & intUserCard & vbCrLf & _
    "Computer: " & intComputerCard & vbCrLf & vbCrLf & _
    "[Click on YES for another card]" & vbCrLf & _
    "[Click on NO to stick]", 4, "Initial Deal")

  Select Case intAnotherCard
    Case 6 'User clicked on Yes
      'MsgBox "You decided to take a hit."
      DealAnotherCard()
    Case 7 'User clicked on No
      strUserDone = "True"
  End Select

  If intUserCard > 21 then
    strUserBusted = "True"
    strUserDone = "True"
  End If

  Loop

End Function
```

Creating the DealAnotherCard() Function

The `DealAnotherCard()` function is called from the `PlayTheGame()` function when the player elects to take a hit (asks for another card). This function consists of two statements. The first statement assigns the card number returned to it from the GetRandomNumber() function to a variable named intUserNextCard. The second statement tallies the player's hand by adding the value of the new card to the cards already in the player's hand.

```
function DealAnotherCard()

  intUserNextCard = GetRandomNumber()
  tinUserCard = intUserCard + intUserNextCard

End Function
```

Creating the ComputerPlay() Function

The ComputerPlay() function, shown here, is responsible for dealing the computer's hand. It uses a Do...While loop to continue dealing the computer's hand until either the computer's hand exceeds a total of 17 but remains under 21, or it busts.

```
function ComputerPlay()

  Do While intComputerCard < 17
    intNewComputerCard = GetRandomNumber()
    intComputerCard = intComputerCard + intNewComputerCard
  Loop
End Function
```

Inside the Do...While loop are two statements. The first statement deals the computer a new card by calling the GetRandomNumber() function. The second statement uses the value returned by the GetRandomNumber() function to update the computer's hand (that is, its total).

Creating the DetermineWinner() Function

The DetermineWinner() function, shown here, checks to see whether the value of strUserBusted is set to True. It also checks to see whether the computer has busted, by checking to see whether the value of intComputerCard is greater than 21. If either of these conditions is true, the script assigns an appropriate text message to the strTextMsg variable. This variable is used as input in an InputBox() pop-up dialog that shows the player the results of the game. If neither of these conditions is true, the DetermineWinner() function performs three tests to determine whether the player won, the computer won, or whether there was a tie; the function then sets the value of strTextMsg accordingly.

```
function DetermineWinner()

  If strUserBusted = "True" Then
    strTextMsg = "The user has busted!"
  Else
    If intComputerCard > 21 then
     strTextMsg = "The Computer has busted!"
    Else
      If intUserCard > intComputerCard Then strTextMsg = "The user wins!"
      If intUserCard = intComputerCard Then strTextMsg = "Push (e.g. Tie)!"
      If intUserCard < intComputerCard Then strTextMsg = "The " & _
        "Computer wins!"
    End If
  End If

  intPlayAgain = MsgBox(strTextMsg & vbCrLf & vbCrLf & "User: " & _
    Space(8) & intUserCard & vbCrLf & "Computer: " & intComputerCard & _
    vbCrLf & vbCrLf & vbCrLf & _
    "Would you like to play another game?", 4, "Initial Deal")

  If intPlayAgain = 6 Then
    strUserBusted = "False"
    strUserDone = "False"
    NowGoPlay()
  End If

  DisplaySplashScreen()

End Function
```

Finally, the game's results are displayed by showing the value of `strTextMsg` and the value of the player's and the computer's final hands. The pop-up dialog also asks the player whether he or she would like to play again. If the player clicks the `Yes` button, then the `NowGoPlay()` function is called and the game starts over again. Otherwise, the `DisplaySplashScreen()` function is called and the game ends.

Creating the DisplaySplashScreen() Function

This final function displays the game's splash screen, providing a little information about the game and its creator, as well as offering an invitation to the player to return and play the game again another time.

```
function DisplaySplashScreen()

  MsgBox "Thank you for playing BlackJack Lite © Jerry Ford 2002." & _
  vbCrLf & vbCrLf & "Please play again soon!", 4144, "BlackJack Lite"

  WScript.Quit()

End Function
```

After displaying the splash screen in a pop-up dialog, the `DisplaySplashScreen()` function ends the game by executing the `WScript Quit()` method.

The Final Result

That's it. You are all done. Your fully assembled script should look as follows.

```
'*************************************************************************
'Script Name: BlackJack.vbs
'Author: Jerry Ford
'Created: 11/28/02
'Description: This script creates a scaled down version of the casino
'version of the BlackJack card game
'*************************************************************************

'Initialization Section

Option Explicit

Dim intPlayGame, strCardImage, intUserCard, intComputerCard, intAnotherCard
Dim intUserNextCard, strUserDone, intNewComputerCard, intPlayAgain
Dim strUserBusted, strTextMsg

strUserDone = "False"
strUserBusted = "False"
```

```
'Main Processing Section

'Ask the user if he or she wants to play
  intPlayGame = DoYouWantToPlay()

  Select Case intPlayGame
    Case 6 'User clicked on Yes
      NowGoPlay()
    Case 7 'User clicked on No
      DisplaySplashScreen()
  End Select

'Procedure Section
function DoYouWantToPlay()

strCardImage = " ===============" & Space(15) & "Rules and " & _
        "Instructions" & vbCrLf & _
        "|   *  " & Space(32) & "|" & Space(15) & "=================" & _
        "========" & vbCrLf & _
        "| *  * " & Space(31) & "|" & Space(15) & "1. Try to get to " & _
        "21 without going over." & vbCrLf & _
        "| *** " & Space(31) & "|" & Space(15) & "2. Aces count as " & _
        "11s (not 1s)." & vbCrLf & _
        "| *  * " & Space(31) & "|" & Space(15) & "3. The dealer " & _
        "must stop at 17 or later." & vbCrLf & _
        "|" & Space(15) & "****" & Space(16) & "|" & vbCrLf & _
        "|" & Space(17) & "**" & Space(18) & "|" & vbCrLf & _
        "|" & Space(14) & "* ** *" & Space(15) &"|" & vbCrLf & _
        "|" & Space(11) & "********" & Space(12) &"|" & vbCrLf & _
        "|" & Space(9) & "**********" & Space(10) & "|" & vbCrLf & _
        "|" & Space(9) & "**********" & Space(10) & "|" & vbCrLf & _
        "|" & Space(11) & "********" & Space(12) & "|" & vbCrLf & _
        "|" & Space(13) & "******" & Space(14) & "|" & vbCrLf & _
        "|" & Space(15) & "****" & Space(16) & "|" & vbCrLf & _
        "|" & Space(17) & " *" & Space(19) & "|" & vbCrLf & _
        "|" & Space(32) & "*  * |" & vbCrLf & _
        "|" & Space(32) & "*** |" & vbCrLf & _
        "|" & Space(32) & "*  * |" & vbCrLf & _
```

```
        "|" & Space(33) & " *    |" & vbCrLf & _
        " ===============" & vbCrLf & vbCrLf & vbCrLf & vbCrLf & _
        "Would you like to play a game of Blackjack Lite?           "

  DoYouWantToPlay = MsgBox(strCardImage, 36, "BlackJack Lite")

End Function

function NowGoPlay()

  DealFirstHand()
  PlayTheGame()
  If strUserBusted = "False" Then
    ComputerPlay()
  End If
  DetermineWinner()

End Function

function DealFirstHand()

  intUserCard = GetRandomNumber()
  intComputerCard = GetRandomNumber()

End Function

function PlayTheGame()

  Do Until strUserDone = "True"

  intAnotherCard = MsgBox("User: " & Space(8) & intUserCard & vbCrLf & _
    "Computer: " & intComputerCard & vbCrLf & vbCrLf & _
    "[Click on YES for another card]" & vbCrLf & _
    "[Click on NO to stick]", 4, "Initial Deal")

  Select Case intAnotherCard
    Case 6 'User clicked on Yes
      'MsgBox "You decided to take a hit."
```

```
      DealAnotherCard()
    Case 7 'User clicked on No
      strUserDone = "True"
  End Select

  If intUserCard > 21 then
    strUserBusted = "True"
    strUserDone = "True"
  End If

  Loop

End Function

function GetRandomNumber()

  Randomize
  GetRandomNumber = Round(FormatNumber(Int((13 * Rnd) + 1)))
  If GetRandomNumber = 1 then GetRandomNumber = 11
  If GetRandomNumber > 10 then GetRandomNumber = 10

End Function

function DealAnotherCard()

  intUserNextCard = GetRandomNumber()
  tinUserCard = intUserCard + intUserNextCard

End Function

function ComputerPlay()

  Do While intComputerCard < 17
    intNewComputerCard = GetRandomNumber()
    intComputerCard = intComputerCard + intNewComputerCard
  Loop
End Function
```

```
function DetermineWinner()

  If strUserBusted = "True" Then
    strTextMsg = "The user has busted!"
  Else
    If intComputerCard > 21 then
     strTextMsg = "The Computer has busted!"
    Else
      If intUserCard > intComputerCard Then strTextMsg = "The user wins!"
      If intUserCard = intComputerCard Then strTextMsg = "Push (e.g. Tie)!"
      If intUserCard < intComputerCard Then strTextMsg = "The " & _
        "Computer wins!"
    End If
  End If

  intPlayAgain = MsgBox(strTextMsg & vbCrLf & vbCrLf & "User: " & _
    Space(8) & intUserCard & vbCrLf & "Computer: " & intComputerCard & _
    vbCrLf & vbCrLf & vbCrLf & _
    "Would you like to play another game?", 4, "Initial Deal")

  If intPlayAgain = 6 Then
    strUserBusted = "False"
    strUserDone = "False"
    NowGoPlay()
  End If

  DisplaySplashScreen()

End Function

function DisplaySplashScreen()

  MsgBox "Thank you for playing BlackJack Lite © Jerry Ford 2002." & _
  vbCrLf & vbCrLf & "Please play again soon!", 4144, "BlackJack Lite"

  WScript.Quit()

End Function
```

Take a few minutes to double-check all your work and then give this game a whirl. This is a pretty big script, so you may have to fix a few syntax errors introduced by typos you may have made when keying in the script. Once everything is working correctly, you should have a really cool game to share with—and impress—all your friends!

SUMMARY

In this chapter you learned how to use procedures to streamline the organization of your VBScripts, allowing you to develop larger and more complex scripts, and, of course, games. In addition, you learned how to create reusable units of code, allowing you to make your scripts smaller and easier to mange. Finally, you learned how to control variable scope by localizing variables within procedures.

CHALLENGES

1. **Give the BlackJack Lite game's splash screen a more polished look by providing additional information in the Rules and Instructions section of the dialog.**
2. **Improve the BlackJack Lite game by adding logic to include the selection of the card's suit (club, heart, spade, or diamond).**
3. **Once you have modified the BlackJack Lite game to assign cards that include both the card's suit and number, add additional logic to ensure that the same card is not used twice in the same hand.**
4. **Add scorekeeping logic to the BlackJack Lite game, and display the number of won and lost hands at the end of each game.**

Part III

Advanced Topics

Storing and Retrieving Data

Now that you've learned the basics of VBScript programming using the WSH, its time to tackle more advanced topics. In this chapter, you'll learn how to work with and administer Windows files and folders, including storing data in reports and creating log files. You'll see how to open up and programmatically read the contents of text files to process script input. You'll learn how to retrieve script configuration settings stored in external files and then use this information to control the way your scripts execute. Finally, I'll show you how to automate file and folder management by using VBScript to copy, move, and delete individual and groups of files and folders. Specifically, you will learn how to

- Create and write data to text files
- Open and process data stored in text files
- Copy, move, and delete files and folders
- Retrieve script configuration settings from external files

Project Preview: The Lucky Lottery Number Picker

This chapter shows you how to create the Lucky Lottery Number Picker game, which assists players by randomly generating lottery ticket numbers. The player only needs to specify how many lottery tickets he or she plans to purchase and the game generates the appropriate amount of numbers. By default, the game assumes that it should generate six numbers for each lottery ticket the player wants to purchase. However, by editing an external configuration file that stores the game's execution settings, the player can modify the game to generate any amount of numbers per play.

Figures 8.1 through 8.4 show the Lucky Lottery Number Picker in action.

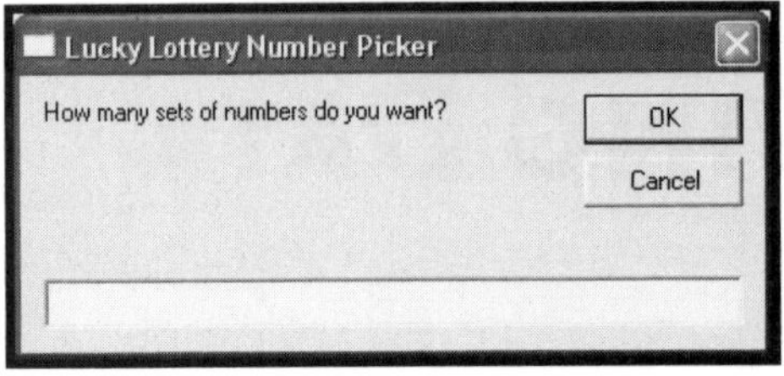

FIGURE 8.1

The game begins by asking the player how many different sets of lottery numbers should be generated.

Lucky Lottery Number Picker

LUCKY LOTTERY NUMBER PICKER

Number of plays: 5

Number of picks per play: 6

Your lottery numbers are:

1)	38	34	23	42	33	24
2)	48	31	18	5	3	15
3)	29	11	28	14	18	43
4)	32	29	23	41	38	10
5)	31	5	7	18	21	35

OK

FIGURE 8.2

By default, the game displays configuration information at the top of its output followed by the lottery numbers.

FIGURE 8.3

By changing script configuration settings stored in an external configuration file, the player can tell the script to provide only summary level information.

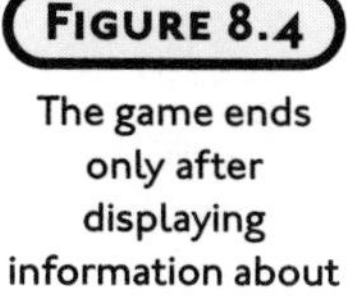

FIGURE 8.4

The game ends only after displaying information about its creator.

By the time you've completed this chapter and created the Lucky Lottery Number Picker game, you will have mastered the building blocks required to work with and administer Windows files and folders. By learning how to store script configuration settings in external files, you'll also learn how to make your VBScripts easier to control and modify.

WORKING WITH THE WINDOWS FILE SYSTEM

The WSH core object model provides the capability to interact with all sorts of Windows resources, such as the Windows desktop and Registry; however, it fails to provide any access to the Windows file system, so you cannot use it to access local disk drives or to work with files and folders. Instead of providing this functionality as part of the WSH core object model, Microsoft chose to implement it via the `FileSystemObject`, which is one of VBScript's run-time objects. Refer to Table 3.4 in Chapter 3, "VBScript Basics" for a complete listing of VBScript's run-time objects.

The `FileSystemObject` is VBScript's primary run-time object. All other run-time objects, except for the `Dictionary` object, are derived from it. To use the `FileSystemObject`, you must instantiate it as shown here:

```
Set objFso = WScript.CreateObject("Scripting.FileSystemObject")
```

The first step in setting up an instance of the `FileSystemObject` is to use the `Set` statement to associate a variable with it. This is accomplished by using the `WScript` object's `CreateObject()` method and specifying the `FileSystemObject` as `Scripting.FileSystemObject`. Once instantiated, you can interact with the `FileSystemObject` by referencing the variable that has been set up, thus providing access to all `FileSystemObject` properties and methods.

To jump-start your understanding of the `FileSystemObject` and how to use it, let's begin with an example. In this example, a VBScript is created that uses the `FileSystemObject` to retrieve and display the properties associated with a file named `Sample.txt`. The script begins by instantiating the `FileSystemObject` and associating it with a variable named `objFso`. Next, the `FileSystemObject` object's `GetFile()` method retrieves a reference to the `File` object that specifically refers to `Sample.txt`, which is located in the computer C:\Temp folder.

The main processing of the script then makes a series of procedure calls. The `CreateDisplayString()` function uses several `File` object properties to collect information about the `Sample.txt` file. The next two functions display the information that has been collected about the file and then terminate the script's execution.

```
'*************************************************************************
'Script Name: ExtractFileProperties.vbs
'Author:      Jerry Ford
'Created:     11/10/04
'Description: This script demonstrates how to retrieve information about
'              a file.
'*************************************************************************


'Initialization Section

Option Explicit

On Error Resume Next

Dim objFso, strInputFile, strDisplayString
```

```
Set objFso = WScript.CreateObject("Scripting.FileSystemObject")

Set strInputFile = objFso.GetFile("C:\Temp\Sample.txt")


'Main Processing Section

CreateDisplayString()

DisplayMessage()

TerminateScript()


'Procedure Section



Function CreateDisplayString()

  strDisplayString = "C:\Temp\Sample.txt" & vbCrLf & _
    vbCrLf & "Created on:     " & vbTab & strInputFile.DateCreated & _
    vbCrLf & "Last Modified: " & vbTab & strInputFile.DateLastModified & _
    vbCrLf & "Last Accessed: " & vbTab & strInputFile.DateLastAccessed & _
    vbCrLf

End Function


Function DisplayMessage()

  MsgBox strDisplayString

End Function


Function TerminateScript()
```

```
  'Stop the execution of this script
  WScript.Quit()

End Function
```

The main thing to take away from this example is that it interacts with the Windows file system using properties belonging to the `File` object to collect information about a given file. To work with the `File` object, you have to use the `FileSystemObject` object's `GetFile()` method, which first requires that you set up an instance of the `FileSystemObject`.

If you run this script, you'll see output similar to that shown in Figure 8.5.

FIGURE 8.5

Using `FileSystemObject` properties to retrieve information about a file.

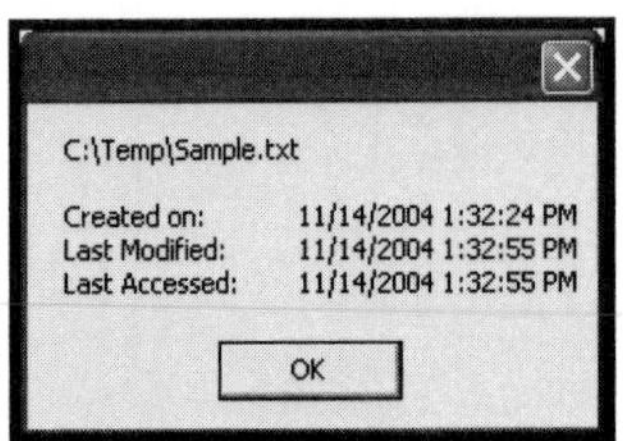

OPENING AND CLOSING FILES

Now that you know how to instantiate the `FileSystemObject` within your VBScripts and have seen an example of how to use it to reference other run-time objects and their associated properties, you are ready to start learning how to work with files and folders.

Before you open a file or create a new file, you must determine whether or not the file already exists. You can do this using the `FileSystemObject` object's `FileExists()` method as demonstrated here:

```
If (objFso.FileExists("C:\Temp\Sample.txt")) Then
   . . .
End If
```

To begin working with a file, you must open it. This is done using the `FileSystemObject` object's `OpenTextFile()` method, which requires that you provide the following pieces of information:

- Name and path of the file
- How to open the file
- Whether to create a new file if the file does not already exist

Table 8.1 defines constants and the values you will use to tell the `OpenTextFile()` method how to open the file.

TABLE 8.1 OPENTEXTFILE() CONSTANTS

Constant	Description	Value
`ForReading`	Opens a file in preparation for reading	1
`ForWriting`	Opens a file in preparation for writing	2
`ForAppending`	Opens a file allowing text to be written to the end of the file	8

Table 8.2 outlines the two available options that determine what the `OpenTextFile()` method should do if the file does not already exist.

TABLE 8.2 OPENTEXTFILE() FILE CREATION OPTIONS

Value	Description
`True`	Open a file if it already exists; create and open a new file if it does not already exist
`False`	Open a file if it already exists; otherwise, take no additional action

You must be careful to always specify the appropriate constant value when telling the `OpenTextFile()` method how to open a file. For example, if you accidentally open a file in `ForWriting` mode when you actually meant to append to the end of the file, then you will overwrite the contents already stored in the file.

Let's look at a VBScript that puts what you have just learned into action. In this example, the script opens a file named `Sample.txt`, which resides in the `Temp` directory on the computer's C: drive. If the file exists, the script opens it. If the file doesn't already exist, the script creates it. Once opened, the script writes a few lines of text and then closes the file.

```
'*************************************************************************
'Script Name: FileCreate.vbs
'Author:      Jerry Ford
'Created:     11/10/04
```

```
'Description: This script demonstrates how to create, open, and write
'a line of text to a text file.
'*********************************************************************

'Initialization Section

Option Explicit

Dim objFso, objFileHandle, strFileName

Set objFso = WScript.CreateObject("Scripting.FileSystemObject")

strFileName = "C:\Temp\Sample.txt"


'Main Processing Section

OpenTextFile()

WriteTextOutput()

CloseTextFile()

TerminateScript()


'Procedure Section

Function OpenTextFile()

  'If exists open it in append mode, otherwise create and open a new file
  If (objFso.FileExists(strFileName)) Then
    Set objFileHandle = objFso.OpenTextFile(strFileName, 8)
  Else
    Set objFileHandle = objFso.OpenTextFile(strFileName, 2, "True")
  End If
```

```
End Function


Function WriteTextOutput()

  'Write 3 lines of text to the text file
  objFileHandle.WriteLine "Once upon a time there was a little boy who"
  objFileHandle.WriteLine "lived in a shoe. Unfortunately it was two sizes"
  objFileHandle.WriteLine "too small!"

End Function


 Function CloseTextFile()

  'Close the file when done working with it
  objFileHandle.Close()

End Function


 Function TerminateScript()

  'Stop the execution of this script
  WScript.Quit()

End Function
```

It is very important that you always remember to close any open files before allowing your scripts to end. You do this by using the `FileSystemObject` object's `Close()` method as shown here:

```
objFileHandle.Close()
```

If you forget to close a file after working with it, the file might become corrupted because the end-of-file marker has not been created for it.

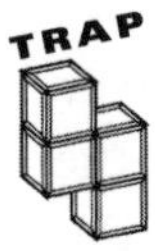

You can only open a file using one mode at a time. In other words, if you open a file in `ForReading` mode, your script cannot write new text to the file unless you first close the file and then open it again in `ForWriting` mode.

If you save and run this script and then open the `Sample.txt` file using Windows Notepad, you'll see the output shown in Figure 8.6.

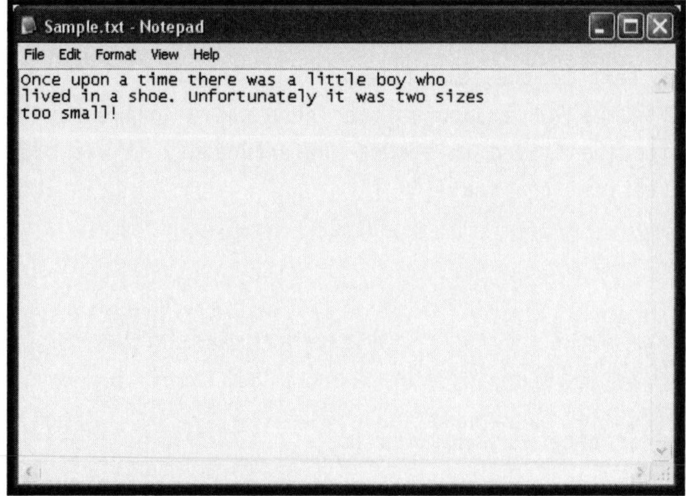

FIGURE 8.6

Writing to a new or existing text file.

WRITING TO FILES

You have a number of different options when it comes to how your VBScripts write text to files:

- Writing one or more characters at a time
- Writing a line at a time
- Writing blank lines

Writing text one or more characters at a time is good when you need to carefully format text output, such as when you want to create reports with data lined up in columns. On the other hand, writing out one line of text at a time is convenient when the format is more free form. Finally, inserting or writing blank lines into text files helps you improve the file's appearance, such as adding space between the heading and the text in a formal report.

Writing Characters

To write text to a file one or more characters at a time, you need to use the `FileSystemObject` object's `Write()` method. This method does not append a carriage return to the end of any text that it writes. If two back-to-back write operations are performed using the `Write()` method, for example, the text from the second write operation is inserted into the text file on the same line immediately following the text written by the first write operation. To see how this works, take at look at the following example:

```
Set objFso = WScript.CreateObject("Scripting.FileSystemObject")
Set objFileHandle = _
  objFso.OpenTextFile("C:\Temp\Sample.txt", 2, "True")
objFileHandle.Write("Once upon a time there ")
objFileHandle.Write("were three little bears.")
objFileHandle.Close()
```

If you save and run this example, you'll see that the output added to the text file by the script is placed on the same line as shown in Figure 8.7.

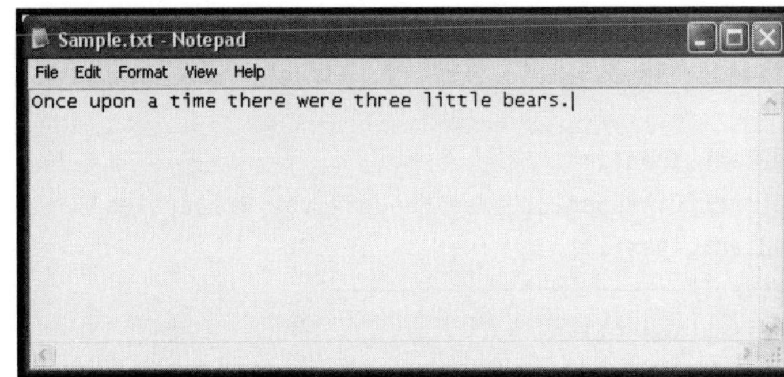

FIGURE 8.7

Writing characters to a text file.

Writing Lines

You can modify the previous example to write text output to the file a line at a time by replacing the `Write()` method with the `WriteLine()` method:

```
Set objFso = WScript.CreateObject("Scripting.FileSystemObject")
Set objFileHandle = _
  objFso.OpenTextFile("C:\Temp\Sample.txt", 2, "True")
objFileHandle.WriteLine("Once upon a time there were three little bears.")
objFileHandle.Close()
```

If you save and run this example, you'll find that the results are almost exactly the same as those produced by the previous example. The one difference is that the cursor is now positioned at the beginning of the next row in the text file when you run this example, whereas the cursor was left at the end of the first row when you ran the previous example. This is because the `WriteLine()` method automatically appends a linefeed to the end of each write operation.

Adding Blank Lines

You can add blank lines to the output generated by your VBScripts to make it look better by using the `FileSystemObject` object's `WriteBlankLines()` method. This method executes by writing a blank line and then advancing the cursor down to the beginning of the next row in the file.

The following example demonstrates how to use the `FileSystemObject` object's `WriteBlankLines()` method:

```
Set objFso = WScript.CreateObject("Scripting.FileSystemObject")

Set strInputFile = objFso.GetFile("C:\VBScriptGames\Hangman.vbs")

Set objFileHandle = _
  objFso.OpenTextFile("C:\Temp\Sample.txt", 2, "True")

objFileHandle.WriteBlankLines(1)
objFileHandle.WriteLine("C:\VBScriptGames\Hangman.vbs Properties")
objFileHandle.WriteBlankLines(1)
objFileHandle.WriteLine("------------------------------")
objFileHandle.WriteBlankLines(1)
objFileHandle.WriteLine("Creation Date: " & strInputFile.DateCreated)
objFileHandle.WriteBlankLines(1)
objFileHandle.WriteLine("Last Modified: " & strInputFile.DateLastModified)
objFileHandle.WriteBlankLines(1)
objFileHandle.WriteLine("------------------------------")

objFileHandle.Close()
```

Figure 8.8 shows how the `Sample.txt` file looks after the script has been executed.

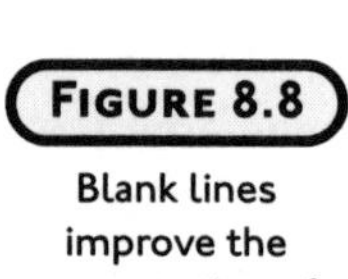

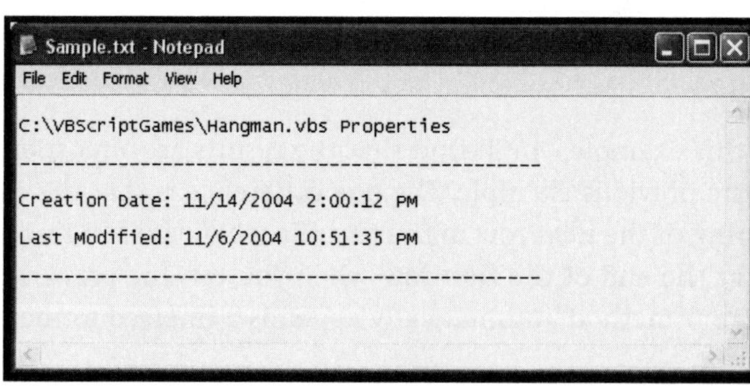

FIGURE 8.8

Blank lines improve the presentation of reports created by your VBScripts.

Reading from Files

VBScript makes it just about as easy to read from a file as it is to write to one. However, before you attempt to read or process the contents of a text file, you should first make sure the file has data in it. If the file has no data, opening the file and attempting to read it is pointless.

You can use the `TestStream` object's `AtEndOfStream` property to determine whether a file contains data. Not only should you check the `AtEndOfStream` property before you begin reading a file, but your script should continue to check this property before each additional read operation to make sure data is still in the file for the script to read. In other words, you need to keep checking to make sure that your script has not reached the end-of-file marker.

To demonstrate how all this works, let's build an example. For starters, create a new VBScript and add the following statements to it:

```
Dim objFso, objFileHandle, strDisplayString
Set objFso = WScript.CreateObject("Scripting.FileSystemObject")
Set objFileHandle = objFso.OpenTextFile("C:\Temp\Sample.txt", 1)
```

The first statement defines variables to be used by the script. The next statement instantiates the `FileSystemObject`. The third statement sets up an object reference to the `Sample.txt` file and opens it in `ForReading` mode. Now add the following statements to the script:

```
Do While objFileHandle.AtEndOfStream = False
  strDisplayString = strDisplayString & objFileHandle.ReadLine() & vbCrLf
Loop
MsgBox strDisplayString
```

The first statement sets up a `Do While` loop that checks on each iteration to determine whether or not the end-of-file marker has been reached. As long as the end of the file has not been reached, another line of the file is read and appended to the end of a variable named `strDisplayString`.

Finally, close the file by adding the following statement:

```
objFileHandle.Close
```

If you run this script, you'll see output similar to that shown in Figure 8.9.

FIGURE 8.9

Creating a VBScript that reads and displays the content of text files.

This example showed you how to read an entire file, a line at a time. Other options that are available to you when reading files include

- Skipping lines
- Reading one or more characters at a time
- Reading the entire file at one time

Skipping Lines

Often text reports and other files begin with some type of heading or other information that you might not be particularly interested in. In these cases, you can skip the reading of these lines using the `FileSystemObject` object's `Skip()` and `SkipLine()` methods. The `Skip()` method allows your script to skip a specific number of characters at a time, whereas the `SkipLine()` allows your script to skip entire lines.

To use the `Skip()` method, you must pass it the number of characters that you want skipped as demonstrated here:

```
objFileHandle.Skip(25)
```

The `SkipLine()` method does not accept any arguments, so it can only be used to skip one line at a time. However, by wrapping the execution of this method up within a loop, you can skip as many lines as you want as demonstrated here:

```
For intCounter = 1 To 5
  objFileHandle.SkipLine()
Next
```

Reading Files Character by Character

To read a file one or more characters at a time, you need to work with the `FileSystemObject` object's `Read()` method. This might be necessary for reading files with fixed length data. For example, you might have a report file that lists a certain category or information in a column that begins at character position 20 and ends at character position 30 on each line of the report. Using the `Read()` method, you could develop a VBScript that reads the file and pulls out only the information stored in that column for each line of the file.

To get a glimpse of the `Read()` method in action, consider the following example. This script uses a `For` loop and the `SkipLine()` method to skip the reading of the first 5 lines of the `Sample.txt` file. The `Skip()` method skips the first 15 characters on the next line in the file (line 6). The `Read()` method reads the next 22 characters from the file. The file is then closed and the text that was read from the file is displayed.

```
Dim objFso, objFileHandle, intCounter, strDisplayString
Set objFso = WScript.CreateObject("Scripting.FileSystemObject")
Set objFileHandle = objFso.OpenTextFile("C:\Temp\Sample.txt", 1)

For intCounter = 1 To 5
 objFileHandle.SkipLine()
Next

objFileHandle.Skip(15)

strDisplayString = objFileHandle.Read(22)

objFileHandle.Close

MsgBox "C:\Temp\Sample.txt was created on " & strDisplayString
```

Reading a File All at Once

Sometimes all you need to do is read an entire file in a single operation, such as when the file to be read is already formatted to produce the output that you want. You can do this using the `FileSystemObject` object's `ReadAll()` method as demonstrated here:

```
Dim objFso, objFileHandle, strDisplayString
Set objFso = WScript.CreateObject("Scripting.FileSystemObject")
Set objFileHandle = objFso.OpenTextFile("C:\Temp\Sample.txt", 1)
```

```
strDisplayString = objFileHandle.ReadAll()

objFileHandle.Close()

MsgBox strDisplayString
```

As you can see, the script reads the entire file using just one `ReadAll()` operation and then displays what it reads using a `MsgBox()` statement. The output displayed when you run this script is exactly the same as that shown previously in Figure 8.9, in which the script read the entire text file a line at a time before displaying the file's contents.

MANAGING FILES AND FOLDERS

In addition to using VBScript and the WSH to read and write to and from text files, you can also use them to help administer all your files and folder. By *administer*, I mean to help keep them organized. Or more specifically, to automate the organization process. For example, if your computer is connected to a local area network, you can create a VBScript that makes copies of all the files it finds in certain folders and stores them on a network server. This way, if something ever happens to your original files, you can always recover by retrieving a backup copy.

The `FileSystemObject` provides several methods for developing scripts that can automate file administration:

- **`CopyFile()`.** Copies one or more files.
- **`MoveFile()`.** Moves one or more files.
- **`DeleteFile()`.** Deletes one or more files.
- **`FileExists()`.** Determines whether or not a file exists.

The `FileSystemObject` also provides a large collection of methods for automating folder administration:

- **`CopyFolder()`.** Copies one or more folders.
- **`MoveFolder()`.** Moves one or more folders.
- **`DeleteFolder()`.** Deletes one or more folders.
- **`FolderExists()`.** Determines whether or not a folder exists.
- **`CreateFolder()`.** Creates a new folder.

As an alternative to working with methods belonging to the FileSystemObject, you also can work with methods that jointly belong to the File and Folder objects:

- **Copy().** Copies a single file or folder.
- **Delete().** Removes a single file or folder.
- **Move().** Moves a single file or folder.

There are a few drawbacks to these methods. First, using these methods requires that you instantiate both the FileSystemObject and the File or Folder object, which is just a little more work. Second, they work with just one file at a time as opposed to the methods belonging to the FileSystemObject, which can work on more than one file or folder at a time. Finally, because the File and Folder objects share the same methods, it's sometimes easy to make a mistake and accidentally mess things up. For example, if you have a file and a folder in the same location with the same or a similar name, it's easy to accidentally delete the wrong one.

Copying, Moving, and Deleting Files

Using the FileSystemObject object's CopyFile() method, you can create VBScript that can copy one or more files as demonstrated in the following example:

```
Dim objFso
Set objFso = WScript.CreateObject("Scripting.FileSystemObject")
objFso.CopyFile "C:\Temp\Sample.txt", "C:\VBScriptGames\Sample.txt"
```

In this example, a file named Sample.txt located in the Temp folder on the computer C: drive is copied to the VBScriptGames folder located on the C: drive. By modifying this example, as shown here, you can change the script so that it copies more than one file. Specifically, this example results in all files named Sample being copied, regardless of their file extensions.

```
Dim objFso
Set objFso = WScript.CreateObject("Scripting.FileSystemObject")
objFso.CopyFile "C:\Temp\Sample.*", "C:\VBScriptGames"
```

Wildcard characters make it possible to copy, move, or delete more than one file or folder at a time. The ? and * wildcard characters enable pattern matching. The ? character is used to specify a single character match. The * character is used to match up against an unlimited number of characters. For example, specifying *.txt results in a match with all files that have a .txt file extension. Specifying sampl?.txt results in a match only with files that have a six-character-long file name, Sampl as the first five characters, and a .txt file extension.

Copying One or More Files

You can copy one or more files using the CopyFile() method. This method also supports an additional parameter that allows you to specify what to do if the script attempts to copy a file to a folder that already contains a file with the same name. You specify a value of either True or False for this parameter. A value of True tells CopyFile() to replace or override files with duplicate file names. A value of False tells CopyFile() to cancel the copy operation for any files with matching file names.

The following example demonstrates how to copy all files with a .txt file extension located in the C:\Temp folder to a folder called C:\VBScriptGames without allowing any duplicate files already located in the destination folder to be overridden:

```
Dim objFso
Set objFso = WScript.CreateObject("Scripting.FileSystemObject")
objFso.CopyFile "C:\Temp\*.txt", "C:\VBScriptGames", "False"
```

This next example does the exact same thing as the previous example, except that it allows duplicate files to be overridden:

```
Dim objFso
Set objFso = WScript.CreateObject("Scripting.FileSystemObject")
objFso.CopyFile "C:\Temp\*.txt", "C:\VBScriptGames", "True"
```

Remember, you can avoid errors by using the FileSystemObject object's FileExists and FolderExists properties to verify whether a file or folder exists before manipulating them.

Moving One or More Files

The difference between moving and copying files is that after you copy a file, you end up with two copies in two places, whereas when you move a file, only the one file exists in its new location. You can move files from one folder to another using the FileSystemObject object's MoveFile() method:

```
Dim objFso
Set objFso = WScript.CreateObject("Scripting.FileSystemObject")
objFso.MoveFile "C:\Temp\*.txt", "C:\VBScriptGames"
```

In this example, all files with a .txt file extension are moved from the C:\Temp folder into the C:\VBScriptGames folder.

Deleting One or More Files

You can delete one or more files using the FileSystemObject object's DeleteFile() method:

```
Dim objFso
Set objFso = WScript.CreateObject("Scripting.FileSystemObject")
objFso.DeleteFile "C:\VBScriptGames\*.txt"
```

In this example, all the files in the C:\VBScriptGames folder with a .txt file extension are deleted.

Creating a New Folder

You can create new folders by using the FileSystemObject object's CreateFolder() method. For example, the following script checks to see whether a folder named VBScriptGames already exists on the computer's C: drive. If it does not exist, the script creates it.

```
Dim objFso, strNewFolder
Set objFso = WScript.CreateObject("Scripting.FileSystemObject")
If (objFso.FolderExists("C:\VBScriptGames") = False) Then
  Set strNewFolder = objFso.CreateFolder("C:\VBScriptGames")
End If
```

Always check to be sure that a folder does not exist before trying to create it. If the folder that you are trying to create already exists, your script will get an error.

Copying Folders

The only differences between copying a folder and a file are that you specify the CopyFolder() method instead of the CopyFile() method and specify a folder name instead of a file name. Of course, not only is the specified folder copied to a new location, but also all its contents are copied as demonstrated in the following example:

```
Dim objFso
Set objFso = WScript.CreateObject("Scripting.FileSystemObject")
objFso.CopyFolder "C:\Temp", "C:\VBScriptGames\Temp"
```

Here, a complete copy of the Temp folder and everything stored in it is replicated inside the C:\VBScriptGames folder.

If you want, you can give the new copy of the specified folder a new name when copying it by simply specifying a new folder name:

```
objFso.CopyFolder "C:\Temp", "C:\VBScriptGames\Temporary"
```

If a folder with the same name already exists in the destination specified by the `CopyFolder()` method, the contents of the source folder are added to the files and folders that are already present. You can tell the `CopyFolder()` method what to do if duplicate file and folder names are found in the destination folder by adding an optional third parameter and setting its value to either `True` or `False`. Specifying a value of `True` causes matching files to be overridden. Specifying a value of `False` prevents matching files from being overridden. For example, the following VBScript statements prevent files with duplicate file names from being overridden:

```
Dim objFso
Set objFso = WScript.CreateObject("Scripting.FileSystemObject")
objFso.CopyFolder "C:\Temp", "C:\VBScriptGames\Temp", "False"
```

This next example allows files with duplicate names to be overridden:

```
Dim objFso
Set objFso = WScript.CreateObject("Scripting.FileSystemObject")
objFso.CopyFolder "C:\Temp", "C:\VBScriptGames\Temp", "True"
```

Moving Folders

You can use the `FileSystemObject` object's `MoveFolder()` method to move folders from one location to another. Of course, when you move a folder, you also move all its contents to the new destination. Take a look at the following example:

```
Dim objFso
Set objFso = WScript.CreateObject("Scripting.FileSystemObject")
objFso.MoveFolder "C:\Temp", "C:\VBScriptGames\Temp"
```

The `Temp` folder and all its contents are copied from the root of the `C:` drive to the `C:\VBScriptGames` folder.

Deleting Folders

You can use the `FileSystemObject` object's `DeleteFolder()` method to delete one or more folders. This method deletes the folder and any subfolders or files stored inside it. To see how it works, look at the following example, which deletes a folder named `Temp` that is located within the `C:\VBScriptGames` folder.

```
Dim objFso
Set objFso = WScript.CreateObject("Scripting.FileSystemObject")
objFso.DeleteFolder "C:\VBScriptGames\Temp"
```

Be extra careful when using the `DeleteFolder()` method. When executed, this method deletes not only the specified folder, but also anything stored within it.

Storing Script Configuration Settings in External Files

Up to this point in the book, all the scripts you've seen have been controlled by configuration settings embedded within the scripts themselves. By *configuration settings*, I mean constants and variables that were set up to store data that was then used to control how the scripts executed. For example, I've controlled the text that the scripts display in pop-up dialogs by assigning a text string to a constant that I've defined at the beginning of each script. To change this display text for a given script, you must open the script and modify it. However, every time you open a script to make even the most simple change, you run the risk of accidentally making a typo that breaks something.

It's often a good idea to remove or externalize script configuration settings. One way of doing this is to store the script configuration settings in external text files that your scripts can then open and retrieve the settings from. This is accomplished using INI (pronounced "eye'n eye") files. *INI* or *initialization* files are plain text files that have an `.ini` file extension. Programmers use INI files to store configuration settings for the operating systems, hardware settings, and software settings.

The nice thing about using INI files is that if you make a mistake when editing them, and as a result your scripts break, it's much easier to find your typo in the INI file than it would be in your script. Also, if you plan on sharing your scripts with other people—especially people without programming backgrounds—once explained, they'll find modifying INI files relatively easy, whereas editing your scripts might overwhelm them.

You also can externalize script configuration settings by storing them in the Windows Registry, which you'll learn how to do in Chapter 10, "Using the Windows Registry to Configure Script Settings."

INI File Structure

INI files have a specific structure that you need to follow when creating them as shown here:

```
;Sample INI file

[Section1]
key1=value1
key2=value2
```

For starters, INI files are organized into sections. Each section's beginning has a section header enclosed within a pair of matching brackets. In the example, `[Section1]` is the only section. Sections are made up of zero or more `key=value` pairs. In the example, there are two `key=value` pairs. You can think of a key as being akin to a variable name and a value as being the data that is assigned to the key.

INI files also can have comments, which begin with the ; character as demonstrated in the previous INI file. INI files also can contain any number of blank lines, which can be added to the INI file to make it easier to read.

INI files are processed in a top-down order. They can have any number of sections and these sections can contain any number of `key=value` pairs. INI files are typically named after the script or program that is associated with them. For example, if you create an INI file to be used by a VBScript named `INIDemo.vbs`, you would probably name its INI file `INIDemo.ini`.

A Working Example

To better understand how to work with INI files, let's look at an example. This example consists of a script named `INIDemo.vbs` that is designed to retrieve configuration settings from an INI file named `INIDemo.ini`. The format of the INI file is shown in Figure 8.10.

The VBScript statements that make up the INIDemo.vbs script are shown here. The script is relatively short, but it is a little involved, so I embedded a lot of comments to help explain what the script is doing.

```
Set objFso = CreateObject("Scripting.FileSystemObject")

strIniFile = "C:\VBScriptGames\INIDemo.ini" 'Specify .ini file location

If (objFso.FileExists(strIniFile)) Then 'Make sure .ini file exists
```

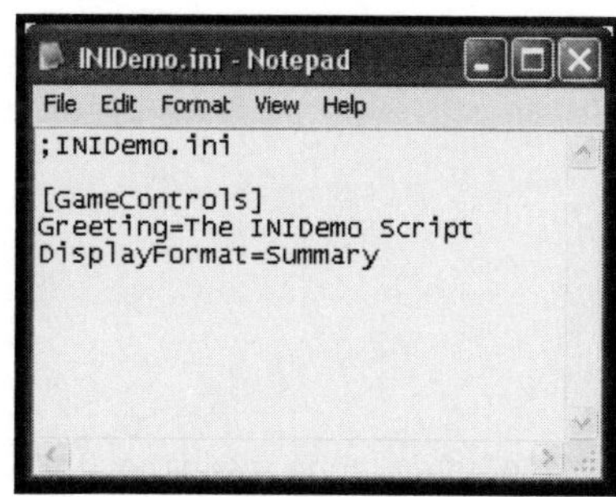
```
;INIDemo.ini

[GameControls]
Greeting=The INIDemo Script
DisplayFormat=Summary
```

FIGURE 8.10 The INI file used by the `INIDemo.vbs` script contains a single section made up of two `key=value` pairs.

```
'Open for reading
Set objOpenFile = objFso.OpenTextFile(strIniFile, 1)

Do Until Mid(strInput, 1, 14) = "[GameControls]" 'Find right section
  strInput = objOpenFile.ReadLine  'Read line from the .ini file
Loop

'Read until end of the file
Do Until objOpenFile.AtEndOfStream = "True"

  strInput = objOpenFile.ReadLine  'Read a line from the file

  If Mid(strInput, 1, 1) = "[" Then
    Exit do   'A new section has been found
  End If

  If Len(strInput) <> 0 Then  'If not a blank line

    intFindEquals = Instr(strInput, "=") 'Locate the equals character

    strKeyName = Mid(strInput, 1, intFindEquals - 1) 'set key value

    Select Case strKeyName  'Match up key value to scripts settings
      Case "Greeting"
        strGreetingMsg = _
          Mid(strInput, intFindEquals + 1, Len(strInput))
      Case "DisplayFormat"
        strDisplayType = _
```

```
            Mid(strInput, intFindEquals + 1, Len(strInput))
        End Select

      End If

    Loop

    objOpenFile.Close()  ' close the .ini file when done reading it

End If

'Display the configuration setting retrieved from the .ini file
MsgBox "Configuration setting: strGreetingMsg = " & strGreetingMsg & _
  vbCrLf & vbCrLf & "Configuration setting: strDisplayType = " & _
  strDisplayType
```

The script begins by instantiating an instance of the `FileSystemObject`. Next, a variable named `strIniFile` is used to store the script's INI file location. The `FileSystemObject` object's `FileExists()` method is used to verify that the INI file exists. The `FileSystemObject` object's `OpenTextFile()` method is then used to open the INI file in `ForReading` mode.

A `Do Until` loop executes until the `[GameControls]` section is located. This is accomplished using the built-in VBScript `Mid()` function. After the section is found, a second `Do Until` loop executes and runs until the end of the file is reached (until `objOpenFile.AtEndOfStream = "True"`). However, if a new section is found while the rest of the INI file is being read, the `Do Until` loop is terminated using an `Exit Do` statement. Next, the VBScript `Len()` function is used to determine whether the current line is blank or not. If it's not blank, then the `key` portion of the `key=value` pair is processed by first locating the equals sign and then assigning all text before the equals sign to a variable named `strKeyName`.

The trick to extracting script configuration setting from `key=value` pairs in INI files is the script's use of the built-in VBScript `MID()` function. This function retrieves or parses out a specified number of characters from a string. The `MID()` function has the following syntax:

```
Mid(string, StartPosition[, Length])
```

`String` represents the string that the `MID()` function is to parse. `StartPosition` identifies the character position within the specified string where the parsing operation should begin. `Length` is optional. When identified, `Length` specifies the number of characters to be returned. If omitted, then all characters from the start position to the end of the string are returned.

After a `key` has been processed, a `Select Case` statement is set up to inspect the value associated with the `key` to determine what it is equal to. After the `[GameControls]` has been processed, the `Do Until` loop terminates and the script displays the configuration settings that were extracted from the INI file as shown in Figure 8.11.

FIGURE 8.11

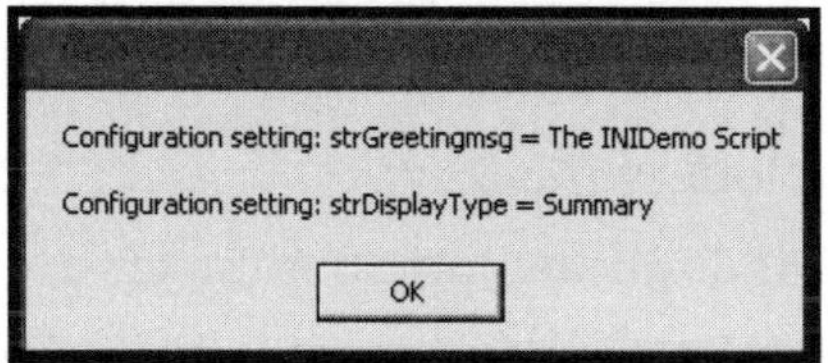

The output displayed by the `INIDemo.vbs` script demonstrates how to extract configuration settings from INI files.

Of course, a script that only displays the configuration settings that it extracts from its INI file isn't really that useful; however, it does provide a working example of how to process INI files. You'll get the chance to modify this example by adapting its logic to work with the Lucky Lottery Number Picker.

BACK TO THE LUCKY LOTTERY NUMBER PICKER

The heart of the Lucky Lottery Number Picker game resides in the script's main processing section, which contains a collection of functions calls and two loops that control the generation of as many sets of lottery numbers as the player asked for. Script configuration settings are stored in an external INI file, which is retrieved by the script at execution. The configuration settings are used to specify the following:

- How many lottery numbers are required to complete a full set
- The message text to be displayed in the title bar or the pop-up dialogs displayed by the script
- The range of numbers from which lottery numbers are to be selected
- Whether to display the results generated by the script in full or summary format

Designing the Game

In total, the script will consist of 10 functions, each of which is designed to perform a specific task. The names of these 10 functions and the tasks they perform are

- **`SetVariableDefaults()`**. Establishes default values for a number of script variables.
- **`ProcessScriptIniFile()`**. Retrieves configuration settings from the script's external INI file.
- **`CollectPlayerInput()`**. Prompts the player to specify the number of lottery numbers to be generated.
- **`GetRandomNumber()`**. Generates random lottery numbers.
- **`ProcessRandomNumber()`**. Makes sure that duplicate lottery numbers are not generated.
- **`DetermineIfSetIsComplete()`**. Determines when a full set of lottery numbers has been generated.
- **`BuildDisplayString()`**. Assembles the display string that will be used to show the player the lottery numbers generated by the script.
- **`ResetVariableDefaults()`**. Resets default variables to prepare the script for the generation of additional sets of lottery numbers.
- **`DisplayFinalResults()`**. Displays the lottery numbers generated by the script.
- **`DisplaySplashScreen()`**. Displays information about the script and its author.

Designing the Script's .ini File

The first step in creating the Lucky Lottery Number Picker game is to create the game's INI file, which will be named `LuckyLotteryNumberPicker.ini`. The complete text of this INI file is shown here:

```
;LuckyLotteryNumberPicker.ini file

[GameControls]
Greeting=Lucky Lottery Number Picker
DisplayFormat=Full
NoOfPicks=6
RangeOfNumbers=50
```

The INI file consists of a single section named `[GameControls]`. A total of four `key=value` pairs have been defined.

Setting Up the Initialization Section

As with all the scripts in this book, development begins with the script's Initialization Section as shown here:

```
'*************************************************************************
'Script Name: LuckyLotteryNumberPicker.vbs
'Author: Jerry Ford
'Created: 11/08/04
'Description: This script randomly picks lottery numbers
'*************************************************************************

'Initialization Section

Option Explicit

Dim aintLotteryArray(10)   'Stores randomly generated lottery numbers

Dim blnAllNumbersPicked    'Determines when a set of #s has been created
Dim blnInputValidated      'Set to True when the player enters a valid number

Dim intNumberCount         'Tracks the number of picks for a given play
Dim intNoOfValidPicks      'Tracks the # of valid selections for a given set
Dim intNoOfPlays           'Determines the # of sets of lottery #s to create
Dim intSetCount            'Used to track how many sets have been generated
Dim intRandomNo            'Used to store randomly generated lottery #s
Dim intNoOfPicksToSelect   'Specifies how many #s to generate for each set
Dim intRangeOfNumbers      'Specifies range to use when generating random #s

Dim strLotteryList         'Displays a string showing 1 set of lottery #s
Dim strDisplayString       'Used to display the list of selected lottery #s
Dim strDisplayType         'Specifies whether to show full or summary data
Dim strTitleBarMsg         'Specifies title bar message in pop-up dialogs
```

Because the script uses an array and a large number of variables, I chose to define them individually and to document each variable's purpose by adding a comment just to the right of each variable.

Developing the Logic for the Main Processing Section

The script's main processing section controls the overall execution of the script. It consists of 10 function calls and two loops:

```
SetVariableDefaults()

ProcessScriptIniFile()

CollectPlayerInput()

For intSetCount = 1 to intNoOfPlays

  Do Until blnAllNumbersPicked = "True"

    GetRandomNumber()

    ProcessRandomNumber()

    DetermineIfSetIsComplete()

  Loop

  BuildDisplayString()

  ResetVariableDefaults()

Next

DisplayFinalResults()

DisplaySplashScreen()
```

The first loop is controlled by a `For` statement that is responsible for making sure that the script generates the number of sets of lottery numbers specified by the player. The second loop is controlled by a `Do Until` and is responsible for making sure that a full count of numbers is generated for each set (or play).

Building the SetVariableDefaults() Function

The `SetVariableDefaults()` function, shown here, is responsible for establishing default values for a number of variables used by the script. The first two variables are `Boolean` and are used to determine when a full set of lottery numbers has been generated and when the player has specified a valid number of plays. The second pair of variables is used to store integer data. The first variable is used to keep track of the number of lottery numbers generated for each play. The second variable is used to track the number of sets of lottery numbers as the script is generating them.

```
Function SetVariableDefaults()

  blnAllNumbersPicked = "False"
  blnInputValidated = "False"

  intNumberCount = 0
  intNoOfValidPicks = 0

End Function
```

Building the ProcessScriptIniFile() Function

The `ProcessScriptIniFile()` function, shown here, is responsible for reading in script configuration settings from the game's INI file. Because of the unique task assigned to this function, I chose to make it completely self contained. Therefore, it begins by defining its own objects and variables. To make the purpose of each variable clear, I documented each one by adding comments to the right of each variable when defined as well as to key statements throughout the function.

```
Function ProcessScriptIniFile()

  Dim FsoObject        'Sets up a reference to the FileSystemObject
  Dim OpenFile         'Sets up a reference to the script's INI file

  Set FsoObject = WScript.CreateObject("Scripting.FileSystemObject")

  Dim intEquals        'Used to parse INI file data

  Dim strKeyName       'Represents a key in the script's INI file
  Dim strSourceFile    'Specifies the name of the script's INI file
  Dim strInput         'Represents a line in the script's INI file
```

```
strSourceFile = "LuckyLotteryMachine.ini"  'Identify script's INI file

If (FsoObject.FileExists(strSourceFile)) Then 'Make sure INI file exists

  'Open for reading
  Set OpenFile = FsoObject.OpenTextFile(strSourceFile, 1)

    Do Until Mid(strInput, 1, 15) = "[GameControls]" 'Find right section
      strInput = OpenFile.ReadLine  'Read line from the INI file
    Loop

    'Read until end of file reached
    Do Until OpenFile.AtEndOfStream = "True"


      strInput = OpenFile.ReadLine  'Read a line from the file

      If Mid(strInput, 1, 1) = "[" Then
        Exit do  'If executed, new sections have been found
      End If

      If Len(strInput) <> 0 Then  'Executes if a blank line is not found

        intEquals = Instr(strInput, "=") 'Locate the equals character

        strKeyName = Mid(strInput, 1, intEquals - 1) 'Set key value

        Select Case strKeyName  'Match up key value to script settings
          Case "Greeting"
            strTitleBarMsg = Mid(strInput, intEquals + 1, Len(strInput))
          Case "DisplayFormat"
            strDisplayType = Mid(strInput, intEquals + 1, Len(strInput))
          Case "NoOfPicks"
            intNoOfPicksToSelect = Cint(Mid(strInput, intEquals + 1, _
            Len(strInput)))
          Case "RangeOfNumbers"
            intRangeOfNumbers = Cint(Mid(strInput, intEquals + 1, _
            Len(strInput)))
```

```
          End Select

        End If

      Loop

    OpenFile.Close()'Close the INI file when done reading it

  Else

    MsgBox "The INI file is missing. Unable to execute."
    WScript.Quit()

  End If

End Function
```

The function begins by instantiating an instance of the `FileSystemObject`. It then specifies the location of its INI file. Next, it checks to make sure that the INI file exists and then opens it. The function then reads the INI file until it finds the `[GameControls]` section. Once found, the function begins reading the rest of the INI file. The function then parses through the `key=value` pairs and assigns values to matching script variables using a `Select Case` statement.

Building the CollectPlayerInput() Function

The `CollectPlayerInput()` function is responsible for collecting and validating player input. The overall execution of this function is controlled by the following `Do While` loop, which executes as long as a `Boolean` variable named `blnInputValidated` is not equal to `True`:

```
Function CollectPlayerInput()

  Do Until blnInputValidated = "True"

    intNoOfPlays = InputBox("How many sets of numbers do " & _
      "you want?", strTitleBarMsg)

    If IsNumeric(intNoOfPlays) <> True Then
      MsgBox "Sorry. You must enter a numeric value. Please " & _
      "try again.", ,strTitleBarMsg
    Else
```

```
      If Len(intNoOfPlays) = 0 Then
        MsgBox "Sorry. You must enter a numeric value. Please " & _
        "try again.", ,strTitleBarMsg
      Else
        If intNoOfPlays = 0 then
          MsgBox "Sorry. Zero is not a valid selection. Please " & _
          "try again.", ,strTitleBarMsg
        Else
          blnInputValidated = "True"
        End If
      End If
    End If

  Loop

End Function
```

Three validation tests are performed. The first test uses the VBScript `IsNumeric()` function to ensure that the input is numeric. The second test uses the `Len()` function to ensure that the player actually typed in input, as opposed to simply clicking on OK or Cancel. The last validation test checks to make sure that the player did not enter a value of zero. If the input provided by the player passes all three of these tests, then a value of `True` is assigned to `blnInputValidated` and the function finishes executing.

Building the GetRandomNumber() Function

The `GetRandomNumber()` function, shown here, is responsible for retrieving random numbers for the script. It begins with the `Randomize` statement to ensure that numbers are randomly generated. Next, a random number is generated. The range from which the number is created is dictated by the value assigned to `intRangeOfNumber`, which was previously established by retrieving its value from the script's INI file.

```
Function GetRandomNumber()

  Randomize

  intRandomNo = cInt(FormatNumber(Int((intRangeOfNumbers * Rnd) + 1)))

End Function
```

Building the ProcessRandomNumber() Function

The `ProcessRandomNumber()` function, shown here, is responsible for ensuring that the same lottery number is not picked twice for a given play or set. It accomplishes this by establishing an array named `aintLotteryArray`. The array is configured to handle up to 11 entries, based on the assumption that this is large enough to handle any amount of lottery numbers a given lottery game might require.

```
Function ProcessRandomNumber()

  Select Case intRandomNo
    Case aintLotteryArray(0)
    Case aintLotteryArray(1)
    Case aintLotteryArray(2)
    Case aintLotteryArray(3)
    Case aintLotteryArray(4)
    Case aintLotteryArray(5)
    Case aintLotteryArray(6)
    Case aintLotteryArray(7)
    Case aintLotteryArray(8)
    Case aintLotteryArray(9)
    Case aintLotteryArray(10)
    Case Else
      strLotteryList = strLotteryList & "   " & intRandomNo & vbTab
      intNoOfValidPicks = intNoOfValidPicks + 1
      aintLotteryArray(intNumberCount) = intRandomNo
      intNumberCount = intNumberCount + 1
  End Select

End Function
```

This function begins by comparing the value of the last lottery number that was generated to the numbers stored in the array. The first time through, there won't be any lottery numbers stored in the array yet. As a result, the lottery number is stored as the first entry in the array. Also, the lottery number is added to a string that is stored in a variable named `strLotteryList`, which is used elsewhere in the script. Finally, the total number of valid lottery numbers is tracked by adding `1` to `intNoOfValidPicks` each time a unique lottery number is generated.

Each time this function is called, it checks to see whether the most recently generated random number matches any of the numbers already stored in the array. If it does, nothing happens; otherwise, that number is added to the array.

Building the DetermineIfSetIsComplete() Function

The DetermineIfSetIsComplete() function, shown here, compares the value stored in intNoOfValidPicks to the value stored in intNoOfPicksToSelect to determine whether a complete set of lottery numbers has been generated. If a complete set has been generated, then DetermineIfSetIsComplete() sets the value assigned to blnAllNumbersPicked equal to True. Otherwise, the value assigned to this variable remains set equal to False.

```
Function DetermineIfSetIsComplete

  If intNoOfValidPicks = intNoOfPicksToSelect Then
    blnAllNumbersPicked = "True"
  End If

End Function
```

Building the BuildDisplayString() Function

The BuildDisplayString() function, shown here, takes the string stored in the strLotteryList variable (which is created by the ProcessRandomNumber() function) and uses it to build a larger string made up of all the sets of lottery numbers generated by the game. This string is later used to display the game's result to the player. To make the displayed output more attractive, this function uses the vbTab constant to organize output into a multi-column format.

```
Function BuildDisplayString()

  strLotteryList = intSetCount & ")" & vbTab & strLotteryList

  strDisplayString = strDisplayString & strLotteryList & _
    vbCrLf & vbCrLf & vbCrLf

End Function
```

Building the ResetVariableDefaults() Function

The ResetVariableDefaults() function, shown here, is used to reset variable values back to their initial default settings after a full set of lottery numbers has been generated. This readies the script to begin generating additional sets of numbers.

```
Function ResetVariableDefaults()

  blnAllNumbersPicked = "False"
  intNoOfValidPicks = 0
  intNumberCount = 0
  strLotteryList = ""

End Function
```

Building the DisplayFinalResults() Function

The `DisplayFinalResults()` function, shown here, is responsible for displaying all the sets of lottery numbers that are generated. It displays this information in one of two formats based on the value assigned to `strDisplayType`, which is a variable whose value was set earlier in the script by retrieving its value from the script's INI file. If `strDisplayType` is equal to `Full`, then the function displays information regarding the number of lottery numbers that was generated per set as well as the total number of sets that were created, followed by the numbers that made up each set. However, if the value assigned to `strDisplayType` is equal to anything other than `Full`, then only the sets of lottery numbers are displayed.

```
Function DisplayFinalResults()

  If strDisplayType = "Full" Then

    MsgBox vbCrLf & _
      "L U C K Y   L O T T E R Y   N U M B E R   P I C K E R" & _
      vbCrLf & vbCrLf & _
      "-----------------------------" & _
      "---------------" & vbCrLf & vbCrLf & _
      "Number of plays: " & intNoOfPlays & vbCrLf &vbCrLf & _
      "Number of picks per play: " & intNoOfPicksToSelect & _
      vbCrLf & vbCrLf & _
      "-----------------------------" & _
      "---------------" & vbCrLf & vbCrLf & vbCrLf & _
      "Your lottery numbers are: " & vbCrLf & vbCrLf & vbCrLf & _
      strDisplayString, , strTitleBarMsg

  Else
```

```
    MsgBox vbCrLf & _
      "L U C K Y   L O T T E R Y   N U M B E R   P I C K E R" & _
      vbCrLf & vbCrLf & _
      "------------------------------" & _
      "----------------" & vbCrLf & vbCrLf & _
      "Your lottery numbers are: " & vbCrLf & vbCrLf & vbCrLf & _
      strDisplayString, , strTitleBarMsg

  End If

End Function
```

Building the DisplaySplashScreen() Function

This last function in the script displays the game's splash screen, providing information about the game and its creator as well as an invitation for the player to return and play again another time.

```
Function DisplaySplashScreen()

  MsgBox "Thank you for using the Lucky Lottery Number Picker " & _
    "© Jerry Ford 2004." & vbCrLf & vbCrLf & "Please play again " & _
    "soon!", 4144, strTitleBarMsg

  WScript.Quit()

End Function
```

The last statement in the function terminates the script's execution using the `WScript` `Quit()` method.

The Final Result

That's it. You're all done. Your fully assembled script should look like this:

```
'*************************************************************************
'Script Name: LuckyLotteryNumberPicker.vbs
'Author: Jerry Ford
'Created: 11/08/04
'Description: This script randomly picks lottery numbers.
'*************************************************************************
```

```
'Initialization Section

Option Explicit

Dim aintLotteryArray(10)   'Stores randomly generated lottery numbers

Dim blnAllNumbersPicked    'Determines when a set of #s has been created
Dim blnInputValidated      'Set to True when the player enters a valid number

Dim intNumberCount         'Tracks the number of picks for a given play
Dim intNoOfValidPicks      'Tracks the # of valid selections for a given set
Dim intNoOfPlays           'Determines the # of sets of lottery #s to create
Dim intSetCount            'Used to track how many sets have been generated
Dim intRandomNo            'Used to store randomly generated lottery #s
Dim intNoOfPicksToSelect   'Specifies how many #s to generate for each set
Dim intRangeOfNumbers      'Specifies range to use when generating random #s

Dim strLotteryList         'Displays a string showing 1 set of lottery #s
Dim strDisplayString       'Used to display the list of selected lottery #s
Dim strDisplayType         'Specifies whether to show full or summary data
Dim strTitleBarMsg         'Specifies title bar message in pop-up dialogs


'Main Processing Section -------------------------


SetVariableDefaults()

ProcessScriptIniFile()

CollectPlayerInput()

For intSetCount = 1 to intNoOfPlays

  Do Until blnAllNumbersPicked = "True"

    GetRandomNumber()
```

```
    ProcessRandomNumber()

    DetermineIfSetIsComplete()

  Loop

  BuildDisplayString()

  ResetVariableDefaults()

Next

DisplayFinalResults()

DisplaySplashScreen()


'Procedure Section -----------------------------


Function SetVariableDefaults()   'Establish default variable settings

  blnAllNumbersPicked = "False"
  blnInputValidated = "False"

  intNumberCount = 0
  intNoOfValidPicks = 0

End Function


Function ProcessScriptIniFile()

  Dim FsoObject           'Sets up a reference to the FileSystemObject
  Dim OpenFile            'Sets up a reference to the script's .ini file

  Set FsoObject = WScript.CreateObject("Scripting.FileSystemObject")

  Dim intEquals           'Used to parse .ini file data
```

```
Dim strKeyName          'Represents a key in the script's .ini file
Dim strSourceFile       'Specifies the name of the script's .ini file
Dim strInput            'Represents a line in the script's .ini file

strSourceFile = "LuckyLotteryNumberPicker.ini"  'Identify script's .ini file

If (FsoObject.FileExists(strSourceFile)) Then

  Set OpenFile = FsoObject.OpenTextFile(strSourceFile, 1)

    Do Until Mid(strInput, 1, 15) = "[GameControls]"
      strInput = OpenFile.ReadLine
    Loop

    Do Until OpenFile.AtEndOfStream = "True"
      strInput = OpenFile.ReadLine

      If Mid(strInput, 1, 1) = "[" Then
        Exit do
      End If

      If Len(strInput) <> 0 Then

        intEquals = Instr(strInput, "=")

        strKeyName = Mid(strInput, 1, intEquals - 1)

        Select Case strKeyName
          Case "Greeting"
            strTitleBarMsg = Mid(strInput, intEquals + 1, Len(strInput))
          Case "DisplayFormat"
            strDisplayType = Mid(strInput, intEquals + 1, Len(strInput))
          Case "NoOfPicks"
            intNoOfPicksToSelect = Cint(Mid(strInput, intEquals + 1, _
            Len(strInput)))
          Case "RangeOfNumbers"
            intRangeOfNumbers = Cint(Mid(strInput, intEquals + 1, _
            Len(strInput)))
```

```
          End Select

        End If

      Loop

    OpenFile.Close()

  Else

    MsgBox "The .ini file is missing. Unable to execute."
    WScript.Quit()

  End If

End Function


Function CollectPlayerInput()   'Ask player how many sets of #s to create

  Do Until blnInputValidated = "True"

    intNoOfPlays = InputBox("How many sets of numbers do " & _
      "you want?", strTitleBarMsg)

    If IsNumeric(intNoOfPlays) <> True Then
      MsgBox "Sorry. You must enter a numeric value. Please " & _
      "try again.", ,strTitleBarMsg
    Else
      If Len(intNoOfPlays) = 0 Then
        MsgBox "Sorry. You must enter a numeric value. Please " & _
        "try again.", ,strTitleBarMsg
      Else
        If intNoOfPlays = 0 then
          MsgBox "Sorry. Zero is not a valid selection. Please " & _
          "try again.", ,strTitleBarMsg
        Else
          blnInputValidated = "True"
        End If
```

```
      End If
    End If

  Loop

End Function


Function GetRandomNumber()   'Generate a random number

  Randomize

  intRandomNo = cInt(FormatNumber(Int((intRangeOfNumbers * Rnd) + 1)))

End Function


Function ProcessRandomNumber()   'Prevent the selection of duplicate #

  Select Case intRandomNo
    Case aintLotteryArray(0)
    Case aintLotteryArray(1)
    Case aintLotteryArray(2)
    Case aintLotteryArray(3)
    Case aintLotteryArray(4)
    Case aintLotteryArray(5)
    Case aintLotteryArray(6)
    Case aintLotteryArray(7)
    Case aintLotteryArray(8)
    Case aintLotteryArray(9)
    Case aintLotteryArray(10)
    Case Else
      strLotteryList = strLotteryList & "  " & intRandomNo & vbTab
      intNoOfValidPicks = intNoOfValidPicks + 1
      aintLotteryArray(intNumberCount) = intRandomNo
      intNumberCount = intNumberCount + 1
  End Select
```

```
End Function


Function DetermineIfSetIsComplete   'Determine if we have a full set of #s

  If intNoOfValidPicks = intNoOfPicksToSelect Then
    blnAllNumbersPicked = "True"
  End If

End Function


Function BuildDisplayString()       'Assemble a string to display lottery #s

  strLotteryList = intSetCount & ")" & vbTab & strLotteryList

  strDisplayString = strDisplayString & strLotteryList & _
    vbCrLf & vbCrLf & vbCrLf

End Function


Function ResetVariableDefaults()    'Reset variables in order to prepare
                                    'for the selection of the next set of #s

  blnAllNumbersPicked = "False"
  intNoOfValidPicks = 0
  intNumberCount = 0
  strLotteryList = ""

End Function


Function DisplayFinalResults()      'Display game's randomly generated #s

  If strDisplayType = "Full" Then

    MsgBox vbCrLf & _
      "L U C K Y   L O T T E R Y   N U M B E R   P I C K E R" & _
```

```
      vbCrLf & vbCrLf & _
      "------------------------------" & _
      "----------------" & vbCrLf & vbCrLf & _
      "Number of plays: " & intNoOfPlays & vbCrLf &vbCrLf & _
      "Number of picks per play: " & intNoOfPicksToSelect & _
      vbCrLf & vbCrLf & _
      "------------------------------" & _
      "----------------" & vbCrLf & vbCrLf & vbCrLf & _
      "Your lottery numbers are: " & vbCrLf & vbCrLf & vbCrLf & _
      strDisplayString, , strTitleBarMsg

  Else

    MsgBox vbCrLf & _
      "L U C K Y   L O T T E R Y   N U M B E R   P I C K E R" & _
      vbCrLf & vbCrLf & _
      "------------------------------" & _
      "----------------" & vbCrLf & vbCrLf & _
      "Your lottery numbers are: " & vbCrLf & vbCrLf & vbCrLf & _
      strDisplayString, , strTitleBarMsg

  End If

End Function


Function DisplaySplashScreen()   'Display splash screen and terminate game

  MsgBox "Thank you for using the Lucky Lottery Number Picker " & _
    "© Jerry Ford 2004." & vbCrLf & vbCrLf & "Please play again " & _
    "soon!", 4144, strTitleBarMsg

  WScript.Quit()

End Function
```

Okay. Why don't you crank it up and see how it works. After you've cleaned out any errors that you might have made when typing, you'll have a pretty cool script.

Summary

In this chapter, you learned how to create and store data in text files. You also learned how to open text files and read or process their contents as input. You also learned how to use properties and methods belonging to the WSH `FileSystemObject` to perform assorted file administration tasks, including copying, moving, and deleting individual and groups of files and folders.

You now understand the fundamentals of working with files and folders and know everything you need to begin developing scripts that can create reports and log files. On top of all this, you also can now develop and leverage the power of INI files as a repository for externalizing script configuration settings.

Challenges

1. **As it is currently written, the Lucky Lottery Number Picker game attempts to display as many sets of lottery numbers as it is asked for. However, depending on the screen resolution, only so many sets of numbers can be displayed at one time. The result is that when too many sets of numbers are specified, some won't be visible to the player. To remedy this, modify the script so that it will only display 10 sets of numbers at a time using as many pop-up dialogs as required to display all the script's output.**
2. **Provide the player with the capability to save the lottery numbers generated by the game to a text file. This allows players to print their numbers and take the list with them when they go to purchase their lottery tickets.**
3. **The Lucky Lottery Number Picker game is set up so that it always displays a closing splash screen before ending. Modify the script and its associated INI file so that the player can enable or disable the display of the splash screen.**
4. **As it is currently written, the Lucky Lottery Number Picker game prevents the player from entering nonnumeric input such as letters and special characters. It also forces the player to enter something (the player can't just click on OK or Cancel). However, there is no logic in the script to prevent negative numbers from being accepted. As unlikely as it may be for the player to enter a negative number, it's a good idea to modify the script to prevent them from being accepted anyway.**

HANDLING SCRIPT ERRORS

Every programmer, no matter how good he or she may be, runs into errors when writing and testing scripts and programs. Like any other programming language, VBScript is subject to many types of errors. Errors may be inevitable, but you can minimize their number or lessen their effects. In this chapter, I'll demonstrate a number of scripting errors and show you how to deal with them. Specifically, you will learn how to

- Fix errors by reading and analyzing error messages
- Write VBScripts that can ignore errors and keep going
- Create error-handling routines to recover from many error situations
- Generate test errors in order to validate the performance of your error-handling routines
- Keep a record of errors using log files and the Windows application event log

PROJECT PREVIEW: THE HANGMAN GAME

This chapter's programming project is the creation of a VBScript version of the classic children's game Hangman. Developing this game will require you to use all the VBScript knowledge that you've accumulated so far, including applying advanced conditional logic, organizing critical processes into procedures, and validating player input to prevent errors from prematurely terminating the game.

The Hangman game begins by presenting the player with a number of blank spaces representing the letters of the game's mystery word. The player is then allowed to begin guessing the letters that make up the word. If the player guesses the word before making six incorrect guesses, he or she wins. Otherwise, the game ends by displaying the mystery word, and the player is asked if he or she would like to play again. Unfortunately, because of the display limitations of the WSH, you won't be able to actually animate a hanging in the event that the player loses. Still, by creating a well-formatted output, the player will probably never even notice.

Figures 9.1 through 9.5 demonstrate the overall flow of the game from beginning to end.

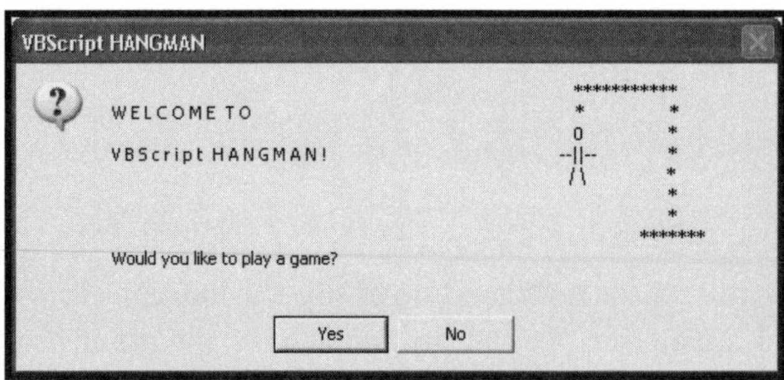

FIGURE 9.1

The Hangman game begins with a graphical welcome message and an invitation to play.

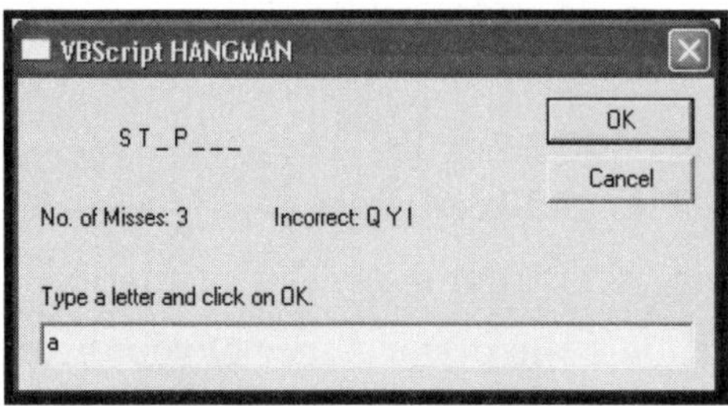

FIGURE 9.2

The game displays both the letters that the player has correctly guessed and the letters the player has incorrectly guessed.

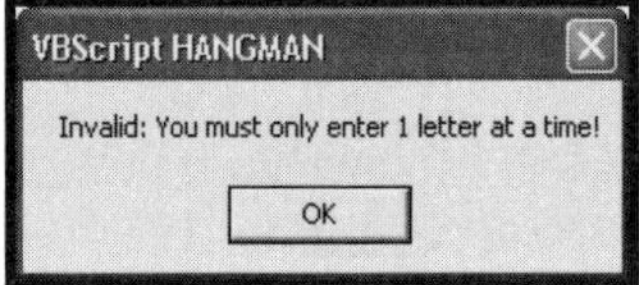

FIGURE 9.3

A number of possible messages may be displayed if the player does not play the game correctly.

FIGURE 9.4

Each game ends by displaying the hidden word, the results of the game, and an invitation to play again.

FIGURE 9.5

A splash screen is displayed when the player decides to stop playing.

UNDERSTANDING VBSCRIPT ERRORS

Errors can appear, even in small scripts, for many reasons. Errors may be generated when a script is first loaded or interpreted. Errors occurring at this stage are referred to as *syntax errors*. Syntax errors are often the result of typos. For example, you might accidentally type a single quote when you meant to type a closing double quote. Syntax errors also occur when you inadvertently mistype a VBScript keyword. Because syntax errors are discovered during the initial loading of a script, they are usually easily caught and corrected during script development.

> **DEFINITION**
>
> A *syntax* error is an error that occurs as a result of improperly formatted statements within scripts.

Errors can also be generated during script execution. These types of errors are referred to as *run-time errors*. Run-time errors only appear when the statements that generate them are executed. As a result, some run-time errors might not be detected when the script executes (if the statement containing the error is not executed). For example, a run-time error might be hidden deep within a function or subroutine that is seldom called.

> **DEFINITION**
>
> A *run-time* error is an error that occurs when a script tries to perform an illegal action, such as multiplying a numeric and a character value.

With proper testing of all the components of a script, most run-time errors can be discovered and fixed during script development. I say "most" because not all run-time errors can be caught—those caused by unforeseen circumstances may be impossible to detect during script development. Perhaps the person running the script incorrectly supplied input in a manner that you could not have anticipated, or perhaps something is wrong with the environment in which the script is being executed. Or maybe the hard disk has become full, preventing your VBScript from writing to a file, or the network goes down as your script is executing a file copy or move operation. In cases such as these, often the best you can do is to end the script gracefully, without confusing the user or making the situation worse.

Another category of error to which scripts are susceptible is logical errors. Logical errors are mistakes made by the script developer. For example, instead of looping 10 times, you might accidentally set up an endless loop. Another example of a logical error is a situation in which a script adds two numbers that should have been multiplied.

DEFINITION

A *logical* error is an error produced as a result of a programming mistake on the part of the script developer.

Understanding Error Messages

VBScript error messages are generated for both syntax and run-time errors. These errors are displayed in the form of pop-up dialogs, as demonstrated in Figure 9.6. Each error message displays information about the error, including a brief description of the error, an error number, and the source of the error.

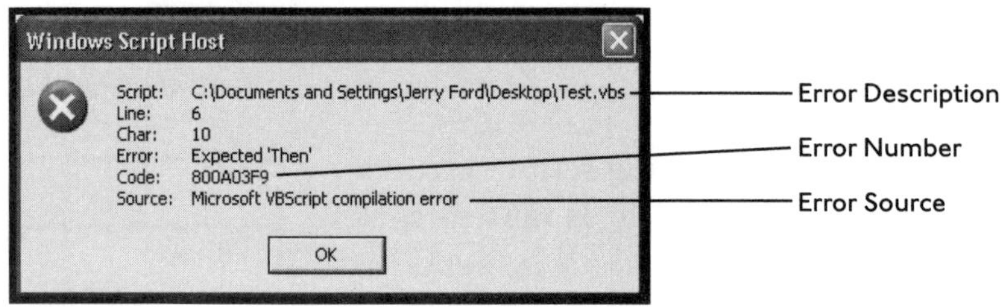

FIGURE 9.6

A typical VBScript error message.

TRICK

Each VBScript syntax and run-time error is assigned an error number. Depending on the execution host, this number may be displayed either as a decimal number or a hexadecimal number. Error messages produced by VBScripts are displayed with a hexadecimal number. Microsoft's VBScript error message documentation, which you will find at http://msdn.microsoft.com/scripting, only lists VBScript's error messages by their decimal numbers.

You can translate between a VBScript error's hexadecimal and decimal number. First, drop the 800A portion of the message. Open the Windows Calculator application in scientific mode, select the hexadecimal setting, and type the last four digits of the hexadecimal number. Select the decimal setting, and the calculator will show the decimal equivalent. In Figure 8.6, 800A03F9 is the hexadecimal equivalent to the decimal number 1017. If this seems like too much work, just refer to Tables 9.1 and 9.2, which list VBScript syntax and run-time errors, and you'll see that I've already done the math for you.

The error message displayed in Figure 8.6 is the result of a syntax error. As you can see, a lot of useful information about the error is automatically provided. The ability to interpret and understand this information is critical for troubleshooting and fixing your VBScripts.

The following information has been provided in this error message:

- **Script.** The name and location of the VBScript that produced the error.
- **Line.** The line number within the VBScript where the error was detected.
- **Char.** The column number position within the line where the error was detected.
- **Error.** A brief description of the error.
- **Code.** An error number identifying the type of error.
- **Source.** The resource that reported the error.

You can see in Figure 9.6 that a VBScript named `X.VBS` located in `C:\Temp` generated the error. Line 6 of the script that generated this error looks like the following statement:

```
If X > 5 MsgBox "Hello World!"
```

This `If` statement uses the VBScript `MsgBox()` function to display a text string. The error message indicates that the problem is that VBScript expected to find the `Then` keyword and did not. If you look at the middle of this statement, you'll see that, in fact, the `Then` keyword is absent. To correct this error, you would add the missing keyword, like this:

```
If X > 5 Then MsgBox "Hello World!"
```

To verify that the error has been eliminated, you could then save and run the script again.

Fixing Syntax Errors

VBScripts are subject to many different types of syntax errors, which Microsoft documents as part of the VBScript documentation available at http://msdn.microsoft.com/scripting. For your convenience, I've provided this information in Table 9.1. I also listed both the decimal and hexadecimal error number associated with each error.

Table 9.1 VBScript Syntax Errors

Hexadecimal	Decimal	Description
800A03E9	1001	Out of Memory
800A03EA	1002	Syntax error
800A03ED	1005	Expected ' ('
800A03EE	1006	Expected ') '
800A03F2	1010	Expected identifier
800A03F3	1011	Expected '='
800A03F4	1012	Expected 'If'
800A03F5	1013	Expected 'To'
800A03F5	1013	Invalid number
800A03F6	1014	Expected 'End'
800A03F6	1014	Invalid character
800A03F7	1015	Expected 'Function'
800A03F7	1015	Unterminated string constant
800A03F8	1016	Expected 'Sub'
800A03F9	1017	Expected 'Then'
800A03FA	1018	Expected 'Wend'
800A03FB	1019	Expected 'Loop'
800A03FC	1020	Expected 'Next'
800A03FD	1021	Expected 'Case'
800A03FE	1022	Expected 'Select'
800A03FF	1023	Expected expression
800A0400	1024	Expected statement
800A0401	1025	Expected end of statement
800A0402	1026	Expected integer constant
800A0403	1027	Expected 'While' or 'Until'
800A0404	1028	Expected 'While', 'Until', or end of statement
800A0405	1029	Expected 'With'
800A0406	1030	Identifier too long
800A040D	1037	Invalid use of 'Me' keyword

Table 9.1 VBScript Syntax Errors (continued)

Hexadecimal	Decimal	Description
800A040E	1038	'loop' without 'do'
800A040F	1039	Invalid 'exit' statement
800A0410	1040	Invalid 'for' loop control variable
800A0411	1041	Name redefined
800A0412	1042	Must be first statement on the line
800A0414	1044	Cannot use parentheses when calling a Sub
800A0415	1045	Expected literal constant
800A0416	1046	Expected 'In'
800A0417	1047	Expected 'Class'
800A0418	1048	Must be defined inside a class
800A0419	1049	Expected Let or Set or Get in property declaration
800A041A	1050	Expected 'Property'
800A041B	1051	Number of arguments must be consistent across properties specification
800A041C	1052	Cannot have multiple default property/method in a class
800A041D	1053	Class initialize or terminate do not have arguments
800A041E	1054	Property Set or Let must have at least one argument
800A041F	1055	Unexpected Next
800A0421	1057	'Default' specification must also specify 'Public'
800A0422	1058	'Default' specification can only be on Property Get

Catching Run-Time Errors

VBScripts are also subject to a wide range of possible run-time errors. Microsoft documents these errors as part of its VBScript documentation, which is available at http://msdn.microsoft.com/scripting. For your convenience, I've provided this information in Table 9.2. I also listed both the decimal and hexadecimal error numbers for each run-time error.

Table 9.2 VBScript Run-Time Errors

Hexadecimal	Decimal	Description
800A0005	5	Invalid procedure call or argument Overflow Out of Memory
800A0006	6	Overflow
800A0007	7	Out of Memory
800A0009	9	Subscript out of range
800A000A	10	This array is fixed or temporarily locked
800A000B	11	Division by zero
800A000D	13	Type mismatch
800A000E	14	Out of string space
800A0011	17	Can't perform requested operation
800A001C	28	Out of stack space
800A0023	35	Sub or function not defined
800A0030	48	Error in loading DLL
800A0033	51	Internal error
800A005B	91	Object variable not set
800A005C	92	For loop not initialized
800A005E	94	Invalid use of Null
800A01A8	424	Object required
800A01AD	429	ActiveX component can't create object
800A01AE	430	Class doesn't support Automation
800A01B0	432	File name or class name not found during Automation operation
800A01B6	438	Object doesn't support this property or method
800A01BD	445	Object doesn't support this action
800A01BF	447	Object doesn't support current locale setting
800A01C0	448	Named argument not found
800A01C1	449	Argument not optional
800A01C2	450	Wrong number of arguments or invalid property assignment
800A01C3	451	Object not a collection
800A01CA	458	Variable uses an Automation type not supported in VBScript
800A01CE	462	The remote server machine does not exist or is unavailable

TABLE 9.2 VBSCRIPT RUN-TIME ERRORS (CONTINUED)

Hexadecimal	Decimal	Description
800A01E1	481	Invalid picture
800A01F4	500	Variable is undefined
800A01F6	502	Object not safe for scripting
800A01F7	503	Object not safe for initializing
800A01F8	504	Object not safe for creating
800A01F9	505	Invalid or unqualified reference
800A01FA	506	Class not defined
800A01FB	507	An exception occurred
800A1390	5008	Illegal assignment
800A1399	5017	Syntax error in regular expression
800A139A	5018	Unexpected quantifier
800A139B	5019	Expected] in regular expression
800A139C	5020	Expected) in regular expression
800A139D	5021	Invalid range in character set

Preventing Logical Errors

Your VBScripts will do exactly what you tell them to do, even if that's not what you really mean for them to do. Therefore, it's extremely important that you plan your VBScript project carefully. For example, you should begin with a pseudo code outline and then translate that into a flowchart, outlining each of the script's major components. You should, as much as possible, develop the script a component at a time, testing each component as you go. I'll show you some different ways to test individual script components as you develop the Hangman game.

Logical errors often make their presence known by presenting incorrect or unexpected results, and can be the most difficult type of error to track down. Unlike syntax and run-time errors, which display messages that describe the nature of their problems, logical errors force you to look through some or all of your script a line at a time to find the faulty logic. The good news is that with careful planning and design, logical errors can be avoided.

DEALING WITH ERRORS

There are many measures you can take to prevent errors from occurring in your VBScripts. I've already mentioned the need to plan and carefully design and test your scripts. In addition, you can avoid many errors by taking the following advice:

- Provide a simple and easy-to-use interface (such as pop-up dialogs).
- Provide clear instructions, so that the user will understand exactly what is expected of him or her.
- Reuse code from existing scripts whenever possible by cutting and pasting code that has already been thoroughly tested.
- Validate input data as much as possible.
- Explicitly declare all your variables.
- Use a consistent naming scheme for all constants, variables, object references, arrays, functions, and subroutines.
- Be on guard for endless loops.
- Do your best to anticipate and handle specific situations where errors are likely to occur.

Unfortunately, errors will occur. You have three basic ways that you can deal with them as they arise in your VBScripts. One option is to simply let them happen and then deal with the consequences, as problems are uncovered. Another option is to tell VBScript to ignore errors and keep going. Finally, you can attempt to anticipate where errors are most likely to occur and try to handle them in a way that either terminates the script's execution gracefully or allows the script to recover and keep going.

Letting Errors Happen

Errors are going to happen. One way of dealing with them is to simply let them happen and instruct users to report them when they occur, along with as much information as possible about what the user was doing when the error occurred. This way, you can attempt to reproduce the error, figure out what caused it, and then fix it.

Normally I would not recommend this approach. After all, your reputation as a VBScript guru depends on the soundness and reliability of your scripts. However, a cost is associated with every VBScript that you write. You may measure this cost in terms of time, effort, or by some other scale. Each time you sit down to create a new script, you must make a judgment call as to how much time and energy you have available to put into the project. You also need to consider the consequences of an error occurring in the script that you're developing. After all, it is entirely possible to develop a simple script in a matter of minutes and spend another hour or more trying to make it bulletproof, only to find that something has gone wrong anyway.

If you're developing an extremely important script that will have high visibility and for which you will be held accountable if a problem arises, then you'll want to do everything that you can to keep errors from happening. On the other hand, if you have been asked to create a "quick and dirty" script to help someone perform a noncritical task, you might be able to get away with ignoring any errors that occur. All you may need to do is tell the person for whom you wrote the script to give you a call if a problem arises, so that you can make a quick modification to the script to fix it.

Just keep this thought in mind: Most users will have no idea what a typical VBScript error message means or what to do if they receive one. It's important to, at a minimum, provide clear instructions on how to use your VBScripts and what to do if an error does occur.

Ignoring Errors

Another option that you might want to consider when developing your scripts is to tell VBScript to ignore any errors that occur. In some cases, this will work just fine. For example, suppose you wrote a VBScript that was supposed to connect to a number of networked computers and copy over a file located in a certain folder at regular intervals throughout the day. As problems sometimes occur on networks, it may be acceptable to ignore situations in which the script is unable to connect to a particular network drive, especially if you know that the script will run again later and get another chance to copy the missing file. This approach, while effective, should be used with caution. There are few situations in which skipping an error will not result in the generation of another error later in a script. For example, if your script was supposed to perform another operation on each file copied from the network drive, then, depending on how you wrote the script, the part of the script that performs this next step might generate an error.

To tell VBScript to ignore errors within your script, add the following statement, exactly as shown, to the beginning of your script:

```
On Error Resume Next
```

However, certain errors will still be reported, even if you have added this statement to your scripts. The key to using the previous statement is that it must be placed in your script before any statements in which you think an error is likely to occur. You can later cancel the effects of this statement using the following statement:

```
On Error GoTo 0
```

For example, the following statement will produce an error message because the keyword `WScript` is misspelled:

```
WScrip.Echo "Hello world!"
```

Adding `On Error Resume Next` before the statement prevents the error from appearing and allows the rest of the script to continue:

```
On Error Resume Next
WScrip.Echo " Hello world!"
```

Now look at two more statements:

```
On Error Resume Next
WScrip.Echo " Hello world!"
On Error Goto 0
WScrip.Echo "Goodbye world!"
```

The `On Error Goto 0` statement nullifies the effects of the `On Error Resume Next` statements for all statements that follow. Therefore, the first error is ignored, but the second error is reported and the script halts its execution.

Like with variables, VBScript allows you to localize the effects of the `On Error Resume Next` statement to the procedure level. In other words, if this statement is placed within a procedure, then it's only in effect for as long as the procedure executes, and is nullified when the procedure (that is, the function or subroutine) finishes executing. Combining the `On Error Resume Next` statement with procedures enables you to significantly limit the effects of this powerful statement.

Creating Error Handlers

The third option that you have for dealing with errors in your VBScripts is to create error handlers. To effectively use error handlers, you must be able to anticipate locations within your scripts where errors are likely to occur and then develop the appropriate programming logic to deal with or handle these errors.

> **DEFINITION**
>
> An *event handler* is an error-triggered routine that alters the execution environment's default handling of an error condition.

You can handle errors in different ways. For example, you can create error handlers that

- Reword cryptic VBScript errors
- Provide the user with instructions
- Give the user another try

- Apologize for the error
- Ask the user to report the error
- Take a corrective action
- Log the occurrence of the error

To set up an error handler, you need to know how to work with the `Err` object. The `Err` object provides a number of properties and methods that allow your scripts to access error information and clear error conditions. To access information about an error, you need to reference the following three properties:

- **`Number`**. Retrieves the last error number.
- **`Description`**. Retrieves the last error message.
- **`Source`**. Retrieves the name of the object that raised (or caused) the error.

You can also modify the contents of any of these three properties, which allows you to reassign a custom error number and message, and even modify source information. For example, in a particularly complex script, you might want to create and document your own custom set of error messages.

The first step in creating an error handler is to add the `On Error Resume Next` statement to your VBScript. You can then add the error handling statements like this:

```
On Error Resume Next

NonExistentFunction()

If Err > 0 then
  Err.Number = 9999
  Err.Description = "This script is still a work in progress."
  MsgBox "Error: " & Err.Number & " - " & Err.description
  Err.Clear
End if
```

Save these statements as a script and execute them. Because the script does not contain a procedure named `NonExistentFunction()`, an error will be generated. However, instead of displaying a VBScript run-time error message, the error-handling routine creates and displays the error message shown in Figure 9.7.

FIGURE 9.7

A custom error message generated by a VBScript error handler.

The `Err` object also provides two very useful methods. One of these methods is the `Clear()` method. This method clears out or removes the previous error, ensuring that the next time a script checks for an error, it will not get a false status (that is, it won't see an already handled error).

To use the `Clear()` method, place it at the end of your error-handling routine, as demonstrated in the previous example. VBScript automatically executes the `Clear()` method on several occasions, including

- Whenever the `On Error Resume Next` statement executes
- Whenever an `Exit Sub` statement executes
- Whenever an `Exit Function` statement executes

The second `Err` object method is the `Raise()` method. This method allows you to generate error messages to test your error-handling routines. Without this method, the only way that you could test your error-handling routines would be to deliberately introduce an error situation into your code. This method is easy to use, as demonstrated by the following:

```
Err.Raise(500)
```

For example, if you save the previous statement as a script and run it, you will see the error message shown in Figure 9.8.

To use the `Raise()` method, add it, along with the error number indicating the error that you want to generate, just before the error-handling procedure that you want to test in your script. After you have validated that the error handler is working as expected, remove the `Raise()` statement from your VBScript.

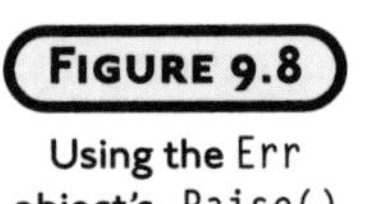

FIGURE 9.8

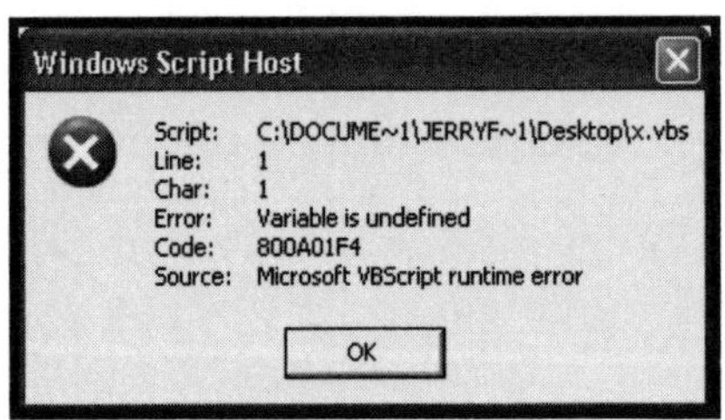

Using the `Err` object's `Raise()` method to generate a test error.

Reporting Errors

The best solution for errors is to prevent them from occurring in the first place; however, that's not always possible. The next best solution is to devise a way of dealing with errors, whether it be handling them or simply ignoring them. Another option is to report errors by recording them to a log file for later review. This allows you to come back and check to see whether any errors have occurred. This is important because many time users do not report errors when they occur, allowing errors to go on forever. By logging error messages, you create an audit log that you can come back to and review from time to time to identify and fix any errors that may have occurred.

When logging error messages, you have two options. The first option is to create your own custom log file. The second option is to record error messages in the Windows application event log. The second option, however, is only available if the script is running on a computer running Windows NT, 2000, or XP.

Creating a Custom Log File

To create a custom log file, you must instantiate the `FileSystemObject` in your VBScript and then use it's `OpenTextFile()` method to open the log file so that your script can write to it as demonstrated in the following example.

```
On Error Resume Next

Err.Raise(7)

Set objFsoObject = WScript.CreateObject("Scripting.FileSystemObject")

If (objFsoObject.FileExists("C:\ScriptLog.txt")) Then
  Set objLogFile = objFsoObject.OpenTextFile("C:\ScriptLog.txt", 8)
Else
  Set objLogFile = objFsoObject.OpenTextFile("C:\ScriptLog.txt", 2, "True")
End If

objLogFile.WriteLine "Test.vbs Error: " & Err.Number & ", Description = " & _
  Err.Description & " , Source = " & Err.Source

objLogFile.Close()
```

In this example, the `On Error Resume Next` statement is used to allow the script to recover from errors and the `Err.Raise(7)` statement is used to simulate an "Out of memory" error.

The rest of the script logs the error in a file called `ScriptLog.txt`, located on the computer's `C:` drive. If the file does not exist, it is created. Error messages are appended to the bottom of the file each time they are written, allowing a running history of information to accumulate. For more information about how to work with the `FileSystemObject` and its methods and properties, refer to Chapter 8, "Storing and Retrieving Data."

You can adapt the previous example as the basis for developing an error-logging routine in your VBScripts. Just copy and paste all but the first two lines into a function and call it whenever errors occur. Just make sure that you call the function before clearing the error. Alternatively, you can modify the example to use variable substitution and pass the function the error number and description as arguments.

Be sure you always close any file that you open before allowing your script to terminate. If you don't, you may have problems with the file the next time you want to open it because its end-of-file marker may be missing.

Recording an Error Message in the Application Event Log

An alternative to creating custom log files for your scripts is to record error messages in the Windows application event log. This is achieved using the `WshShell` object's `LogEvent()` method:

```
On Error Resume Next

Err.Raise(7)

Set objWshShl = WScript.CreateObject("WScript.Shell")

objWshShl.LogEvent 1, "Test.vbs Error: " & Err.Number & ", Description = " & _
  Err.Description & " , Source = " & Err.Source
```

In this example, an "Out of memory" error has again been simulated, only this time, the error has been written to the Windows application event log using the `WshShell` object's `LogEvent()` method. Only two arguments were processed. The first is a number indicating the type of event being logged. Table 9.5 lists the different types of events that are supported by Windows. The second argument was the message to be recorded. Figure 9.9 shows how the message will appear when viewed from the Event Viewer.

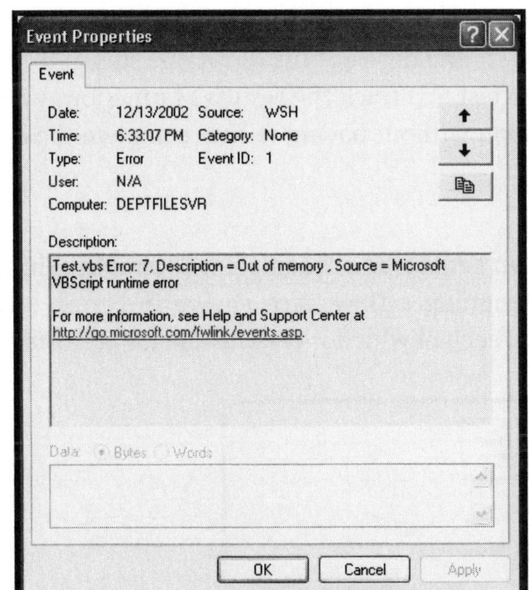

FIGURE 9.9 Writing error messages to the Windows application event log using the `WshShell` object's `LogEvent()` method.

TABLE 9.5 EVENT LOG ERROR INDICATORS

Value	Description
0	Indicates a successful event
1	Indicates an error event
2	Indicates a warning event
4	Indicates an informational event
8	Indicates a successful audit event
16	Indicates a failed audit event

BACK TO THE HANGMAN GAME

Now that you've reviewed the basic steps involved in overcoming VBScript errors, let's return to the Hangman game and begin its development. I'm going to cover the development of this game from a different angle than in previous chapters. By now, you should have a pretty good idea of how things work, and you should be able to read and understand the scripts that you'll see throughout the remainder of this book (just in case, I'll leave plenty of comments in the code to help you along). This time, I'll provide a much higher explanation of what is going on and offer suggestions for ways to test and develop this script one step at a time. I'll also point out techniques that you can use to test and track the results of functions within the script, so that you can validate their operation without having to first complete the entire script.

Designing the Game

The overall design of the Hangman game is fairly complex. To simplify things, I'll begin the game-development process by designing a flowchart, shown in Figure 9.10, which breaks the game down into distinct units, each of which is responsible for performing a unique task.

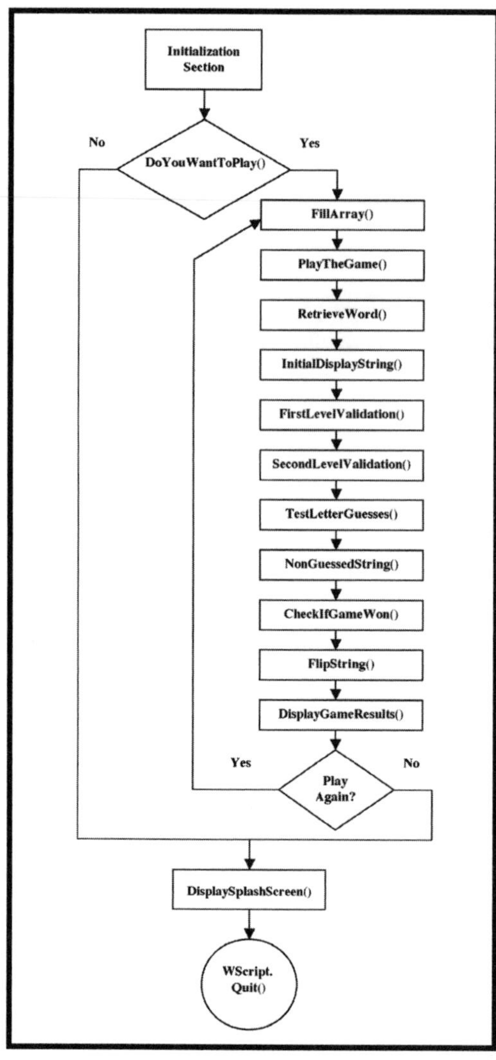

FIGURE 9.10

A flowchart providing a high-level design for the Hangman game.

In addition to the Initialization Section and Main Processing Section, this script is made up of 13 separate procedures. Therefore, you will develop this game in 15 steps, as follows:

1. Create a new script, adding your VBScript template and defining the variables, constants, and arrays that are used by this script.
2. Develop the controlling logic for the Main Processing Section.
3. Using the `DoYouWantToPlay()` function, create an introductory game splash screen and determine whether the user wants to play.
4. Assign a list of game words to an array using the `FillArray()` function.
5. Create a loop in the `PlayTheGame()` function that controls the actual flow of the game, collecting player guesses and calling other functions as required.
6. Retrieve a randomly selected game word using the `RetrieveWord()` function.
7. Display space-separated underscore characters representing each letter in the game word using the `InitialDisplayString()` function.
8. Using the `FirstLevelValidation()` function, validate the player's input to make sure the player is providing valid guesses.
9. Using the `SecondLevelValidation()` function, test to determine whether the player has already tried guessing a letter before accepting it as input.
10. Using the `TestLetterGuess()` function, check to see whether the player made an incorrect guess.
11. Using the `NonGuessedString()` function, create a temporary string blanking out the letters correctly guessed by the player.
12. Using the `CheckIfGameWon()` function, check to see whether the player has guessed all the letters that make up the mystery word.
13. Using the `FlipString()` function, spin through the script created in step 11, and reverse the display of each character of the string (that is, now only show the correctly guessed letters).
14. Tell the player whether he or she won or lost using the `DisplayGameResults()` function.
15. Display information about the game as it finishes using the `SplashScreen()` function.

Setting Up the Script Template and Initialization Section

This portion of the script, shown here, should look pretty familiar to you by now, and does not require much explanation. As you can see from the code, this section consists of the script template and the definition of the script's constant, variables, and array.

```
'*************************************************************************
'Script Name: Hangman.vbs
'Author:      Jerry Ford
'Created:     02/30/02
'Description: This script demonstrates how to create a game of Hangman
'              using VBScript and the WSH.
'*************************************************************************

'Initialization Section

Option Explicit

Const cTitlebarMsg = "VBScript HANGMAN"

Dim strChoice, strGameWord, intNoMisses, intNoRight, strSplashImage
Dim intPlayOrNot, strMsgText, intPlayAgain, strWrongGuesses
Dim strRightGuesses, blnWordGuessed, intLetterCounter
Dim strTempStringOne, strTempStringTwo, strWordLetter, strDisplayString
Dim intFlipCounter, intRandomNo, strProcessGuess, blnGameStatus
Dim strCheckAnswer

Dim astrWordList(9)  'Define an array that can hold 10 game words
```

Putting Together the Logic for the Main Processing Section

Like the other scripts that you have seen in this book, the logic located in the script's Main Processing Section is very straightforward. It calls upon procedures that determine whether the user wants to play, loads the game words into an array, starts the game, and ultimately ends the game by displaying a splash screen and executing the `WScript.Quit()` statement.

```
'Main Processing Section

intPlayOrNot = DoYouWantToPlay()

If intPlayOrNot = 6 Then 'User elected to play the game
  FillArray()
  PlayTheGame()
End If

SplashScreen()

WScript.Quit()
```

At this point in the script, you have enough code in place to run your first test and see whether there are any syntax errors. For now, I recommend that you go ahead and define a procedure for each of the preceding functions, placing a `MsgBox()` function that simply displays the name of the function inside each one. Save and execute the script and make sure that the pop-up dialogs all appear when they should. You can leave the functions as they are until you are ready to complete them.

Using the `WScript.Quit()` method, as I did in this section, is not required. Script execution would have ceased after the display of the splash screen anyway. I added this statement for the sake of clarity, and to prevent any statements that I might have inadvertently left outside of a function in the Procedure Section from accidentally being executed.

Building the DoYouWantToPlay() Function

You've seen functions very similar to this one in previous chapters. All the `DoYouWantToPlay()` function does is display a clever graphic and ask the user if he or she wants to play a game of Hangman.

```
Function DoYouWantToPlay()

  'Display the splash screen and ask the user if he or she wants to play
'Display the splash screen and ask the user if he or she wants to play
  strSplashImage = Space(100) & "***********" & vbCrLf & _
    "W E L C O M E  T O  " & Space(68) & "*" & Space(18) & "*" & _
    vbCrLf & Space(100) & "O" & Space(18) & "*" & vbCrLf & _
    "V B S c r i p t  H A N G M A N !" & Space(50) & "--||--" & _
    Space(15) & "*" & vbCrLf & Space(99) & "/" & Space(1) & "\" & _
    Space(17) & "*" & vbCrLf & Space(120) & "*" & vbCrLf & Space(120) & _
    "*" & vbCrLf & space(113) & " *******             " & vbCrLf & _
    "Would you like to play a game?" & vbCrLf & " "

  DoYouWantToPlay = MsgBox(strSplashImage, 36, cTitlebarMsg)
End Function
```

This is a good place to pause and perform another test of your script to ensure that this function looks and works like it should. This test allows you to evaluate the operation of all the controlling logic in the Main Processing Section.

Building the FillArray() Function

The `FillArray()` function, shown next, simply loads a list of words into an array. Later, another procedure will randomly select a game word from the array.

```
Function FillArray()

  'Add the words to the array
  astrWordList(0) = "AUTOMOBILE"
  astrWordList(1) = "NETWORKING"
  astrWordList(2) = "PRACTICAL"
  astrWordList(3) = "CONGRESS"
  astrWordList(4) = "COMMANDER"
  astrWordList(5) = "STAPLER"
  astrWordList(6) = "ENTERPRISE"
  astrWordList(7) = "ESCALATION"
  astrWordList(8) = "HAPPINESS"
  astrWordList(9) = "WEDNESDAY"

End Function
```

You can't perform much of a test on this function at this point, but you can always save and run the script again to see whether you have any syntax problems. You should create a temporary script, copy this function into it, and then create a `For...Next` loop that processes and displays the contents of the array to ensure that the function is loading as expected. Next delete the `For...Next` loop and add the following statements to the beginning of the temporary script:

```
Dim astrWordList(9)  'Define an array that can hold 10 game words
FillArray()
```

Save this script again. A little later, I'll show you how to modify and use this temporary script to perform another test.

Building the PlayTheGame() Function

The `PlayTheGame()` function, shown next, controls the play of the Hangman game. When I developed this function, I wrote a few lines, stopped and tested it, and then wrote some more. Specifically, each time I added a call to an external function I stopped, wrote the function that I called, and then did a test to be sure that everything worked before continuing. However, it would take me too long to guide you through every step along the way. Instead,

I'll leave it up to you to follow this basic process, and will instead focus on the development of the other functions that make up the script, most of which are called from within the `PlayTheGame()` function.

```
Function PlayTheGame()

  'Initialize variables displayed by the game's initial pop-up dialog
  intNoMisses = 0
  intNoRight = 0
  strWrongGuesses = ""
  strRightGuesses = ""

  'Get the game a mystery word
  strGameWord = RetrieveWord()

  'Call function that formats the initial pop-up dialog's display string
  strDisplayString = InitialDisplayString()

  strTempStringOne = strGameWord

  'Let the player start guessing
  Do Until intNoMisses = 6

    'Collect the player's guess
    strChoice = InputBox(vbCrLf & vbTab & strDisplayString & vbCrLf & _
                vbCrLf & vbCrLf & "No. of Misses: " & intNoMisses & _
                "   " & vbTab & "Incorrect:" & strWrongGuesses & vbCrLf _
                & vbCrLf & vbCrLf & _
                "Type a letter and click on OK." , cTitleBarMsg)

    'Determine if the player has quit
    If strChoice = "" Then
      Exit Function
    End If

    strProcessGuess = FirstLevelValidation()
```

```
'The Player wants to quit the game
If strProcessGuess = "ExitFunction" Then
  Exit Function
End If

'The player typed invalid input
If strProcessGuess <> "SkipRest" Then

  strProcessGuess = SecondLevelValidation()

  Select Case strProcessGuess
    Case "DuplicateWrongAnswer"
      MsgBox "Invalid: You've already guessed this incorrect letter."
    Case "DuplicateRightAnswer"
      MsgBox "Invalid: You've already guessed this correct letter."
    Case Else
      strCheckAnswer = TestLetterGuess()
      If strCheckAnswer <> "IncorrectAnswer" Then

        'Reset the value of variable used to build a string containing
        'the interim stage of the word as currently guessed by player
        strTempStringTwo = ""

        NonGuessedString()

        'Check to see if the player has guessed the word
        blnGameStatus = CheckIfGameWon()
        If blnGameStatus = "True" Then
          blnWordGuessed = "True"
          Exit Do
        End If

        'Set the value of the temporary string equal to the string
        'created by the Previous For...Next loop
        strTempStringOne = strTempStringTwo

        'Clear out the value of the strDisplayString variable
```

```
            strDisplayString = ""

            FlipString()

          End If
        End Select
      End If
    Loop

    DisplayGameResults()

End Function
```

Building the RetrieveWord() Function

This function is designed to retrieve a randomly selected word to be used by the game. `RetrieveWord()` first selects a random number between 1 and 10, and then uses that number to retrieve a game word from the `WordList()` array. This function randomly retrieves a word from an array.

```
Function RetrieveWord()

  Randomize
  intRandomNo = FormatNumber(Int(10 * Rnd))
  RetrieveWord = astrWordList(intRandomNo)

End Function
```

This is a good place to perform another test. This time, open the temporary script that you created a little earlier and cut and paste it into the statements located in the previous function. Paste the three statements into the temporary file, making them lines 3 though 5 in the script. Next, add the following statement as line 6:

```
MsgBox RetrieveWord
```

Save and run the script. Each time you execute the temporary script, a different randomly selected word should be displayed. If this is not the case, then something is wrong. Locate and fix any errors that may occur until the temporary script works as expected. Then, cut and paste any corrected script statements back into your Hangman script and move on to the next section.

Building the InitialDisplayString() Function

This function is used to display a series of underscore characters representing each letter that makes up the mystery game word:

```
Function InitialDisplayString()

  'Create a loop that processes each letter of the word
  For intLetterCounter = 1 to Len(strGameWord)
    'Use underscore characters to display a string representing each
    'letter
    InitialDisplayString = InitialDisplayString & "_ "
  Next

End Function
```

You can run a quick test of this function by creating a new temporary VBScript, cutting and pasting the statements from within this function into the temporary script, and modifying it.

```
For intLetterCounter = 1 to Len("DOG")
  'Use underscore characters to display a string representing each letter
  InitialDisplayString = InitialDisplayString & "_ "
Next

MsgBox InitialDisplayString
```

You should see three underscore characters separated by blank spaces, indicating the length of the word. If anything is wrong, fix it and then copy the corrected statement(s) back into the Hangman script.

Building the FirstLevelValidation() Function

The `FirstLevelValidation()` function, shown next, ensures that the player is providing valid input. It checks to make sure that the player typed in something, that the player did not type in more than one character, and that a number was not provided as input.

```
'Validate the player's input
Function FirstLevelValidation()

  'See if the player clicked on Cancel or failed to enter any input
  If strChoice = "" Then
```

```
    FirstLevelValidation = "ExitFunction"
    Exit Function
  End If

  'Make sure the player only typed 1 letter
  If Len(strChoice) > 1 Then
    MsgBox "Invalid: You must only enter 1 letter at a time!"
    FirstLevelValidation = "SkipRest"
  Else
    'Make sure the player did not type a number by accident
    If IsNumeric(strChoice) = "True" Then
      MsgBox "Invalid: Only letters can be accepted as valid input!"
      FirstLevelValidation = "SkipRest"
    Else
      FirstLevelValidation = "Continue"
    End If
  End If

End Function
```

Building the SecondLevelValidation() Function

Like the previous function, the `SecondLevelValidation()` function, shown here, performs additional tests on the player's guess to make sure that the player is not trying to guess the same letter twice.

```
Function SecondLevelValidation()

  'Check to see if this letter is already on the incorrectly guessed list
  If Instr(1, strWrongGuesses, UCase(strChoice), 1) <> 0 Then
    SecondLevelValidation = "DuplicateWrongAnswer"
  Else
    'Check to see if this letter is already on the correctly guessed list
    If Instr(1, strRightGuesses, UCase(strChoice), 1) <> 0 Then
      SecondLevelValidation = "DuplicateRightAnswer"
    End If
  End If

End Function
```

Building the TestLetterGuess() Function

The `TestLetterGuess()` function, shown here, checks to see whether the letter is part of the word and keeps track of missed guesses. If the total number of missed guesses equals `6`, then this function assigns a value of `False` to the `blnWordGuessed` variable. This variable is a flag that is later checked to see whether the player has lost the game.

```
Function TestLetterGuess()

  If Instr(1, UCase(strGameWord), UCase(strChoice), 1) = 0 Then
    'Add the letter to the list of incorrectly guessed letters
    strWrongGuesses = strWrongGuesses & " " & UCase(strChoice)
    'Increment the number of guesses that the player has made by 1
    intNoMisses = intNoMisses + 1
    'If the player has missed 6 guesses then he has used up all chances
    If intNoMisses = 6 Then
      blnWordGuessed = "False"
    End If
    TestLetterGuess = "IncorrectGuess"
  Else
    TestLetterGuess = "CorrectGuess"
  End If

End Function
```

Building the NonGuessedString() Function

This game displays as a string the letters that make up the game's mystery word and uses VBScript string manipulation functions to control the display of correctly and incorrectly guessed letters. As I was creating the game, I wanted an easy way of seeing what game word had been randomly selected and of tracking which letters had yet to be guessed. The `NonGuessedString()` function, shown next, builds a string that, if it were displayed, would show all the letters that make up the word, less the letters that the player has correctly guessed. This function gave me a tool for displaying how the game was keeping track of the game word.

```
Function NonGuessedString()

  'Loop through the temporary string
  For intLetterCounter = 1 to Len(strTempStringOne)
```

```
    'Examine each letter in the word one at a time
    strWordLetter = Mid(strTempStringOne, intLetterCounter, 1)
    'Otherwise add an underscore character indicating a nonmatching guess
    If UCase(strWordLetter) <> UCase(strChoice) Then
      strTempStringTwo = strTempStringTwo & strWordLetter
    Else
      'The letter matches player's guess. Add it to the temporary string
      intNoRight = intNoRight + 1
      strRightGuesses = strRightGuesses & " " & UCase(strChoice)
      strTempStringTwo = strTempStringTwo & "_"
    End If
  Next

End Function
```

After I developed this function, I added the following statement as the last statement in the function:

```
MsgBox " **** = " & strTempStringTwo
```

This way, each time the function ran, I was able to see the contents of the string. For example, if the game word is DOG and the player has missed his or her first guess, this string would be displayed in a pop-up dialog as `D O G`. If the player then guessed the letter `O`, then the string would display as `D_G` the next time this function ran. This function allowed me to visually track the progress of the string as the game ran and manipulated its contents.

Building the CheckIfGameWon() Function

The `CheckIfGameWon()` function checks to see whether the number of correctly guessed letters is equal to the length of the word. If this is the case, then the player has guessed all the letters that make up the word and won the game.

```
Function CheckIfGameWon()

  'Check and see if the player has guessed all the letters that make up
  'the word. If so, set indicator variable and exit the Do...Until loop
  If intNoRight = Len(strGameWord) Then
    CheckIfGameWon = "True"
  End If

End Function
```

Again, a well-placed `MsgBox()` in this function can be used to track the value of the `blnCheckIfGameWon` variable.

Building the FlipString() Function

The problem with the string produced by the `NonGuessedString()` function was that it displayed a string in exactly the opposite format that I wanted to ultimately display. In other words, if the game word was `DOG` and the player had correctly guessed the letter O, then I wanted the game to display the word as `_O_` and not as `D_G`. So I developed the `FlipString()` function. It loops through each character of the string created by the `NonGuessedString()` function and reverses the display of character data.

```
Function FlipString()

  'Spin through and reverse the letters in the strTempStringTwo variable
  'In order to switch letters to underscore characters and underscore
  'characters to the appropriate letters
  For intFlipCounter = 1 to Len(strTempStringTwo)
    'Examine each letter in the word one at a time
    strWordLetter = Mid(strTempStringTwo, intFlipCounter, 1)
    'Replace each letter with the underscore character
    If strWordLetter <> "_" Then
      strDisplayString = strDisplayString & "_ "
    Else
      'Replace each underscore with its appropriate letter
      strDisplayString = strDisplayString & _
        Right(Left(strGameWord,intFlipCounter),1) & " "
    End If
  Next

End Function
```

Here again, a well-placed statement that contains the `MsgBox()` function can be used to display the activity of this function as it attempts to spin through and reverse the display of the letters that make up the game word.

Building the DisplayGameResults() Function

The `DisplayGameResults()` function, shown here, determines whether the player won or lost the game and is responsible for displaying the results of the game and for determining whether the player wants to play again. If the user elects to play another game, the strings that are used to track the status of the game word are blanked out and the `PlayTheGame()` function is called. Otherwise, the function ends and processing control is passed back to the end of the current iteration of the `PlayTheGame()` function, which then returns control to the Main Processing Section where the `SplashScreen()` function is called.

```
'Determine if the player won or lost and display game results
Function DisplayGameResults()

  'Select message based on whether or not the player figured out the word
  If blnWordGuessed = "True" Then
    strMsgText = "Congratulations, You Win!"
  Else
    strMsgText = "Sorry, You Lose."
  End If

  'Display the results of the game
  intPlayAgain = MsgBox(vbCrLf & "The word was:  " & _
    UCase(strGameWord) & vbCrLf & vbCrLf & vbCrLf & strMsgText & _
    vbCrLf & vbCrLf & vbCrLf & _
    "Would you like to play again?" , 4, cTitleBarMsg)

  'Find out if the player wants to play another game
  If intPlayAgain = 6 Then
    'If the answer is yes reset the following variables & start a new game
    strDisplayString = ""
    strTempStringTwo = ""
    PlayTheGame()
  End If

End Function
```

Building the SplashScreen() Function

The `SplashScreen()` function is the last function in the script. As you have seen in other games in this book, this function displays some information about the game and its creator. After this function is processed, the Main Processing Section executes the `WScript.Quit()` method, terminating the game's execution.

```
'This function displays the game splash screen
Function SplashScreen()
```

```
  MsgBox "Thank you for playing VBScript Hangman © Jerry Ford 2002." & _
    vbCrLf & vbCrLf & "Please play again soon!", , cTitlebarMsg

End Function
```

The Final Result

By now you should have all the pieces and parts of the Hangman script assembled and ready for execution. Save your work and give it a shot. After you have everything working correctly, you can remove or comment out any of the extra statements that use the `MsgBox()` function to track the game's intermediate results.

```
'*************************************************************************
'Script Name: Hangman.vbs
'Author:      Jerry Ford
'Created:     02/30/02
'Description: This script demonstrates how to create a game of Hangman
'              using VBScript and the WSH.
'*************************************************************************


'Initialization Section

Option Explicit

Const cTitlebarMsg = "VBScript HANGMAN"

Dim strChoice, strGameWord, intNoMisses, intNoRight, strSplashImage
Dim intPlayOrNot, strMsgText, intPlayAgain, strWrongGuesses
Dim strRightGuesses, blnWordGuessed, intLetterCounter
Dim strTempStringOne, strTempStringTwo, strWordLetter, strDisplayString
Dim intFlipCounter, intRandomNo, strProcessGuess, blnGameStatus
Dim strCheckAnswer

Dim astrWordList(9)  'Define an array that can hold 10 game words


'Main Processing Section

intPlayOrNot = DoYouWantToPlay()
```

```
If intPlayOrNot = 6 Then 'User elected to play the game
  FillArray()
  PlayTheGame()
End If

SplashScreen()

WScript.Quit()


'Procedure Section

Function DoYouWantToPlay()

  'Display the splash screen and ask the user if he or she wants to play
  strSplashImage = Space(100) & "***********" & vbCrLf & _
    "W E L C O M E  T O  " & Space(68) & "*" & Space(18) & "*" & _
    vbCrLf & Space(100) & "0" & Space(18) & "*" & vbCrLf & _
    "V B S c r i p t  H A N G M A N !" & Space(50) & "--||--" & _
    Space(15) & "*" & vbCrLf & Space(99) & "/" & Space(1) & "\" & _
    Space(17) & "*" & vbCrLf & Space(120) & "*" & vbCrLf & Space(120) & _
    "*" & vbCrLf & space(113) & " *******       " & vbCrLf & _
    "Would you like to play a game?" & vbCrLf & " "

  DoYouWantToPlay = MsgBox(strSplashImage, 36, cTitlebarMsg)

End Function


Function FillArray()

  'Add the words to the array
  astrWordList(0) = "AUTOMOBILE"
  astrWordList(1) = "NETWORKING"
  astrWordList(2) = "PRACTICAL"
  astrWordList(3) = "CONGRESS"
  astrWordList(4) = "COMMANDER"
  astrWordList(5) = "STAPLER"
```

```
  astrWordList(6) = "ENTERPRISE"
  astrWordList(7) = "ESCALATION"
  astrWordList(8) = "HAPPINESS"
  astrWordList(9) = "WEDNESDAY"

End Function


Function PlayTheGame()

  'Initialize variables displayed by the game's initial pop-up dialog
  intNoMisses = 0
  intNoRight = 0
  strWrongGuesses = ""
  strRightGuesses = ""

  'Get the game a mystery word
  strGameWord = RetrieveWord()

  'Call function that formats the initial pop-up dialog's display string
  strDisplayString = InitialDisplayString()

  strTempStringOne = strGameWord

  'Let the player start guessing
  Do Until intNoMisses = 6

    'Collect the player's guess
    strChoice = InputBox(vbCrLf & vbTab & strDisplayString & vbCrLf & _
                vbCrLf & vbCrLf & "No. of Misses: " & intNoMisses & _
                "   " & vbTab & "Incorrect:" & strWrongGuesses & vbCrLf _
                & vbCrLf & vbCrLf & _
                "Type a letter and click on OK." , cTitleBarMsg)

    'Determine if the player has quit
    If strChoice = "" Then
      Exit Function
    End If
```

```
strProcessGuess = FirstLevelValidation()

'The player wants to quit the game
If strProcessGuess = "ExitFunction" Then
  Exit Function
End If

'The player typed invalid input
If strProcessGuess <> "SkipRest" Then

  strProcessGuess = SecondLevelValidation()

  Select Case strProcessGuess
    Case "DuplicateWrongAnswer"
      MsgBox "Invalid: You've already guessed this incorrect letter."
    Case "DuplicateRightAnswer"
      MsgBox "Invalid: You've already guessed this correct letter."
    Case Else
      strCheckAnswer = TestLetterGuess()
      If strCheckAnswer <> "IncorrectAnswer" Then

        'Reset the value of variable used to build a string containing
        'the interim stage of the word as currently guessed by player
        strTempStringTwo = ""

        NonGuessedString()

        'Check to see if the player has guessed the word
        blnGameStatus = CheckIfGameWon()
        If blnGameStatus = "True" Then
          blnWordGuessed = "True"
          Exit Do
        End If

        'Set the value of the temporary string equal to the string
        'created by the Previous For...Next loop
        strTempStringOne = strTempStringTwo
```

```
          'Clear out the value of the strDisplayString variable

          strDisplayString = ""

          FlipString()

        End If
      End Select
    End If
  Loop

  DisplayGameResults()

End Function


'This function randomly retrieves a word from an array
Function RetrieveWord()

  Randomize
  intRandomNo = FormatNumber(Int(10 * Rnd))
  RetrieveWord = astrWordList(intRandomNo)

End Function

Function InitialDisplayString()

  'Create a loop that processes each letter of the word
  For intLetterCounter = 1 to Len(strGameWord)
    'Use underscore characters to display string representing each letter
    InitialDisplayString = InitialDisplayString & "_ "
  Next

End Function


'Validate the player's input
Function FirstLevelValidation()
```

```
  'See if the player clicked on Cancel or failed to enter any input
  If strChoice = "" Then
    FirstLevelValidation = "ExitFunction"
    Exit Function
  End If

  'Make sure the player only typed 1 letter
  If Len(strChoice) > 1 Then
    MsgBox "Invalid: You must only enter 1 letter at a time!"
    FirstLevelValidation = "SkipRest"
  Else
    'Make sure the player did not type a number by accident
    If IsNumeric(strChoice) = "True" Then
      MsgBox "Invalid: Only letters can be accepted as valid input!"
      FirstLevelValidation = "SkipRest"
    Else
      FirstLevelValidation = "Continue"
    End If
  End If

End Function


Function SecondLevelValidation()

  'Check to see if this letter is already on the incorrectly guessed list
  If Instr(1, strWrongGuesses, UCase(strChoice), 1) <> 0 Then
    SecondLevelValidation = "DuplicateWrongAnswer"
  Else
    'Check to see if this letter is already on the correctly guessed list
    If Instr(1, strRightGuesses, UCase(strChoice), 1) <> 0 Then
      SecondLevelValidation = "DuplicateRightAnswer"
    End If
  End If

End Function
```

```
Function TestLetterGuess()

  If Instr(1, UCase(strGameWord), UCase(strChoice), 1) = 0 Then
    'Add the letter to the list of incorrectly guessed letters
    strWrongGuesses = strWrongGuesses & " " & UCase(strChoice)
    'Increment the number of guesses that the player has made by 1
    intNoMisses = intNoMisses + 1
    'If the player has missed 6 guesses then he has used up all chances
    If intNoMisses = 6 Then
      blnWordGuessed = "False"
    End If
    TestLetterGuess = "IncorrectGuess"
  Else
    TestLetterGuess = "CorrectGuess"
  End If

End Function


Function NonGuessedString()

  'Loop through the temporary string
  For intLetterCounter = 1 to Len(strTempStringOne)
    'Examine each letter in the word one at a time
    strWordLetter = Mid(strTempStringOne, intLetterCounter, 1)
    'Otherwise add an underscore character indicating a nonmatching guess
    If UCase(strWordLetter) <> UCase(strChoice) Then
      strTempStringTwo = strTempStringTwo & strWordLetter
    Else
      'The letter matches player's guess. Add it to the temporary string
      intNoRight = intNoRight + 1
      strRightGuesses = strRightGuesses & " " & UCase(strChoice)
      strTempStringTwo = strTempStringTwo & "_"
    End If
  Next

End Function
```

```
Function CheckIfGameWon()

  'Check and see if the player has guessed all the letters that make up
  'the word. If so, set indicator variable and exit the Do...Until loop
  If intNoRight = Len(strGameWord) Then
    CheckIfGameWon = "True"
  End If

End Function


Function FlipString()

  'Spin through and reverse the letters in the strTempStringTwo variable
  'In order to switch letters to underscore characters and underscore
  'characters to the appropriate letters
  For intFlipCounter = 1 to Len(strTempStringTwo)
    'Examine each letter in the word one at a time
    strWordLetter = Mid(strTempStringTwo, intFlipCounter, 1)
    'Replace each letter with the underscore character
    If strWordLetter <> "_" Then
      strDisplayString = strDisplayString & "_ "
    Else
      'Replace each underscore with its appropriate letter
      strDisplayString = strDisplayString & _
        Right(Left(strGameWord,intFlipCounter),1) & " "
    End If
  Next

End Function


'Determine if the player won or lost and display game results
Function DisplayGameResults()

  'Select message based on whether or not the player figured out the word
  If blnWordGuessed = "True" Then
    strMsgText = "Congratulations, You Win!"
```

```
  Else
    strMsgText = "Sorry, You Lose."
  End If

  'Display the results of the game
  intPlayAgain = MsgBox(vbCrLf & "The word was:  " & _
    UCase(strGameWord) & vbCrLf & vbCrLf & vbCrLf & strMsgText & _
    vbCrLf & vbCrLf & vbCrLf & _
    "Would you like to play again?" , 4, cTitleBarMsg)

  'Find out if the player wants to play another game
  If intPlayAgain = 6 Then
    'If the answer is yes reset the following variables & start a new game
    strDisplayString = ""
    strTempStringTwo = ""
    PlayTheGame()
  End If

End Function


'This function displays the game splash screen
Function SplashScreen()

  MsgBox "Thank you for playing VBScript Hangman © Jerry Ford 2002." & _
    vbCrLf & vbCrLf & "Please play again soon!", , cTitlebarMsg

End Function
```

Although the script, as shown here, should work just fine, there is always the chance that you'll miss something or make a typo when creating it. After all, this is a rather large script and with size generally comes complexity, which only increases the probability that something will go wrong.

After you've thoroughly tested the script, give it to somebody else to test. Ask your tester to play the game according to the rules, and then ask him to play it by not following the rules. Ask your tester to keep track of any problems that he experiences and to record any error messages that might appear. If an error does appear, get the player to write down exactly what steps he took, so that you can go back and generate the error yourself and begin debugging it.

Summary

In this chapter, you learned how to add programming logic to your scripts to help deal with errors. This included everything from rewriting error messages to making them more user friendly to ignoring errors or creating error-handling routines that allow your scripts to recover from certain types of errors. I also provided advice that can help you prevent errors from occurring in the first place, or at least minimize their number. Finally, I reviewed the different ways of reporting errors that cannot otherwise be handled. On top of all this, you learned how to create the Hangman game and how to test it at various stages of development.

Challenges

1. **Make the Hangman game more fun and interesting by expanding the pool of game words.**
2. **Improve the Hangman program by keeping track of the number of games played during a session and displaying a summary of the overall number of times the player won and lost.**
3. **Add logic to the Hangman game that allows you to track its use. For example, prompt the player for his or her name, and then write a message to either a log file or the Windows application event log each time the player plays the game.**

Using the Windows Registry to Configure Script Settings

So far, all the scripts you've worked with in this book collected configuration information and input from three places: from the user, from within the script itself, or from INI files. In this chapter, I'll show you another option for externalizing script settings by storing and retrieving configuration data using the Windows Registry. As a bonus, in the chapter's game project, I'll also demonstrate how to retrieve input data from files. Specifically, you will

- Review the overall organization and design of the Windows Registry
- Learn how to programmatically create, modify, and delete Registry keys and values
- Learn how to read data stored in external files and process it as input

Project Preview: Part 2 of the Hangman Game

In this chapter, you will enhance the Hangman game that you began developing in Chapter 9, "Handling Script Errors." You'll begin by creating a new setup script that uses the Windows Registry to store the location of the folder where new external word files are stored. You'll then modify the Hangman script by removing the array that stores game words within the script and tweaking the script so that it retrieves words from the external word files. You will also modify the game to allow the player to select the category of words to play in. For example, you might want to create different word files for categories such as Foods or Places.

Figures 10.1 through 10.6 demonstrate the overall flow of the game from beginning to end.

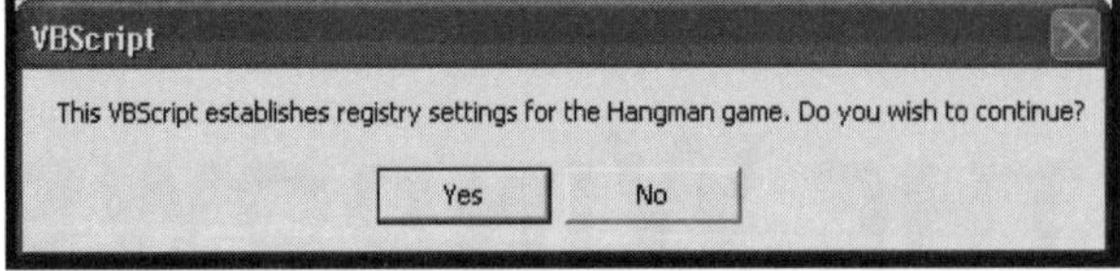

FIGURE 10.1

First, you need to run the Hangman setup script once to establish the game's new Registry setting.

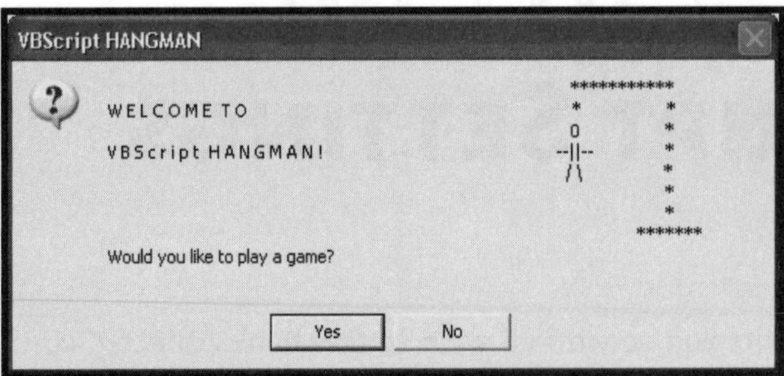

FIGURE 10.2

The Hangman game begins exactly as it did before, by inviting the user to play a game.

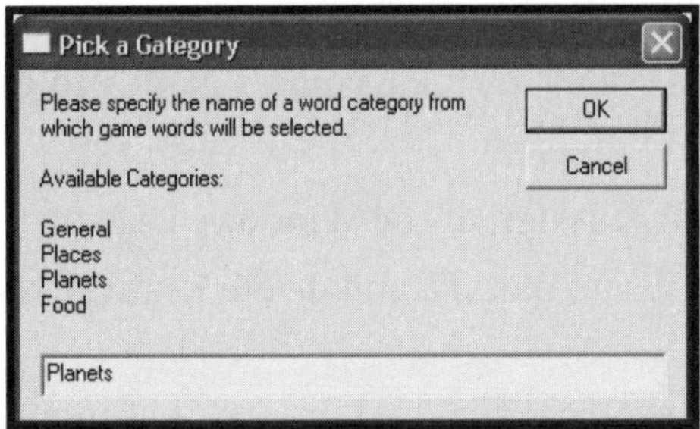

FIGURE 10.3

Now a list of word categories is dynamically generated, allowing the player to select a category of words to play in.

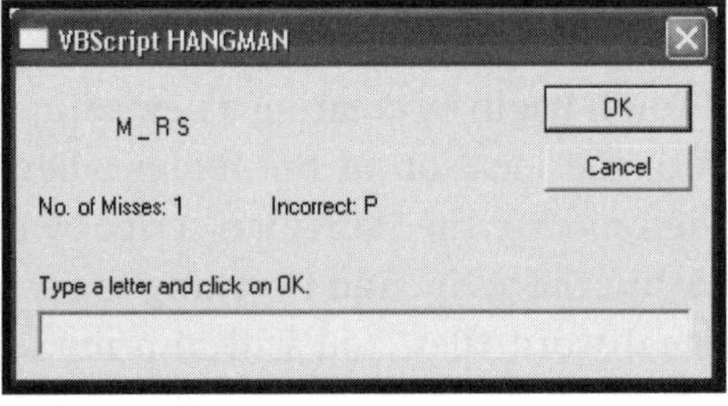

FIGURE 10.4

The flow of the game runs exactly as it did before, by randomly selecting a word from whichever word category the player selected.

FIGURE 10.5

When the game ends, the results are displayed and the player is invited to guess a new word.

FIGURE 10.6

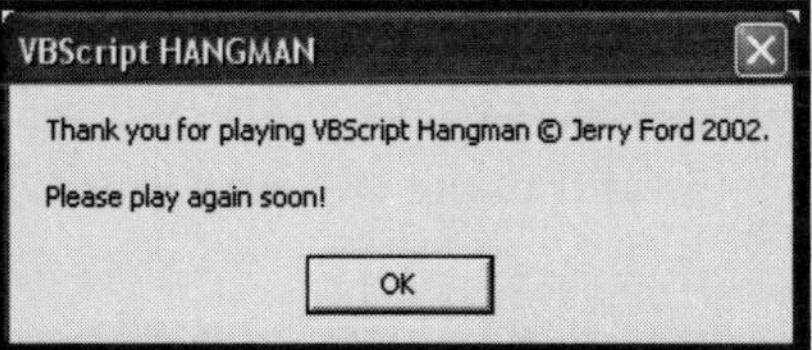

Eventually, the game's closing splash screen is displayed, providing information about the game and its author.

By the time you've finished writing the new Hangman setup script and modifying the original Hangman game, you'll have a basic understanding of the Windows Registry and what it means to access and modify its contents. You will also know how to retrieve data stored in external files to use it as input in your VBScripts.

Introducing the Windows Registry

Since the introduction of Windows 95, the Registry has been the central repository for configuration information on all Microsoft operating systems. The *Registry* is a type of built-in database that acts as a central repository for configuration settings. Windows uses it to store information that affects every component of the computer, including

- Windows operating system configuration settings
- Software configuration settings
- User configuration settings
- Windows services configuration settings
- Hardware configuration settings
- Software device driver configuration settings

As you can see, the Registry is used to store information regarding just about every aspect of the computer and its operation. It only makes sense then, that by making changes to the Registry, you can configure the appearance, behavior, and operation of just about anything that affects the computer. For example, you could directly change the appearance and behavior of the Windows desktop or screen saver by making the appropriate changes to the Registry.

The Registry is so critical to the operation of Windows computers that you actually interact with it just about every day, perhaps without ever even realizing it. For example, just about every time you open the Windows Control Panel and make a change using one its utilities or applets, you end up changing a configuration setting stored in the Registry. In the case of the Control Panel applets, Microsoft has just made things easy for you by creating a collection of specialized graphical interfaces, each of which is designed to help you change the way the computer is configured. Alternatively, you can use the Windows Regedit Registry editor utility that comes with Windows to view and make changes to the Registry.

Because the Registry is a very reliable repository for storing and retrieving information, many application developers take advantage of it by storing their application's settings there. In a similar fashion, you can migrate settings from your VBScripts into the Registry.

You can also create VBScripts that can manipulate Registry contents to affect virtually every aspect of your computer's operation.

DEFINITION

The Windows *Registry* is a built-in database that the operating system uses to store configuration information about itself, as well as the computer's software, hardware, and applications.

How Is the Registry Organized?

The Registry is organized as a collection of five root or parent keys, which are defined in Table 10.1. All the data in the Registry is stored in a tree-like fashion under one of these keys.

If you are still working with Windows 98 or Me, you'll see that that operating system supports a sixth root key name `HKEY_DYN_DATA`. This key manages configuration settings that reference plug and play information.

Although the Registry is logically organized into five root keys, physically it consists of many files. On computers running Windows 2000 or Windows XP, files belonging to the Registry can be found in `%systemroot%\system32\config`. These files include

- `DEFAULT`
- `SYSTEM`
- `SECURITY`

- SAM
- SOFTWARE
- Userdiff

%systemroot% is an environment variable created and maintained by the operating system. This variable identifies the location of the folder where Windows stores system files and folders. By default, this is C:\Windows on Windows 2000 and XP.

Table 10.1 Registry Root Keys

Key	Short Name	Description
HKEY_CLASSES_ROOT	HKCR	Stores information about Windows file associations
HKEY_CURRENT_USER	HKCU	Stores information about the currently logged-on user
HKEY_LOCAL_MACHINE	HKLM	Stores global computer settings
HKEY_USERS	-	Stores information about all users of the computer
HKEY_CURRENT_CONFIG	-	Stores information regarding the computer's current configuration

Information managed by the Windows Registry also consists of data stored about each user of the computer. This data is stored in user profiles, which are located in the Documents and Settings folder belonging to each user of the computer.

Even though the Registry has five root keys, as a VBScript programmer, chances are you'll only need to work with three of them. To help make things easier on you, Microsoft has created a short name reference for each of these three keys. You can see these shortcut names listed in the second column of Table 10.1. You can, however, still interact with the remaining two keys by specifying their full names (HKEY_CURRENT_CONFIG and HKEY_USERS).

Understanding How Data Is Stored in the Registry

Data stored in the Windows Registry is organized into a hierarchy. This hierarchy consists of keys and values. A *key* is a container that holds values or other keys. *Values* are used to store actual data. All data stored in the Windows Registry has the following format:

```
Key : key_type : value
```

Key specifies the name of a Registry key. For example, to reference the `Control Panel` subkey, you would specify `HKCU\Control Panel\`. To reference the `Desktop` subkey, which is located under the `Control Panel` subkey, you would specify `HKCU\Control Panel\Desktop\`. Note that in both examples, the name of the last subkey is followed by the \ character. This character identifies that what is being referenced is a key and not a value.

DEFINITION

A Registry *key* is a container that stores other Registry keys and values. You can think of a key as being akin to a folder in the Windows file system.

Value specifies the container used to store actual data. To reference a value, instead of the key that stores it, you must add the name of the value without the closing \ character. For example, to reference the `ScreenSaveActive` value stored in the `Desktop` subkey, you would specify `HKCU\Control Panel\Desktop\ScreenSaveActive`.

DEFINITION

Within the context of the Windows Registry, a *value* represents the name of an element to which data is assigned. Therefore, a Registry value acts in many ways like a file, which is a container for storing data in a Windows file system.

Key_type identifies the type of data that has been stored. The Registry is capable of storing many types of data, as shown in Table 10.2.

TABLE 10.2 DATA TYPES SUPPORTED BY THE WINDOWS REGISTRY

Data Type	Description
REG_BINARY	Stores a binary value
REG_DWORD	Stores a hexadecimal DWORD value
REG_EXPAND_SZ	Stores an expandable string
REG_MULTI_SZ	Stores multiple strings
REG_SZ	Stores a string

Every value within the Registry falls into one of two types, either `named` or `unnamed`. The most common type of value is `named`. `Named` values have been assigned an explicit name. This allows you to retrieve the data stored in the value by specifying its name. `Unnamed` values, as the name implies, do not have a name assigned to them. One `unnamed` value is stored under every key. This value represents the key's default value. In other words, it's the value that would be retrieved if you did not specify a specific value by name. Windows graphically identifies `unnamed` values by displaying a label of `Default` as demonstrated in Figure 10.7.

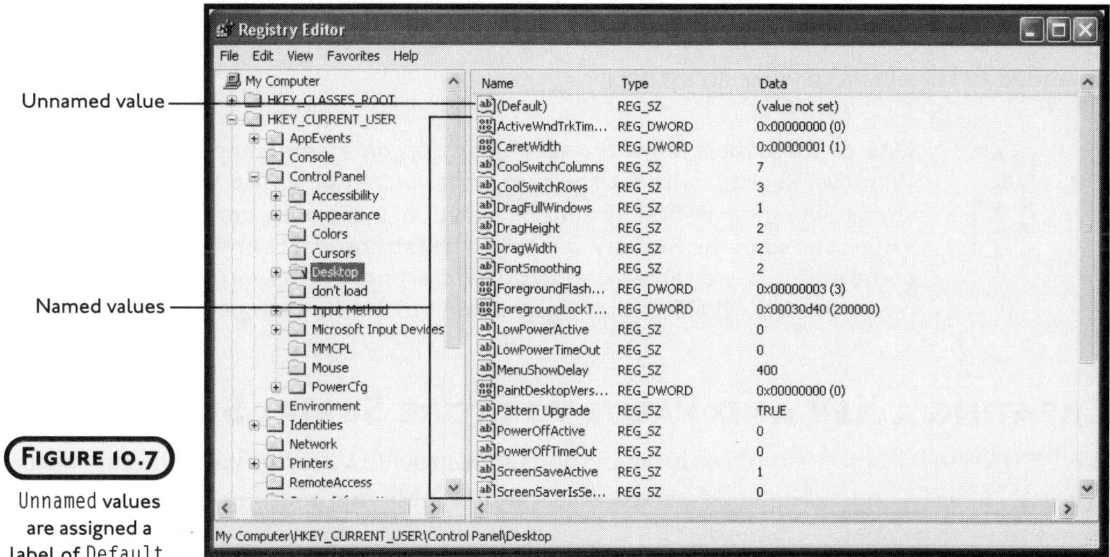

FIGURE 10.7

`Unnamed` values are assigned a label of `Default`.

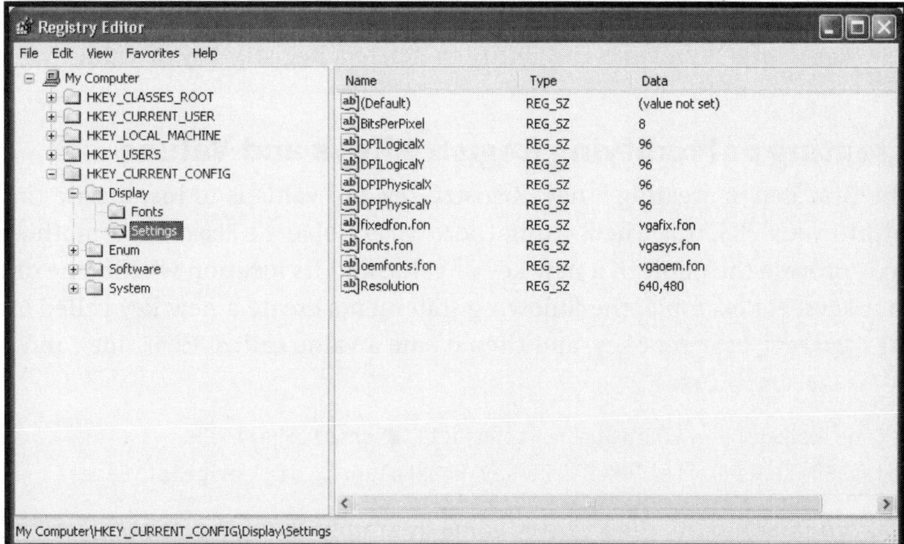

FIGURE 10.8

Examining the Windows Registry using the Regedit utility.

Accessing Registry Keys and Values

You can manually view the contents of the Windows Registry using the Regedit utility supplied with every version of Windows. In addition, if you're using Windows NT, 2000, or XP, you can also use the Regedt32 utility, which looks and works like the Regedit utility. For example, Figure 10.8 provides a high-level view of the Registry using the Regedit utility. As you can see, the five root keys are visible, and one of the root keys has been partially expanded to reveals its tree-like structure.

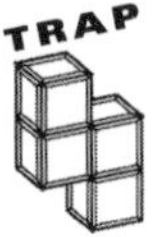

One of the easiest ways to mess things up on a computer is to modify the Windows Registry without knowing what you're doing. The Windows Registry stores extremely critical system information. Incorrectly configuring keys and values stored in the Registry can have a disastrous effect on the computer, and could potentially disable Windows from starting. Unless you're absolutely sure how a change will affect the Registry, don't make the change.

Creating a Key and Value to Store Script Settings

The WSH `WshShell` object supplies three methods that provide VBScript with the capability to access, modify, and delete Registry keys and values. These methods are demonstrated in the sections that follow.

- **`RegWrite()`**. Provides the ability to create and modify a Registry key or value.
- **`RegRead()`**. Provides the ability to retrieve a Registry key or value.
- **`RegDelete()`**. Provides the ability to delete a Registry key or value.

Creating or Modifying Registry Keys and Values

The first step in creating a new Registry key and value is to instantiate the `WshShell` object within your VBScript. Then, using the `WshShell` object's `RegWrite()` method, all you have to do is provide the name of a new key or value and its location within one of the five Registry root keys. For example, the following statements create a new key called `GameKey` under the `HKEY_Current_User` root key, and then create a value called `HomeFolder` and assign it a string of `"C:\VBScript\Games"`.

```
Set objWshShell = WScript.CreateObject("WScript.Shell")
objWshShell.RegWrite "HKCU\GameKey\HomeFolder", "C:\VBScript\Games"
```

You can later modify the Registry value by simply changing its assignment like this:

```
Set objWshShell = WScript.CreateObject("WScript.Shell")
objWshShell.RegWrite "HKCU\GameKey\HomeFolder", "C:\MyGames\VBScript"
```

A single Registry key can be used to store any number of values. For example, the following statements establish a second value named `FileType` under the `GameKey` key and assign it a string of `".txt"`:

```
Set objWshShell = WScript.CreateObject("WScript.Shell")
objWshShell.RegWrite "HKCU\GameKey\FileType", ".txt"
```

Accessing Information Stored in the Registry

After a Registry key and one or more values have been established, you can read them using the `WshShell` object's `RegRead()` method. For example, the following statements read and then display the value stored in the previous example:

```
Set objWshObject = WScript.CreateObject("WScript.Shell")
strResults = objWshObject.RegRead("HKCU\GameKey\FileType")
MsgBox strResults
```

Deleting Keys and Values

Now let's delete one of the two Registry values that we've just created using the `WshShell` object's `RegDelete()` method, as follows:

```
Set objWshObject = WScript.CreateObject("WScript.Shell")
objWshObject.RegDelete "HKCU\GameKey\FileType"
```

In similar fashion, you can delete the `GameKey` key, thus deleting all the values that it stores, like this:

```
Set objWshObject = WScript.CreateObject("WScript.Shell")
objWshObject.RegDelete "HKCU\GameKey\"
```

Take note of the \ character that follows the word `GameKey` in the previous statement. This character tells the `RegDelete()` method that the specified element is a Registry key and not a value.

Retrieving System Information Stored in the Registry

Now that you know the basics of reading, writing, modifying, and deleting Registry keys and values, look at the following example. In this example, the `ProcessorInfo.vbs` script shows how to retrieve information about the processor (that is, the CPU) of the computer on which the script is run.

```
'*************************************************************************
'Script Name: ProcessorInfo.vbs
'Author: Jerry Ford
'Created: 12/13/02
'Description: This script collects CPU information about the computer that
'it is running on.
'*************************************************************************

'Initialization Section

Option Explicit

Dim objWshShl, intResponse, strCpuSpeed, strCpuVendor, strCpuID

'Set up an instance of the WshShell object
Set objWshShl = WScript.CreateObject("WScript.Shell")


'Main Processing Section

'Prompt for permission to continue
intResponse = MsgBox("This VBScript gathers information about your " & _
   "processor from the Windows registry." & vbCrLf & vbCrLf & _
  "Do you wish to continue?", 4)

'Call the function that collects CPU information
If intResponse = 6 Then
  GetProcessorInfo()
End If

WScript.Quit()

'Procedure Section

Function GetProcessorInfo()

  'Get the processor speed
  strCpuSpeed = objWshShl.RegRead _
    ("HKLM\HARDWARE\DESCRIPTION\System\CentralProcessor\0\~MHz")
```

```
  'Get the manufacturer name
  strCpuVendor = objWshShl.RegRead _
    ("HKLM\HARDWARE\DESCRIPTION\System\CentralProcessor\0\VendorIdentifier")

  'Get processor ID information
  strCpuID = objWshShl.RegRead _
    ("HKLM\HARDWARE\DESCRIPTION\System\CentralProcessor\0\Identifier")

  MsgBox "Speed:  " & strCpuSpeed & vbCrLf & "Manufacturer:  " & _
    strCpuVendor & vbCrLf & "ID:  " & strCpuID

End Function
```

The script's Initialization Section defines its variables and instantiates the `WshShell` object. The Main Processing Section prompts the user for confirmation before continuing, and then calls the `GetProcessorInfo()` function before executing the `WScript.Quit()` method, thus terminating the script's execution.

The `GetProcessorInfo()` function performs three Registry read operations using the `WshShell` object's `RegRead()` method. Each read operation retrieves a different piece of information about the computer's processor. The function then uses the VBScript `MsgBox()` function to display a text string of the information collected about the computer's processor.

For additional examples of how to use VBScript to interact with the Windows Registry, refer to the "Desktop Administration" section in Appendix A, "WSH Administrative Scripting." You'll find two scripts that demonstrate how to perform desktop administration by manipulating Registry settings to configure the Windows desktop and screen saver.

Back to Part 2 of the Hangman Game

Now that you've had a review of the Windows Registry, including its overall structure and design, let's modify the Hangman game to work with the Registry. You might want to take a few minutes to review the design of the Hangman script as shown at the end of Chapter 9.

Because you already have the basic Hangman script written, all you have to do to complete this chapter's project is to focus on creating the new Hangman setup script, and on modifying the parts of the original Hangman script affected by the changes. You tackle this project in two stages: creating a setup script that establishes registry settings and updating the Hangman script to retrieve the registry settings each time the game executes.

Creating the Setup Script

In stage 1, you'll create a VBScript called `HangmanSetup.vbs`. This script will create and store a Registry key called `Hangman` in the `HKEY_CURRENT_USER` root key (referred to in the script as `HKCU`). Within this key, a value called `ListLocation` will be created and assigned a string identifying the location where you plan to store your Hangman word files. The `HangmanSetup.vbs` script will be developed in three steps.

1. Create a new script, adding your VBScript template and defining the variables and objects used by this VBScript.
2. Set up the controlling logic in the Main Processing Section, first prompting for confirmation before continuing, and then finally calling the procedure that creates the Registry key and value.
3. Set up the Procedure Section by adding the `SetHangmanKeyAndValue()` function, which performs the actual modification of the Registry.

Defining Variables and Objects

By now, this step should be very familiar to you. Begin by copying over your VBScript template and filling in information about the new script.

```
'*************************************************************************
'Script Name: HangmanSetup.vbs
'Author: Jerry Ford
'Created: 12/14/02
'Description: This script configures Registry entries for the Hangman.vbs
'game.
'*************************************************************************


'Initialization Section

Option Explicit
```

Next, define the variables and objects required by the script. As you can see here, this is a very simple script, with only a few items that need to be defined:

```
Dim objWshShl, intResponse

Set objWshShl = WScript.CreateObject("WScript.Shell")
```

The first variable represents the `WshShell` object, and the second variable stores the user's response when asked whether he or she wants to make the Registry change.

Get Confirmation First

The Main Processing Section prompts the user for confirmation and then tests the results returned by the `InputBox()` function before proceeding. If the value returned is equal to `6`, then the user elected to continue. Otherwise, the `WScript` object's `Quit()` method terminates script execution.

```
'Main Processing Section

'Ask for confirmation before proceeding
intResponse = MsgBox("This VBScript establishes registry settings " & _
  "for the Hangman game. Do you wish to continue?", 4)

If intResponse = 6 Then
  SetHangmanKeyAndValue()
End If

WScript.Quit()
```

Modify the Registry

The final step in creating this script is to define a function that creates the new Registry key and value. As you saw earlier in this chapter, this operation is accomplished using the `WshShell` object's `RegWrite()` method.

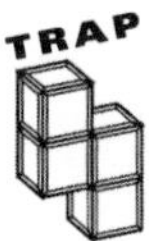

When deciding what Registry key and value to create in situations like this, it's critical that you take steps to ensure that you don't accidentally overwrite an already existing key or value of the same name. Otherwise, you might accidentally disable another application or even a Windows component. In the case of this script, it's virtually certain that the key and value I defined will not be in use. However, if there is any doubt, you can add logic to your VBScripts that first check to determine whether the key and value already exist before proceeding.

```
'Procedure Section

Function SetHangmanKeyAndValue()

  objWshShl.RegWrite "HKCU\VBGames\Hangman\ListLocation", "c:\Hangman"

End Function
```

Assembling the Entire Setup Script

Now let's put the three sections of this script together; then run the script and click on Yes when prompted for confirmation. If you want to, you can use the Regedit utility to go behind your script and make sure that it created the new Registry key and value as expected.

```
'*************************************************************************
'Script Name: HangmanSetup.vbs
'Author: Jerry Ford
'Created: 12/14/02
'Description: This script configures Registry entries for the Hangman.vbs
'game.
'*************************************************************************


'Initialization Section

Option Explicit

Dim objWshShl, intResponse

Set objWshShl = WScript.CreateObject("WScript.Shell")


'Main Processing Section

'Ask for confirmation before proceeding
intResponse = MsgBox("This VBScript establishes registry settings " & _
  "for the Hangman game. Do you wish to continue?", 4)

If intResponse = 6 Then
  SetHangmanKeyAndValue()
End If

WScript.Quit()


'Procedure Section

Function SetHangmanKeyAndValue()
```

```
  objWshShl.RegWrite "HKCU\VBGames\Hangman\ListLocation", "c:\Hangman"

End Function
```

You only need to run this script one time to set up a computer to play the Hangman game. However, you need to modify and rerun this script if you decide to change the location of the folder in which you plan to store your Hangman word files.

Updating the Hangman Game

In this second part of the project's development, you will modify the original Hangman script so that it retrieves from the Registry the location of the folder that stores the Hangman word files. You'll also add logic that enables the script to open and read the contents of the word files. To accomplish this goal, the original Hangman script needs to be modified in five steps.

1. Open the Hangman script and modify its Initialization Section to include additional variables and object references required to support the script's new functionality.
2. Delete the `FillArray()` function, which was responsible for retrieving a randomly selected word from an internal array, from the script.
3. Modify the `RetrieveWord()` function to call two new functions, `GetWordFileLocation()` and `SelectAWordCategory()`. Add logic that processes the word file specified by the player to randomly select a game word.
4. Create the `GetWordFileLocation()` function, which retrieves the location of the folder where the word files are stored from the Windows Registry.
5. Create the `SelectAWordCategory()` function, which presents the player with a list of word categories based on the word files that it finds in the folder.

You should make a copy of your current Hangman script and modify the copy instead of the original script. This way, if something goes wrong, you'll still have your original working version of the game to play.

Updating the Initialization Section

You need to make several changes to the Hangman script's Initialization Section. These include defining new variables used by new portions of the script. These variables appear in boldface in the following:

```
'Initialization Section
```

```
Option Explicit

Const cTitlebarMsg = "VBScript HANGMAN"

Dim strChoice, strGameWord, intNoMisses, intNoRight, strSplashimage
Dim intPlayOrNot, strMsgText, intPlayAgain, strWrongGuesses
Dim strRightGuesses, blnWordGuessed, intLetterCounter
Dim strTempStringOne, strTempStringTwo, strWordLetter, strDisplayString
Dim strFlipCounter, intRandomNo, strProcessGuess, blnGameStatus
Dim strCheckAnswer, objWshShl, strGameFolder, objFsoObject, objGameFiles
Dim strSelection, strFileString, strCharactersToRemove
Dim blnValidResponse, strSelectCategory, strInputFile, strWordFile
Dim intNoWordsInFile, intLinesInFile, strWordList
```

In addition, you need to delete the following statement because the array that held the game words used in the original version of the script is no longer supported:

```
Dim astrWordList(9)  'Define an array that can hold 10 game words
```

Finally, you need to instantiate both the `FileSystemObject` and the `WshShell` object like this:

```
'Set up an instance of the FileSystemObject

Set objFsoObject = CreateObject("Scripting.FileSystemObject")

'Set up an instance of the WshShell object
Set objWshShl = WScript.CreateObject("WScript.Shell")
```

Methods and properties belonging to the `FileSystemObject` object are required to read and process the words stored in the game's word files. In addition, the `WshShell` object's `RegRead()` method is needed to retrieve the location of the folder where the game's word files are stored.

Removing Obsolete Statements

The next thing to do is delete the `FillArray()` function, shown next, from the VBScript. Before doing so, copy and paste each of the words defined by this array into a blank Notepad file, each on its own separate line. Save the file in a folder called Hangman on your computer's `C:` drive and name the file `General.txt` (that is, save it as `C:\Hangman\General.txt`). This text file will be used to retrieve game words for the new and improved version of the game.

```
FillArray()

Function FillArray()

  'Add the words to the array
  astrWordList(0) = "AUTOMOBILE"
  astrWordList(1) = "NETWORKING"
  astrWordList(2) = "PRACTICAL"
  astrWordList(3) = "CONGRESS"
  astrWordList(4) = "COMMANDER"
  astrWordList(5) = "STAPLER"
  astrWordList(6) = "ENTERPRISE"
  astrWordList(7) = "ESCALATION"
  astrWordList(8) = "HAPPINESS"
  astrWordList(9) = "WEDNESDAY"

End Function
```

While you're at it, you might want to create one or two other word files, give them names that describe their contents, and then save them in the Hangman folder. This way, the player will have more than one category of words to choose from when playing the game.

Modifying the RetrieveWord() Function

You should begin modifying the `RetrieveWord()` function by first deleting all its statements and then adding the statements shown next. As you can see, I have added a number of comments to this code to explain its construction in detail.

```
'This function retrieves a randomly selected word from a word file
Function RetrieveWord()

  'Locate the folder where collections of game words are stored
  strGameFolder = GetstrWordFileLocation()

  'Get the player to select a word category
  strSelectCategory = SelectAWordCategory(strGameFolder)

  'Create the complete path and file name for the selected word file
  strInputFile = strGameFolder & "\" & strSelectCategory

  'Open the file for reading
```

```
  Set strWordFile = objFsoObject.OpenTextFile(strInputFile, 1)

  'Set this variable to zero. It represents the No of words in the file
  intNoWordsInFile = 0

  'Count the number of words in the file
  Do while False = strWordFile.AtEndOfStream
    'Read a line
    strWordFile.ReadLine()
    'Keep count of the number of words (or lines) read
    intNoWordsInFile = intNoWordsInFile + 1
    'If the loop iterates more than 50 times something is wrong
    If intNoWordsInFile > 50 Then
      Exit Do
    End If
  Loop

  'Close the file when done counting the number of words (or lines)
  strWordFile.Close

  'Pick a random number between 1 and the number of words in the file
  Randomize
  intRandomNo = FormatNumber(Int((intNoWordsInFile + 1) * Rnd),0)

  'Open the file for reading
  Set strWordFile = objFsoObject.OpenTextFile(strInputFile, 1)

  'Skip the reading of all words prior to the randomly selected word
  For intLinesInFile = 1 to intRandomNo - 1
    'Read the randomly selected word
    strWordFile.SkipLine()
  Next

  'Return the randomly selected word to the calling statement
  RetrieveWord = strWordFile.ReadLine()

  'Close the file when done
  strWordFile.Close

End Function
```

Create the GetWordFileLocation() Function

The `RetrieveWord()` function calls upon the `GetWordFileLocation()` function, shown here, to retrieve the location of the folder where the Hangman game's word files are stored (that is, the function retrieves the information stored in the Windows Registry by the `HangmanSetup.vbs` script).

```
'This function retrieves the location of folder where word files are stored
Function GetstrWordFileLocation()

  'Get the folder name and path from its assigned Registry value
  GetstrWordFileLocation = _
    objWshShl.RegRead("HKCU\VBGames\Hangman\ListLocation")

End Function
```

Create the SelectAWordCategory() Function

The `RetrieveWord()` function also calls upon the `SelectAWordCategory()` function, shown next, to prompt the player to select a word category from which the game's mystery word should be randomly selected. This function takes one argument, `TargetFolder`, which is the location of the folder where the word files are stored. The function then displays a list of word categories based on the word files stored in the folder and prompts the player to select one. If the player fails to make a selection, the function automatically specifies the `General` category as the default. Again, I've added plenty of comments to the function to document its construction.

```
'This function returns a word category
Function SelectAWordCategory(TargetFolder)

  'Specify the location of the folder that stores the word files
  Set strGameFolder = objFsoObject.GetFolder(TargetFolder)
  'Get a list of files stored in the folder
  Set objGameFiles = strGameFolder.Files

  strSelection = ""

  'Loop through the list of word files
  For Each strWordList In objGameFiles
```

```
    'Build a master string containing a list of all the word files
    strFileString = strFileString & strWordList.Name

    'Remove the .txt portion of each file's file name.
    strCharactersToRemove = Len(strWordList.Name) - 4

    'Build a display string showing the category names of each word file
    strSelection = strSelection & _
      Left(strWordList.Name, strCharactersToRemove) & vbCrLf

  Next

  blnValidResponse = "False"

  'Loop until a valid category strSelection has been made
  Do Until blnValidResponse = "True"

    'Prompt the player to select a word category
    strChoice = InputBox("Please specify the name of a word category " & _
      "from which game words will be selected." & vbCrLf & vbCrLf & _
      "Available Categories:" & vbCrLf & vbCrLf & _
      strSelection, "Pick a Category" , "General")

    'If input is not in master string the player must try again
    If InStr(UCase(strFileString), UCase(strChoice)) = 0 Then
      MsgBox "Sorry but this is not a valid category. Please try again."
    Else
      blnValidResponse = "True"
    End If

  Loop

  'If the player typed nothing then specify a default word category
  If Len(strChoice) = 0 Then
    strChoice = "General"
  End If

  'Add the .txt portion of the file name back
  SelectAWordCategory = strChoice & ".txt"

End Function
```

Viewing the Completed Hangman Script

That's it! Your new and improved version of the Hangman script, shown next, should be ready for testing. Don't forget to test it thoroughly and to have someone else test it as well.

```
'*************************************************************************
'Script Name: Hangman-2.vbs
'Author: Jerry Ford
'Created: 12/14/02
'Description: This is a Registry-enabled version of Hangman.vbs.
'*************************************************************************


'Initialization Section

Option Explicit

Const cTitlebarMsg = "VBScript HANGMAN"

Dim strChoice, strGameWord, intNoMisses, intNoRight, strSplashimage
Dim intPlayOrNot, strMsgText, intPlayAgain, strWrongGuesses
Dim strRightGuesses, blnWordGuessed, intLetterCounter
Dim strTempStringOne, strTempStringTwo, strWordLetter, strDisplayString
Dim strFlipCounter, intRandomNo, strProcessGuess, blnGameStatus
Dim strCheckAnswer, objWshShl, strGameFolder, objFsoObject, objGameFiles
Dim strSelection, strFileString, strCharactersToRemove
Dim blnValidResponse, strSelectCategory, strInputFile, strWordFile
Dim intNoWordsInFile, intLinesInFile, strWordList

'Set up an instance of the FileSystemObject
Set objFsoObject = CreateObject("Scripting.FileSystemObject")

'Set up an instance of the WshShell object
Set objWshShl = WScript.CreateObject("WScript.Shell")

'Main Processing Section

intPlayOrNot = DoYouWantToPlay()
If intPlayOrNot = 6 Then 'User elected to play the game
  PlayTheGame()
```

```
End If

SplashScreen()

WScript.Quit()


'Procedure Section

Function DoYouWantToPlay()

  'Display the splash screen and ask the user if he or she wants to play
  strSplashimage = Space(100) & "***********" & vbCrLf & _
    "W E L C O M E  T O  " & Space(68) & "*" & Space(18) & "*" & _
    vbCrLf & Space(100) & "O" & Space(18) & "*" & vbCrLf & _
    "V B S c r i p t  H A N G M A N !" & Space(50) & "--||--" & _
    Space(15) & "*" & vbCrLf & Space(99) & "/" & Space(1) & "\" & _
    Space(17) & "*" & vbCrLf & Space(120) & "*" & vbCrLf & _
    Space(120) & "*" & vbCrLf & space(113) & " *******                " & _
    vbCrLf & "Would you like to play a game?" & vbCrLf & " "

  DoYouWantToPlay = MsgBox(strSplashimage, 36, cTitlebarMsg)

End Function


Function PlayTheGame()

  'Initialize variables displayed in the game's initial pop-up dialog
  intNoMisses = 0
  intNoRight = 0
  strWrongGuesses = ""
  strRightGuesses = ""

  'Get the game a mystery word
  strGameWord = RetrieveWord()
```

```
'Call the function that formats the initial pop-up dialog display string
strDisplayString = InitialDisplayString()

strTempStringOne = strGameWord

'Let the player start guessing
Do Until intNoMisses = 6

  'Collect the player's guess
  strChoice = InputBox(vbCrLf & vbTab & strDisplayString & vbCrLf & _
    vbCrLf & vbCrLf & "No. of Misses: " & intNoMisses & "   " & vbTab & _
           "Incorrect:" & strWrongGuesses & vbCrLf & vbCrLf & vbCrLf & _
           "Type a letter and click on OK." , cTitleBarMsg)

  'Determine if the player has quit
  If strChoice = "" Then
    Exit Function
  End If

  strProcessGuess = FirstLevelValidation()

  'The Player wants to quit the game
  If strProcessGuess = "ExitFunction" Then
    Exit Function
  End If

  'The player typed invalid input
  If strProcessGuess <> "SkipRest" Then

    strProcessGuess = SecondLevelValidation()

    Select Case strProcessGuess
      Case "DuplicateWrongAnswer"
        MsgBox "Invalid: You've already guessed this incorrect letter."
      Case "DuplicateRightAnswer"
        MsgBox "Invalid: You've already guessed this correct letter."
      Case Else
```

```
          strCheckAnswer = TestLetterGuess()
          If strCheckAnswer <> "IncorrectAnswer" Then

            'Reset the value of the variable used to build a string
            'containing the interim stage of the word as currently
            'guessed by the player
            strTempStringTwo = ""

            NonGuessedString()

            'Check to see if the player has guessed the word
            blnGameStatus = CheckIfGameWon()
            If blnGameStatus = "yes" Then
              blnWordGuessed = "True"
              Exit Do
            End If

            'Set the value of the temporary string equal to the string
            'created by the 'Previous For...Next loop
            strTempStringOne = strTempStringTwo

            'Clear out the value of the strDisplayString variable

            strDisplayString = ""

            FlipString()

          End If
      End Select
    End If
  Loop

  DisplayGameResults()

End Function

Function InitialDisplayString()
```

```
  'Create a loop that processes each letter of the word
  For intLetterCounter = 1 to Len(strGameWord)
    'Use underscore characters to display string representing each letter
    InitialDisplayString = InitialDisplayString & "_ "
  Next

End Function

'Determine if the player won or lost and display game results
Function DisplayGameResults()

  'Set message depending on whether or not player figured out the word
  If blnWordGuessed = "True" Then
    strMsgText = "Congratulations, You Win!"
  Else
    strMsgText = "Sorry, You Lose."
  End If

  'Display the results of the game
  intPlayAgain = MsgBox(vbCrLf & "The word was:  " & _
    UCase(strGameWord) & vbCrLf & vbCrLf & vbCrLf & strMsgText & vbCrLf & _
    vbCrLf & vbCrLf & "Would you like to play again?" , 4, cTitleBarMsg)

  'Find out if the player wants to play another game
  If intPlayAgain = 6 Then
    'If answer is yes reset the following variables and start a new game
    strDisplayString = ""
    strTempStringTwo = ""
    PlayTheGame()
  End If

End Function

'This function retrieves a randomly selected word from a word file
Function RetrieveWord()

  'Locate the folder where collections of game words are stored
  strGameFolder = GetstrWordFileLocation()
```

```
'Get the player to select a word category
strSelectCategory = SelectAWordCategory(strGameFolder)

'Create the complete path and file name for the selected word file
strInputFile = strGameFolder & "\" & strSelectCategory

'Open the file for reading
Set strWordFile = objFsoObject.OpenTextFile(strInputFile, 1)

'Set this variable to zero. It represents the No of words in the file
intNoWordsInFile = 0

'Count the number of words in the file
Do while False = strWordFile.AtEndOfStream
  'Read a line
  strWordFile.ReadLine()
  'Keep count of the number of words (or lines) read
  intNoWordsInFile = intNoWordsInFile + 1
  'If the loop iterates more than 50 times something is wrong
  If intNoWordsInFile > 50 Then
    Exit Do
  End If
Loop

'Close the file when done counting the number of words (or lines)
strWordFile.Close

'Pick a random number between 1 and the number of words in the file
Randomize
intRandomNo = FormatNumber(Int((intNoWordsInFile + 1) * Rnd),0)

'Open the file for reading
Set strWordFile = objFsoObject.OpenTextFile(strInputFile, 1)

'Skip the reading of all words prior to the randomly selected word
For intLinesInFile = 1 to intRandomNo - 1
  'Read the randomly selected word
  strWordFile.SkipLine()
```

```
  Next

  'Return the randomly selected word to the calling statement
  RetrieveWord = strWordFile.ReadLine()

  'Close the file when done
  strWordFile.Close

End Function

'This function retrieves location of folder where word files are stored
Function GetstrWordFileLocation()

  'Get the folder name and path from its assigned Registry value
  GetstrWordFileLocation = _
    objWshShl.RegRead("HKCU\VBGames\Hangman\ListLocation")

End Function

'This function returns a word category
Function SelectAWordCategory(TargetFolder)

  'Specify the location of the folder that stores the word files
  Set strGameFolder = objFsoObject.GetFolder(TargetFolder)
  'Get a list of files stored in the folder
  Set objGameFiles = strGameFolder.Files

  strSelection = ""

  'Loop through the list of word files
  For Each strWordList In objGameFiles

    'Build a master string containing a list of all the word files
    strFileString = strFileString & strWordList.Name

    'Remove the .txt portion of each file's file name.
    strCharactersToRemove = Len(strWordList.Name) - 4
```

```
    'Build a display string showing the category names of each word file
    strSelection = strSelection & _
      Left(strWordList.Name, strCharactersToRemove) & vbCrLf

  Next

  blnValidResponse = "False"

  'Loop until a valid category strSelection has been made
  Do Until blnValidResponse = "True"

    'Prompt the player to select a word category
    strChoice = InputBox("Please specify the name of a word category " & _
      "from which game words will be selected." & vbCrLf & vbCrLf & _
      "Available Categories:" & vbCrLf & vbCrLf & _
      strSelection, "Pick a Category" , "General")

    'If input is not in master string the player must try again
    If InStr(UCase(strFileString), UCase(strChoice)) = 0 Then
      MsgBox "Sorry but this is not a valid category. Please try again."
    Else
      blnValidResponse = "True"
    End If

  Loop

  'If the player typed nothing then specify a default word category
  If Len(strChoice) = 0 Then
    strChoice = "General"
  End If

  'Add the .txt portion of the file name back
  SelectAWordCategory = strChoice & ".txt"

End Function

'This function displays the game splash screen
Function SplashScreen()
```

```
  MsgBox "Thank you for playing VBScript Hangman © Jerry Ford 2002." & _
    vbCrLf & vbCrLf & "Please play again soon!", , cTitlebarMsg
End Function

'Validate the player's input
Function FirstLevelValidation()

  'See if the player clicked on cancel or failed to enter any input
  If strChoice = "" Then
    FirstLevelValidation = "ExitFunction"
    Exit Function
  End If

  'Make sure the player only typed 1 letter
  If Len(strChoice) > 1 Then
    MsgBox "Invalid: You must only enter 1 letter at a time!"
    FirstLevelValidation = "SkipRest"
  Else
    'Make sure the player did not type a number by accident
    If IsNumeric(strChoice) = "True" Then
      MsgBox "Invalid: Only letters can be accepted as valid input!"
      FirstLevelValidation = "SkipRest"
    Else
      FirstLevelValidation = "Continue"
    End If
  End If

End Function

Function SecondLevelValidation()

  'Check to see if this letter is already on the incorrectly guessed list
  If Instr(1, strWrongGuesses, UCase(strChoice), 1) <> 0 Then
    SecondLevelValidation = "DuplicateWrongAnswer"
  Else
    'Check to see if this letter is already on the correctly guessed list
    If Instr(1, strRightGuesses, UCase(strChoice), 1) <> 0 Then
      SecondLevelValidation = "DuplicateRightAnswer"
```

```
    End If
  End If

End Function

Function CheckIfGameWon()

  'Check and see if player has guessed all the letters that make up the
  'word. If so set the indicator variable and exit the Do...Until loop
  If intNoRight = Len(strGameWord) Then
    CheckIfGameWon = "yes"
  End If

End Function

Function NonGuessedString()

  'Loop through the temporary string
  For intLetterCounter = 1 to Len(strTempStringOne)
    'Examine each letter in the word one at a time
    strWordLetter = Mid(strTempStringOne, intLetterCounter, 1)
    'Otherwise add a underscore character indicating a nonmatching guess
    If UCase(strWordLetter) <> UCase(strChoice) Then
      strTempStringTwo = strTempStringTwo & strWordLetter
    Else
      'The letter matches the guess so add it to the temporary string
      intNoRight = intNoRight + 1
      strRightGuesses = strRightGuesses & " " & UCase(strChoice)
      strTempStringTwo = strTempStringTwo & "_"
    End If
  Next

End Function

Function FlipString()

  'Spin through and reverse the letters in the strTempStringTwo variable
  'In order to switch letters to underscore characters and underscore
```

```
  'characters to the appropriate letters
  For strFlipCounter = 1 to Len(strTempStringTwo)
    'Examine each letter in the word one at a time
    strWordLetter = Mid(strTempStringTwo, strFlipCounter, 1)
    'Replace each letter with the underscore character
    If strWordLetter <> "_" Then
      strDisplayString = strDisplayString & "_ "
    Else
      'Replace each underscore with its appropriate letter
      strDisplayString = strDisplayString & _
        Right(Left(strGameWord,strFlipCounter),1) & " "
    End If
  Next

End Function

Function TestLetterGuess()

  If Instr(1, UCase(strGameWord), UCase(strChoice), 1) = 0 Then
    'Add the letter to the list of incorrectly guessed letters
    strWrongGuesses = strWrongGuesses & " " & UCase(strChoice)
    'Increment the number of guesses that the player has made by 1
    intNoMisses = intNoMisses + 1
    'If player has missed 6 guesses then he has used up all his chances
    If intNoMisses = 6 Then
      blnWordGuessed = "False"
    End If
    TestLetterGuess = "IncorrectGuess"
  Else
    TestLetterGuess = "CorrectGuess"
  End If

End Function
```

SUMMARY

In this chapter, you learned how to write scripts that programmatically interact with the Windows Registry; this included reading, writing, and modifying Registry keys and values.

These new programming techniques provide you with tools for externalizing script configuration information, allowing you to change your script configuration settings without having to make direct modifications to your scripts, and without having to worry about making mistakes while you do it. In addition, I showed you how to use text files as another source of data input for your VBScripts.

CHALLENGES

1. **Create new collection of word files to increase the number of categories available to the player.**
2. **Add an error-handling routine to the `HangmanSetup.vbs` script and use it to report any problems that may occur when the script attempts to perform the `RegWrite()` method.**
3. **Modify `HangmanSetup.vbs` to display a pop-up dialog that asks the user to agree to abide by any terms that you choose to specify to play the game. Store a value indicating whether or not the user has accepted the terms in the Registry. Check this value each time the Hangman game is started, allowing the user to play only if the terms have been accepted and prompting the user to accept the terms again if they have not been accepted yet.**
4. **Create and store a variable in the Registry and modify `Hangman.vbs` to increment it every time the game is started. Use this value to track the number of games played. Check this value each time the game starts to determine whether it exceeds a value of 20. Then, if the user has not yet accepted your terms, prevent the game from running and force the user to accept your terms to play.**

Working with Built-In VBScript Objects

To get any real work done VBScript depends on access to objects and their associated properties and methods. So far, you have learned how to work with objects provided by the WSH and the VBScript run-time object model. Besides these collections of objects, your VBScripts have access to a small collection of built-in or core objects. Using these built-in VBScript objects, you can create scripts that react to errors, create their own custom objects, and perform a host of complex parsing operations when dissecting the contents of strings. Besides discussing VBScript's built-in objects, this chapter also assists you in creating a Tic-Tac-Toe game. Specifically, you will

- Review VBScript's built-in objects and collections
- Learn how to define your own custom objects
- Learn how to associate properties and methods with custom objects
- Learn how to trigger events associated with custom objects
- Learn how to perform advanced string parsing operations

Project Preview: The Tic-Tac-Toe Game

In this chapter you will learn how to develop a Tic-Tac-Toe game. Through the development of this game you will learn how to create and control a two-player game. To do this you will have to develop the logic that controls who goes next, while simultaneously making sure that every player's move is valid. Figures 11.1 through 11.6 demonstrate the overall flow of the game from beginning to end.

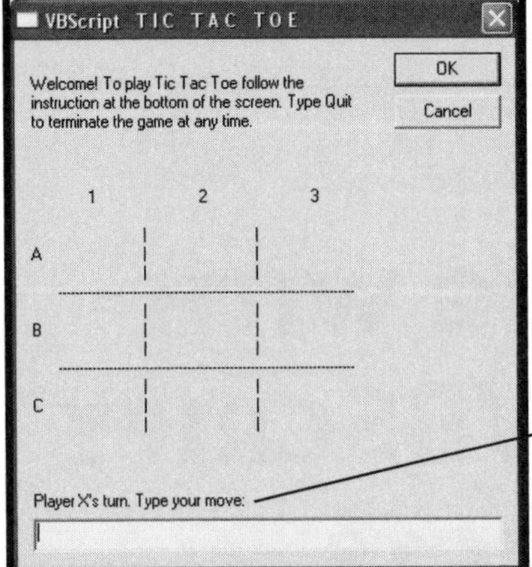

FIGURE 11.1

The game begins by displaying a blank game board and prompting the first player to make a move.

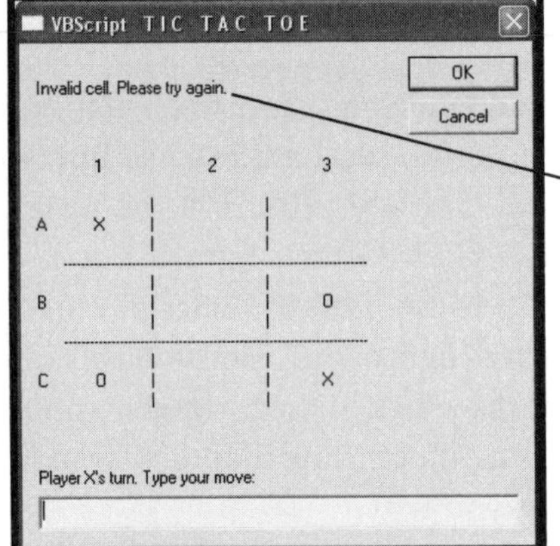

FIGURE 11.2

The game automatically updates the game board after each player's move.

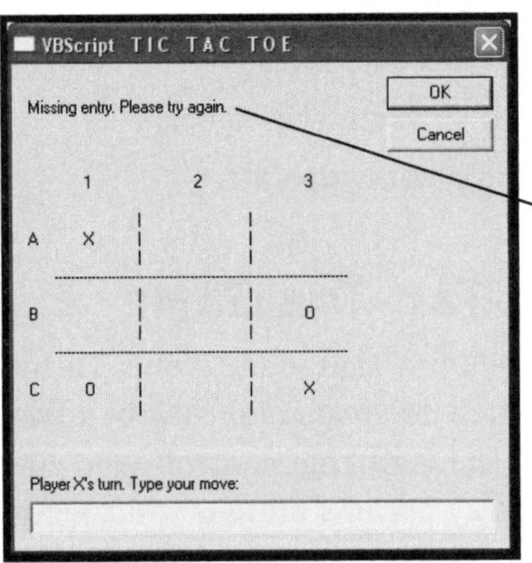

FIGURE 11.3

Messages that provide players with additional instruction when needed are posted at the top of the game board.

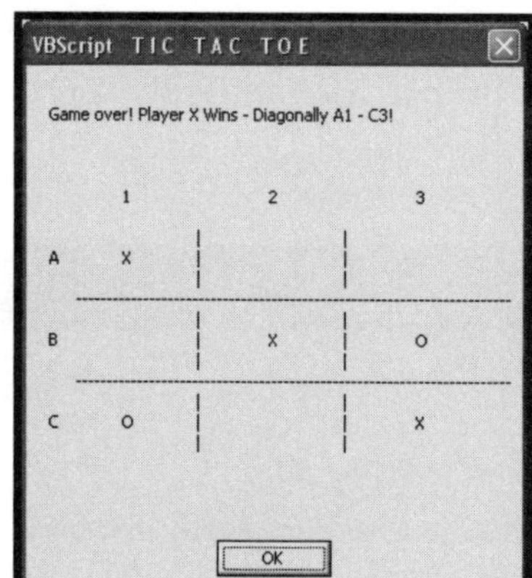

FIGURE 11.4

The results of each game are posted at the top of the game board.

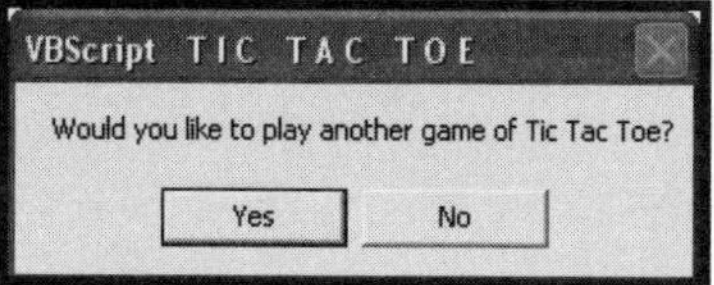

FIGURE 11.5

At the end of each game, players are prompted to play again.

FIGURE 11.6

The game ends by displaying information about itself and its author.

By the end of this chapter you will have learned a great deal about how to work with VBScript's built-in collection of objects. You will also have developed your first multi-player VBScript game.

Leveraging VBScript's Built-In Collection of Objects

VBScript provides a small collection of built-in objects. The VBScript interpreter provides access to these objects. Therefore, they are available to any VBScript regardless of the execution host running it. This collection of objects, though not numerous, provide VBScript with a powerful arsenal of capabilities, including:

- Creating customized objects complete with their own properties and methods
- Intercepting and deal with run-time errors that your VBScripts may encounter
- Performing complex regular expression pattern matching

Table 11.1 displays a list of VBScript's built-in objects and provides a description of each object, as well as a complete listing of all the properties, methods, and events associated with the objects.

TABLE 11.1 VBSCRIPT'S COLLECTION OF BUILT-IN OBJECTS

Object	Description
`Class`	Used to create new custom objects
	Properties: This object does not have any associated properties.
	Methods: This object does not have any associated methods.
	Events: `Initialize`, `Terminate`
`Err`	Used to retrieve information about run-time errors.
	Properties: `Description`, `HelpContext`, `HelpFile`, `Number`, `Source`
	Methods: `Clear`, `Raise`
	Events: This object does not have any associated events.
`Match`	Used to access read-only properties associated with a regular expression match strings.
	Properties: `FirstIndex`, `Length`, `Value`
	Methods: This object does not have any associated methods.
	Events: This object does not have any associated events.
`Matches Collection`	Represents a collection of regular expression `Match` objects.
	Properties: This object does not have any associated properties.
	Methods: This object does not have any associated methods.
	Events: This object does not have any associated events.
`RegExp`	Provides the ability to work with regular expressions.
	Properties: `Global`, `IgnoreCase`, `Pattern`
	Methods: `Execute`, `Replace`, `Test`
	Events: This object does not have any associated events.
`SubMatches Collection`	Used to access read-only values associated with regular expression `submatch` strings.
	Properties: This object does not have any associated properties.
	Methods: This object does not have any associated methods.
	Events: This object does not have any associated events.

Built-In Object Properties

As you can see in Table 11.1, VBScript's built-in objects have a number of associated properties. A description of each of these properties is provided in Table 11.2.

TABLE 11.2 BUILT-IN VBSCRIPT OBJECT PROPERTIES

Property	Description
`Description`	Returns error messages associated with the `Err` object
`FirstIndex`	Returns the starting character location of a substring within a string
`Global`	Returns a `Boolean` value
`HelpContext`	Returns the context ID associated with Help file topic
`HelpFile`	Retrieves the path of the specified Help file
`IgnoreCase`	Returns a value of `True` or `False` depending on whether a pattern search is case-sensitive
`Length`	Retrieves the number of characters associated with a search string match
`Number`	Retrieves an error number
`Pattern`	Returns a regular expression pattern from a search operation
`Source`	Returns the object name responsible for generating an error
`Value`	Retrieves a value from a search string match

Built-In Object Methods

Of all the VBScript built-in objects, only the `Err` object and the `RegExp` objects have methods associated with them. Methods associated with the `Err` object generate and clear errors as outlined here:

- **`Clear()`**. Clears out `Err` object property settings.
- **`Raise()`**. Provides the ability to simulate a run-time error.

Methods associated with the `RegExp` object provide the ability to search strings and to replace portions of strings as outlined here:

- **`Execute()`**. Performs a regular expression search.
- **`Replace()`**. Replaces specified text during a regular expression search.
- **`Test()`**. Returns a Boolean value indicating whether a matching pattern is located within a string.

Creating Custom Objects

VBScript enables you to store data in constants, variables, and arrays. VBScript supports a wide variation of variable subtypes, such as date, string, and integer. However, VBScript does not provide for strict enforcement of variable subtypes, meaning that you can store any type of value in any variable and then change the value type and value later on without raising any errors. Although all this flexibility is great, it also makes it easy to introduce errors. That's why it's best to use strict discipline when working with variables to ensure that you don't allow your scripts to mix data types. VBScript's support for arrays provides for the storage and retrieval of more complex data structures. But again, there is nothing built-in to VBScript to prevent you from mixing and matching data types within your arrays.

By providing you with access to the `Class` object, VBScript gives you the capability to create complex data structures in the form of custom objects. You can then define properties and methods for your custom objects. Once created, you can access custom objects just like you do with any other objects. Custom objects help to improve data consistency because they give you the capability to establish validation procedures that ensure data consistency and enforce strict control over object manipulation.

Defining a Custom Object

You can create a custom object using the `Class...End Class` statements. The `Class` object provides a template for the creation of new objects. Once defined, custom objects must be instantiated just like any other object. The syntax of the `Class...End Class` statement follows:

```
Class ClassName
   Statements
End Class
```

`ClassName` is used to specify the name assigned to the new object. *`Statements`* are variables, properties, and methods that you define within the object. Object properties are defined for objects by adding any of the following statements within the `Class...End Class` statement:

- **`Property Get`**. Enables the retrieval of a value assigned to a private variable.
- **`Property Let`**. Enables the modification of a value assigned to a private variable.
- **`Property Set`**. Enables the modification of a value assigned to a public variable.

Defining Object Properties and Methods

Within the `Class...End Class` statements, variables, properties, and methods can be defined as either private or public using the `Private` and `Public` keywords. Labeling a variable, property or method as `Private` restricts access to only within the `Class`. Labeling a variable, property, or method as `Public` makes it accessible throughout a script.

When not specified, it is assumed that variables, properties, and methods are public. However, it is generally not a good idea to allow variables to be defined with a public scope. Making variables public removes the capability to strictly control their value within an object. Instead, it's better to make object variables private and then allow them to be accessed using the `Property Get` and `Property Let` statements.

To best demonstrate how all this works, let's look at an example. Here a new custom object is defined and assigned the name of `SuperHero`.

```
Class SuperHero

  Private strName

  Public Property Let Name(strIdentity)
    strName = strIdentity
  End property

  Function DisplayName
    MsgBox "Our new hero's name is " & strName & "!"
   End Function

End Class
```

The first statement defines the object and assigns its name. The next statement defines a private variable named `strName`. The three statements that follow define an object property and make it writable by the rest of the script. The next three statements define a method for the object called `DisplayName()`. The last statement ends the definition of the `SuperHero` object.

To exercise your new object definition, create a new script and add the preceding statements to the script's procedure section. Then add the following statements to the Initialization section. These statements define a variable, and then use the variable to instantiate a new `SuperHero` object.

```
Dim objFirstHero
Set objFirstHero = New SuperHero
```

Once instantiated, you can assign a value to the object's Name property by adding the following statement to the script's Main Processing section:

```
objFirstHero.Name = "Captain Adventure"
```

You then can execute the object's DisplayName() method by adding the following statement to the main processing section:

```
objFirstHero.DisplayName()
```

Once assembled, the previous example displays the output shown in Figure 11.7 when executed.

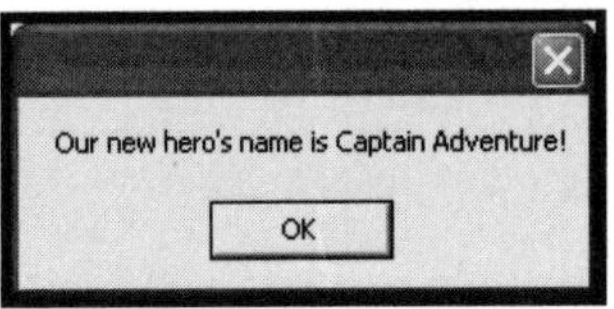
Our new hero's name is Captain Adventure!
OK

FIGURE 11.7 Creating and instantiating a new SuperHero object.

Creating Event Procedures

Custom VBScript objects automatically support two events. These events execute as follows:

- **Class_Initialize**. Executes whenever a new instance of an object is instantiated.
- **Class_Terminate**. Executes whenever an instance of an object is destroyed.

The defining of these procedures is optional. When defined, the Class_Initialize procedure performs tasks such as the definition of variable default values. Similarly, the Class_Terminate procedure performs any cleanup that may be required once an object is no longer needed. For example, the following statements define an initialization procedure for the SuperHero object from the previous example.

```
Private Sub Class_Initialize
    MsgBox "In a blast of smoke and lightning another new super " & _
           "hero is born!"
  End Sub
```

These statements must be added inside the Class...End Class statements. Once defined, they will automatically execute any time a new instance of the SuperHero object is established.

If your script instantiates an object that it does not need anymore, it can destroy that object instance as shown here.

```
Set objFirstHero = Nothing
```

In this example, the object instance is set equal to `Nothing`. This disassociates the specified object variable from an object, releasing any memory allocated to it.

The following example further demonstrates how to define a custom object complete with multiple properties and its own method and event definition.

```
'*************************************************************************
'Script Name: NewObjectDemo.vbs
'Author:      Jerry Ford
'Created:     11/20/04
'Description: This script demonstrates how to create a custom object
'             with its own properties, methods, and events
'*************************************************************************

'Initialization Section

Option Explicit

Dim objFirstHero   'Object variable representing the first super hero
Dim objSecondHero  'Object variable representing the second super hero


'Main Processing Section

ProcessFirstHero()

ProcessSecondHero()

WScript.Quit()


'Procedure Section
```

```
Function ProcessFirstHero()

  Set objFirstHero = New SuperHero  'Instantiate a new SuperHero object

  objFirstHero.Name = "Captain Adventure"  'Assign value to Name property
  objFirstHero.Power = "Laser Vision"   'Assign value to Power property
  objFirstHero.Weakness = "Dog Whistle" 'Assign value to Weakness property
  objFirstHero.Identity = "Bruce Tracy" 'Assign value to Identity property

  objFirstHero.DisplayIdentity()  'Execute the SuperHero object's method

End Function


Function ProcessSecondHero()

  Set objSecondHero = New SuperHero

  objSecondHero.Name = "Captain Marvelous" 'Assign value to Name property
  objSecondHero.Power = "Lightning Speed" 'Assign value to Power property
  objSecondHero.Weakness = "Blue Jello" 'Assign value to Weakness property
  objSecondHero.Identity = "Rob Denton" 'Assign value to Identity property

  objsecondHero.DisplayIdentity()  'Execute the SuperHero object's method

End Function


Class SuperHero

  Private strName, strPower, strWeakness, strIdentity  'Define variables
                                                       'used by this class

  Public Property Let Name(strIdentity) 'Define the Name property
    strName = strIdentity
  End property
```

```
  Public Property Let Power(strSuperPower) 'Define the Power property
    strPower = strSuperPower
  End property

  Public Property Let Weakness(strHurtBy) 'Define the Weakness property
    strWeakness = strHurtBy
  End property

  Public Property Let Identity(strSecretIdentity) 'Define the Identity
    strIdentity = strSecretIdentity                'property
  End property

  Function DisplayIdentity   'This function defines the SuperHero object's
                             'DisplayIdentity() method
    MsgBox strName & vbCrLf & vbCrLf & _
           "Hero Power: " & vbTab & strPower & vbCrLf & _
           "Hero Weakness: " & vbTab & strWeakness & vbCrLf & _
           "Hero Identity: " & vbTab & strIdentity
  End Function

  Private Sub Class_Initialize 'This event automatically executes when
                               'the SuperHero object is instantiated
    MsgBox "In a blast of smoke and lightning another new super " & _
           "hero is born!"
  End Sub

End Class
```

As the script runs, pop-up dialogs will be displayed as shown in Figures 11.8 and 11.9 demonstrating the execution of the `Class_Initialize` event and the object's `DisplayIdentity()` method.

FIGURE 11.8

The `Class_Initialize` event occurs every time a new instance of the `SuperHero` object is established.

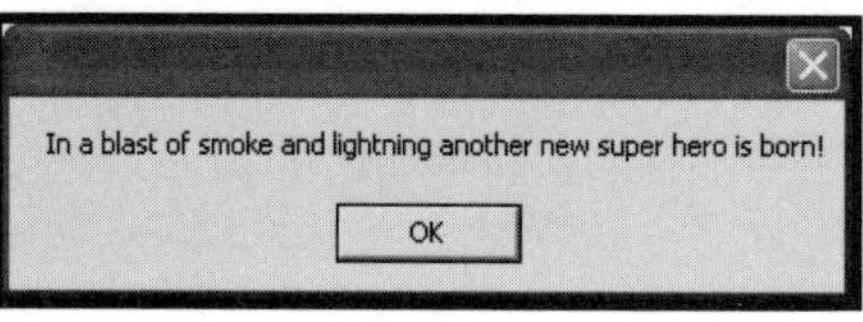

FIGURE 11.9

The SuperHero object's Display Identity() method displays the value of all properties assigned to an instance of an object.

WORKING WITH THE ERR OBJECT

The Err object provides access, via its properties, to information about run-time errors. For example, using the Err object's Description property you can retrieve a string containing an error's description. Using the Err object's Number property you can retrieve the error number associated with an error and using the Err object's Source property you can retrieve the name of the resource that reported the error.

The Err object also provides access to two methods. The Clear() method clears out the properties belonging to the Err object. This is handy in situations where you can develop an effective error handling routine that enables your script to recover from an error and keep running. The Raise() method is equally useful, giving you the capability to simulate run-time errors so that you can test out your script's error handling procedures.

For additional information and examples on how to work with the Err object, refer to Chapter 9, "Handling Script Errors."

WORKING WITH REGULAR EXPRESSIONS

All remaining VBScript built-in objects and collections deal with regular expressions. A *regular expression* is a pattern consisting of characters and metacharacters. Regular expressions are used as a means of searching and replacing patterns within strings.

The first step in preparing your VBScripts to work with regular expressions is to instantiate the RegExp object. This object provides access to the remaining built-in VBScript objects. The RegExp object is instantiated as follows:

```
Dim objRegExp
Set objRegExp = New RegExp
```

The `RegExp` object provides access to the following properties:

- **`Pattern`**. Identifies the pattern to be matched.
- **`IgnoreCase`**. Contains a value of `True` or `False` depending on whether a case-sensitive search is performed.
- **`Global`**. An optional Boolean value used to specify whether all occurrences of the specified pattern are to be replaced.

The RegExp object provides access to several methods, including:

- **`Replace()`**. Replaces matching string patterns.
- **`Test()`**. Performs a pattern search, generating a Boolean value based on whether a match is found.
- **`Execute()`**. Provides the ability to generate a `Matches` collection.

Replacing Matching Patterns

Using the `RegExp` object's `Replace()` method, you can replace matching patterns within a string. The syntax for this method is

```
RegExp.Replace(String1, String2)
```

`String1` identifies the string to search and `String2` identifies the replacement string. To demonstrate how to work with the `Replace()` method, look at the following example:

```
Dim objRegExp
Set objRegExp = New RegExp

objRegExp.Pattern = "planet"

MsgBox objRegExp.Replace("A long time ago on a far away planet", "world")
```

In this example, a variable name `objRegExp` is defined, and then used to instantiate a reference to the `RegExp` object. Next a value of `planet` is assigned to the `RegExp` object's `Pattern` property to define a search pattern. Finally, the `Replace()` method is used to force the replacement of the word `planet` with the word `world`. Figure 11.10 shows the output generated when this example is run.

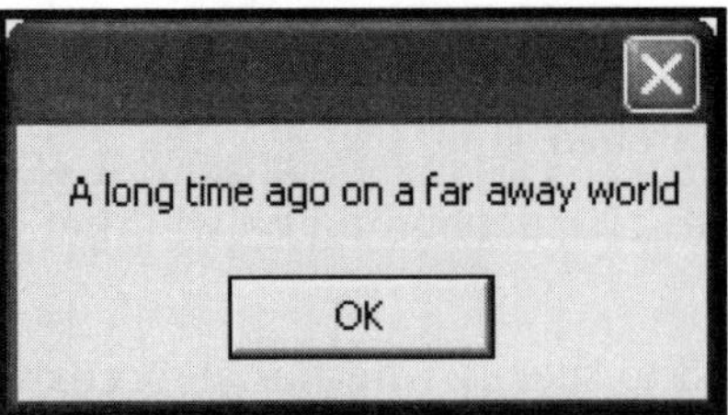

FIGURE 11.10 Using regular expression matching you can substitute a portion of any string.

By default, the `Replace()` method only replaces the first occurrence of a match within the specified search string. However, by setting the value of the `RegExp` object's `Global` property to `True` you can force the replacement of all matching patterns. To see this in action, modify the previous example as follows.

```
Dim objRegExp
Set objRegExp = New RegExp

objRegExp.Pattern = "planet"
objRegExp.Global = "True"

MsgBox objRegExp.Replace("A long time ago on a far away planet", "world")
```

VBScript's support for regular expressions includes the capability to define a host of complex pattern matches through the use of metacharacters. Table 11.3 lists all the metacharacters supported by VBScript.

> **DEFINITION**
>
> A *metacharacter* is a special character used to provide information about other characters. In the case of regular expression, metacharacters specify how a matching pattern is to be processed.

TABLE 11.3 VBSCRIPT REGULAR EXPRESSION METACHARACTERS

Character	Description
\	Sets the next character as a special character, a back reference, a literal, or an octal escape
^	Matches the beginning of the input string
$	Matches the end of the input string
*	Matches the preceding expression (zero or more times)

Table 11.3 VBScript Regular Expression Metacharacters (continued)

Character	Description
+	Matches the preceding expression (one or more times)
?	Matches the preceding expression (zero or one time)
{n}	Matches exactly n times
{n,}	Matches a minimum of n times
{n,m}	Matches a minimum of n times and a maximum of m times
.	Matches any individual character except the newline character
(pattern)	Matches a pattern and allows the matched substring to be retrieved from the Matches collection.
x|y	Matches x or y
[xyz]	Matches any of the specified characters
[^xyz]	Matches any character except those specified
[a-z]	Matches character specified in the range
[^a-z]	Matches character except for those specified in the range
\b	Matches on a word boundary
\B	Matches on a non-word boundary
\cx	Matches the control character specified as x
\d	Matches a single digit number
\D	Matches any single non-numeric character
\f	Matches the form-feed character
\n	Matches the newline character
\r	Matches the carriage return character
\s	Matches any white space character (for example, space, tab, form-feed)
\S	Matches any non-white-space character
\t	Matches the tab character
\v	Matches the vertical tab character
\w	Matches any word character
\W	Matches any non-word character
\xn	Matches n, where n is a two-digit hexadecimal escape value

(continues)

Table 11.3 VBScript Regular Expression Metacharacters (continued)

Character	Description
\num	Matches num, where num is a positive integer in a backward reference to captured matches
\n	Specifies an octal escape value or a back reference
\nml	Matches octal escape value nml where n is an octal digit in the range of 0–3 and m and l are octal digits in the range of 0–7
\un	Matches n, where n is a four-digit hexadecimal Unicode character

To better understand how to take advantage of metacharacters, take a look at the following example:

```
Dim objRegExp
Set objRegExp = New RegExp

objRegExp.Pattern = "[\d]"
objRegExp.Global = "True"

MsgBox objRegExp.Replace("1 years ago on a far away planet", "1000")
```

In this example, specifying the `\d` metacharacter as the value assigned to the `RegExp` object's `Pattern` property results in a replacement operation where any single numeric character is identified as a match. Figure 11.11 shows the output generated when you run this example. As you can see, in this example the number 1 is replaced by the number 1000.

Testing for Matching Patterns

The `RegExp` object's `Test()` method performs a pattern match without actually performing a replacement operation. The syntax for the `Test()` method is

```
RegExp.Test(string)
```

The following statements demonstrate how to use this method. In this example, the script displays one of two messages, depending on whether the string assigned to the `Pattern` property is found within the search string.

Using metacharacters enables you to perform complex substitutions.

```
Dim objRegExp
Set objRegExp = New RegExp

objRegExp.Pattern = "planet"

If objRegExp.Test("A long time ago on a far away planet") = "True" Then
  MsgBox "The word " & objRegExp.Pattern & " was found!"
Else
  MsgBox "The word " & objRegExp.Pattern & " was not found!"
End If
```

Creating Matches Collections

Using the `RegExp` object's `Execute()` method, you can generate a `Matches` collection as a result of a regular expression search. The syntax of the `Execute()` method is

```
RegExp.Execute(string)
```

Once generated, the `Matches` collection is read-only. It is made up of individual `Match` objects. Each `Match` object has its own set of properties, which include:

- **FirstIndex.** Retrieves the starting character positions of a match within a string
- **Length.** Returns the length of a match found within a string
- **Value.** Retrieves the text of the match found within a string

Once a `Matches` collection has been generated, you can process all the members of the collection using a loop, as demonstrated by the next example.

```
Dim objRegExp, objMatchCollection, objMatch, strStory, strDisplayMsg
Set objRegExp = New RegExp
```

```
objRegExp.Pattern = "bear"
objRegExp.Global = "True"

strStory = "Once upon a time there were three little bears. There " & _
  "was mama bear, papa bear and baby bear. There was cousin bear too!"

Set objMatchCollection = objRegExp.Execute(strStory)

For Each objMatch in objMatchCollection
  strDisplayMsg = strDisplayMsg & "An instance of " & _
    objRegExp.Pattern & " found at position " & objMatch.FirstIndex & _
    vbCrLf
Next

MsgBox strDisplayMsg
```

In this example, a `For Each...Next` loop was set up to process each `Match` object in the collection. The `Match` object's `FirstIndex` property was used to retrieve the starting position of each matching pattern in the search string, which was then used to generate the output shown in Figure 11.12.

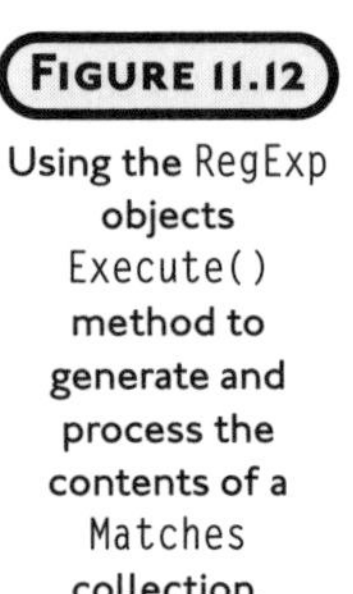
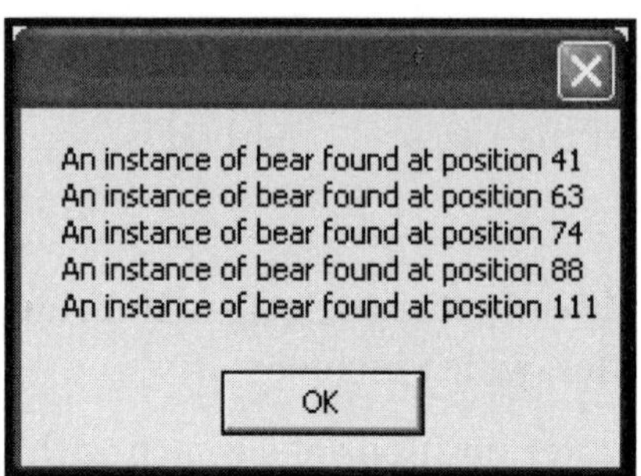
An instance of bear found at position 41
An instance of bear found at position 63
An instance of bear found at position 74
An instance of bear found at position 88
An instance of bear found at position 111
OK

FIGURE 11.12
Using the `RegExp` objects `Execute()` method to generate and process the contents of a `Matches` collection.

Back to the Tic-Tac-Toe Game

The heart of the Tic-Tac-Toe game lies in the design of its game board, which is divided into three sections. Status and error messages are displayed at the top of the board to assist players when mistakes are made playing the game.

In the middle of the board is an image of a traditional Tic-Tac-Toe board. To the right and top of the Tic-Tac-Toe board are letters and numbers, the coordinates of each cell that make up the game board. Players play the game by using these letters and numbers to specify what cell they want to select as their next move. Embedded within the board are variables representing each cell on the board. The values assigned to these variables are set to either an `X` or `O` based on the moves made by each player as the game progresses.

The bottom of the game board is made up of an input text field that enables players to enter their moves. In addition, instruction is provided just above this text field in the form of a text message that is used to keep track of player turns.

Designing the Game

Besides its Initialization and Main Processing sections, the game is made up of nine functions. Each function performs a specific task. Here is a list of the script's functions along with a brief description of their associated tasks:

- **`SetVariableDefaults()`.** Establishes default values for various script variables.
- **`ClearGameBoard()`.** Resets each cell on the Tic-Tac-Toe game board so that it appears as blank or empty.
- **`ManageGamePlay()`.** Controls the overall execution of the game, calling on other functions as necessary.
- **`DisplayBoard()`.** Displays the game board along with instruction, error messages, and any moves already made by each player.
- **`DisplayGameResults()`.** Displays the final results of each game, identifying who won or whether the game results in a tie.
- **`ValidateInput()`.** Ensures that players are only allowed to enter valid cell coordinates when taking their turns.
- **`MarkPlayerSelection()`.** Associates input provided by players with the appropriate cell coordinates on the game board.
- **`SeeIfWon()`.** Checks the game board to determine whether a player has won or whether the game has ended in a tie.
- **`DisplaySplashScreen()`.** Displays information about the script and its author.

Setting Up the Script's Template and Initialization Section

The Tic-Tac-Toe game begins by defining the constants and variables used by the game. Because the game uses a large number of variables, I embedded comments to the right of each variable to identify its purpose.

```
'*************************************************************************
'Script Name:   TicTacToe.vbs
'Author:        Jerry Ford
'Created:       11/15/04
'Description:   This script is a VBScript implementation of the
'                Tic-Tac-Toe game
'*************************************************************************


'Initialization Section

Option Explicit

Const cTitleBarMsg = "VBScript   T I C   T A C   T O E"

Dim A1, A2, A3, B1, B2, B3, C1, C2, C3  'Variables representing sections
                                        'of the Tic Tac Toe game board

Dim blnGameOver              'Boolean variable that determines when to end game
Dim blnPlayerTypedQuit       'Variable used to track whether a player typed Quit
Dim blnStopGame              'Variable used in Main Processing section to
                             'determine when to stop the game
Dim blnValidCell             'Boolean variable that determines whether a player
                             'specified a valid cell

Dim intNoMoves               'Variable used to keep track of the number of plays
Dim intPlayAgain             'Variable holds player response when asked to play
                             'again

Dim strNotificationMsg       'Variable used to display messages to player
Dim strPlayer                'Variable used to identify whose turn it is
Dim strWinner                'Variable used to determine whether the game is won
Dim strPlayerInput           'Variable used to hold the player's cell selection
Dim strDirection             'Variable identifies how the player won the game

blnStopGame = "False"
```

Developing the Logic for the Main Processing Section

The game's main processing section is made up of a Do Until loop and a series of procedure calls. The loop is set up to execute until the players decide to stop playing the game as tracked using a Boolean variable named blnStopGame.

```
Do Until blnStopGame = "True"  'Keep playing until players decide to stop

  SetVariableDefaults()

  ClearGameBoard()

  ManageGamePlay()

  If blnPlayerTypedQuit = "True" Then  'One of the players typed Quit
    blnStopGame = "True"
  Else  'The game is over. Ask the players whether they'd like to play again

    intPlayAgain = MsgBox("Would you like to play another game of " & _
      "Tic Tac Toe?", 4, cTitleBarMsg)

    If intPlayAgain = 7 Then 'A player clicked on No. B break out of loop
      blnStopGame = "True"
    End If

  End If

Loop

DisplaySplashScreen()
```

Building the SetVariableDefaults() Function

The SetVariableDefaults() function, shown here, is straightforward and is responsible for setting default variable values.

```
Function SetVariableDefaults()   'Establish default variable settings

  blnGameOver = "False"
  blnPlayerTypedQuit = "False"
  blnValidCell = "False"
```

```
  intNoMoves = 0

  strNotificationMsg = "Welcome! To play Tic Tac Toe follow the " & _
    "instruction at the bottom of the screen. Type Quit to terminate " & _
    "the game at any time."
  strPlayer = "X"
  strWinner = "None"
  strDirection = ""

End Function
```

Building the ClearGameBoard() Function

The `ClearGameBoard()` function that follows is executed to clear out the contents of the game board to prepare it for a new game. As you can see, the game board is cleared by assigning a blank space to each cell of the board, thus removing any `X`s or `O`s that may be present from a previous game.

```
Function ClearGameBoard()  'Reset the game board

  A1 = " "
  A2 = " "
  A3 = " "
  B1 = " "
  B2 = " "
  B3 = " "
  C1 = " "
  C2 = " "
  C3 = " "

End Function
```

Building the ManageGamePlay() Function

The `ManageGamePlay()` function that follows is controlled by a `Do Until` loop that executes until the value assigned to a variable name `blnGameOver` is set equal to `True`. Within the loop, the function begins by performing a series of checks to determine whether the game has already been won. The first check looks to see whether player `X` has won. If this is the case, the value assigned to `strNotificationMsg` is set to `Game over! Player X Wins` and the value assigned to a variable named `strDirection` is used to identify how the game was won. The display string assigned to `strNotificationMsg` is later used by the `DisplayGameResults()` function. The next check looks to see whether player `0` won. The last check looks to see whether the game has ended in a tie.

```
Function ManageGamePlay()  'Manage the overall execution of the game

  Do Until blnGameOver = "True"

    'Start by checking to see if the game has already been completed
    If strWinner = "X" Then
      strNotificationMsg = "Game over! Player X Wins " & strDirection
      DisplayGameResults()
      blnGameOver = "True"
    End If

    If strWinner = "O" Then
      strNotificationMsg = "Game over! Player O Wins " & strDirection
      DisplayGameResults()
      blnGameOver = "True"
    End If

    If strWinner = "Nobody" Then
      strNotificationMsg = "Game over. It's a tie!"
      DisplayGameResults()
      blnGameOver = "True"
    End If

    If blnGameOver <> "True" Then 'If game is not over display the board
      DisplayBoard()              'in order to collect next player's input
      ValidateInput()             'Validate the input

      If UCase(strPlayerInput) = "QUIT" Then  'See if a player type Quit
        blnPlayerTypedQuit = "True"
        blnValidCell = "False"
        blnGameOver = "True"
      End If

    End If
```

```
    'Count the number of valid cell selections
    If blnValidCell = "True" Then

      intNoMoves = intNoMoves + 1
      MarkPlayerSelection()

    End If

    'If all 9 cells have been filled in we have a tie
    If intNoMoves = 9 Then
      SeeIfWon()
      If strWinner = "None" Then
        strWinner = "Nobody"
      End If
    Else
      SeeIfWon()
    End If

    'Time to switch player turns
    If blnValidCell = "True" Then
      If strPlayer = "X" Then
        strPlayer = "O"
      Else
        strPlayer = "X"
      End If
    End If

  Loop

End Function
```

If the game is not over yet (e.g., `blnGameOver <> "True"`), then the game board is displayed and a player is prompted to make a move. The player's move is then validated. If the player typed `Quit`, then the script sets a number of controlling variables to indicate that the game is about to be terminated. Otherwise, the value assigned to `intNoMoves` is incremented by 1 to keep track of the game's progress and the `MarkPlayerSelection()` function is called to associate the player's move with a specific cell on the game board. Next the value assigned to `intNoMoves` is examined. If it is equal to `9`, then the game is over and the script calls on `SeeIfWon()` to ascertain whether there was a winner. If nine moves were made and no winner is identified, the game is declared a tie and the value assigned to `strWinner` is set equal to `Nobody`. If nine moves have not been made yet, the script still executes the `SeeIfWon()` function to see whether player `X` or `O` has managed to line up three cells in a row. Finally, the last set of statements inside the loop controls player turns by switching the value assigned to `strPlayer` to either `X` or `O`.

Building the DisplayBoard() Function

The `DisplayBoard()` function consists of text designed to provide a graphic-like display. Embedded inside the game board displayed by this function are nine variables named `A1 - A3`, `B1 - B3`, and `C1 - C3`—each of which represent a different cell on the game board.

```
Function DisplayBoard()  'Display the game board

    strPlayerInput = UCase(InputBox(vbCrLf & _
      strNotificationMsg & _
      vbCrLf & vbCrLf & vbCrLf & vbCrLf & _
      vbTab & "1" & vbTab & vbTab & "2" & vbTab & vbTab & "3" & vbCrLf & _
      vbCrLf & vbTab & vbTab & "|" & vbTab & vbTab & "|" & vbTab & _
      vbCrLf & "A" & vbTab & A1 & vbTab & "|" & vbTab & A2 & vbTab & _
      "|" & vbTab & A3 & vbCrLf & vbTab & vbTab & "|" & vbTab & vbTab & _
      "|" & vbTab & vbCrLf & "      ------------------" & _
      "------------------" & vbCrLf & vbTab & _
      vbTab & "|" & vbTab & vbTab & "|" & vbTab & vbCrLf & "B" & vbTab & _
      B1 & vbTab & "|" & vbTab & B2 & vbTab & "|" & vbTab & B3 & _
      vbCrLf & vbTab & vbTab & "|" & vbTab & vbTab & "|" & vbTab & _
      vbCrLf & "      ----------------------" & _
      "-------------" & vbCrLf & vbTab & vbTab & "|" & _
      vbTab & vbTab & "|" & vbTab & vbCrLf & "C" & vbTab & C1 & vbTab & _
      "|" & vbTab & C2 & vbTab & "|" & vbTab & C3 & vbCrLf & vbTab & _
      vbTab & "|" & vbTab & vbTab & "|" & vbTab & vbCrLf & vbCrLf & _
      vbCrLf & vbCrLf & "Player " & strPlayer & _
      "'s turn. Type your move:", cTitleBarMsg))

End Function
```

Whenever this function is called it displays the game board, including the values assigned to each of its nine embedded variables (as either `X`s or `O`s). This gives the game the capability to dynamically display each move made as the game progresses.

Building the DisplayGameResults() Function

The `DisplayGameResults()` function that follows is responsible for displaying the final results of the game. The dialog generated by this function is not much different than the dialog created by the `DisplayBoard()` function, except that this function uses the `MsgBox()` function in place of the `InputBox()` function. The `MsgBox()` function is more appropriate for this function because it can be used to display a dialog with a single `OK` button, whereas using the `InputBox()` function would have resulted in the unnecessary display on a text input field at the bottom of the dialog.

```
Function DisplayGameResults()  'Game is over. Display the results.

  MsgBox vbCrLf & _
    strNotificationMsg & _
    vbCrLf & vbCrLf & vbCrLf & vbCrLf & _
    vbTab & "1" & vbTab & vbTab & "2" & vbTab & vbTab & "3" & vbCrLf & _
    vbCrLf & vbTab & vbTab & "|" & vbTab & vbTab & "|" & vbTab & _
    vbCrLf & "A" & vbTab & A1 & vbTab & "|" & vbTab & A2 & vbTab & _
    "|" & vbTab & A3 & vbCrLf & vbTab & vbTab & "|" & vbTab & vbTab & _
    "|" & vbTab & vbCrLf & _
    "        -----------------------------" & _
    "---------" & vbCrLf & vbTab & vbTab & "|" & vbTab & vbTab & _
    "|" & vbTab & vbCrLf & "B" & vbTab & B1 & vbTab & "|" & vbTab & _
    B2 & vbTab & "|" & vbTab & B3 & vbCrLf & vbTab & vbTab & "|" & _
    vbTab & vbTab & "|" & vbTab & vbCrLf & "        ---------" & _
    "-----------------------------" & vbCrLf & _
    vbTab & vbTab & "|" & vbTab & vbTab & "|" & vbTab & vbCrLf & _
    "C" & vbTab & C1 & vbTab & "|" & vbTab & C2 & vbTab & "|" & vbTab & _
    C3 & vbCrLf & vbTab & vbTab & "|" & vbTab & vbTab & "|" & vbTab & _
    vbCrLf & vbCrLf & vbCrLf & vbCrLf, , cTitleBarMsg

End Function
```

Building the ValidateInput() Function

The `ValidateInput()` function, shown here, uses a `Select Case` statement to process the input provided by players to determine whether valid input has been provided. Input is valid only if it is provided in the form of a valid cell range. Next, the function checks to be sure the player did not accidentally click on `OK` before entering a move. The last validation test performed by this function checks to make sure that the cell specified by the player has not already been selected. This is done by checking to see whether the value assigned to the cell is anything other than a blank space. If it is, then regardless of whether a value of X or O has been assigned, the cell not available.

```
Function ValidateInput()  'Run several tests valid correct player input

  Select Case strPlayerInput  'Ensure a valid cell was specified
    Case "A1"
      blnValidCell = "True"
    Case "A2"
      blnValidCell = "True"
    Case "A3"
      blnValidCell = "True"
    Case "B1"
      blnValidCell = "True"
    Case "B2"
      blnValidCell = "True"
    Case "B3"
      blnValidCell = "True"
    Case "C1"
      blnValidCell = "True"
    Case "C2"
      blnValidCell = "True"
    Case "C3"
      blnValidCell = "True"
    Case Else
      blnValidCell = "False"
      strNotificationMsg = "Invalid cell. Please try again."
  End Select

  If strPlayerInput = "" Then  'Player must type something
    strNotificationMsg = "Missing entry. Please try again."
    blnValidCell = "False"
  End If

  'Check each cell to make sure that it has not already been selected
  If strPlayerInput = "A1" Then
    If A1 <> " " Then
      blnValidCell = "False"
```

```
    strNotificationMsg = "Invalid entry. Cell already selected. " & _
      "Please try again."
  End If
End If

If strPlayerInput = "A2" Then
  If A2 <> " " Then
    blnValidCell = "False"
    strNotificationMsg = "Invalid entry. Cell already selected. " & _
      "Please try again."
  End If
End If

If strPlayerInput = "A3" Then
  If A3 <> " " Then
    blnValidCell = "False"
    strNotificationMsg = "Invalid entry. Cell already selected. " & _
      "Please try again."
  End If
End If

If strPlayerInput = "B1" Then
  If B1 <> " " Then
    blnValidCell = "False"
    strNotificationMsg = "Invalid entry. Cell already selected. " & _
      "Please try again."
  End If
End If

If strPlayerInput = "B2" Then
  If B2 <> " " Then
    blnValidCell = "False"
    strNotificationMsg = "Invalid entry. Cell already selected. " & _
      "Please try again."
  End If
End If

If strPlayerInput = "B3" Then
```

```
    If B3 <> " " Then
      blnValidCell = "False"
      strNotificationMsg = "Invalid entry. Cell already selected. " & _
        "Please try again."
    End If
  End If

  If strPlayerInput = "C1" Then
    If C1 <> " " Then
      blnValidCell = "False"
      strNotificationMsg = "Invalid entry. Cell already selected. " & _
        "Please try again."
    End If
  End If

  If strPlayerInput = "C2" Then
    If C2 <> " " Then
      blnValidCell = "False"
      strNotificationMsg = "Invalid entry. Cell already selected. " & _
      "Please try again."
    End If
  End If

  If strPlayerInput = "C3" Then
    If C3 <> " " Then
      blnValidCell = "False"
      strNotificationMsg = "Invalid entry. Cell already selected. " & _
        "Please try again."
    End If
  End If

End Function
```

Building the MarkPlayerSelection() Function

The `MarkPlayerSelection()` function that follows, is responsible for associating the player's move with the appropriate cell on the game board. It does this by assigning the value stored in `strPlayer` to the specified cell. Remember, the value assigned to `strPlayer` is either an `X` or an `O`, depending on whose turn it is.

```
Function MarkPlayerSelection()  'Mark an X or O in the appropriate cell

  If strPlayerInput = "A1" Then
    A1 = strPlayer
  End If
  If strPlayerInput = "A2" Then
    A2 = strPlayer
  End If
  If strPlayerInput = "A3" Then
    A3 = strPlayer
  End If
  If strPlayerInput = "B1" Then
    B1 = strPlayer
  End If
  If strPlayerInput = "B2" Then
    B2 = strPlayer
  End If
  If strPlayerInput = "B3" Then
    B3 = strPlayer
  End If
  If strPlayerInput = "C1" Then
    C1 = strPlayer
  End If
  If strPlayerInput = "C2" Then
    C2 = strPlayer
  End If
  If strPlayerInput = "C3" Then
    C3 = strPlayer
  End If

End Function
```

Building the SeeIfWon() Function

The `SeeIfWon()` function, shown here, performs a series of eight tests to see whether the game has been won by one of the players. These tests include checking all three cells in each row and in each column to see whether the same player has selected them. The function also checks diagonally to see whether there is a winner.

```
Function SeeIfWon()

  'Check across the first row
  If A1 = strPlayer Then
    If A2 = strPlayer Then
      If A3 = strPlayer Then
        strWinner = strPlayer
        strDirection = "- First row across!"
      End If
    End If
  End If

  'Check across the second row
  If B1 = strPlayer Then
    If B2 = strPlayer Then
      If B3 = strPlayer Then
        strWinner = strPlayer
        strDirection = "- Second row across!"
      End If
    End If
  End If

  'Check across the third row
  If C1 = strPlayer Then
    If C2 = strPlayer Then
      If C3 = strPlayer Then
        strWinner = strPlayer
        strDirection = "- Third row across!"
      End If
    End If
  End If

  'Check the first column
  If A1 = strPlayer Then
    If B1 = strPlayer Then
      If C1 = strPlayer Then
        strWinner = strPlayer
        strDirection = "- First column down!"
```

```
      End If
    End If
  End If

  'Check the second column
  If A2 = strPlayer Then
    If B2 = strPlayer Then
      If C2 = strPlayer Then
        strWinner = strPlayer
        strDirection = "- Second column down!"
      End If
    End If
  End If

  'Check the third column
  If A3 = strPlayer Then
    If B3 = strPlayer Then
      If C3 = strPlayer Then
        strWinner = strPlayer
        strDirection = "- Third column down!"
      End If
    End If
  End If

  'Check diagonally
  If A1 = strPlayer Then
    If B2 = strPlayer Then
      If C3 = strPlayer Then
        strWinner = strPlayer
        strDirection = "- Diagonally A1 - C3!"
      End If
    End If
  End If

  'Check the diagonally
  If A3 = strPlayer Then
    If B2 = strPlayer Then
      If C1 = strPlayer Then
```

```
        strWinner = strPlayer
        strDirection = "- Diagonally C1 - A3!"
      End If
    End If
  End If

End Function
```

Building the DisplaySplashScreen() Function

The script's final function, `DisplaySplashScreen()` is shown here. This function displays information about the script and its author and then terminates the script's execution by using the `WScript` object's `Quit()` method.

```
Function DisplaySplashScreen()   'Display splash screen and terminate game

  MsgBox "Thank you for playing Tic-Tac-Toe" & _
    "© Jerry Ford 2004." & vbCrLf & vbCrLf & "Please play again " & _
    "soon!", 4144, cTitleBarMsg

  WScript.Quit()

End Function
```

The Final Result

That's it. You have all the necessary pieces to assemble the game. Once you have keyed everything, your fully assembled script should like the one that follows.

```
'*************************************************************************
'Script Name:   TicTacToe.vbs
'Author:        Jerry Ford
'Created:       11/15/04
'Description:   This script is a VBScript implementation of the
'                Tic-Tac-Toe game
'*************************************************************************


'Initialization Section

Option Explicit
```

```
Const cTitleBarMsg = "VBScript   T I C   T A C   T O E"

Dim A1, A2, A3, B1, B2, B3, C1, C2, C3  'Variables representing sections
                                        'of the Tic Tac Toe game board

Dim blnGameOver          'Boolean variable that determines when to end game
Dim blnPlayerTypedQuit   'Variable used to track whether a player typed Quit
Dim blnStopGame          'Variable used in Main Processing section to
                         'determine when to stop the game
Dim blnValidCell         'Boolean variable that determines whether a player
                         'specified a valid cell

Dim intNoMoves           'Variable used to keep track of the number of plays
Dim intPlayAgain         'Variable holds player response when asked to play
                         'again

Dim strNotificationMsg   'Variable used to display messages to player
Dim strPlayer            'Variable used to identify whose turn it is
Dim strWinner            'Variable used to determine whether the game is won
Dim strPlayerInput       'Variable used to hold the player's cell selection
Dim strDirection         'Variable identifies how the player won the game

blnStopGame = "False"


'Main Processing Section --------------------------

Do Until blnStopGame = "True"  'Keep playing until players decide to stop

  SetVariableDefaults()

  ClearGameBoard()

  ManageGamePlay()

  If blnPlayerTypedQuit = "True" Then  'One of the players typed Quit
    blnStopGame = "True"
  Else  'The game is over. Ask the players if they'd like to play again
```

```
    intPlayAgain = MsgBox("Would you like to play another game of " & _
      "Tic Tac Toe?", 4, cTitleBarMsg)

    If intPlayAgain = 7 Then 'A player clicked on No. B break out of loop
blnStopGame = "True"
    End If

  End If

Loop

DisplaySplashScreen()


'Procedure Section ------------------------------

Function SetVariableDefaults()   'Establish default variable settings

  blnGameOver = "False"
  blnPlayerTypedQuit = "False"
  blnValidCell = "False"

  intNoMoves = 0

  strNotificationMsg = "Welcome! To play Tic Tac Toe follow the " & _
    "instruction at the bottom of the screen. Type Quit to terminate " & _
    "the game at any time."
  strPlayer = "X"
  strWinner = "None"
  strDirection = ""

End Function


Function ClearGameBoard()  'Reset the game board
```

```
  A1 = " "
  A2 = " "
  A3 = " "
  B1 = " "
  B2 = " "
  B3 = " "
  C1 = " "
  C2 = " "
  C3 = " "

End Function


Function ManageGamePlay()  'Manage the overall execution of the game

  Do Until blnGameOver = "True"

    'Start by checking to see if the game has already been completed
    If strWinner = "X" Then
      strNotificationMsg = "Game over! Player X Wins " & strDirection
      DisplayGameResults()
      blnGameOver = "True"
    End If

    If strWinner = "O" Then
      strNotificationMsg = "Game over! Player O Wins " & strDirection
      DisplayGameResults()
      blnGameOver = "True"
    End If

    If strWinner = "Nobody" Then
      strNotificationMsg = "Game over. It's a tie!"
      DisplayGameResults()
      blnGameOver = "True"
    End If

    If blnGameOver <> "True" Then 'If game is not over display the board
      DisplayBoard()               'in order to collect next player's input
      ValidateInput()              'Validate the input
```

```
      If UCase(strPlayerInput) = "QUIT" Then  'See if a player type Quit
        blnPlayerTypedQuit = "True"
        blnValidCell = "False"
        blnGameOver = "True"
      End If

    End If

    'Count the number of valid cell selections
    If blnValidCell = "True" Then

      intNoMoves = intNoMoves + 1
      MarkPlayerSelection()

    End If

    'If all 9 cells have been filled in we have a tie
    If intNoMoves = 9 Then
      SeeIfWon()
      If strWinner = "None" Then
        strWinner = "Nobody"
      End If
    Else
      SeeIfWon()
    End If

    'Time to switch player turns
    If blnValidCell = "True" Then
      If strPlayer = "X" Then
        strPlayer = "O"
      Else
        strPlayer = "X"
      End If
    End If

  Loop

End Function
```

```
Function DisplayBoard()  'Display the game board

    strPlayerInput = UCase(InputBox(vbCrLf & _
      strNotificationMsg & _
      vbCrLf & vbCrLf & vbCrLf & vbCrLf & _
      vbTab & "1" & vbTab & vbTab & "2" & vbTab & vbTab & "3" & vbCrLf & _
      vbCrLf & vbTab & vbTab & "|" & vbTab & vbTab & "|" & vbTab & _
      vbCrLf & "A" & vbTab & A1 & vbTab & "|" & vbTab & A2 & vbTab & _
      "|" & vbTab & A3 & vbCrLf & vbTab & vbTab & "|" & vbTab & vbTab & _
      "|" & vbTab & vbCrLf & "      ------------------" & _
      "--------------------" & vbCrLf & vbTab & _
      vbTab & "|" & vbTab & vbTab & "|" & vbTab & vbCrLf & "B" & vbTab & _
      B1 & vbTab & "|" & vbTab & B2 & vbTab & "|" & vbTab & B3 & _
      vbCrLf & vbTab & vbTab & "|" & vbTab & vbTab & "|" & vbTab & _
      vbCrLf & "      -----------------------" & _
      "-------------" & vbCrLf & vbTab & vbTab & "|" & _
      vbTab & vbTab & "|" & vbTab & vbCrLf & "C" & vbTab & C1 & vbTab & _
      "|" & vbTab & C2 & vbTab & "|" & vbTab & C3 & vbCrLf & vbTab & _
      vbTab & "|" & vbTab & vbTab & "|" & vbTab & vbCrLf & vbCrLf & _
      vbCrLf & vbCrLf & "Player " & strPlayer & _
      "'s turn. Type your move:", cTitleBarMsg))

End Function


Function DisplayGameResults()  'Game is over. Display the results.

  MsgBox vbCrLf & _
    strNotificationMsg & _
    vbCrLf & vbCrLf & vbCrLf & vbCrLf & _
    vbTab & "1" & vbTab & vbTab & "2" & vbTab & vbTab & "3" & vbCrLf & _
    vbCrLf & vbTab & vbTab & "|" & vbTab & vbTab & "|" & vbTab & _
    vbCrLf & "A" & vbTab & A1 & vbTab & "|" & vbTab & A2 & vbTab & _
    "|" & vbTab & A3 & vbCrLf & vbTab & vbTab & "|" & vbTab & vbTab & _
    "|" & vbTab & vbCrLf & _
    "      -----------------------------" & _
    "--------" & vbCrLf & vbTab & vbTab & "|" & vbTab & vbTab & _
```

```
    "|" & vbTab & vbCrLf & "B" & vbTab & B1 & vbTab & "|" & vbTab & _
    B2 & vbTab & "|" & vbTab & B3 & vbCrLf & vbTab & vbTab & "|" & _
    vbTab & vbTab & "|" & vbTab & vbCrLf & "      ----------" & _
    "---------------------------" & vbCrLf & _
    vbTab & vbTab & "|" & vbTab & vbTab & "|" & vbTab & vbCrLf & _
    "C" & vbTab & C1 & vbTab & "|" & vbTab & C2 & vbTab & "|" & vbTab & _
    C3 & vbCrLf & vbTab & vbTab & "|" & vbTab & vbTab & "|" & vbTab & _
    vbCrLf & vbCrLf & vbCrLf & vbCrLf, , cTitleBarMsg

End Function


Function ValidateInput()  'Run several tests valid correct player input

  Select Case strPlayerInput  'Ensure a valid cell was specified
    Case "A1"
      blnValidCell = "True"
    Case "A2"
      blnValidCell = "True"
    Case "A3"
      blnValidCell = "True"
    Case "B1"
      blnValidCell = "True"
    Case "B2"
      blnValidCell = "True"
    Case "B3"
      blnValidCell = "True"
    Case "C1"
      blnValidCell = "True"
    Case "C2"
      blnValidCell = "True"
    Case "C3"
      blnValidCell = "True"
    Case Else
      blnValidCell = "False"
      strNotificationMsg = "Invalid cell. Please try again."
  End Select
```

```
If strPlayerInput = "" Then  'Player must type something
  strNotificationMsg = "Missing entry. Please try again."
  blnValidCell = "False"
End If

'Check each cell to make sure that it has not already been selected
If strPlayerInput = "A1" Then
  If A1 <> " " Then
    blnValidCell = "False"
    strNotificationMsg = "Invalid entry. Cell already selected. " & _
      "Please try again."
  End If
End If

If strPlayerInput = "A2" Then
  If A2 <> " " Then
    blnValidCell = "False"
    strNotificationMsg = "Invalid entry. Cell already selected. " & _
      "Please try again."
  End If
End If

  If strPlayerInput = "A3" Then
  If A3 <> " " Then
    blnValidCell = "False"
    strNotificationMsg = "Invalid entry. Cell already selected. " & _
      "Please try again."
  End If
End If

If strPlayerInput = "B1" Then
  If B1 <> " " Then
    blnValidCell = "False"
    strNotificationMsg = "Invalid entry. Cell already selected. " & _
      "Please try again."
  End If
End If
```

```
  If strPlayerInput = "B2" Then
    If B2 <> " " Then
      blnValidCell = "False"
      strNotificationMsg = "Invalid entry. Cell already selected. " & _
        "Please try again."
    End If
  End If

  If strPlayerInput = "B3" Then
    If B3 <> " " Then
      blnValidCell = "False"
      strNotificationMsg = "Invalid entry. Cell already selected. " & _
        "Please try again."
    End If
  End If

  If strPlayerInput = "C1" Then
    If C1 <> " " Then
      blnValidCell = "False"
      strNotificationMsg = "Invalid entry. Cell already selected. " & _
        "Please try again."
    End If
  End If

  If strPlayerInput = "C2" Then
    If C2 <> " " Then
      blnValidCell = "False"
      strNotificationMsg = "Invalid entry. Cell already selected. " & _
      "Please try again."
    End If
  End If

  If strPlayerInput = "C3" Then
    If C3 <> " " Then
      blnValidCell = "False"
      strNotificationMsg = "Invalid entry. Cell already selected. " & _
        "Please try again."
    End If
  End If

End Function
```

```
Function MarkPlayerSelection()  'Mark an X or O in the appropriate cell

  If strPlayerInput = "A1" Then
    A1 = strPlayer
  End If
  If strPlayerInput = "A2" Then
    A2 = strPlayer
  End If
  If strPlayerInput = "A3" Then
    A3 = strPlayer
  End If
  If strPlayerInput = "B1" Then
    B1 = strPlayer
  End If
  If strPlayerInput = "B2" Then
    B2 = strPlayer
  End If
  If strPlayerInput = "B3" Then
    B3 = strPlayer
  End If
  If strPlayerInput = "C1" Then
    C1 = strPlayer
  End If
  If strPlayerInput = "C2" Then
    C2 = strPlayer
  End If
  If strPlayerInput = "C3" Then
    C3 = strPlayer
  End If

End Function


Function SeeIfWon()

  'Check across the first row
  If A1 = strPlayer Then
    If A2 = strPlayer Then
```

```
    If A3 = strPlayer Then
      strWinner = strPlayer
      strDirection = "- First row across!"
    End If
  End If
End If

'Check across the second row
If B1 = strPlayer Then
  If B2 = strPlayer Then
    If B3 = strPlayer Then
      strWinner = strPlayer
      strDirection = "- Second row across!"
    End If
  End If
End If

'Check across the third row
If C1 = strPlayer Then
  If C2 = strPlayer Then
    If C3 = strPlayer Then
      strWinner = strPlayer
      strDirection = "- Third row across!"
    End If
  End If
End If

'Check the first column
If A1 = strPlayer Then
  If B1 = strPlayer Then
    If C1 = strPlayer Then
      strWinner = strPlayer
      strDirection = "- First column down!"
    End If
  End If
End If
```

```
  'Check the second column
  If A2 = strPlayer Then
    If B2 = strPlayer Then
      If C2 = strPlayer Then
        strWinner = strPlayer
        strDirection = "- Second column down!"
      End If
    End If
  End If

  'Check the third column
  If A3 = strPlayer Then
    If B3 = strPlayer Then
      If C3 = strPlayer Then
        strWinner = strPlayer
        strDirection = "- Third column down!"
      End If
    End If
  End If

  'Check diagonally
  If A1 = strPlayer Then
    If B2 = strPlayer Then
      If C3 = strPlayer Then
        strWinner = strPlayer
        strDirection = "- Diagonally A1 - C3!"
      End If
    End If
  End If

  'Check diagonally
  If A3 = strPlayer Then
    If B2 = strPlayer Then
      If C1 = strPlayer Then
        strWinner = strPlayer
        strDirection = "- Diagonally C1 - A3!"
      End If
    End If
  End If

End Function
```

```
Function DisplaySplashScreen()    'Display splash screen and terminate game

  MsgBox "Thank you for playing Tic-Tac-Toe" & _
    "© Jerry Ford 2004." & vbCrLf & vbCrLf & "Please play again " & _
    "soon!", 4144, cTitleBarMsg

  WScript.Quit()

End Function
```

Okay, run through the Tic-Tac-Toe game a few times to be sure that you haven't accidentally made a few typos when keying in the script. After you have everything working just right, go out and get a friend to play with and show off what you have learned.

Summary

In this chapter, you learned how to work with built-in VBScript objects. This included learning how to create custom objects with their own unique set of properties and methods. You also learned how to trigger events associated with custom objects. On top of all this, you learned how to perform complex parsing operations by working with the `RegExp` object and you created your first multi-player VBScript game.

Challenges

1. Enhance the Tic-Tac-Toe game by adding options that allow the players to get help.

2. If you have a Web site, consider modifying the game's closing splash screen to display its address.

3. Try making a computerized version of this game where a single player goes head to head against the computer.

4. Add logic that keeps track of the total number of games played and display this information, along with the total number of games won by each player, at the end of the final game.

Combining Different Scripting Languages

Welcome to the final chapter of this book. In this chapter, you will learn how to develop a new type of script, called a Windows Script File, which enables you to combine VBScript with one or more other WSH-supported scripting languages to create a single executable script. Doing so enables you to create scripts that can take advantage of the strengths of each individual scripting language. Specifically, in this chapter I'll demonstrate how to develop Windows Script Files that combine VBScript and JScript. Along the way, you'll be introduced to the Extensible Markup Language, or XML, which allows different scripting languages to be combined into Windows Script Files. Specifically, you will

- Learn how to combine VBScript with another scripting language to create Windows Script Files
- Learn how XML is used to format Windows Script Files
- Get a sneak peek at the JScript scripting language
- Learn how to execute Windows Script Files

Project Preview: The VBScript Game Console

In your final project, you will learn how to create Windows Script Files that combine VBScript with a little bit of JScript to create a game console for all your VBScript games. Once started, the game console displays a dynamically created numbered list of your VBScript games and enables the user to choose which game to play by either typing in the name of the game or typing its assigned number.

When started, the game console appears in the upper-left corner of the display area. As games are selected, they will appear in the middle of the screen. This keeps the game console handy without making it intrusive. Figures 12.1 through 12.5 demonstrate the overall operation of the game console from beginning to end.

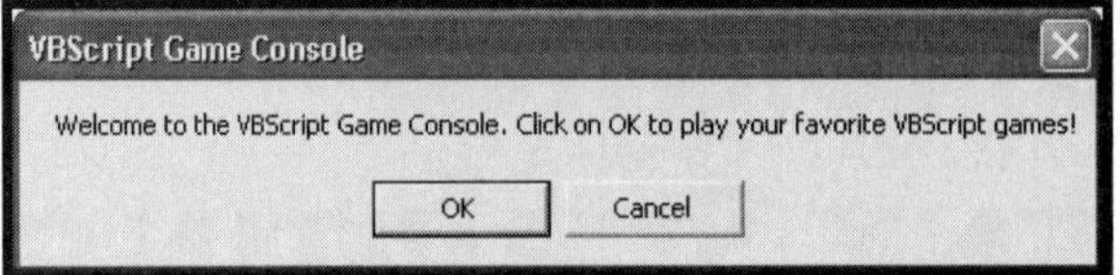

FIGURE 12.1

A JScript that displays the game console's initial splash screen is executed.

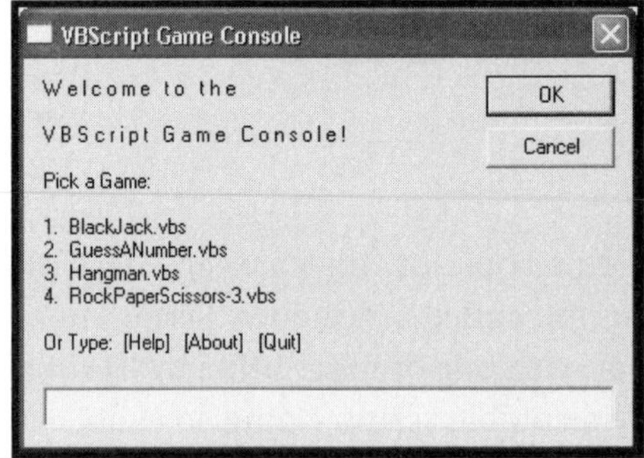

FIGURE 12.2

The core logic for the game console is provided by a VBScript, which is responsible for displaying and controlling the execution of your VBScript games.

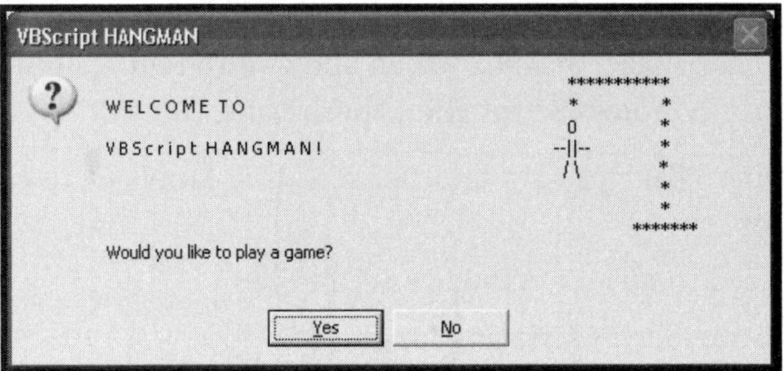

FIGURE 12.3

The game console remains tucked away in the corner while the player enjoys playing your VBScript game.

FIGURE 12.4

By selecting the `About` option, the user can get more information about the game console and its author.

FIGURE 12.5

When the game console is finally closed, another JScript is run to display a closing splash screen.

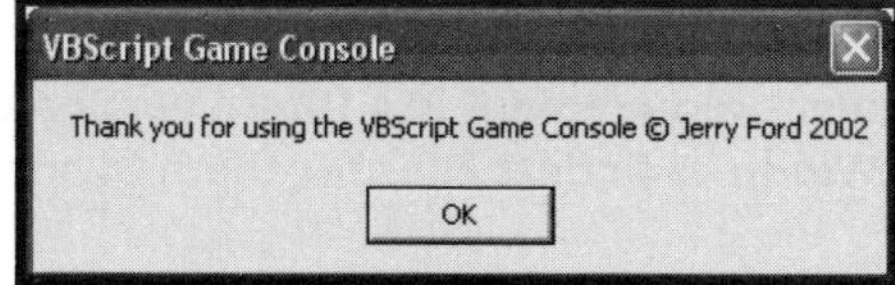

INTRODUCING WINDOWS SCRIPT FILES

One of the strengths of the WSH is that it supports a number of different scripting languages, including VBScript, JScript, Perl, Python, and REXX. Microsoft automatically equips the WSH with VBScript and JScript. Third-party software developers provide support for the other scripting languages. Besides executing scripts written in any of these scripting languages, the WSH enables you to put any combination of these languages into a single script file known as a *Windows Script File.*

XML provides the glue for combining different scripts into a Windows Script File. In this chapter, I'll cover some of the more commonly used WSH-supported XML statements. However, there simply is not enough space available in this book to completely cover every single XML element supported by the WSH. To learn more about the WSH's support for XML, visit http://www.msdn.microsoft.com/scripting and read through the Windows Script Host documentation posted there.

> **DEFINITION**
>
> A *Windows Script File* is a type of script that allows multiple scripts, written in any WSH-supported scripting language, to be combined to create a single script.

> **DEFINITION**
>
> *Extensible Markup Language,* or XML, is a language similar in design and syntax to HTML. It is used within the context of the WSH to define the structure of Windows Script Files.

Using XML, you specify the components that make up Windows Script Files. For example, you use XML to mark the locations within Windows Script Files where individual scripts (written in scripting languages such as VBScript and JScript) are embedded. Windows Script Files are saved as plain text files with a .wsh file extension and can be created using any plain text or script editor.

XML is case-sensitive and imposes a strict set of rules on the format of Windows Script Files. For example, within the context of the WSH, most XML tags occur in pairs with one opening and one closing tag. Failure to include a matching closing tag will result in an error.

The WSH currently supports XML version 1.0. Version 1.0 supports both uppercase and lowercase spelling of tag elements. However, lowercase spelling is preferred, and I recommend that you do use only lowercase spelling. This way, if lowercase spelling becomes a requirement in a future version of XML, you will not have to retrofit your Windows Scripts Files for them to continue to run.

Examining WSH Supported XML Tags

XML represents an extensive and powerful multipurpose markup language. XML is therefore often used in many environments, including the WSH. In this chapter, I'll introduce you to a number of commonly used XML tags, and I'll provide examples of how they're used to build Windows Script Files.

To begin, take a look at Table 12.1, which shows the XML tags that you'll see demonstrated in this chapter's examples.

TABLE 12.1 XML TAGS COMMONLY USED IN WINDOWS SCRIPT FILES

Tag	Description
`<?job ?>`.	Enables or disabled error handling and debugging for a specified job.
`<?XML ?>`.	Specifies the Windows Script File's XML level.
`<comment> </comment>`.	Embeds comments within Windows Script Files.
`<script> </script>`.	Identifies the beginning and ending of a script within a Windows Script File.
`<job> </job>`.	Identifies the beginning and ending of a job inside a Windows Script File.
`<package> </package>`.	Enables multiple jobs to be defined within a single Windows Script File.
`<resource> </resource >`.	Defines static data (constants) that can be referenced by script within a Windows Script File.

Using the <?job ?> Tag

The `<?job ?>` tag allows you to enable or disable error reporting and debugging within your Windows Script Files. The use of this tag is optional. Unlike most tags, the `<?job ?>` tag does not have a closing tag. The syntax for this tag is as follows:

```
<?job error="flag" debug="flag" ?>
```

Both error and debug are Boolean values. By default, both are set equal to false. Setting error="true" turns on error reporting, thus allowing syntax and run-time error messages to be reported. Setting debug="true" turns on debugging for Windows Script Files, allowing them to start the Windows script debugger.

To take advantage of the <?job ?> tags' debug capability, you'll need to install the Microsoft Windows script debugger utility. This utility is designed to assist programmers in debugging script errors. To learn more about this utility, check out msdn.microsoft.com/scripting.

The following example demonstrates how to use the <?job ?> tag within a Windows Script File:

```
<job>
  <?job error="true" debug="true"?>
  <script language="VBScript">
    MsgBox "Error handling and debugging have been enabled."
  </script>
</job>
```

As you can see, both error reporting and script debugging have been enabled.

Using the <?XML ?> Tag

The <?XML ?> tag is used to specify the version of XML required to support a Windows Script File. As with the <?job ?> tag, the use of this tag is optional.

When used, the <?XML ?> tag must be the first tag defined as the first statement in the Windows Script File. The syntax for the <?XML ?> tag is as follows:

```
<?XML version="version" standalone="DTDflag"  ?>
```

Version specifies the version of XML required to support the Windows Script File. The current version is 1.0. Standalone is used to specify an external Document Type Definition, which is a feature not currently supported by the WSH. However, you can still include it if you want, but you'll have to specify it as having a value of Yes (but it will still be ignored).

When used, the <?XML ?> tag enforces stricter interpretation of all XML statements; it also enforces case-sensitivity, while requiring that all values be specified within either single or double quotes. Omitting this tag provides for a less restrictive syntax. Let's look at the following example, which demonstrates the placement of a <?XML ?> tag at the beginning of a small Windows Script File.

```
<?XML version="1.0" standalone="yes" ?>
<job>
  <?job error="true" debug="true"?>
  <script language="VBScript">
    MsgBox "Error handling and debugging have been enabled."
  </script>
</job>
```

The <comment> </comment> Tags

You can document the XML statements used within your Windows Script Files using the XML `<comment>` and `</comment>` tags. Using these tags, you can spread comments over multiple lines. The syntax for the `<comment>` and `</comment>` tags is as follows:

```
<comment> Comment Text  </comment>
```

The following example demonstrates the use of the XML `<comment>` and `</comment>` tags.

```
<?XML version="1.0" standalone="yes" ?>
<job>
  <?job error="true" debug="true"?>
  <comment>The following VBScript displays an information message</comment>
  <script language="VBScript">
    MsgBox "Error handling and debugging have been enabled File. "
  </script>
</job>
```

The <job> </job> Tags

To embed a script into a Windows Script File, you must first define a pair of root tags. The `<job>` and `</job>` tags provide one type of root tag pair.

All Windows Script Files are composed of at least one job. The beginning and ending of a job are identified by the `<job>` and `</job>` tags. The syntax for the tags is as follows:

```
<job [id=JobID]>
  . . .
</job>
```

When only one job is defined within a Windows Script File, the `id=JobID` parameter can be omitted from the opening `<job>` tag. However, if two or more jobs are defined within a single Windows Script File, each must be given a unique `ID` assignment. This assignment allows you to execute any job within the Windows Script File.

The following example shows a Windows Script File that contains a single job. The job itself is made up of two different scripts:

```
<?XML version="1.0" standalone="yes" ?>
<job>

  <?job error="true" debug="true"?>

  <comment>The following VBScript displays a information message</comment>
  <script language="VBScript">
    MsgBox "VBScript has displayed this message."
  </script>

  <comment>The following JScript displays an information message</comment>
  <script language="JScript">
    WScript.Echo("JScript has displayed this message.");
  </script>

</job>
```

If you double-click on the file, you'll see two pop-up dialogs appear, as shown in Figures 12.6 and 12.7. The VBScript generates the first pop-up dialog, and the JScript generates the other. To place more than one job within a Windows Script File, you must use the `<package>` and `</package>` tags, which I'll explain next.

FIGURE 12.6 A pop-up dialog displayed by the Windows Script File's VBScript.

FIGURE 12.7 A pop-up dialog displayed by the Windows Script File's JScript.

The <package> </package> Tags

To place more than one job within a Windows Script File, you must enclose the jobs within the <package> and </package> tags. The syntax for these tags is as follows:

```
<package>
   . . .
</package>
```

To understand their use, look at the following example:

```
<?XML version="1.0" standalone="yes" ?>

<package>

  <comment>The following job contains a VBScript and a JScript</comment>
  <job id="job1">
    <?job error="true" debug="true"?>
    <comment>The following VBScript displays an information message</comment>
    <script language="VBScript">
      MsgBox "A VBScript has displayed this message."
    </script>
    <comment>The following JScript displays an information message</comment>
    <script language="VBScript">
      WScript.Echo "A JScript has displayed this message."
    </script>
  </job>

  <comment>The following job contains one VBScript</comment>
  <job id="job2">
    <script language="VBScript">
      MsgBox "A second VBScript has displayed this message."
    </script>
  </job>

</package>
```

In this Windows Script File, the <package> and </package> tags are used to define two jobs. The first job is assigned an ID of job1, and the second job has been assigned an ID of job2.

The <resource> </resource> Tags

You have already learned about the advantages of defining constants within your VBScripts. However, these constants are only available within the script that defines them. Using the XML <resource> and </resource> tags, you can define constants within your Windows Script Files that can then be accessed by every script located within the same job. Therefore, when used, these tags must be placed within the <job> and </job> tags.

The syntax of the <resource> and </resource> tags is as follows:

```
<resource id="resourceID">
  . . .
</resource>
```

Id specifies the name of the constant whose value is then assigned when you type it between the opening and closing tags, as demonstrated in the following example:

```
<job>

  <resource id="cTitleBarMsg">TestScript.wsh</resource>

  <script language="VBScript">

    Set objWshShl = WScript.CreateObject("WScript.Shell")

    MsgBox "Greetings", , getResource("cTitleBarMsg")

  </script>

</job>
```

The <script> </script> Tags

You've already seen the <script> and </script> tags in action a number of times in this chapter. They are used to mark the beginning and ending of individual scripts embedded within jobs in Windows Script Files. The syntax for these tags is as follows:

```
<script language="language" [src="externalscript"]>
  ...
</script>
```

`language` specifies the scripting language used to create a script. The `src` argument is used to specify an optional reference to an external script. If used, the external script is called and executed just as if it were embedded within the Windows Script File.

In the Real World

In the real world, time is money. Saving time during script development means that you can get more done in less time. One of the ways that experienced programmers save time is by creating reusable code. You can use Windows Script Files to save development time by externalizing scripts that perform common tasks. This way, you can set up a reference to those scripts in any number of Windows Script Files without having to reinvent the wheel. In addition, you'll save yourself a lot of maintenance work because if you ever need to modify a commonly used external script, you'll only have to make the change to the script once. This is preferable to making the same change over and over again in any scripts where you embedded copies of the script.

Let's look at an example of how to create a Windows Script File that includes both an embedded VBScript and one that is externally referenced. As you can see, the following Windows Script File includes a reference to two VBScripts:

```
<job>

  <script language="VBScript">
    MsgBox "This message is being displayed by an embedded VBScript"
  </script>

  <script language="VBScript" src="TestScript.vbs" />

</job>
```

The embedded VBScript simply displays a text message stating that it has executed. Similarly, the external VBScript might consist of a single statement that uses the `MsgBox()` function to display a similar message.

```
MsgBox "This message is being displayed by an external VBScript"
```

If you create both of these scripts and then double-click on the Windows Script File, you'll see that both scripts will execute and display their pop-up dialog in sequence.

Executing Your Windows Script Files

As you know, you can run a Windows Script File by double-clicking on it. When started this way, the Windows Script File runs the first job that has been defined. If more than one job has been defined within the Windows Script File, you can execute any job by running the script from the Windows command prompt and specifying the job's `ID`, as demonstrated next. Of course, every script contained within the job that is run will be executed.

Let's look at some examples of how to run Windows Script Files from the Windows command prompt. To run the first script in a Windows Script File that contains two jobs, just type the name of an execution host, followed by the name of the Windows Script File.

```
cscript TestWsfScript.wsf
```

If the two jobs in the Windows Script Files have been assigned job IDs of `job1` and `job2`, you can selectively execute either job by specifying its `ID`.

```
wscript TestWsfScript.wsf //job:job2
```

Back to the VBScript Game Console

The VBScript Game Console project is actually a Windows Script File designed to display a list of VBScript games that is dynamically generated based on the contents of a game folder. Once started, the VBScript Game Console gives the user easy access to any VBScript games that you have stored in the game folder.

The VBScript Game Console is actually made up of three different scripts, two written in JScript, and the other, written in VBScript. The rest of this chapter explains how the VBScript Game Console is built.

Designing the Game

The VBScript Game Console consists of three different scripts written using two different WSH-supported scripting languages, VBScript and JScript. Because JScript is a full-featured scripting language in its own right, I won't be able to go into great detail about its syntax or structure. However, I've tried to organize this Windows Script File in such a way as to ensure that the JScript you see is not overly complex. Hopefully, given the comments that I have added to each script, you will be able to understand what's happening in each JScript.

The VBScript Game Console will be created in four stages:

- **Stage 1:** Create a `.wsf` file and add the XML statements required to define the script's structure.

- **Stage 2:** Create the first JScript, which will be responsible for displaying the VBScript Game Console's initial splash screen and determining whether the user wants to open the console.
- **Stage 3:** Design the Windows Script File's VBScript, wherein the logic that controls the operation of the game console is stored.
- **Stage 4:** Create a second JScript, which is responsible for displaying the VBScript Game Console's closing splash screen.

Using XML to Outline the Script's Structure

The first stage in developing the VBScript Game Console involves two activities. First, create a new file and save it with a `.wsf` file extension, thus creating a new Windows Script File. Second, add the XML tags required to outline the overall structure of the Windows Script File, like this:

```
<package>
  <comment>This .WSF file builds a VBScript Game Console</comment>
  <job>
    <resource id="cTitlebarMsg">VBScript Game Console</resource>

    <script language="JScript">

    </script>

    <script language="VBScript">

    </script>

    <script language="JScript">

    </script>

    <script language="JScript">

    </script>

  </job>
</package>
```

The <package> and </package> tags were not required because this Windows Script File only contains one job. I added them anyway, just in case I ever decide to expand the script by adding another job. For example, if script configurations are ever migrated to the Windows registry, it might be helpful to define a second job to the Windows Script File specifying a setup script.

The <comment> and </comment> tags were added to help document the function of the Windows Script File. The opening <job> and closing </job> tags define the Windows Script File's only job. As only one job was defined, I did not bother to add the <job> tag's ID attribute. Finally, three separate sets of <script> and </script> tags have been created, marking the location at which each script that makes up the Windows Script File will be placed.

Writing the First JScript

Because the focus of this book is on VBScript as a WSH scripting language and not on JScript, I'm not going to attempt to explain in detail the following JScript. This script is relatively simple, and you should be able to tell what's going on by looking at the comments embedded within the script itself.

```
//*********************************************************************
//Script        Name: N/A
//Author:       Jerry Ford
//Created:      12/20/02
//Description: This JScript displays the .WSF file's initial splash
//              screen
//*********************************************************************

//Initialization Section

var objWshShl = WScript.CreateObject("WScript.Shell");
var strWelcome;
var strInstructions;
var intResults;
var intReply;
var strTitleBarMsg;

strWelcome = "Welcome to the VBScript Game Console. ";
strInstructions = "Click on OK to play a VBScript game!";
```

```
//Main Processing Section

//Verify that the user wants to open the VBScript Game Console
intReply = DisplayInitialSplashScreen();

//intReply will be set equal to 2 if the user clicks on the Cancel
if (intReply == 2) {
  //Close the VBScript Game Console
  WScript.Quit();
}


//Procedure Section

//This procedure prompts the user for confirmation
function DisplayInitialSplashScreen() {

  strTitleBarMsg = getResource("cTitlebarMsg");

  //Display popup dialog using the WshShell object's Popup() method
  intResults = +
    objWshShl.Popup(strWelcome +
      strInstructions, 0, strTitleBarMsg, 1);

  //Return the result to the calling statement
  return intResults

}
```

One way to develop each of the three scripts used in this Windows Script File is to create each script as a stand-alone script and get them all working as expected, and then to cut and paste the scripts into the Windows Script File in the areas identified for each script by the XML tags.

As you can see, this JScript is broken down into the same three sections that I've been using to organize this book's VBScripts (that is, the initialization section, the main processing section, and the procedure section). Comments in JScript are created using the // characters, and I have added a number of them to the script to explain its operation. The script's only function, DisplayInitialSplashScreen(), is responsible for displaying the VBScript Game Console's initial splash screen, which it does using the WshShell object's Popup() method. JScript does not provide any functions that work similarly to the VBScript MsgBox() or InputBox() functions. Therefore, to display text in a pop-up dialog using JScript, you must use either the WshShell object's Popup() method or the WScript object's Echo() method.

Developing the VBScript Game Console

The VBScript portion of the VBScript Game Console contains the bulk of the complexity and programming logic. The first step in developing this VBScript is to insert your VBScript template and fill it in, as follows:

```
'*************************************************************************
'Script Name: N/A
'Author:      Jerry Ford
'Created:     12/20/02
'Description: This VBScript displays the actual VBScript
'             Game Console interface and interacts with the user
'*************************************************************************

'Initialization Section

Option Explicit
```

Defining the Elements in the Initialization Section

Next, let's define the variables, objects, and the array used by the VBScript. In most of the VBScripts that you've seen in this book, I've included a constant that defines the titlebar message to be displayed in the script's pop-up dialogs. However, this time I've omitted this constant in the VBScript because I have, instead, defined this value using the <reference> and </reference> tags at the beginning of the Windows Script File. This allows me to retrieve the constant and create a standard titlebar message for every script defined in the Windows Script File.

```
Dim objFsoObject, objWshShl, strPlayOrNot, strConsoleStatus
Dim objGameFolder, objGames, strSelection, objWordList
Dim strFileString, intCount, strDisplayString, intNoFilesFound
Dim strTitleBarMsg, intResults

Dim ConsoleArray()
```

```
'Set up an instance of the FileSystemObject
Set objFsoObject = CreateObject("Scripting.FileSystemObject")

'Set up an instance of the WshShell
Set objWshShl = WScript.CreateObject("WScript.Shell")

'Retrieve the titlebar message to the displayed in popup dialogs
strTitleBarMsg = getResource("cTitlebarMsg")
```

Building the Main Processing Section

The statements listed in the Main Processing section are straightforward. I began by first checking the value of `intResults`, which was set by the previous JScript. If `intResults` is equal to 2, then the player told the JScript to shut down the game console. However, after executing the `WScript` object's `Quit()` method, inside the JScript, the WSF script keeps running, executing the VBScript. Therefore, you'll need to include this additional check and execute the `WScript` object's `Quit()` method a second time to prevent the VBScript from displaying the game console.

I then used the `FileSystemObject` object's `GetFolderMethod()` to establish a reference to the location where the VBScript games to be displayed in the game console are stored. A `For Each` loop that spins through the list of files stored in this folder, keeping a record of the number of files counted, is executed.

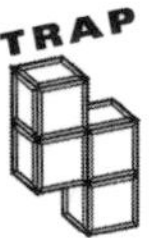

Note as the VBScript is currently written, it expects to find only VBScript files stored in the game folder. Therefore, no steps have been taken to filter out other file types. If you plan to store different files in the game folder, you will need to add additional logic to the VBScript to prevent it from displaying those files as well.

Next, the VBScript's array is resized according to the number of files found. This array is used to store the names of each VBScript game and to associate each VBScript game with its assigned number as shown in the game console's dialog. Finally, the `ConsoleLoop()` function is called. This function is responsible for the overall operation of the VBScript game console.

```
'Main Processing Section

If intResults = 2 Then
  WScript.Quit()
End If
```

```
'Specify the location of the folder where word files are stored
Set objGameFolder = objFsoObject.GetFolder("C:\VBScriptGames")

'Get a list of files stored in the folder
Set objGames = objGameFolder.Files

'Look and count the number of words files
For Each objWordList In objGames
  intNoFilesFound = intNoFilesFound + 1
Next

'Redefine the script's array based on number of word files found
ReDim ConsoleArray(intNoFilesFound)

'Call the function that displays the VBScript Game Console
ConsoleLoop()
```

Creating the ConsoleLoop() Function

The VBScript Game Console is controlled by the `ConsoleLoop()` function. This function is responsible for assigning a number to each VBScript, for loading the VBScript's array, for interrogating user input, and for performing the appropriate action based on that input.

```
'This function displays the VBScript Game Console, accepts user
'input, validates the input and starts other VBScript games
Function ConsoleLoop()

  'This string contains a list of all the word files discovered
  'in the target folder
  strSelection = ""

  'This counter will be used to track individual word files and
  'will be kept in sink with array entries
  intCount = 0

  'Loop through the list of word files
  For Each objWordList In objGames

    'Build a master string containing a list of all the word files
```

```
    'But exclude the VBScriptGameConsole.wsf file from this list
    If objWordList.Name <> "VBScriptGameConsole.wsf" Then

      'Increment count each time through the loop
      intCount = intCount + 1

      strFileString = strFileString & " " & objWordList.Name

      'Build another list, adding number for later display
      strSelection = strSelection & intCount & ".  " & _
        objWordList.Name & vbCrLf

      'Load the name of each script into the array
      ConsoleArray(intCount) = objWordList.Name

    End If

  Next

  'This variable is used to determine when to close the console
  strConsoleStatus = "Active"

  'Create loop & keep it running until the user decides to close it
  Do Until strConsoleStatus = "Terminate"

    'Interrogate the user's input
    strPlayOrNot = UCase(PickAGame())

    'If the user did not type anything or if he or she clicked on
    'Cancel then exit the function let things come to an end
    If strPlayOrNot = "" Then
      Exit Function
    End If

    'Define a Select Case statement and use it to test the various
    'possible types of user input
    Select Case UCase(strPlayOrNot)
```

```
      'If the user typed QUIT then exit the function let things
      'come to an end
      Case "QUIT"
        Exit Function

      'If the user typed ABOUT call the function that displays
      'additional information abut the VBScript Game Console
      Case "ABOUT"
        AboutFunction()

      'If the user typed HELP call the function that provides
      'additional help information
      Case "HELP"
        HelpFunction()

      'Otherwise call the function that runs the selected VBScript
      Case Else
        ValidateAndRun()'

    End Select

  Loop

End Function
```

Creating the ValidateAndRun() Function

When called by the `ConsoleLoop()` function, the `ValidateAndRun()` function, shown below, validates user input by making sure that the user has supplied either a valid game number or valid game name. If a valid number or name is not supplied, then the function calls the `InvalidChoice()` function, which displays a generic error message telling the user how to properly operate the VBScript Game Console. If a valid number or name is supplied, then the function calls the `RunScript()` function, which then executes the specified VBScript game.

```
'This function validates user input and if appropriate calls
'functions that display further instructions or run the selected
'VBScript
Function ValidateAndRun()
```

```
'Check to see if the user provided a valid game number
If IsNumeric(strPlayOrNot) <> 0 Then
  'Make sure that the user did not type a negative number
  If strPlayOrNot > 0 Then
    'Make sure that the user did not type a invalid number
    If CInt(strPlayOrNot) < CInt(intCount) Then
      'If the number is valid then find the associated script
      strPlayOrNot = ConsoleArray(strPlayOrNot)
      'Call the procedure that will then run the selected script
      RunScript()
    Else
      'Call this procedure if the user hast not typed a valid
      'script number
      InvalidChoice()
    End If
  Else
    InvalidChoice()
  End If

'Check to see instead if the user provided a valid game name
Else
  'Proceed only if the input typed by the user is a valid VBScript
  'game (e.g. its name appears in the previously built list of
  'VBScript game names
  If InStr(1, strSelection, strPlayOrNot, 1) > 1 Then
    'If the user didn't type the .vbs file extension add it
    If InStr(1, strPlayOrNot, ".VBS", 1) = 0 Then
      strPlayOrNot = strPlayOrNot & ".vbs"
      'Recheck to make sure that the script name is still valid
      If InStr(1, strSelection, strPlayOrNot, 1) > 1 Then
        'Call the procedure that runs the selected script
        RunScript()
      Else
        'Call this procedure if the user  has not typed a valid
        'script name
        InvalidChoice()
      End If
    Else
```

```
          'If the user specified the script's .vbs file extension and
          'it is found in the previously built list of VBScript game
          'names then go ahead and call the procedure that will run
          'the script
          If InStr(1, strSelection, strPlayOrNot, 1) > 1 Then
            RunScript()
          Else
            'Run this procedure if user fails to supply valid input
            InvalidChoice()
          End If
        End If
      Else
        'If user supplied input is not found in the previously
        'built list of VBScript game names call this procedure
        InvalidChoice()
      End If
    End If

End Function
```

Creating the PickAGame() Function

The `PickAGame()` function, shown next, is charged with displaying the contents of the VBScript game console whenever it is called. It does this by first building a primary display string that consists of a list of all VBScript games that have been found, as well as instructions for getting Help, information about the script and its author, and for closing the game console.

The display string, which is aptly named `DisplayString`, is then plugged into a VBScript `InputBox()` function, thus displaying information about your VBScript games and providing the user with a means of selecting those games.

```
'This function displays the main VBScript game Console and collects
'user input
Function PickAGame()

  strDisplayString = strSelection & vbCrLf & _
  "Or Type:  [Help]   [About]   [Quit]" & vbCrLf

  PickAGame = InputBox("W e l c o m e   t o   t h e" & vbCrLf & _
```

```
    vbCrLf & "V B S c r i p t   G a m e   C o n s o l e !" & _
    vbCrLf & vbCrLf & "Pick a Game:" & vbCrLf & vbCrLf & _
    strDisplayString, strTitleBarMsg, "", 50, 50)

End Function
```

By default, all WSH and VBScript pop-up dialogs are displayed in the middle of the display area. However, in the previous example I specified values of 50 and 50 as the last two attributes of the `InputBox()` function. These two values specify the location where the pop-up dialog should be displayed on the user's screen. In this case, the pop-up dialog will be displayed in the upper-left corner of the screen. This keeps it handy without crowding the display area in the middle of the screen, where the VBScript games are displayed.

Creating the RunScript() Function

The `RunScript()` function, shown here, is very straightforward. When called, it uses the `WshShell` object's `Run()` method to execute the VBScript selected by the user, as specified in the variable called `PlayOrNot`.

```
'This function starts the VBScript selected by the user
Function RunScript()

  objWshShl.Run "WScript " & strPlayOrNot

End Function
```

Creating the InvalidChoice() Function

The `InvalidChoice()` function, shown next, is responsible for displaying a generic error message using the VBScript `MsgBox()` function whenever the user provides the VBScript Game Console with invalid input. Examples of invalid input include numbers that have not been assigned to a VBScript listed in the console, such as –4 or 9999, as well as misspelled names of listed VBScript games.

```
'This function is called whenever the user provides invalid input
Function InvalidChoice()

  MsgBox "Sorry. Your selection was not valid. A valid " & _
    "selection consists of one of the following:" & vbCrLf & _
    vbCrLf & "* The number associated with one of the listed " & _
    "VBScript games" & vbCrLf & "* The name of a listed " & _
```

```
    "VBScript game" & vbCrLf & "* The name of a listed " & _
    "VBScript game plus its file extension" & vbCrLf & _
    "* Help - To view help information." & vbCrLf & _
    "* About - To view additional information about this game " & _
    "and its Author" & vbCrLf & "* Quit - To close the " & _
    "VBScript Game Console" & vbCrLf & vbCrLf & _
    "Please try again.", , strTitleBarMsg

End Function
```

Creating the HelpFunction() Function

The `HelpFunction()` function, shown next, uses the VBScript `MsgBox()` function to display additional help information about the VBScript Game Console. It is called anytime the user types **help** and clicks OK.

```
'This function displays help information in a popup dialog
Function HelpFunction()

MsgBox "Additional help information for the VBScript Game " & _
  "Console can be found at:" & vbCrLf & vbCrLf & _
  "www.xxxxxxxx.com.", , strTitleBarMsg

End Function
```

Creating the AboutFunction() Function

The final function in the VBScript, shown next, is responsible for displaying information about the VBScript Game Console and its author. It is called whenever the user types **about** in the VBScript Game Console and clicks OK. As you can see, the function consists of a single statement that uses the `MsgBox()` function. The information included here is really just a brief template; I leave it to you to finish adding whatever content you think is appropriate.

```
'This function displays information about the VBScript Game Console
'and its author
Function AboutFunction()

  MsgBox "VBScript Game Console © Jerry Ford 2002" & vbCrLf & _
    vbCrLf & "Email the author at: xxxxx@xxxxxxxx.com.", , strTitleBarMsg

End Function
```

Writing the Second JScript

The final script defined in this Windows Script File, shown next, is JScript. It displays the game's closing splash screen and is designed in the same basic manner as the first JScript, using the `WshShell` object's `Popup()` method to display its graphical pop-up dialog.

```
//*************************************************************************
//Script Name: N/A
//Author:       Jerry Ford
//Created:      12/20/02
//Description: This JScript displays the .WSF file's closing splash
//              screen
//*************************************************************************

//Initialization Section

var objWshShl = WScript.CreateObject("WScript.Shell");
var strMessage;
var strAuthor;
var dtmDate;
var strTitleBarMsg;

strMessage = "Thank you for using the VBScript Game Console © ";
strAuthor = "Jerry Ford ";
dtmDate = "2002";

//Main Processing Section

strTitleBarMsg = getResource("cTitlebarMsg");

//Display a popup dialog using the WshShell object's Popup() method
objWshShl.Popup(strMessage + strAuthor + dtmDate, 0, strTitleBarMsg);
```

The Final Result

That's it. Let's assemble the entire Windows Script File as shown next. Before you run it for the first time, be sure that you've first created a folder called `C:\VBScriptGames` and that you've copied both the VBScript game console script as well as a few other of your VBScript games into the folder.

```
<package>

  <comment>This .WSF file builds a VBScript Game Console</comment>

  <job>

    <resource id="cTitlebarMsg">VBScript Game Console</resource>

    <script language="JScript">

      //*****************************************************************
      //Script       Name: N/A
      //Author:      Jerry Ford
      //Created:     12/20/02
      //Description: This JScript displays the .WSF file's initial splash
      //              screen
      //*****************************************************************

      //Initialization Section

      var objWshShl = WScript.CreateObject("WScript.Shell");
      var strWelcome;
      var strInstructions;
      var intResults;
      var intReply;
      var strTitleBarMsg;

      strWelcome = "Welcome to the VBScript Game Console. ";
      strInstructions = "Click on OK to play a VBScript game!";


      //Main Processing Section

      //Verify that the user wants to open the VBScript Game Console
      intReply = DisplayInitialSplashScreen();

      //intReply will be set equal to 2 if the user clicks on the Cancel
      if (intReply == 2) {
```

```
    //Close the VBScript Game Console
    WScript.Quit();
  }



  //Procedure Section

  //This procedure prompts the user for confirmation
  function DisplayInitialSplashScreen() {

    strTitleBarMsg = getResource("cTitlebarMsg");

    //Display popup dialog using the WshShell object's Popup() method
    intResults = +
    objWshShl.Popup(strWelcome +
      strInstructions, 0, strTitleBarMsg, 1);

    //Return the result to the calling statement
    return intResults

  }

</script>

<script language="VBScript">

  '*************************************************************************
  'Script Name: N/A
  'Author:      Jerry Ford
  'Created:     12/20/02
  'Description: This VBScript displays the actual VBScript
  '             Game Console interface and interacts with the user
  '*************************************************************************

  'Initialization Section

   Option Explicit
```

```
Dim objFsoObject, objWshShl, strPlayOrNot, strConsoleStatus
Dim objGameFolder, objGames, strSelection, objWordList
Dim strFileString, intCount, strDisplayString, intNoFilesFound
Dim strTitleBarMsg, intResults

Dim ConsoleArray()

'Set up an instance of the FileSystemObject
Set objFsoObject = CreateObject("Scripting.FileSystemObject")

'Set up an instance of the WshShell
Set objWshShl = WScript.CreateObject("WScript.Shell")

'Retrieve the titlebar message to the display in popup dialogs
strTitleBarMsg = getResource("cTitlebarMsg")


'Main Processing Section

If intResults = 2 Then
  WScript.Quit()
End If

'Specify the location of the folder where word files are stored
Set objGameFolder = objFsoObject.GetFolder("C:\VBScriptGames")

'Get a list of files stored in the folder
Set objGames = objGameFolder.Files

'Look and count the number of word files
For Each objWordList In objGames
  intNoFilesFound = intNoFilesFound + 1
Next

'Redefine the script's array based on number of word files found
ReDim ConsoleArray(intNoFilesFound)

'Call the function that displays the VBScript Game Console
ConsoleLoop()
```

```
'Procedure Section

'This function displays the VBScript Game Console, accepts user
'input, validates the input and starts other VBScript games
Function ConsoleLoop()

  'This string contains a list of all the word files discovered
  'in the target folder
  strSelection = ""

  'This counter will be used to track individual word files and
  'will be kept in sync with array entries
  intCount = 0

  'Loop through the list of word files
  For Each objWordList In objGames

    'Build a master string containing a list of all the word files
    'But exclude the VBScriptGameConsole.wsf file from this list
    If objWordList.Name <> "VBScriptGameConsole.wsf" Then

      'Increment count each time through the loop
      intCount = intCount + 1

      strFileString = strFileString & " " & objWordList.Name

      'Build another list, adding number for later display
      strSelection = strSelection & intCount & ".  " & _
        objWordList.Name & vbCrLf

      'Load the name of each script into the array
      ConsoleArray(intCount) = objWordList.Name
    End If

  Next

  'This variable is used to determine when to close the console
  strConsoleStatus = "Active"
```

```
  'Create loop & keep it running until the user decides to close it
  Do Until strConsoleStatus = "Terminate"

    'Interrogate the user's input
    strPlayOrNot = UCase(PickAGame())

    'If the user did not type anything or if he or she clicked on
    'Cancel then exit the function let things come to an end
    If strPlayOrNot = "" Then
      Exit Function
    End If

    'Define a Select Case statement and use it to test the various
    'possible types of user input
    Select Case UCase(strPlayOrNot)

      'If the user typed QUIT then exit the function let things
      'come to an end
      Case "QUIT"
        Exit Function

      'If the user typed ABOUT call the function that displays
      'additional information about the VBScript Game Console
      Case "ABOUT"
        AboutFunction()

      'If the user typed HELP call the function that provides
      'additional help information
      Case "HELP"
        HelpFunction()

      'Otherwise call the function that runs the selected VBScript
      Case Else
        ValidateAndRun()'

    End Select

  Loop

End Function
```

```
'This function validates user input and if appropriate calls
'functions that display further instructions or runs the selected
'VBScript
Function ValidateAndRun()

  'Check to see if the user provided a valid game number
  If IsNumeric(strPlayOrNot) <> 0 Then
    'Make sure that the user did not type a negative number
    If strPlayOrNot > 0 Then
      'Make sure that the use did not type a invalid number
      If CInt(strPlayOrNot) < CInt(intCount) Then
        'If the number is valid then find the associated script
        strPlayOrNot = ConsoleArray(strPlayOrNot)
        'Call the procedure that will then run the selected script
        RunScript()
      Else
        'Call this procedure if the user has not typed a valid
        'script number
        InvalidChoice()
      End If
    Else
      InvalidChoice()
    End If

  'Check to see instead if the user provided a valid game name
  Else
    'Proceed only if the input typed by the user a valid VBScript
    'game (e.g. its name appears in the previously built list of
    'VBScript game names
    If InStr(1, strSelection, strPlayOrNot, 1) > 1 Then
      'If the user didn't type the .vbs file extension add it
      If InStr(1, strPlayOrNot, ".VBS", 1) = 0 Then
        strPlayOrNot = strPlayOrNot & ".vbs"
        'Recheck to make sure that the script name is still valid
        If InStr(1, strSelection, strPlayOrNot, 1) > 1 Then
          'Call the procedure that runs the selected script
          RunScript()
        Else
```

```
        'Call this procedure if the user has not typed a valid
        'script name
          InvalidChoice()
        End If
      Else
        'If the user specified the script's .vbs file extension and
        'it is found in the previously built list of VBScript game
        'names then go ahead and call the procedure that will run
        'the script
        If InStr(1, strSelection, strPlayOrNot, 1) > 1 Then
          RunScript()
        Else
          'Run this procedure if user fails to supply valid input
          InvalidChoice()
        End If
      End If
    Else
      'If user supplied input is not found in the previously
      'built list of VBScript game names call this procedure
      InvalidChoice()
    End If
  End If

End Function

'This function displays the main VBScript game Console and collects
'user input
Function PickAGame()

  strDisplayString = strSelection & vbCrLf & _
  "Or Type:  [Help]   [About]   [Quit]" & vbCrLf

  PickAGame = InputBox("W e l c o m e   t o   t h e" & vbCrLf & _
    vbCrLf & "V B S c r i p t   G a m e   C o n s o l e !" & _
    vbCrLf & vbCrLf & "Pick a Game:" & vbCrLf & vbCrLf & _
    strDisplayString, strTitleBarMsg, "", 50, 50)

End Function
```

```
'This function starts the VBScript selected by the user
Function RunScript()

  objWshShl.Run "WScript " & strPlayOrNot

End Function

'This function is called whenever the user provides invalid input
Function InvalidChoice()

  MsgBox "Sorry. Your selection was not valid. A valid " & _
    "selection consists of one of the following:" & vbCrLf & _
    vbCrLf & "* The number associated with one of the listed " & _
    "VBScript games" & vbCrLf & "* The name of a listed " & _
    "VBScript game" & vbCrLf & "* The name of a listed " & _
    "VBScript game plus its file extension" & vbCrLf & _
    "* Help - To view help information." & vbCrLf & _
    "* About - To view additional information about this game " & _
    "and its Author" & vbCrLf & "* Quit - To close the " & _
    "VBScript Game Console" & vbCrLf & vbCrLf & _
    "Please try again.", , strTitleBarMsg

End Function

'This function displays help information in a popup dialog
Function HelpFunction()

  MsgBox "Additional help information for the VBScript Game " & _
  "Console can be found at:" & vbCrLf & vbCrLf & _
  "www.xxxxxxxx.com.", , strTitleBarMsg

End Function

'This function displays information about the VBScript Game Console
'and its author
Function AboutFunction()

  MsgBox "VBScript Game Console © Jerry Ford 2002" & vbCrLf & _
```

```
        vbCrLf & "Email the author at: xxxxx@xxxxxxxx.com.", , strTitleBarMsg

      End Function

    </script>

    <script language="JScript">

      //*****************************************************************
      //Script Name: N/A
      //Author:      Jerry Ford
      //Created:     12/20/02
      //Description: This JScript displays the .WSF file's closing splash
      //              screen
      //*****************************************************************

      //Initialization Section

      var objWshShl = WScript.CreateObject("WScript.Shell");
      var strMessage;
      var strAuthor;
      var dtmDate;
      var strTitleBarMsg;

      strMessage = "Thank you for using the VBScript Game Console © ";
      strAuthor = "Jerry Ford ";
      dtmDate = "2002";

      //Main Processing Section

      strTitleBarMsg = getResource("cTitlebarMsg");

      //Display a popup dialog using the WshShell object's Popup() method
      objWshShl.Popup(strMessage + strAuthor + dtmDate, 0, strTitleBarMsg);

    </script>

  </job>

</package>
```

Summary

In this final chapter you learned how to combine two or more different scripts into a single script using Windows Script Files. Windows Script Files are created using XML and a combination of different scripting languages. In addition, you got the opportunity to demonstrate your ability to work with Windows Script Files by developing the VBScript Game Console.

At this point, you should have a solid understanding of both VBScript and the Windows Script Host and should feel confident, not just of your game development capabilities, but also in your ability to apply the knowledge and skills that you've learned here in real-world situations.

Challenges

1. **Modify the information presented in the `AboutFunction()` and `HelpFunction()` procedures to make them more useful.**
2. **Modify the Windows Script File so the Windows Game Console script does not have to reside in the same folder as the games it supports, and then modify the script to retrieve the location of VBScript game folder from the Windows registry.**
3. **Right now, the VBScript Game Console script only works with VBScripts. Modify it so it will support any other script types you plan to work with (such as Windows Script Files).**

Part IV

Appendices

WSH Administrative Scripting

In this book, you learned a great deal about both VBScript and the WSH by developing computer games. In the real world, of course, VBScript and the WSH are used to automate tasks. These tasks are typically mundane, repetitive, and time-consuming, or extremely complex and therefore subject to human error. Automating such tasks using VBScript and the WSH makes perfect sense. The purpose of this appendix is to provide you with a collection of sample scripts that demonstrate some real-world tasks that can be scripted.

None of the VBScripts that you will see in this appendix should be considered finished products. For example, you won't see any complex programming logic or a lot of error checking. These scripts were developed on a computer running Windows XP; you should review and test the scripts before running them on other operating systems. My intention for providing these sample scripts is to give you a feel for some of the real-world tasks that you can automate using VBScript and the WSH. I wanted to provide you with a collection of starter scripts from which you can begin to create and develop your own collection of scripts.

I won't spend a lot of time going over the development of these scripts, nor will I attempt to explain every operation they perform. By now, you should be able to look at each of these scripts and determine what it is doing. To help you out a little, I made sure to include plenty of comments.

Desktop Administration

The administration of the Windows desktop on a single computer isn't terribly time-consuming. However, for those responsible for the maintenance and care of a large number of computers, scripting is a godsend. For example, a lot of small companies purchase their computers directly from the manufacturer. These computers arrive with the operating system already installed. However, desktop settings such as the color of the Windows desktop background or screen saver settings will vary depending on just how the computer manufacturer chose to set them up.

Companies often try to keep the configuration of their computer settings standardized. This makes maintaining their computers easier and reduces a lot of user confusion. One way of configuring computers in this scenario is to develop VBScripts that automate the configuration of desktop settings according to company policy. Then, all you need to do to prepare a new computer for deployment is to copy over the scripts and have the user run them the first time he or she logs on to the computer.

Configuring the Desktop Background

The following VBScript demonstrates how to use the `WshShell` object's `RegWrite()` method to configure values that are stored in the Windows Registry and affect the Windows desktop background:

```
'*************************************************************************
'Script Name: Background.vbs
'Author: Jerry Ford
'Created: 12/07/02
'Description: This script changes the user's background selection to none
'and sets the default background color to white.
'*************************************************************************


'Initialization Section

Option Explicit

On Error Resume Next

Dim objWshShl, intChangeSettings

Set objWshShl = WScript.CreateObject("WScript.Shell")
```

```
'Main Processing Section

'Verify that the user intends to change his or her screen saver settings
intChangeSettings = PromptForConfirmation()

If intChangeSettings = 6 Then
  ModifySettings()
End If

WScript.Quit()


'Procedure Section

'This function determines if the user wishes to proceed

Function PromptForConfirmation()
  PromptForConfirmation = MsgBox("Set standard desktop background?", 36)
End Function


'This subroutine alters screen saver settings

Sub ModifySettings()
  'Turn off the wallpaper setting
  objWshShl.RegWrite "HKCU\Control Panel\Desktop\Wallpaper", ""

  'Setting the background color to white
  objWshShl.RegWrite "HKCU\Control Panel\Colors\Background", "255 255 255"
End Sub
```

The script begins by prompting for confirmation and then proceeds to modify the following Registry values:

```
objWshShl.RegWrite "HKCU\Control Panel\Desktop\Wallpaper", ""
objWshShl.RegWrite "HKCU\Control Panel\Colors\Background", "255 255 255"
```

The first statement sets the Windows `Wallpaper` setting to `""`. This is equivalent to right-clicking on the Windows desktop, selecting Properties, and then setting the Background setting on the Desktop property sheet of the Windows Display Properties dialog to `None`.

The second statement sets the value of the Background setting to 255 255 255. This is the equivalent of selecting white as the color setting on the Desktop property sheet.

To test this script, run it and then log off and on again.

Configuring the Screen Saver

The following VBScript demonstrates how to change the configuration of the Windows screen saver. The overall construction of this script is very similar to the previous example, the only difference being which Registry keys are edited.

```
'*************************************************************************
'Script Name: ScreenSaver.vbs
'Author: Jerry Ford
'Created: 12/07/02
'Description: This script changes the user's screen saver to a default
'collection of settings.
'*************************************************************************


'Initialization Section

Option Explicit

On Error Resume Next

Dim objWshShl, intChangeSettings

Set objWshShl = WScript.CreateObject("WScript.Shell")


'Main Processing Section

'Verify that the user intends to change his or her screen saver settings
intChangeSettings = PromptForConfirmation()

If intChangeSettings = 6 Then
  ModifySettings()
End If
```

```
WScript.Quit()


'Procedure Section

'This function determines if the user wishes to proceed

Function PromptForConfirmation()
  PromptForConfirmation = _
    MsgBox("Set standard screen saver settings?", 36)
End Function


'This subroutine alters screen saver settings

Sub ModifySettings()
    'Enables the Windows screen saver
    objWshShl.RegWrite "HKCU\Control Panel\Desktop\ScreenSaveActive", 1

    'Turns on password protection
    objWshShl.RegWrite "HKCU\Control Panel\Desktop\ScreenSaverIsSecure", 1

    'Establishes a 10-minute inactivity period
    objWshShl.RegWrite "HKCU\Control Panel\Desktop\ScreenSaveTimeOut", 600

    'Enable the Starfield screen saver
    objWshShl.RegWrite "HKCU\Control Panel\Desktop\SCRNSAVE.EXE", _
      "C:\Windows\System32\ssstars.scr"
End Sub
```

As you can see, this script modifies four Registry values. The modification of the first value enables the Windows screen saver. The modification of the second value enables screen saver password protection, which means that if the screen saver kicks in, the user has to retype his password to get back into Windows. The third modification sets up the screen saver to begin running after a 10-minute period of user inactivity. Finally, the last modification selects the screen saver that is to be run.

To test this script, run it and then log off and on again.

Network Administration

Network administration means many things to many people. For one thing, it may mean establishing connections to network drives so that a script can move, copy, create, and delete files and folders residing on network computers. Network management also means establishing or removing connections to network printers. In the next several sections, I'll provide you with scripts that demonstrate how to connect to, and disconnect from, network drives and printers.

Mapping Network Drives

When you create a connection to a network drive (known as *mapping*), you make the network drive look as if it were local to your computer by assigning it a local drive letter—that is, as long as you have the appropriate set of security permissions on the network drive. Connecting to and disconnecting from a network drive is achieved using methods belonging to the `WshNetwork` object.

Mapping to Network Drives

To create a drive mapping, you must use the `WshNetwork` object's `MapNetworkDrive()` method:

```
WshNetwork.MapNetworkDrive letter, name, [persistent], [username],
[password]
```

`Letter` is an available logical disk drive letter on your computer. *`Name`* is the UNC (universal naming convention) name and network path of the network drive. *`Persistent`* is optional; it determines whether or not the mapping is permanent. A value of `True` creates a permanent mapping. The default value of this setting is *`False`*, which causes the connection to last only for the current working session. *`Username`* and *`password`* are optional and are used to supply the username and password required to access the drive.

When you run scripts from the Windows desktop or command line, they execute using your security credentials. However, if you schedule the execution of your VBScript, then your scripts will not have the authority that you have and will be unable to establish a network drive connection. One way to get around this is to embed a username and password inside your script. However, doing so is really bad for security. Another option is to set up your script to prompt for a valid username and password at execution time and authorize someone who might be around to supply these credentials.

The following VBScript demonstrates how to establish a temporary network drive mapping:

```
'*************************************************************************
'Script Name: DriveMapper.vbs
'Author: Jerry Ford
'Created: 12/07/02
'Description: This script demonstrates how to add logic to VBScripts in
'order to support network drive mapping.
'*************************************************************************


'Initialization Section

Option Explicit

On Error Resume Next

Dim objWshNet

'Instantiate the objWshNetwork object
Set objWshNet = WScript.CreateObject("WScript.Network")


'Main Processing Section

'Call the procedure that maps drive connections passing it an available
'drive letter and the UNC pathname of the drive
MapNetworkDrive "z:", "\\ICS_Server\D"

WScript.Quit()  'Terminate script execution


'Procedure Section


'This subroutine creates network drive mappings
Sub MapNetworkDrive(DriveLetter, NetworkPath)
```

```
  'use the objWshNetwork object's MapNetworkDrive() method to map to drive
  objWshNet.MapNetworkDrive DriveLetter, NetworkPath

End Sub
```

Disconnecting Mapped Drives

You can use the `WshNetwork` objects' `RemoveNetworkDrive()` method to disconnect a mapped drive when it's no longer needed. For example, you might want to do this at the end of the script that created the drive mapping, after it has completed its assigned task. The syntax of the `RemoveNetworkDrive()` method is as follows:

```
WshNetwork.RemoveNetworkDrive letter, [kill], [persistent]
```

Letter is the drive that has been assigned to the mapped drive. `Kill` is an optional setting with a value of either `True` or `False`. Setting it to `True` disconnects a mapped drive even if it is currently in use. `Persistent` is also optional. Set it to `True` to disconnect a permanently mapped drive.

The following VBScript demonstrates how to disconnect the network drive that was mapped by the previous script:

```
'*************************************************************************
'Script Name: DriveBuster.vbs
'Author: Jerry Ford
'Created: 12/07/02
'Description: This script demonstrates how to add logic to VBScripts in
'order to terminate a network drive mapping.
'*************************************************************************


'Initialization Section

Option Explicit

On Error Resume Next

Dim objWshNet

'Instantiate the objWshNetwork object
Set objWshNet = WScript.CreateObject("WScript.Network")
```

```
'Main Processing Section

'Call procedure that deletes network drive connections, passing it the
'the drive letter to be removed
MapNetworkDrive "z:"

WScript.Quit()  'Terminate script execution


'Procedure Section

'This subroutine disconnects the specified network drive connection

Sub MapNetworkDrive(DriveLetter)

  'Use the objWshNetwork object's RemoteNetworkDrive() method to disconnect
  'the specified network drive
  objWshNet.RemoveNetworkDrive DriveLetter

End Sub
```

Printer Administration

Printer administration involves many tasks. One task is setting up network printer connections. Other tasks include managing print jobs and physically managing the printer, including refilling its paper, ink, ribbon, or toner supply. Another task includes removing printer connections when they are no longer needed. The next two sections demonstrate how to use VBScript and the WSH to set up and disconnect network printer connections.

Connecting to a Network Printer

To create a connection to a network printer, you need to use the `WshNetwork` object's `AddWindowsPrinterConnection()` method. This method has two different types of syntax, depending on the operating system on which the script is executed.

The syntax for the `AddWindowsPrinterConnection()` method when used on a computer running Windows NT, 2000, or XP is

```
WshNetwork.AddWindowsPrinterConnection(strPrinterPath)
```

The syntax for the `AddWindowsPrinterConnection()` method when used on a computer running Windows 95, 98, or Me is as follows:

```
WshNetwork.AddWindowsPrinterConnection(strPrinterPath, strDriverName
[, strPort])
```

StrPrinterPath is the UNC path and name for the network printer. *StrDriverName* is the name of the appropriate printer software driver, and `StrPort` is an optional port assignment for the printer connection.

The following VBScript demonstrates how to set up a network printer connection:

```
'*************************************************************************
'Script Name: PrinterMapper.vbs
'Author: Jerry Ford
'Created: 12/07/02
'Description: This script demonstrates how to use a VBScript to set up a
'connection to a network printer.
'*************************************************************************


'Initialization Section

Option Explicit

Dim objWshNet

'Instantiate the objWshNetwork object
Set objWshNet = WScript.CreateObject("WScript.Network")


'Main Processing Section

'Call the procedure that creates network printer connections passing
'it a port number and the UNC pathname of the network printer
SetupNetworkPrinterConnection "\\ICS_Server\CanonPrinter"

WScript.Quit()  'Terminate script execution
```

```
'Procedure Section

Sub SetupNetworkPrinterConnection(NetworkPath)

  'Use the objWshNetwork object's AddWindowsPrinterConnection() method
  'to connect to the network printer
  objWshNet.AddWindowsPrinterConnection NetworkPath

End Sub
```

Disconnecting from a Network Printer

As with network drives, removing a printer connection is a little easier to do than connecting it initially. Printer connections need to be removed for a number of reasons. For example, every printer eventually breaks and must be replaced. Sometimes people move from one location to another, necessitating changes to printer connections. By scripting the setup and removal of printer connections, you can automate this process. To remove a network printer connection, you need to use the `WshNetwork` object's `RemovePrinterConnection()` method:

```
WshNetwork.RemovePrinterConnection resource, [kill], [persistent]
```

`Resource` identifies the printer connection and may be either the connection's assigned port number or its UNC name and path. `Kill` is an optional setting with a value of either `True` or `False`. Setting it to `True` disconnects a printer connection even if it is currently in use. `Persistent` is also optional. Set it to `True` to disconnect a permanent printer connection.

The following VBScript demonstrates how to remove the printer connection established by the previous VBScript:

```
'*************************************************************************
'Script Name: PrinterBuster.vbs
'Author: Jerry Ford
'Created: 12/07/02
'Description: This script demonstrates how to use a VBScript to disconnect
'a network printer connection.
'*************************************************************************


'Initialization Section
```

```
Option Explicit

Dim objWshNet

'Instantiate the objWshNetwork object
Set objWshNet = WScript.CreateObject("WScript.Network")


'Main Processing Section

'Call the procedures that disconnect network printer connections passing
'it the UNC pathname of the network printer
SetupNetworkPrinterConnection "\\ICS_Server\CanonPrinter"

'Terminate script execution
WScript.Quit()


'Procedure Section

Sub SetupNetworkPrinterConnection(NetworkPath)

  'Use the objWshNetwork object's RemovePrinterConnection() method to
  'disconnect from a network printer
  objWshNet.RemovePrinterConnection NetworkPath, "True", "True"

End Sub
```

Computer Administration

The term *computer administration* represents a very broad category of tasks. Rather than try to list or explain them all, I'll simply present you with two computer administration examples. The first example demonstrates how to use VBScript and the WSH to manage Windows services, and the second example demonstrates automated user account creation.

Managing Services

On computers running Windows NT, 2000, and XP operating systems, much of the operating system's core functionality is provided in the form of services. These services perform tasks, such as managing Windows plug and play, handling the spooling of printer jobs, and administering the execution of scheduled tasks. By starting and stopping Windows services, you can enable and disable specific Windows functions (that is, control just what users can and cannot do).

You can use the Windows `NET STOP` and `NET START` commands to stop and start Windows services. To execute these commands from within a VBScript, you can use the `WshShell` object's `Run()` method, as demonstrated in the following script:

```
'*************************************************************************
'Script Name: ServiceCycler.vbs
'Author: Jerry Ford
'Created: 12/07/02
'Description: This script demonstrates how to use VBScript to stop and
'start Windows services.
'*************************************************************************


'Initialization Section

Option Explicit

On Error Resume Next

Dim objWshShl, strServiceToManage

'Instantiate the WshShell object
Set objWshShl = WScript.CreateObject("WScript.Shell")


'Main Processing Section

'Prompt the user to specify the name of the service to cycle
strServiceToManage = InputBox("What service would you like to cycle?")

'Call the procedure that stops a service
StopService(strServiceToManage)
```

```
'Pause for 5 seconds
WScript.Sleep(15000)

'Call the procedure that starts a service
StartService(strServiceToManage)

'Terminate script execution
WScript.Quit()


'Procedure Section

'This subroutine stops a specified service
Function StopService(ServiceName)

  objWshShl.Run "net stop " & ServiceName, 0, "True"

End Function

'This subroutine starts a specified service
Function StartService(ServiceName)

  objWshShl.Run "net start " & ServiceName, 0, "True"

End Function
```

User Account Administration

User administration involves many tasks, including creating, modifying, and removing user accounts from the computer or the Windows domain to which the computer is a member. To perform user account administration, you need to have administrative privileges within the context that the script will execute (that is, on the computer or at the domain level).

One way to create a new user account is with the Windows `NET USER` command.

You also can use the `NET GROUP` command to add a newly created user account into a global domain group account or the `NET LOCALGROUP` command to add the user account to a local group.

For example, the following VBScript uses the `WshShell` object's `Run()` method and the `NET USER` command to create a new user account on the Windows NT, 2000, or XP computer on which the script is executed.

```
'*************************************************************************
'Script Name: AccountCreator.vbs
'Author: Jerry Ford
'Created: 12/07/02
'Description: This script demonstrates how to use VBScript to create new
'user accounts.
'*************************************************************************


'Initialization Section

Option Explicit

On Error Resume Next

Dim objFsoObject, objWshShl, strNewAccts, strAcctName

'Instantiate the FileSystemObject object
Set objFsoObject = CreateObject("Scripting.FileSystemObject")

'Instantiate the WshShell object
Set objWshShl = WScript.CreateObject("WScript.Shell")

'Specify the location of the file containing the new user account name
Set strNewAccts = _
  objFsoObject.OpenTextFile("c:\Temp\UserNames.txt", 1, "True")


'Main Processing Section

CreateNewAccts()  'Call the procedure that creates new user accounts

WScript.Quit()    'Terminate script execution
```

```
'Procedure Section

Sub CreateNewAccts()  'This procedures creates new accounts

  'Create a Do While loop to process each line in the input file
  Do while False = strNewAccts.AtEndOfStream

    'Each line of the file specifies a unique username
    strAcctName = strNewAccts.ReadLine()

    'Create the new account
    objWshShl.Run "net user " & strAcctName & " " & strAcctName & _
      " /add", 0

  Loop

  'Close the input file
  strNewAccts.Close

End Sub
```

To make the script more flexible, it has been set up to use VBScript `FileSystemObject` methods, which allow it to open and retrieve a list of names from an external file called `UserNames.txt`, located in the `C:\Temp` folder. This way, the script can be used over and over again without any modification. All you need to do is modify the script's input text file.

Scheduling the Execution of Administrative Scripts

Windows operating systems provide two means of scheduling script execution. The first option is the `AT` command, which is executed from the Windows command prompt. The second option is to use the Scheduled Task Wizard, which provides a step-by-step walk-through of the scheduling process. In addition, you can also use either of these two options to automate the execution of a single master scheduling script, from which you can programmatically control the execution of other VBScripts.

The AT Command

The Windows `AT` command allows you to set up and manage scheduled tasks from the Windows command prompt, which you can access from within your VBScripts using the `WshShell` object's `Run()` method.

There are two different types of syntax for the AT command. The syntax used to delete scheduled tasks:

```
at [\\computername] [[id] [/delete] | /delete [/yes]]
```

To view a list of currently scheduled tasks, type the AT command at the Windows command prompt and press the Enter key.

To set the computer at which a new scheduled task is to be executed, specify the computer's name in place of `\\computername`. *Id* identifies a numbered task ID assigned to every task by the scheduler service. `/Delete` performs a task deletion. `/Yes` is used to supply a confirmation for a delete operation.

The syntax used to create a new scheduled task is

```
at [\\computer] time [/interactive] [/every:date[,...] | /next:date[,...]]

command
```

`\\Computer` specifies the computer where the task is to be scheduled. *Time* specifies the time that task is to be executed in the format of `hh:mm` on a 24-hour clock. Specify `/interactive` to allow the script to interact with the desktop and the logged on user. `/Every:date[,...]` specifies the task's schedule using specified days of the week or month. For example, dates are specified as M, T, W, Th, F, S, Su, and days of the month are specified as `1 - 31`. `/Next:date[,...]` sets the tasks to run on the next occurrence of a specified day or date. Finally, *command* specifies the name of the application or script to be scheduled.

The following VBScript demonstrates how to use the Windows AT command to set up scheduled tasks for three VBScripts:

```
'*************************************************************************
'Script Name: AtScheduler.vbs
'Author: Jerry Ford
'Created: 12/07/02
'Description: This script demonstrates how to use the Windows AT command
'within a VBScript to schedule the execution of other scripts.
'*************************************************************************


'Initialization Section

Option Explicit
```

```
On Error Resume Next

Dim objWshShl

'Instantiate the WshShell object
Set objWshShl = WScript.CreateObject("WScript.Shell")


'Main Processing Section

'Call the procedure that schedules the execution of VBSCripts
ScheduleTheScripts()

WScript.Quit()  'Terminate script execution


'Procedure Section

Sub ScheduleTheScripts()

  'Use the WshShell object's Run() method to run the AT command
  objWshShl.Run "at 20:00 /every:M,T,W,Th,F cmd /c GenerateRpts.vbs", 0, "True"
  objWshShl.Run "at 21:00 /every:M,T,W,Th,F cmd /c CopyFiles.vbs", 0, "True"
  objWshShl.Run "at 22:00 /every:M,T,W,Th,F cmd /c ClearOutFolders.vbs", 0, "True"

End Sub
```

The Windows Scheduler

If you prefer to point and click your way through the setup of an automation schedule for your VBScripts, then you can use the Windows Scheduled Task Wizard. To start this wizard on a computer running Windows XP, click on Start, Control Panel, Performance and Maintenance, and then Scheduled Tasks. This opens the Scheduled Tasks folder, as shown in Figure A.1.

To set up a new scheduled task for one of your VBScripts, double-click on the Add Scheduled Task icon. This starts the Scheduled Task Wizard. Click on Next and follow the instructions presented by the wizard.

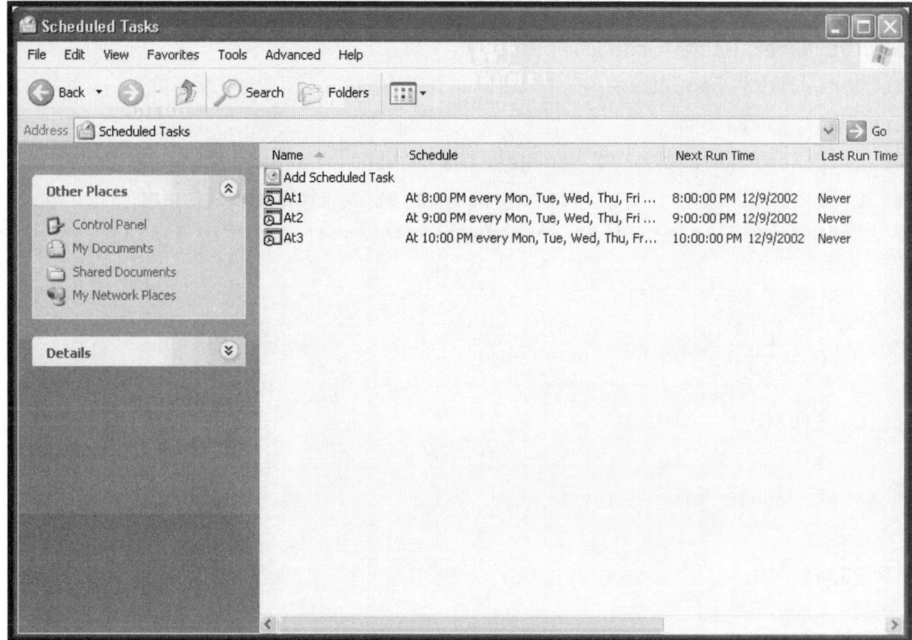

FIGURE A.1

Using the Scheduled Tasks folder to view the three scheduled tasks set up by the previous VBScript.

IN THE REAL WORLD

Scripts that you execute manually run using the security permissions assigned to you. However, tasks run using the Windows Task Scheduler services will not, by default, have this same level of access. One way to get around this problem is to associate a specific username and password with each scheduled task. You can do this from the Scheduled Tasks folder by right-clicking on a scheduled task and specifying a username in the Run as field, and then clicking on Password and typing in the password associated with the account.

Creating a Master Scheduling Script

Another option for managing the execution of your VBScripts is to create a single script that you schedule using either the `AT` command or the Windows Scheduler. This master scheduling script can then manage the execution of your other scripts as demonstrated in the following example:

```
'*************************************************************************
'Script Name: MasterScheduler.vbs
'Author: Jerry Ford
'Created: 11/13/04
'Description: This script manages the controlled execution of other
'VBScripts. It runs these VBScripts one at a time in sequential order.
'*************************************************************************


'Initialization Section

Option Explicit

On Error Resume Next

Dim objWshShl

Set objWshShl = WScript.CreateObject("WSCript.shell")


'Main Processing Section

RunScript("TestScript1.vbs")
RunScript("TestScript2.vbs")
RunScript("TestScript3.vbs")

WScript.Quit()  'Terminate script execution


'Procedure Section

Function RunScript(ScriptName)

  objWshShl.Run ScriptName, 1, True

End Function
```

The WshShell object's Run() method makes this script work. You can use this method to start a VBScript and then wait for it to finish executing before starting the execution of another script. This example is fairly basic; you can easily adapt it to selectively executing your VBScripts. For example, the following statements could be added to the script to limit the execution of a VBScript to the 15th day of the month:

```
If Day(Date()) = 15 Then
  RunScript("TestScript4.vbs")
End If
```

Disk Management

VBScripts provide an excellent tool for automating the execution of various Windows system administration utilities. Examples of two such utilities are the Windows Disk Cleanup and Defrag utilities. Like many Windows utilities, these utilities provide a command-line interface, meaning that you can control their execution via your scripts using the WshShell object's Run() method.

The Disk Cleanup and Disk Defrag utilities are perfect candidates for VBScript automation because they consume so many system resources when they execute that it's difficult to use the computer while they are running. By scripting their execution and then scheduling your scripts to run when you are not using your computer, you can keep your computer's disk drive in good shape without major inconvenience.

Automating Disk Cleanup

The Windows disk cleanup utility recovers lost disk space by deleting unnecessary files stored on the computer's disk drive. When executed, the disk cleanup utility deletes the following files:

- Files found in the Recycle Bin
- Temporary files
- Downloaded program files
- Temporary Internet files
- Catalog files for the Content Indexer
- WebClient/Publisher temporary files

Before you can automate the execution of the disk cleanup utility, you must perform a one-time configuration process as outlined here:

1. Click on Start and then Run. The Run dialog opens.
2. Type `cleanmgr /sageset:1` and then click on OK.
3. The Disk Cleanup dialog opens. Select the types of files that you want the disk cleanup process to remove and then click on OK.

After you've completed the configuration process, you can create your disk cleanup execution script using the following example as a template:

```
'*************************************************************************
'Script Name: VBSCleanup.vbs
'Author:      Jerry Ford
'Created:     11/13/04
'Description: This script automates the execution of the Windows Cleanup
'              utility.
'*************************************************************************


'Initialization Section

Option Explicit

Dim objWshShl

Set objWshShl = WScript.CreateObject("WScript.Shell")


'Main Processing Section

ExecuteCleanupUtility()

RecordMsgToAppEventLog()

WScript.Quit()  'Terminate the script's execution


'Procedure Section
```

```
Function ExecuteCleanupUtility()  'Run the Windows Disk Cleanup utility

  objWshShl.Run "C:\WINDOWS\SYSTEM32\cleanmgr /sagerun:1"

End Function


Function RecordMsgToAppEventLog() 'Record message in Application event log

  objWshShl.LogEvent 4, "VBSCleanup.vbs - Disk cleanup has been started."

End Function
```

When you create your script make sure that you specify the `/sagerun:1` parameter exactly as shown here:

```
WshShl.Run "C:\WINDOWS\SYSTEM32\cleanmgr /sagerun:1"
```

Automating the Disk Defrag Process

The disk defrag process speeds up the time it takes for your computer to store and retrieve files on the hard drive by reorganizing files that become scattered all over the drive as space becomes scarce. To run the Windows defrag process from within a VBScript, you need to know the syntax of the `defrag.exe` command, which is listed here:

```
defrag <volume:> [/a] [/f] [/v]
```

`Volume` specifies the disk drive to be worked on. The `/a` parameter displays an analysis of the drive's fragmentation status. By default, the defrag command will not run unless at least 15 percent of free space is available on the specified disk drive. When specified, the `/f` parameter forces `defrage.exe` to execute when less than 15 percent of free space is available. When specified, the `/v` parameter causes verbose output to be displayed.

If disk space is tight, schedule the execution of the disk cleanup process before running your disk defrag script to ensure that as much free space as possible is available.

The following script demonstrates how you can automate the execution of the defrag process:

```
'*************************************************************************
'Script Name: DiskDefrag.vbs
'Author:      Jerry Ford
'Created:     11/13/04
'Description: This script executes the Defrag.exe (Windows Defrag
'              utility).
'*************************************************************************


'Initialization Section

Option Explicit

Dim objWshShl

Set objWshShl = WScript.CreateObject("WScript.Shell")


'Main Processing Section

RunDefragUtility()

RecordMsgToAppEventLog()

WScript.Quit()  'Terminate the script's execution


'Procedure Section


Function RunDefragUtility()  'Run the defrag.exe command-line utility

  objWshShl.Run "c:\Windows\System32\defrag C: /f"

End Function


Function RecordMsgToAppEventLog() 'Record message in Application event log

  objWshShl.LogEvent 4, "VBSCleanup.vbs - Disk cleanup has been started."

End Function
```

As you can see, the script executes the defrag command using the `WshShell` object's `Run()` method, specifying the `/f` parameter.

Integrating VBScript with Other Applications

In addition to creating VBScripts that can interact with and control Windows resources, you can also create VBScripts that automate the execution of popular Windows applications such as Microsoft Word, Microsoft Excel, and WinZip. In this section you'll see examples of how to use VBScript and the WSH to create a Word document, an Excel spreadsheet, and a Zip file.

Automating Microsoft Word Reports Generation

To use VBScript to automate Word tasks, you need to know a little something about the Word object model. The `Application` object resides at the top of the Word object model. The `Application` object is automatically instantiated when Word is started. Using properties and methods associated with the `Application` object, you can access lower-level objects and collections in the Word model, and using the properties and methods associated with the lower-level objects, you can automate any number of Word tasks.

The following script provides you with a working example of how to use VBScript and the WSH to automate the creation of a Word document. Comments embedded within the script provide additional information about the Word object model.

The Word object model is far too large and detailed to be covered in this book. You can learn more about it by visiting http://msdn.Microsoft.com/office.

```
'*************************************************************************
'Script Name:  WordObjectModelExample.vbs
'Author:       Jerry Ford
'Created:      11/13/04
'Description:  This script demonstrates how to use integrate VBScript and
'               the Microsoft Word Object model.
'*************************************************************************


'Initialization Section

Option Explicit
```

```
On Error Resume Next

Dim objWord  'Used to establish a reference to Word Application object

Set objWord = WScript.CreateObject("Word.Application") 'Instantiate Word


'Main Processing Section

CreateNewWordDoc()

WriteWordReport()

SaveWordDoc()

CloseDocAndEndWord()

TerminateScript()


'Procedure Section

Function CreateNewWordDoc()

  'Documents is a collection. Add() is a method belonging to the Documents
  'collection that opens a new empty Word document
  objWord.Documents.Add()

End Function

Function WriteWordReport()

  'Specify Font object's Name, Size, Underline, & Bold properties
  objWord.Selection.Font.Name = "Arial"
  objWord.Selection.Font.Size = 16
  objWord.Selection.Font.Underline = True
  objWord.Selection.Font.Bold = True
```

```
    'Use the Selection object's Typetext() method to write text output
    objWord.Selection.Typetext("Sample VBScript Word Report")

    'Use the Selection object's TypeParagraph() method to insert linefeeds
    objWord.Selection.TypeParagraph
    objWord.Selection.TypeParagraph
    objWord.Selection.TypeParagraph

    'Use the Font object's Underline & Bold properties
    objWord.Selection.Font.Underline = False
    objWord.Selection.Font.Bold = False

    'Use the Font object's Size & Bold properties
    objWord.Selection.Font.Size = 12
    objWord.Selection.Font.Bold = False

    'Use the Selection object's Typetext() method to write text output
    objWord.Selection.Typetext("Prepared on " & Date())

    'Use the Selection object's TypeParagraph() method to insert linefeeds
    objWord.Selection.TypeParagraph
    objWord.Selection.TypeParagraph

    'Use the Selection object's Typetext() method to write text output
    objWord.Selection.Typetext("CopyRight - Jerry Lee Ford, Jr.")

End Function


Function SaveWordDoc()

    'The Applications object's ActiveDocument property established a
    'reference to the current Word document.

    'The Document object's SaveAs() method provides the ability to save
    'the Word file
```

```
  'Save the new document to C:\Temp
  objWord.ActiveDocument.SaveAs("c:\Temp\TextFile.doc")

End Function


Function CloseDocAndEndWord()

  'Use the Document object's Close() method to close the document
  objWord.ActiveDocument.Close()

  'Terminate Word
  objWord.Quit()

End Function


Function TerminateScript()

  WScript.Quit()  'Terminate script execution

End Function
```

Figure A.2 shows how the Word document created by this script looks after it has been created.

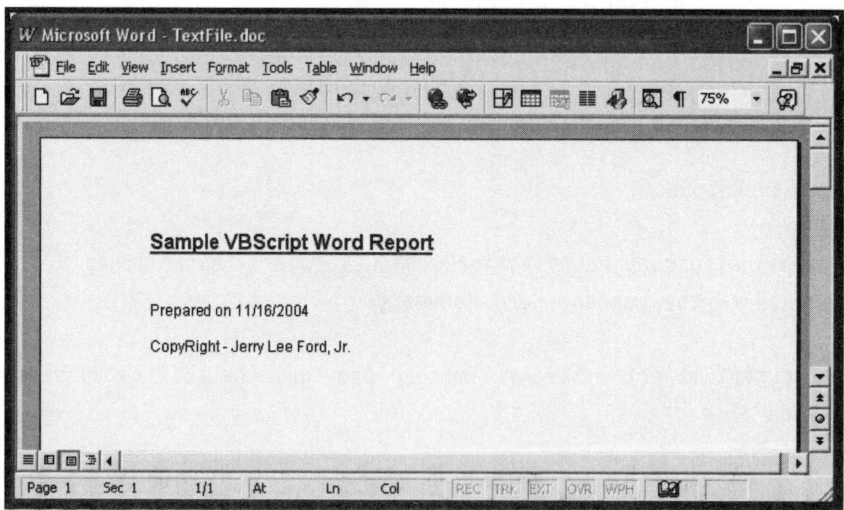

FIGURE A.2

Automating the creation of a Word document.

Automating the Creation of Microsoft Excel Spreadsheets

As you probably expect, the Excel object model is very similar to the Word object model. At the top of its model is the `Application` object, which is automatically instantiated when Excel is started. Using the properties and methods associated with the `Application` object, you can access lower-level objects and collections. Using the properties and methods associated with the lower-level objects, you can automate any number of Excel tasks.

The following script provides you with a working example of how to use VBScript and the WSH to automate the creation of an Excel spreadsheet. Refer to comments embedded throughout the script for more detailed information about the Excel object model.

```
'*************************************************************************
'Script Name:  ExcelObjectModelDemo.vbs
'Author:       Jerry Ford
'Created:      11/13/04
'Description:  This script demonstrates how to use VBScript to interact
'               with the Microsoft Excel object model.
'*************************************************************************


'Initialization Section

Option Explicit

On Error Resume Next

Dim objExcel  'Used to establish a reference to Excel Application object

Set objExcel = WScript.CreateObject("Excel.Application")'Instantiate Excel


'Main Processing Section

CreateAndHideNewSheet()

WriteExcelData()

SaveExcelSheet()
```

```
CloseSheetAndEndExcel()

TerminateScript()


'Procedure Section

Function CreateAndHideNewSheet()

  'Visible is a property of the Application object. It cab be used to
  'prevent Excel from appearing as the script executes
  objExcel.Visible = False

  'WorkBooks is a collection. Add() is a method belonging to the
  'WorkBooks collection that opens a new empty spreadsheet
  objExcel.WorkBooks.Add

End Function


Function WriteExcelData()

  'Use the Columns object's ColumnWidth property to set column widths
  objExcel.Columns(1).ColumnWidth = 15
  objExcel.Columns(2).ColumnWidth = 35
  objExcel.Columns(3).ColumnWidth = 6

  'Use the Range object's Select method to select a range of cells
  objExcel.Range("A1:C1").Select()

  'Set the Font object's Bold property
  objExcel.Selection.Font.Bold = True

  'Use the Cells object's Value property to enter text into the
  'spreadsheet
  objExcel.Cells(1,1).Value = "Name"
  objExcel.Cells(1,2).Value = "Description"
  objExcel.Cells(1,3).Value = "Rating"
```

```
  'Enter additional text
  objExcel.Cells(2,1).Value = "Hangman"
  objExcel.Cells(2,2).Value = "A word guessing game"
  objExcel.Cells(2,3).Value = "5"

  'Enter additional text
  objExcel.Cells(3,1).Value = "TicTacToe"
  objExcel.Cells(3,2).Value = "Two player board game"
  objExcel.Cells(3,3).Value = "5"

  'Enter additional text
  objExcel.Cells(4,1).Value = "Blackjack"
  objExcel.Cells(4,2).Value = "Player versus computer card came"
  objExcel.Cells(4,3).Value = "5"

End Function


Function SaveExcelSheet()

  'Use the ActiveWorkBook property to reference the current WorkBook.
  'Use the WorkBook object's SaveAs() method to save the WorkBook.
  objExcel.ActiveWorkBook.SaveAs("C:\Temp\ExcelFile.xls")

End Function


Function CloseSheetAndEndExcel()

  'Use the WorkBook object's Close() method to close the spreadsheet
  objExcel.ActiveWorkBook.Close()

  objExcel.Quit()  'Terminate  Excel

End Function


Function TerminateScript()
```

```
  WScript.Quit()  'Terminate script execution

End Function
```

Figure A.3 shows how the Word document created by this script appears after it has been created.

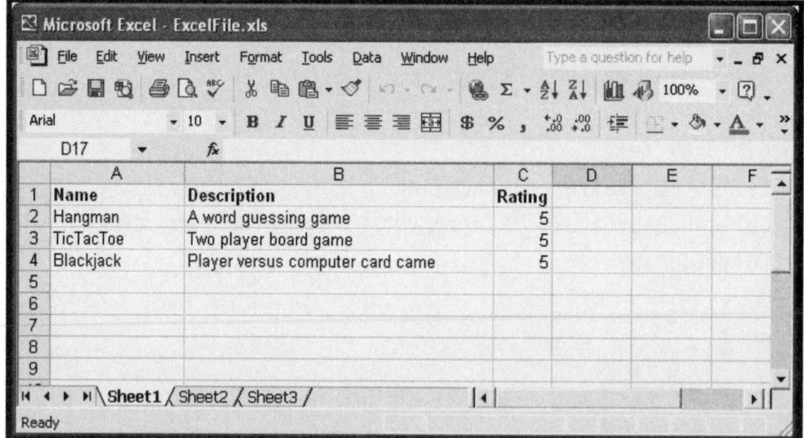

FIGURE A.3

Automating the creation of an Excel spreadsheet.

Automating the Execution of Third-Party Applications

Using VBScript and the WSH, you can automate the functionality of any application that exposes its object model. However, not every Windows application does this. Instead, many applications provide the capability to automate function via built-in command line interfaces, meaning that you can send commands to the application that the application then processes. A good example of one such application is WinZip. For example, you can send command to WinZip by executing its `WinZip32.exe` program and passing it arguments. The following VBScript demonstrates how to create a script that automates the creation of a new Zip file named `VBScripts.Zip`. The syntax for `WinZip32.exe` is embedded as comments within the script.

```
'*************************************************************************
'Script Name:  WinZipDemo.vbs
'Author:        Jerry Ford
'Created:       11/13/04
'Description:  This script creates a new Zip file made up of all the
'               VBScripts found in the C:\VBScriptsGames folder.
'*************************************************************************
```

```
'Initialization Section

Option Explicit

Dim intUserResponse, objWshShl

'Instantiate the Windows Shell Object
Set objWshShl = WScript.CreateObject("WScript.Shell")


'Main Processing Section

PromptForPermission()

If intUserResponse = vbYes Then
  CreateZipFile()
End If

TerminateScriptExecution()


'Procedure Section

Function PromptForPermission()  'Ask user for permission to continue

  intUserResponse = MsgBox("This script creates a ZIP file containing" & _
    " all the VBScripts found in C:\VBScriptGames." & vbCrLf & vbCrLf & _
    "Do you wish to continue?", 36, "VBScript Zipper!")

End Function


Function CreateZipFile()  'Create the new Zip file

  'WINZIP32 Command Syntax:
  'WINZIP32 [-min] action [options] filename[.zip] files
  ' -min   - Tells WinZip to run minimized
  ' action - Represents any one of the following arguments
```

```
  '          -a   Create new Zip file
  '          -f   Refresh existing archive
  '          -u   Update an existing archive
  '          -m   Move archive to specified location
  ' options  - Optional arguments that include
  '          -r   Add files and folders when adding to Zip file
  '          -p   Include information about any added folders
  ' filename[.zip]  - name of Zip file to be created
  ' files  - names of file to be added to the Zip file

  objWshShl.Run _
    "WINZIP32 -a C:\Temp\VBScripts.zip D:\VBScriptGames\*.vbs", 0, True

End Function


Function TerminateScriptExecution()  'Terminate the script's execution

  WScript.Quit()

End Function
```

Built-In VBScript Functions

VBScript provides an enormous collection of built-in functions as outlined in Table B.1. You can use these functions in your VBScripts to shorten your development time and save yourself from having to reinvent the wheel.

VBScript Functions

Table B.1 Built-In VBScript Functions

Function Name	Description
`Abs`	Returns a number's absolute value
`Array`	Returns an array based on the supplied argument list
`Asc`	Returns the ANSI code of the first letter in the supplied argument
`Atn`	Inverse trigonometric function that returns the arctangent of the argument
`CBool`	Converts an expression to a Boolean value and returns the result
`CByte`	Converts an expression to a variant subtype of `Byte` and returns the result
`CCur`	Converts an expression to a variant subtype of `Currency` and returns the result
`Cdate`	Converts an expression to a variant subtype of `Date` and returns the result

(continues)

TABLE B.1 BUILT-IN VBSCRIPT FUNCTIONS (CONTINUED)

Function Name	Description
CDbl	Converts an expression to a variant subtype of Double and returns the result
Chr	Returns a character based on the supplied ANSI code
Cint	Converts an expression to a variant subtype of Integer and returns the result
CLng	Converts an expression to a variant subtype of Long and returns the result
Cos	Trigonometric function that returns the cosine of the argument
CreateObject	Creates an automation object and returns a reference to it
CSng	Converts an expression to a variant subtype of Single and returns the result
Date	Returns the current date
DateAdd	Adds an additional time interval to the current date and returns the result
DateDiff	Compares two dates and returns the number of intervals between them
DatePart	Returns a portion of the specified date
DateSerial	Returns a variant (subtype Date) based on the supplied year, month, and day
DateValue	Converts a string expression into a variant of type Date and returns the result
Day	Converts an expression representing a date into a number between 1 and 31 and returns the result
Eval	Returns the results of an evaluated expression
Exp	Returns the value of an argument raised to a power
Filter	Returns an array based on a filtered set of elements using supplied filter criteria
FormatCurrency	Returns an expression that has been formatted as a currency value
FormatDateTime	Returns an expression that has been formatted as a date or time value
FormatNumber	Returns an expression that has been formatted as a numeric value
FormatPercent	Returns an expression that has been formatted as a percentage (including the accompanying %)
GetLocale	Returns the locale ID
GetObject	Returns a reference for an automation object
GetRef	Returns a reference for a procedure
Hex	Returns a hexadecimal string that represents a number
Hour	Returns a whole number representing an hour in a day (0 to 23)
InputBox	Returns user input from a dialog box

Table B.1 Built-In VBScript Functions (continued)

Function Name	Description
InStr	Returns the starting location of the first occurrence of a substring within a string
InStrRev	Returns the ending location of the first occurrence of a substring within a string
Int	Returns the integer portion from the supplied number
IsArray	Returns a value of True or False, depending on whether a variable is an array
IsDate	Returns a value of True or False, depending on whether an expression is properly formatted for a data conversion
IsEmpty	Returns a value of True or False, depending on whether a variable is initialized
IsNull	Returns a value of True or False, depending on whether an expression is set to Null
IsNumeric	Returns a value of True or False, depending on whether an expression evaluates to a number
IsObject	Returns a value of True or False, depending on whether an expression has a valid reference for an automation object
Join	Returns a string that has been created by concatenating the contents of an array
Lbound	Returns the smallest possible subscript for the specified array dimension
Lcase	Returns a lowercase string
Left	Returns characters from the left side of a string
Len	Returns a number or string's character length
LoadPicture	Returns a picture object
Log	Returns the natural log of the specified argument
LTrim	Trims any leading blank spaces from a string and returns the result
Mid	Returns a number of characters from a string based on the supplied start and length arguments
Minute	Returns a number representing a minute within an hour in range of 0 to 59
Month	Returns a number representing a month within a year in the range of 1 to 12
MonthName	Returns a string containing the name of the specified month
MsgBox	Returns a value specifying the button users click in a dialog box
Now	Returns the current date and time

(continues)

TABLE B.1 BUILT-IN VBSCRIPT FUNCTIONS (CONTINUED)

Function Name	Description
`Oct`	Returns a string containing an octal number representation
`Replace`	Returns a string after replacing occurrences of one substring with another substring
`RGB`	Returns a number that represents an RGB color
`Right`	Returns characters from the right side of a string
`Rnd`	Returns a randomly generated number
`Round`	Returns a number after rounding it by a specified number of decimal positions
`RTrim`	Trims any trailing blank spaces from a string and returns the result
`ScriptEngine`	Returns a string identifying the current scripting language
`ScriptEngineBuildVersion`	Returns the scripting engine's build number
`ScriptEngineMajorVersion`	Returns the scripting engine's major version number
`ScriptEngineMinorVersion`	Returns the scripting engine's minor version number
`Second`	Returns a number representing a second within a minute in range of 0 to 59
`Sgn`	Returns the sign of the specified argument
`Sin`	Trigonometric function that returns the sine of the argument
`Space`	Returns a string consisting of a number of blank spaces
`Split`	Organizes a string into an array
`Sqr`	Returns a number's square root
`StrComp`	Returns a value that specifies the results of a string comparison
`String`	Returns a character string made up of a repeated sequence of characters
`Tan`	Trigonometric function that returns the tangent of the argument
`Time`	Returns a variant of subtype `Date` that has been set equal to the system's current time
`Timer`	Returns a value representing the number of seconds that have passed since midnight
`TimeSerial`	Returns a variant of subtype `Date` that has been set equal to containing the specified hour, minute, and second

Table B.1 Built-In VBScript Functions (continued)

Function Name	Description
`TimeValue`	Returns a variant of subtype `Date` that has been set using the specified time
`Trims`	Returns a string after removing any leading or trailing spaces
`TypeName`	Returns a string that specified the variant subtype information regarding the specified variable
`Ubound`	Returns the largest subscript for the specified array dimension
`Ucase`	Returns an uppercase string
`VarType`	Returns a string that specified the variant subtype information regarding the specified variable
`Weekday`	Returns a whole number in the form of 1 to 7, which represents a given day in a week
`WeekdayName`	Returns a string identifying a particular day in a week
`Year`	Returns a number specifying the year

What's on the Companion Web Site?

The best way to become a good script developer is to spend time writing new scripts. However, it helps to have a collection of scripts from which you can cut and paste when starting out. Hopefully, you've been creating the scripts that you've seen in this book as you've gone along. But just in case you missed some, I've added copies of each script to the book's companion Web site. In this appendix, I'll provide a brief reference to each of the scripts that you'll find on the companion Web site.

The book's companion Web site also contains copies of three editors that you may want to try. I'll provide a high-level overview of each editor and tell you where you can go for more information.

Script Examples

Table C.1 provides a quick overview of all the sample scripts from this book that are located on the companion Web site.

Table C.1 Sample Scripts on the Companion Web Site

Reference	Script	Description
Chapter 1	Greeting.vbs	Collects the user's name and displays a greeting message
	Hello-1.vbs	Displays the classic "Hello World!" message
	Hello-2.vbs	Displays a message using the `WshShell` object's `Popup()` method
	Hello-3.vbs	Displays a message using the `WScript` object's `Echo()` method
	KnockKnock.vbs	A "Knock Knock" joke game
Chapter 2	EventLogger.vbs	Demonstrates how to write messages to the Windows application event log
	Greeting.vbs	Another example of how to use the `WScript` object's `Echo()` method
	Messenger.vbs	Demonstrates how to use VBScript and the WSH as a wrapper for the Windows `NET SEND` command
	NetInfo.vbs	Demonstrates how to collect network information
	RockPaperScissors.vbs	A "Rock, Paper, and Scissors" game
Chapter 3	FreeSpace.vbs	Demonstrates how to determine how much free space is left on a disk drive
	MathGame.vbs	Prompts the user to solve a mathematical equation and demonstrates how to solve it in the event that the user cannot do so
	SquareRootCalc – 1.vbs	Demonstrates how to solve square root calculations using a mathematic solution devised by Sir Isaac Newton
	SquareRootCalc – 2.vbs	Demonstrates how to solve square root calculations using VBScript's built-in `Sqr()` function
Chapter 4	ArgumentProcessor.vbs	Demonstrates how to work with arguments passed to the script by the user at execution time
	ArrayDemo.vbs	Demonstrates how to store and retrieve data using a single-dimension VBScript array
	BigBadWolf.vbs	Demonstrates how to use the `Option Explicit` statement
	CaptainAvenger.vbs	Prompts the user to answer a number of questions and then uses the answers to create a comical action adventure story
	ComputerAnalyzer.vbs	Demonstrates how to access environment variables using the WSH
	HappyHour.vbs	Tells the user whether it's Friday

Table C.1 Sample Scripts on the Companion Web Site (continued)

Reference	Script	Description
Chapter 4 *(continued)*	LittlePigs.vbs	Demonstrates how to use a constant to create a standardized title bar message for pop-up dialogs displayed by the script
	MathDemo.vbs	Demonstrates how to use various VBScript arithmetic operators
	MsgFormatter.vbs	Demonstrates how to use VBScript string constants to control how text messages are displayed
	ResizeArray.vbs	Demonstrates how to resize an array during execution
Chapter 5	RockPaperScissors – 2.vbs	Revisits the `RockPaperScissors.vbs` script first introduced in Chapter 2 and updates it using advanced conditional logic
	RockPaperScissors – 3.vbs	Revisits the `RockPaperScissors-2.vbs` script, replacing some of the `If` statment logic with a `Select Case` statement
	StarTrekQuiz.vbs	Creates a *Star Trek* Quiz game
Chapter 6	GuessANumber.vbs	Plays a number guessing game with the user
	ShortcutMaker.vbs	Creates shortcuts on the Windows desktop, Programs menu. and Quick Launch Toolbar for the GuessaNumber.vbs VBScript
Chapter 7	BlackJack.vbs	Creates a scaled-down version of Casino BlackJack
	GuessANumber – 2.vbs	Plays a number guessing game with the user
Chapter 8	LuckyLotteryMachine.vbs	Assists players by automating the generation of any number of randomly generated lottery numbers
	ExtractFileProperties.vbs	Demonstrates how to access any file's properties
	FileCreate.vbs	Demonstrates how to create and write to a new text file
	INIDemo.vbs	Demonstrates how to read and process the content of an INI file
Chapter 9	Hangman.vbs	Demonstrates how to create a game of Hangman using VBScript and the WSH
Chapter 10	Hangman – 2.vbs	Completes the Chapter 9 Hangman game by configuring it to store and retrieve game settings using the Windows registry
	HangmanSetup.vbs	Loads configuration settings for the Hangman game into the Windows registry
	ProcessorInfo.vbs	Demonstrates how to retrieve information about the computer's processor

(continues)

Table C.1 Sample Scripts on the Companion Web Site (continued)

Reference	Script	Description
Chapter 11	NewObjectDemo.vbs	Demonstrates how to create customized objects
	TicTacToe.vbs	Creates a two player Tic-Tac-Toe game
Chapter 12	VBScriptGameConsole.vbs	Creates a game console that builds a dynamic list of VBScript games for the player to select from
Appendix A	ScreenSaver.vbs	Changes the user's screen saver settings
	BackGround.vbs	Changes the user's background selection to "None" and sets the default background color to white
	DriveMapper.vbs	Demonstrates how to add logic to VBScripts to set up a network drive mapping
	MapBuster.vbs	Demonstrates how to add logic to VBScripts to terminate a network drive mapping
	PrinterMapper.vbs	Demonstrates how to use a VBScript to set up a connection to a network printer
	PrinterBuster.vbs	Demonstrates how to use a VBScript to disconnect a network printer connection
	ServiceCycler.vbs	Demonstrates how to use VBScript to stop and start Windows services
	AccountCreator.vbs	Demonstrates how to use VBScript to create new user accounts
	AtScheduler.vbs	Demonstrates how to use the Windows AT command within a VBScript to schedule the execution of other scripts
	MasterScheduler.vbs	Demonstrates how to automate the execution of multiple scripts using a single scheduled VBScript
	DiskDefrag.vbs	Demonstrates how to use VBScript to automate the execution of the Windows Disk Defrag utility
	VBSCleanup.vbs	Demonstrates how to use VBScript to automate the execution of the Windows Disk Cleanup utility
	ExcelObjectModelExample.vbs	Demonstrates how to use VBScript to automate the creation of a new Excel spreadsheet
	WordObjectModelExample.vbs	Demonstrates how to use VBScript to automate the creation of a new Word document
	WinZipDemo.vbs	Demonstrates how to use VBScript to automate the creation a new Zip file

VBScript Editors

You'll also find three good script editors located on the book's companion Web site. Unless you already have a script editor that you really like, I recommend that you take a look at each of these editors.

Unlike simple text editors such as Windows Notepad, these editors provide a number of advanced features that you'll soon find essential when writing your own scripts. For example, keyword color-coding should be considered an essential requirement for any good editor. Color-coding highlights different components in your scripts by displaying text using different colors. For example, comments may appear in green, whereas other VBScript keywords appear in blue, and your variables, objects, and constants appear in black.

Another important feature to look for is line numbering, or identification. VBScript error messages provide the line number of the statement on which an error occurs. Therefore, a VBScript editor helps you to zoom right in on the source of the error.

Another convenient feature of editors is the capability to save and execute your VBScripts from within the editor. This saves you a lot of time and effort because you no longer have to jump from the editor to either the Windows desktop or Command Console every time you need to test your script.

Adersoft VbsEdit

Adersoft VbsEdit, shown in Figure C.1, is a script editor designed specifically for the development of VBScript. It is distributed as shareware with a limited period of free trial use. At the time of this writing, a licensed copy of version 2.0 of Adersoft VbsEdit can be downloaded and purchased along with the JsEdit JScript editor for just $30.

Major features provided by VbsEdit include:

- Statement color-coding
- Built-in debugger
- Line and column numbering
- Find and replace
- Undo and redo
- Dynamic help
- Print and print preview
- Execution from within the editor using CScript
- Execution from within the editor using WScript

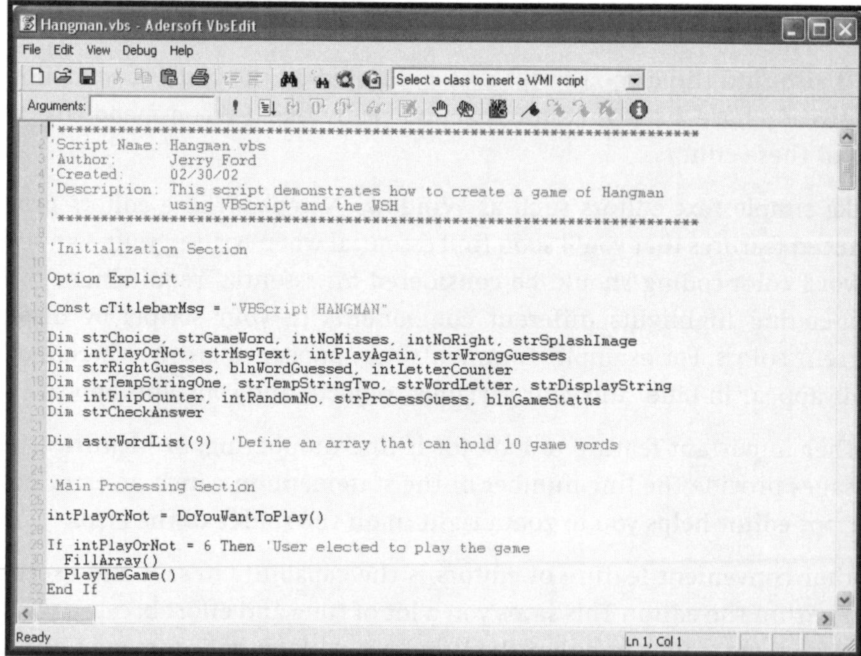

FIGURE C.1

The Adersoft VbsEdit 2.0 VBScript editor.

To learn more about Adersoft VbsEdit, or to purchase a licensed copy, visit http://www.vbsedit.com.

VBSEditor

Another good VBScript editor is the Koala VBSEditor (see Figure C.2). This script editor is designed specifically to support VBScript development. Best of all, as of the writing of this book, VBSEditor is freeware, which means that you do not have to purchase it to use it.

Major features provided by this VBSEditor include:

- Statement color-coding
- Line and column numbering
- Search and replace
- Undo and redo
- Print and print preview
- Indent and unindent
- Comment and uncomment
- Book marking of specific lines
- Custom color configuration

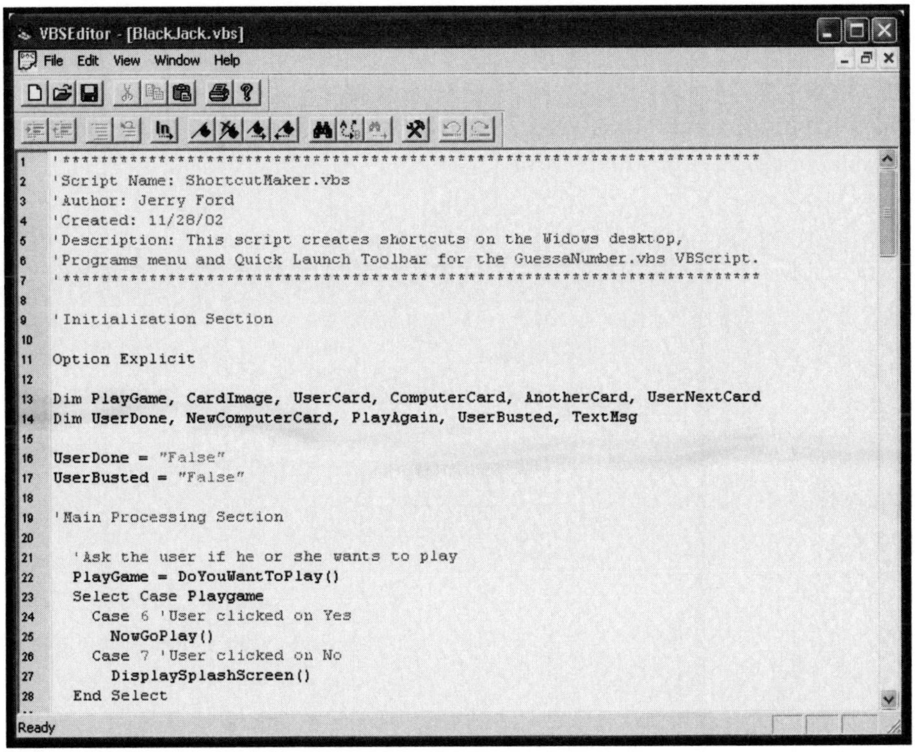

```
'***************************************************************************
'Script Name: ShortcutMaker.vbs
'Author: Jerry Ford
'Created: 11/28/02
'Description: This script creates shortcuts on the Widows desktop,
'Programs menu and Quick Launch Toolbar for the GuessaNumber.vbs VBScript.
'***************************************************************************

'Initialization Section

Option Explicit

Dim PlayGame, CardImage, UserCard, ComputerCard, AnotherCard, UserNextCard
Dim UserDone, NewComputerCard, PlayAgain, UserBusted, TextMsg

UserDone = "False"
UserBusted = "False"

'Main Processing Section

  'Ask the user if he or she wants to play
  PlayGame = DoYouWantToPlay()
  Select Case Playgame
    Case 6 'User clicked on Yes
      NowGoPlay()
    Case 7 'User clicked on No
      DisplaySplashScreen()
  End Select
```

FIGURE C.2

The Koala VBSEditor.

You can download a copy of the VBSEditor at http://www.koansoftware.com/upload/VBSeditor.zip.

SitePad Pro

The third editor that you find on this book's companion Web site is ModelWorks SitePad Pro, shown in Figure C.3. SitePad Pro is distributed as shareware, which means you can try it for free for a limited period of time before purchasing a licensed copy. This editor provides advanced support for a number of programming languages, including Java, HTML, VRML, JavaScript, and VBScript. Its support for VBScript includes the following features:

- Statement color-coding
- Line and column numbering
- Search and replace
- Undo and redo
- Print
- Indent and unindent

- Project management
- Syntax checking

To learn more about ModelWorks SitePad Pro, or to purchase a licensed copy, visit http://www.modelworks.com/products.html.

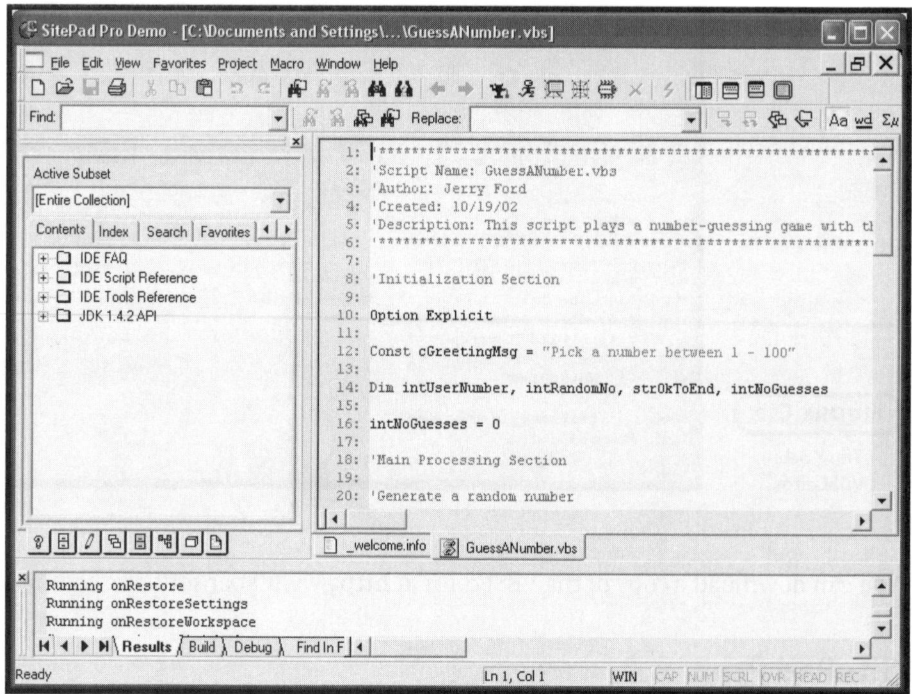

FIGURE C.3

The ModelWorks SitePad Pro editor.

What Next?

This book represents the beginning, not the end, of your VBScript programming experience. To become an effective and sought-after programmer, it is important you work diligently to continue learning as much as possible. The best way to do this is to start writing your own scripts and to experiment and try new things as you go. It's equally important that you continue to read and learn more about VBScript, the WSH, and programming in general. To help you on this journey, I have assembled a list of books and Web sites where you can learn more and find tons of sample scripts.

Recommended Reading

The following list of books will provide you with additional information about both VBScript and the WSH. Also included in this list are books covering VBScript's close relatives, VBA and Visual Basic.

- *Learn VBScript In a Weekend.* ISBN: 1931841705; Premier Press, 2002. This book provides additional beginner-level coverage of VBScript. It splits its focus between the use of VBScript in Web page development and as a scripting language for use with the WSH, providing a next step in the event that you're interested in spicing up your Web site using VBScript.
- *Microsoft Windows Shell Scripting and WSH Administrator's Guide.* ISBN: 1931841268; Premier Press, 2002. This book is designed to assist you in continuing your VBScript and WSH education by preparing you to use both in the real world. It's a great guide for current or future system administrators, programmers, and power users. Besides covering VBScript, this book also provides you with a foundation for developing scripts using JScript.

- *Microsoft Visual Basic .NET Programming for the Absolute Beginner.* ISBN: 1592000029; Premier Press, 2002. This book is an excellent next step, should you want to use your knowledge of VBScript as a stepping stone for learning Microsoft Visual Basic .Net. You will find that you have been well-served by your new VBScript background as you add Visual Basic to your bag of programming tricks.
- *Microsoft Excel VBA Programming for the Absolute Beginner.* ISBN: 1931841047; Premier Press, 2002. This book provides you with everything you need to learn to apply Microsoft VBA to Microsoft Excel. Thanks to its close relationship with VBScript, you'll find that you have a head start on your VBA learning curve, and that you're developing VBA games in no time as you learn to become a VBA programmer.
- *VBScript in a Nutshell.* ISBN: 1565927206; O'Reilly & Associates, 2000. This book provides experienced VBScript programmers with a complete language reference. Here you will find a detailed element-by-element breakdown of every aspect of VBScript, including the syntax of every VBScript statement, constant, operator, and function.
- *Microsoft VBScript Professional Projects.* ISBN: 1592000568; Premier Press, 2003. This book demonstrates advanced VBScript programming concepts in the form of four hands-on projects. Each project focuses on a specific set of concepts based on real word situations.

Locating WSH and VBScript Resources Online

There is more to VBScript than can be found in books alone. Much of the information about this topic is free and can be found on the Internet. The following section discusses Web sites that provide you with a place to begin your research.

The MSDN Scripting Web page (at http://www.msdn.microsoft.com/scripting), shown in Figure D.1, is Microsoft's official site for all things VBScript and WSH. Here you'll find language references for both VBScript and JScript, as well as detailed documentation on the WSH. You also can download and install the latest version of the WSH, join scripting newsgroups, and view sample scripts.

The Win32 Scripting Web site (at http://cwashington.netreach.net), shown in Figure D.2, provides an abundance of information for a number of scripting languages, including VBScript. Here you will find plenty of documentation, a chat room, and tons of downloadable sample script examples.

Another good site, shown in Figure D.3, is http://www.windowsitpro.com/WindowsScripting. This site provides access to *Windows Scripting Solutions* magazine. You have to pay to subscribe to this service to access its articles on scripting. But even if you don't, you'll still be able to access free articles and plenty of sample scripts.

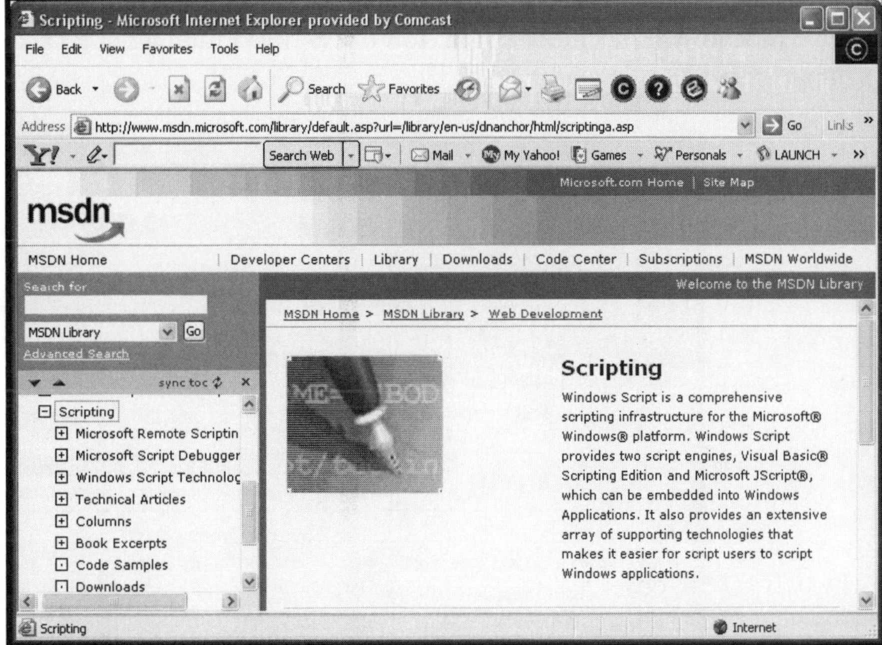

FIGURE D.1

The MSDN Scripting page.

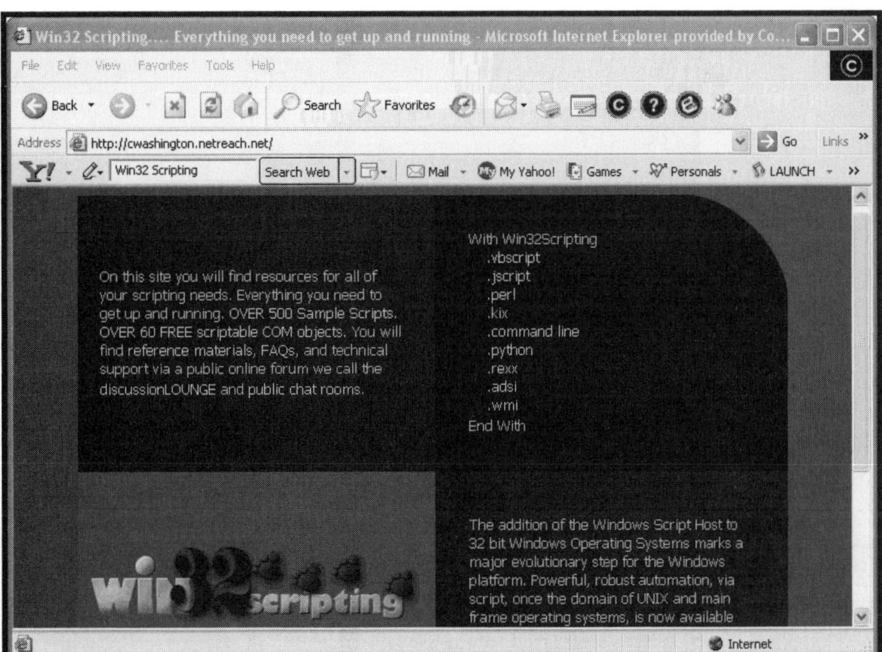

FIGURE D.2

The Win32 Scripting Web site.

WSHScripting.com (at http://www.wshscripting.com), shown in Figure D.4, is another good site for Windows WSH documentation. You'll also find a number of good articles and plenty of sample scripts.

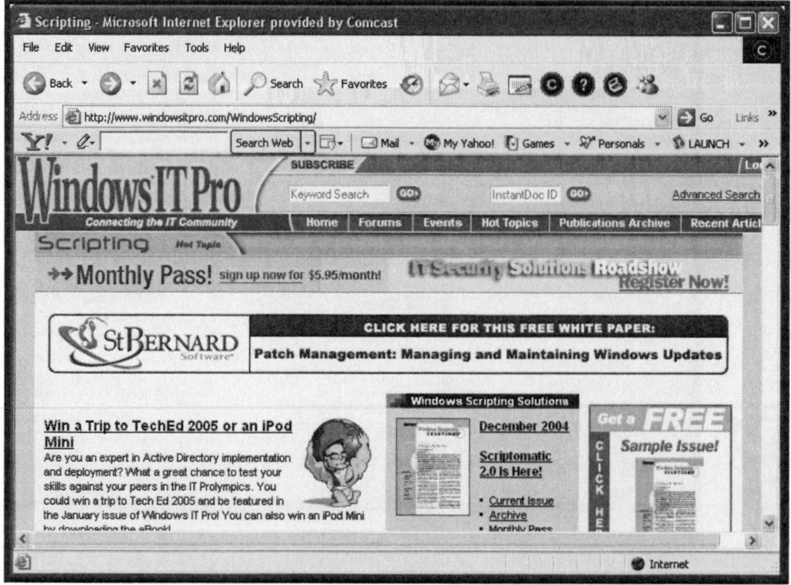

FIGURE D.3

WindowsIT Pro Web site.

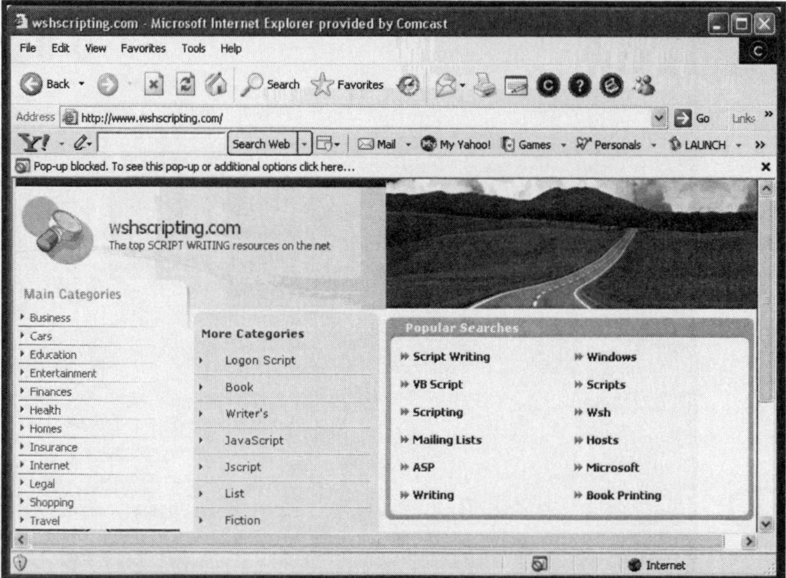

FIGURE D.4

WSHScripting.com Web site.

Another good site is Winscripter, which is located at http://www.winscripter.com and is shown in Figure D.5. Here you will find articles, sample scripts, and an online message board where you can post and receive answers to your questions. In addition, you will find an abundance of WSH documentation and links to other helpful Web sites.

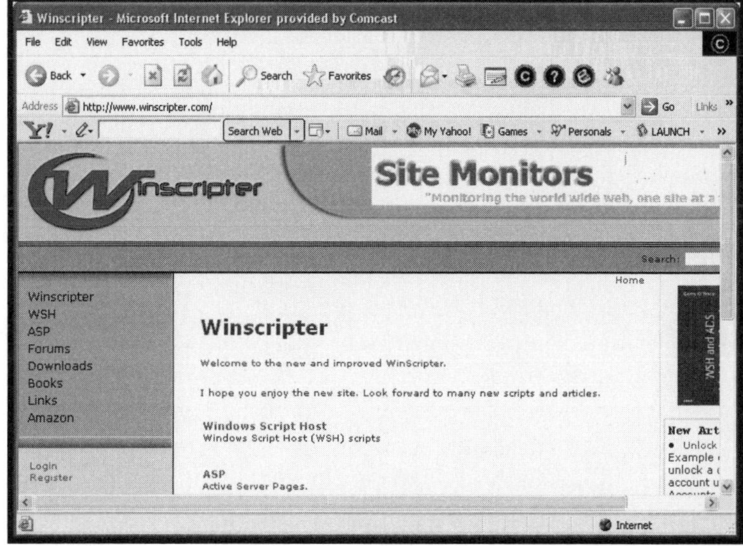

FIGURE D.5
The Winscripter site.

One other site you may want to visit is http://www.w3schools.com/vbscript. Here you will find a VBScript tutorial as well as access to plenty of sample scripts.

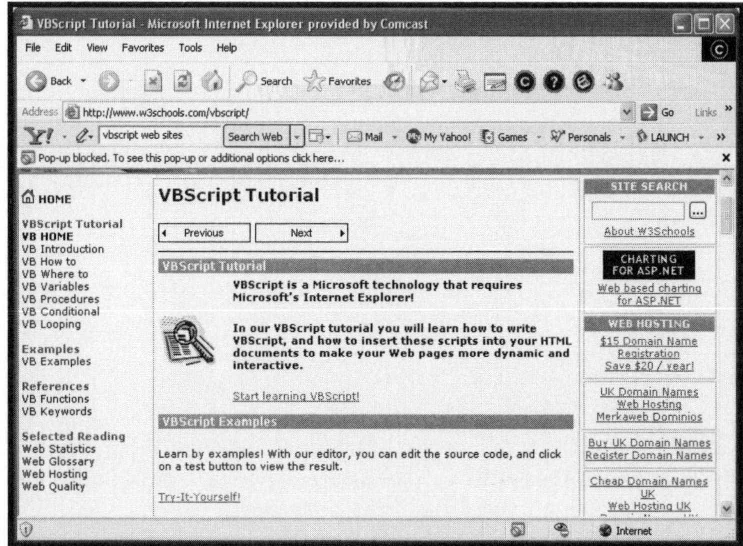

FIGURE D.6
http://www.w3schools.com/vbscript.

INDEX

A

B

C

D

T

U

V

W

X

Y